AT THE HEARTH OF THE CROSSED RACES

At the Hearth of the Crossed Races ✳ *A French-Indian Community in Nineteenth-Century Oregon, 1812–1859*

MELINDA MARIE JETTÉ

FIRST PEOPLES
New Directions in Indigenous Studies

Oregon State University Press   *Corvallis*

Publication of this book was made possible, in part, with a grant from the Andrew W. Mellon Foundation.

The paper in this book meets the guidelines for permanence and durability of the Committee on Production Guidelines for Book Longevity of the Council on Library Resources and the minimum requirements of the American National Standard for Permanence of Paper for Printed Library Materials Z39.48-1984.

Library of Congress Cataloging-in-Publication Data

Jetté, Melinda Marie.

At the hearth of the crossed races : a French-Indian community in nineteenth-century Oregon, 1812–1859 / Melinda Marie Jetté.

pages cm

ISBN 978-0-87071-597-6 (original trade paperback : alkaline paper) — ISBN 978-0-87071-598-3 (e-book)

1. French Prairie (Or.)—Race relations—History—19th century. 2. Acculturation—Oregon—French Prairie—History—19th century. 3. Indians of North America—Mixed descent—Oregon—French Prairie—History—19th century. 4. French Americans—Oregon—French Prairie—History—19th century. 5. Kalapuya Indians—Oregon—French Prairie—History—19th century. 6. British Americans—Oregon—French Prairie—History--19th century. 7. Pioneers—Oregon—French Prairie—History—19th century. 8. Frontier and pioneer life—Oregon—French Prairie. 9. French Prairie (Or.)—Colonization. 10. French Prairie (Or.)—History—19th century. I. Title.

F882.W6J47 2015

305.8009795'3709034—dc23

2015009745

Oregon State University Press
121 The Valley Library
Corvallis OR 97331-4501
541-737-3166 • fax 541-737-3170
www.osupress.oregonstate.edu

For my family in memory of my father,

Kenneth Reynolds Jetté Jr. (1935–2013)

Contents

Maps

Figures

Tables

Preface

I cannot recall when I first became aware of my family origins. Perhaps an early initiation came during holiday outings to French Prairie, that small corner of Oregon once home to a French-Indian community. Perhaps the process began with visits to my aged great-grandfather who (so the story goes) disavowed his Indian heritage. Whatever its beginnings, this education continued through my adolescence. On occasion, my father would recite the family lineage and recount stories about his paternal ancestors, French Canadian fur trappers and their Indian and *métis* wives who resettled the Oregon Country before the arrival of the Oregon Trail emigrants. These stories provided a special link with the past and afforded our family legitimacy in the present. The secret knowledge that my ancestors "were here first" allowed me to see myself as different from other Oregonians.

After high school I studied in France for a year before returning to the United States and completing a degree in history and French literature. This formal education later came to overshadow earlier memories and gradually infused a sense of ambiguity into my perception of my ancestral past. The family lore provided a linkage with the past, but this link felt increasingly tenuous because the French-Indian heritage seemed so distant, so unrelated to the present. Unlike our forebears, my family spoke only English, we looked more or less Germanic, and we lived in the suburbs rather than in the countryside.

I spent some years away from academe, mulling over the decision to pursue graduate studies in history. During that time, I occasionally returned to the question of my family heritage. I would ask myself if it were possible to have a meaningful connection to my ancestors, seemingly so different from myself. I wondered if it might be worthwhile to delve into that French-Indian past. I did eventually pursue graduate work in history, completing a master's degree at Université Laval in Quebec City and a doctorate at the University of British Columbia. At the start of my graduate studies, I was loath to admit that they were inextricably linked to my own personal search for identity. I believed that I wanted only to learn how the experience of my family might serve as a guide to the history of French Prairie. Fortunately, instinct later dictated that unless I honestly addressed the issue of my desire for self-knowledge, my research would lack credibility. And so, where has the search led? I had hoped to make some startling discoveries or develop a newfound sense of identity. However, the outcome was not so spectacular. If anything, I find that this research has led to a greater sense of ambiguity, though an ambiguity tempered with some understanding.

I am keenly aware of my "Americanness," though I admit that a clear definition of this American identity eludes me. I do not feel a sense of ethnic kinship with French Canadians or Native people. I possess no direct ties to the world of my Indian grandmothers or my francophone grandfathers. My family no longer speaks their languages nor remembers their cultural traditions. Although I became fluent in French by studying and living in France and Quebec, I cannot undo generations of assimilation. Nonetheless, who I am remains rooted in where I come from. In her essay titled "The Search for Generational Memory," Tamara Hareven noted that one of the main motivations in such a search is the desire to connect the experience of one's ancestors to larger historical events. This is the crux of the issue. I cannot forget my ancestral origins because it is this history that binds me to the land, to the American West. My French Canadian grandfathers crossed the continent, and my Native and *métis* grandmothers joined their destinies to these French Canadian voyageurs. They were thus all involved in the meeting of two cultures, Euro-American and Native American, a meeting that was ultimately beneficial for Euro-American settlers and devastating for indigenous peoples. My forebears resettled the West, and the path they chose—or were forced to choose—was integration. And so I am American, but I still feel a sense of loss, a strange nostalgia for something that I never knew.

Therein lies the value of this ancestral past. It binds me to America, yet offers an alternative to the historical myths and popular images of American Western culture. After assimilation, after the waning of ethnic distinctions and our cultural heritage, what remains is memory. For myself and my family, this memory contains both what we remember and the traces of what we have forgotten: the knowledge of having forgotten what it meant to be French Canadian and Walla Walla during the 1800s. Ultimately it is this memory, these fragments of memory, that allow us to distinguish ourselves from others. On a personal level, the tension between memory and identity provides an impetus to seek out more knowledge. It serves as a guide in the task of unearthing chapters in American history that still need to be investigated: the experience of French North Americans in the

Trans-Mississippi West and of French-Indian communities born of the Euro-American conquest.

I am indebted to a number of scholars for their assistance over the past several years. From the beginning of my entry into the doctoral program at the University of British Columbia, Arthur J. Ray took a keen interest in my professional development, and he provided unwavering support as well as constructive criticism that allowed me to progress as a historian. Dianne Newell and Paul Krause consistently offered incisive comments that created a stimulating intellectual environment.

Any research project ultimately benefits from the assistance and cooperation of a wide group of scholars and professionals. For this reason, I would like to acknowledge the assistance of mentors and colleagues, whose intellectual insights and professional support have been immeasurable: Katrine Barber, Joshua Binus, Robert Boyd, Eliza Canty-Jones, Andrew Fisher, Shawna Gandy, Max Geier, Kimberly Jensen, Marianne Keddington-Lang, the late H. Lloyd Keith, Mary C. Kelly, William Lang, Douglas Ley, Dean Louder, Theresa Schenck, Eric Waddell, and Henry Zenk. I would also like to express my gratitude to the anonymous reviewers who provided incisive comments and constructive criticism to improve the original manuscript.

In conducting the research for this project, I was fortunate to make the acquaintance, either in person or via the Internet, of several library and archival specialists who willingly lent their expertise to my numerous queries. During the more than six months that I spent in the Archdiocese of Portland in Oregon Archives, former archivist Mary Grant-Doty graciously helped me search through the Francis N. Blanchet Collection. The staff members of the Oregon Historical Society Research Library and the H. H. Bancroft Library also guided my inquiries on nineteenth-century manuscripts. Marie Reidke of the Hudson's Bay Company Archives provided useful reference information. And finally, the staff members of the Multnomah County Library's Interlibrary Loan Department, the UBC Library's Extension Library division, and the Franklin Pierce University Library demonstrated a high standard of professionalism by providing access to numerous books, articles, and microforms over the years.

A special thanks goes to the incomparable staff of Oregon State University Press, especially to Mary Braun. This book would not have been possible without the financial support of the Andrew W. Mellon Foundation, major sponsor of the First Peoples: Indigenous Studies joint publishing initiative and the Franklin Pierce University Faculty Development Research Fund.

My family has supported my educational and career goals since I took the first step on a long and winding road when I left home to spend a year studying abroad in France after high school. For their encouragement in following that path, I thank my father, the late Kenneth R. Jetté Jr., and my mother, R. Eileen (Willett) Jetté. I also thank my siblings and their spouses for providing unconditional financial, moral, and logistical support throughout my ten years of graduate schooling: Catherine Jetté, Don Limbaugh, Hazen Jetté, and Chieko Sone Jetté. My niece, Summer Jetté-Gray, and my nephews Chihiro Hazen Jetté and Naoki Kenneth Jetté have been a source of joy and inspiration for us all. I have also been blessed with wonderful friendships that have provided encouragement over the years: Jean Dawson, Michele Korb, Martin Payne, Doreen Ramirez, Amar Sangha, and Dayanthie Weeraratne. *Merci mille fois!*

Abbreviations

AAQ	Archives of the Archdiocese of Quebec
AHR	*American Historical Review*
APOA	Archdiocese of Portland in Oregon Archives
BAN	H. H. Bancroft Library
BCHQ	*British Columbia Historical Quarterly*
CHR	*Canadian Historical Review*
CCRPNW-SL	*Catholic Church Records of the Pacific Northwest-Saint Louis*
CCRPNW-SP	*Catholic Church Records of the Pacific Northwest-Saint Paul*
CCRPNW-V	*Catholic Church Records of the Pacific Northwest-Vancouver*
DBC	*Dictionnaire biographique du Canada*
HBC	Hudson's Bay Company
HBCA	Hudson's Bay Company Archives
MCH	*Marion County History*
MCPCF	Marion County Probate Case Files
MVHR	*Mississippi Valley Historical Review*
NWC	North West Company
OHS	Oregon Historical Society Research Library
OHQ	*Oregon Historical Quarterly*
OSA	Oregon State Archives
PFC	Pacific Fur Company
PHR	*Pacific Historical Review*
PNQ	*Pacific Northwest Quarterly*
TOPA	*Transactions of the Oregon Pioneer Association*
WaHQ	*Washington Historical Quarterly*
WHQ	*Western Historical Quarterly*

Introduction

In the summer of 1851, the French traveler Pierre Fournier de Saint Amant visited the Oregon Territory, spending several weeks with French-Indian families living in a corner of the Willamette Valley known as French Prairie.[1] In the account of his travels published in 1854, Saint Amant painted a fanciful portrait of French Prairie as a pastoral backwater settlement. In one passage, he noted that while "seated at the hearth of the crossed races," he had observed the "patriarchal" customs of the settlers that bespoke contentment with the present and an apparent absence of concern about the future. Saint Amant also noted with a tinge of annoyance that the settlers rarely discussed the "rise and fall of empires," not even the violent revolutions that had erupted across Europe just a few years earlier.[2]

Given the class distinctions between the French-Indian families and Saint Amant—a former world chess champion and a French foreign service envoy—the Frenchman's social background colored his perceptions of the settlers. Their preoccupations appeared local and immediate, common for a class of unlettered former fur laborers and their Native wives. Indeed, Saint Amant's observations were not unusual for his day. Educated observers who happened to mention French Canadian voyageurs in their writings often portrayed them as simple and carefree, even childlike. This stereotype of the happy-go-lucky French Canadian voyageur was then becoming a staple of early fur trade and pioneer chronicles.[3]

While such an image may indicate the education level of the French Canadian men retired from the fur trade and the semi-isolated nature of life in a contact zone (frontier), it evokes a romanticized vision of the Far West. The French Canadians—whom Saint Amant portrays as blithely unaware of larger historical events—were in reality the vanguard of international commercial interests that set out to exploit the Pacific Northwest in the early 1800s. These fur laborers, together with their Indian wives, literally propelled British and American imperial interests into the region by staffing vital canoe brigades and fur-trapping expeditions for ten, twenty, and even thirty years. Following their permanent move to French Prairie, these French-Indian families contributed to the agrarian colonization of the Willamette Valley, assisted early Methodist and Catholic missionary efforts, and participated in local debates about the nature of civil governance and national authority during the years preceding large-scale American migration to Oregon in the mid-1840s.

Saint Amant's inclination to overlook the role of the French Canadian trappers—and by extension their bicultural families and Native kin—in the sweep of larger historical events illustrates a common perception in the historical writing of the nineteenth century. Nicolas Biddle (editor of the Lewis and Clark journals), Oregon boosters, and overland pioneers who recorded the Euro-American exploration and settlement of Oregon inaugurated a tenacious "founding mythology" of the Pacific Northwest, a historical interpretation later reproduced and modified in succeeding generations. Akin to Frederick Jackson Turner's frontier thesis articulated in the 1890s, this mythology followed a predominant theme in American letters rendering Anglo-Americans as the central actors in a progressive, triumphant settlement of the western regions.[4]

The original "Oregon Country" was the vast region west of the Rocky Mountains that stretched from Russian Alaska to Spanish California. Following the international boundary treaty of 1846, the Oregon Territory encompassed the present-day states of Oregon, Washington, Idaho, and part of western Montana. Even before Americans ventured into the region in large numbers, there was an American "Oregon of the mind" shaped by both cartography and the printed word.[5] This mental geography was expansive enough to hold the dreams of a diverse citizenry, no matter how fanciful. As the nineteenth century progressed, American visions of Oregon came to encompass Edenic landscapes, republican virtues, true religion, economic prosperity, and individual liberty. James Ronda has noted that Oregon was "one more part of an American tradition to include Oleanna, the Big Rock Candy Mountains, Paradise Valley, and the Peaceable Kingdom."[6] This mental act of territorial possession was in keeping with the vision of President Thomas Jefferson, who had dispatched Lewis and Clark on their expedition to the Far West in 1803. Jefferson believed that the United States must continue to expand westward in order to ensure the economic stability and social vitality of a republic built upon yeoman farmers. By cultivating new lands, westward expansion—the American brand of colonialism—offered "cultural salvation and imperial power" to the young nation.[7]

A few notable figures—Robert Gray, Lewis and Clark, John McLoughlin, Jason Lee, and Marcus Whitman—laid the foundation for this "inevitable"

Anglo-American colonization and resettlement of the Far West. The Oregon story was portrayed as particularly heroic and celebratory owing to the great hardships endured by American overlanders on their 2,000-mile trek from Missouri to Oregon. The emigrants found their primary destination, Oregon's Willamette Valley, to be a land providentially depopulated of its Indian population due to disease. The newcomers thereupon set out to create a progressive, agricultural-based economy and establish American law and governance. Over the next two decades, the Anglo-American settlers gained ascendancy over the emerging economic and political institutions in the region, instituted a racialized social hierarchy, and forced most Native American groups onto reservations, small portions of their once vast ancestral territories.[8]

This marginalization of Native groups, fur trade personnel, and their families had several ramifications for Pacific Northwest historiography. First and foremost, analysis of the historical experiences of Indian peoples and fur trade laborers remained cursory into the twentieth century, as did knowledge about the relations *between* Natives and newcomers during the early colonial period.[9] In turn, American historians tended to overlook the relationship between the British North American fur trade and the Anglo-American resettlement of the Pacific Northwest, thereby obscuring long-term colonizing processes in the region.[10] A common practice consisted of portraying Native peoples and fur trade personnel as obstacles rather than as precursors to Anglo-American settlement. Thus, if not fully absent from historical texts, these groups were depicted as maintaining an inherently conflictual relationship with the incoming American settlers. A classic case in point is the standard interpretation of the development of a provisional government in Oregon. Pioneer chronicles and historians alike viewed French Canadian opposition to a provisional government in the early 1840s in highly nationalistic terms, portraying the French Canadians as spoilers intent on demonstrating their loyalty to the Hudson's Bay Company and the British cause in Oregon.[11]

The notion of French Canadians—then second-class citizens in British North America— opposing a provisional government out of loyalty to the territorial and mercantile interests of Great Britain and the Hudson's Bay Company would be comical if this interpretation were not so ingrained in Oregon's founding mythology.[12] As Chad Reimer has observed, nationalist perspectives and racial ideologies played a central role in shaping the early historiography of the Pacific Northwest. During the 1830s and 1840s, Americans writing in support of the U.S. territorial claims in the Oregon Country attacked the Hudson's Bay Company (HBC), portraying it as a tainted organization because of its monopolistic trade policies, its position as a representative of the antidemocratic British establishment, and its tolerance of sexual relations between company employees and Indian women. Ignorant of the company's sometimes troubled relations with French Canadian laborers, aboriginal peoples, and Métis groups in Rupert's Land (the present-day Canadian Prairies), the American chroniclers conceived of a close, conspiratorial relationship between the HBC, Indian groups, and French Canadians in the Pacific Northwest. Thus, the long-standing interpretation of French Canadian settlers in the Willamette Valley as representatives of the HBC and the British Crown flowed not only from notions of Anglo-Saxon, Protestant religious and ethnic superiority but also from the American settlers' antipathy toward Britain and her representative in Oregon, the HBC.[13]

During the decades that saw the Anglo-American colonization of the Pacific Northwest, Native peoples, fur trade laborers, and their bicultural families were at another disadvantage in having their experiences recorded. They were largely illiterate, and Americans chronicling the resettlement of the Pacific Northwest were not particularly interested in writing about these groups in a substantive manner. Both scholars and popular historians relied on traditional written sources left by Anglo-Canadian fur trade officers and by Anglo-American explorers and pioneers that at best marginalized the historical experiences of those who were not white, male, Protestant, and English-speaking, and at worse effaced them from the historical record.[14]

The dominance of Oregon's founding mythology endured into the latter decades of the twentieth century, its staying power resting on an ability to meet the needs of Anglo-Americans who had dominated the state and the Pacific Northwest—demographically, politically, and economically—since the 1850s. The heroic, celebratory, and ultimately reassuring tone of this mythology answered the cultural needs of the majority ethnic group, while also providing ideological support for an economy based on the exploitation of the region's natural resources. In this sense, the Euro-American resettlement of the Pacific Northwest was inevitable and progressive, and this view held together into the 1970s.[15]

The present study follows developments in Pacific Northwest historiography over the past generation, particularly the work of scholars who spotlight Native history, intercultural relations, women's history, and gender dynamics within the context of British and American colonialism during the nineteenth century.[16] This volume's particular contribution is its focus on French Prairie, the bicultural community at the heart of Oregon's Willamette Valley—the homeland of the Kalapuyan peoples and the central focus of the American settlers' colonizing efforts in the 1840s and 1850s. Culture, language, religion, geography, nearly universal endogamy for the three generations, and a shared historical experience bound the interethnic families as a community. My choice of French Prairie is based on several factors: its prime location in the Willamette Valley, its place as the largest concentration of French-Indian families in the Pacific Northwest, and the existence of archaeological research on the area.[17] I must also note my familial connection to French Prairie, the home of my paternal French-Indian ancestors.[18] This study is narrower in scope than Jean Barman's recent transnational study, *French Canadians, Furs, and Indigenous Women in the Making of the Pacific Northwest*, and John C. Jackson's narrative survey, *Children of the Fur Trade: Forgotten Métis of the Pacific Northwest*, both of which examine French-Indian communities in the larger Pacific Northwest region at locations such as Cowlitz Prairie, Fort Colvile, Fort Nisqually, Fort Walla Walla (Frenchtown), and Fort Victoria.[19]

By examining the social, economic, and political dynamics that shaped family and community in French Prairie from the start of the overland fur trade through Oregon's achievement of statehood (1812–1859), this study recovers continuities and changes that marked the initial phase of Euro-American colonization in the Pacific Northwest, the ascendancy of Anglo-Americans in the region, and Oregon's incorporation into the United States on the eve of the Civil War.[20] As recent studies have demonstrated, the incorporation of western territories into the United States during the nineteenth century was a discordant, unsteady process that included periods of armed violence, interracial strife, strident disagreements among American settlers, and multilayered forms of accommodation and resistance by Native, Mexican, and French-speaking groups.[21] This history of French Prairie adds another layer to this story by highlighting the agency of French-Indian westerners responding to the social, political, and economic pressures that accompanied Anglo-American westward expansion and the sectional crisis during the antebellum period. It is in keeping with recent studies on women, family, and community that explore how gender, race, and ethnic relations shaped Western history.[22]

In the decades preceding large-scale American resettlement, several historical forces structured relations between the nascent French-Indian community, the Kalapuyans, and the initial collection of Americans in the Willamette Valley: the indigenous trade networks of the Columbia-Willamette region, the centuries-old North American fur trade, the French Canadian diaspora, competing visions of global commerce and national conquest, Protestant and Catholic missionary zeal, and cultural values and community interests. Social relations in French Prairie were marked by tension, miscommunication, mutual self-interest, cooperation, and genuine compassion. Drawing on their experience in the fur trade, as well their connections with both aboriginal and Euro-American cultures, the French Prairie settlers tried to negotiate a middle course within the context of competing forces, especially at times when cross-cultural tensions were high.

Following the Oregon Trail migration of 1843, Anglo-Americans gained a demographic advantage in the valley and later achieved political dominance with the signing of the Oregon Treaty of 1846 and the establishment of the territorial government in 1849. Under the Anglo-American regime of the 1840s and the 1850s, the French-Indian families, like their Native kin, faced a host of challenges: political marginalization, the ripple effects of mining frontiers on the Pacific Slope, settler-Indian wars, Indian removal, religious intolerance, an increasingly racialized society, and tensions over land, resources, and civil rights.[23] In response to these changing circumstances, the French Prairie settlers devised family strategies that included participation in the developing economic and political systems, contributions to military expeditions against regional Native groups, and the exercise of legal tools at their disposal. The French Prairie settlers sought to advance and preserve their own community interests within an Anglo-American settler society that coveted the Oregon Country and had little room for these bicultural people of French-Indian ancestry and their Native kin.[24]

Recent landmark studies have demonstrated that the balance of power in Native-newcomer relations during early colonial periods was not necessarily weighted in favor of European imperial interests. European and Native societies were relatively evenly matched so long as the Europeans remained at a disadvantage demographically, economically, and militarily, and in regions where the newcomers' presence was tenuous, Indian groups held the upper hand in shaping intercultural relations. Native and newcomers utilized socioeconomic relationships and cultural practices to construct systems of communication, accommodation, and exchange over several generations—a "middle ground" within the context of European imperialism.[25] Once later generations of Euro-Americans gained an upper hand in a region, they sought to dictate the terms of intercultural relations. In the Trans-Mississippi West, shifts in power relations ultimately resulted from large-scale Anglo-American migrations and the territorial expansion of the United States. Beginning in the nineteenth century, Native groups struggled to fend off the effects of disease, loss of control over natural resources, structural economic change, and social dislocation as they confronted Anglo-American settler colonialism.[26]

Similar forces were at play in the Willamette Valley during the first half of the nineteenth century. Mercantile capitalism in the form of the overland fur trade gave rise to the French-Indian settlement in French Prairie, while Americans supporting westward expansion advocated various schemes of economic, religious, and military intervention in the Oregon Country. Given the scholarship on Euro-American colonization and intercultural relations, it is important to consider how French Prairie compares with other contact zones in North America. As in other regions, both the indigenous Kalapuyans and the French-Indian settlers adapted long-standing aboriginal trade and kinship practices to changing economic circumstances. While the Kalapuyans did not have the economic clout of the Chinookan peoples who controlled the Columbia River, nor the advantages of the equestrian cultures of the Plateau peoples, the Willamette Valley peoples demonstrated a willingness to engage in both local and regional resistance against the newcomers until some accommodation could be reached. On the other hand, the Willamette Valley was unique in several respects.

The catastrophic decline of the Kalapuyan population due to "intermittent fever" in the 1830s—just twenty years after the first direct contact with Euro-Americans—played a pivotal role in shaping fanciful notions of an untouched idyllic landscape in Oregon. The "Oregon Fever" that resulted, together with social and economic conditions in the Midwest, led to the massive migration of American settlers into the valley in the 1840s. Following the Rogue River War (1850s), a genocidal campaign against the indigenous peoples of southwestern Oregon, Anglo-American officials confined nearly all of the Native groups of western Oregon on Indian reservations.[27] Thus, in comparison with other contact zones such as the Great Lakes region, the Canadian prairies, and the Southwest, the early colonial period in the Willamette Valley was compressed into a much shorter time span. Although the French Prairie settlers labored under historical forces similar to those in other regions, it was this compression of the early colonial period combined with the juggernaut of American migration that ultimately influenced the ethnic identity of their descendants.

Over the past decades, scholars have studied the connections between intermarriage, Native women's roles in the fur trade, bicultural community formation, and the emergence of Métis ethnic identity and nationalism in Canada and the United States. Their research suggests that although mixed-race populations developed in every contact situation (a process known as *métissage* in French), the emergence of a separate Métis ethnic identity was the result of specific historical circumstances.[28] Key components in the process of Métis ethnogenesis included the long-term viability of the fur trade and related mercantile economies, intermarriage between Native/bicultural women and French Canadian men over several generations, matrifocal residence, the centrality of kinship networks and geographic mobility, a prioritization of family and community interests, a layering of indigenous and French Canadian culture and religious practices, and a markedly slow pace of Anglo settlement and economic penetration.[29]

Sleeper-Smith's research on the western Great Lakes illustrates the long persistence of ethnic French-Indian families from the late seventeenth century through the late nineteenth century.[30] This persistence of bicultural families was due in large part to the role of Native women in incorporating French Canadian men into their indigenous communities and in acting as cultural mediators in the fur trade. Martha Foster has demonstrated that the development and maintenance of a distinctive Métis identity and culture in Montana was a long-term process spanning more than one hundred years—a process that continued well into the twentieth century despite a lack of federal recognition. In Tanis Thorne's work on the French and Indian peoples of the Lower Missouri from 1750 to 1880, she found that people of bicultural ancestry "may have shared a collective identity as members of a community, but not necessarily a nationalistic identity as a 'new people.'"[31]

In the Pacific Northwest, Anglo-Americans established a settler society relatively quickly in the mid-1800s. They institutionalized white supremacy and racial exclusion both socially and geographically, and as the nineteenth century progressed, this system of classification increasingly placed "mixed-bloods" in the racial category of "Indian" rather than in the category of "white," a racial distinction comparable to the black/white dualism in nineteenth-century America.[32] Such restrictive circumstances, at odds with both the indigenous world and the multiethnic society of the fur trade, prompted French-Indian families to make differing decisions as to their racial affiliation. Some families distanced themselves from their Indian heritage and outwardly acculturated into white society, while others chose an opposite route and joined their kinfolk on Indian reservations.[33]

The initial experience of the French Prairie settlers parallels that of the early bicultural communities in the Great Lakes region, the Lower Missouri, and Canada. There is little evidence, however, to suggest the development of separate Métis ethnic identity in the Willamette Valley over the relatively short thirty-year period of intercultural contact preceding the Oregon Treaty of 1846. Especially significant is the demographic factor: the French-Indian community, which ranged between 75 and 120 families in the 1840s and 1850s, remained relatively small in comparison to the thousands of American settlers who came to Oregon during the same period. For this reason, I have elected to use the term "French-Indian" when referring to the bicultural families and individuals who settled in the Willamette Valley. I employ more specific terms such as "French-Algonquin" when more information is available on individual historical figures. Following previous researchers, I occasionally use the French term *métis* when referring to people of French Canadian and Native ancestry. I use this approach in order to avoid confusion with the Métis peoples of North America, who developed and maintain a distinctive indigenous identity.[34]

In *At the Hearth of the Crossed Races*, it is my aim to recover the experience and the role of the French Prairie settlers in early Oregon history. As a social historian, I have taken a microhistorical approach that examines women, family, and community and considers the importance of gender, race, and ethnicity. The central place of women, family, and community is especially significant given the interethnic heritage of the French Prairie settlers and their social, economic, and cultural ties to their maternal Native communities in the Pacific Northwest. Although historians have produced microhistories focusing on educated individuals and well-documented events, microhistory is perhaps best known as an approach for illuminating the lives of marginalized groups and individuals whose historical experiences were less documented and of less interest to academic historians in North America prior to the emergence of social history in the 1960s.

The advantage of a microhistorical approach in this study is its emphasis on tracing the behaviors, decisions, and agency of the men and women of French Prairie.[35] Such an approach has allowed me to elucidate the settlers' society, economy, and culture and to some extent their self-identity, all historical realties that have either been obscured or previously unremarked.[36] Although the frame of reference for microhistory is smaller—the individual, the family, and the community—it should have significance for the larger macrohistory. Tamara Hareven argued that the challenge for historians of the family is "the reconstruction of a multi-tiered reality—the lives of individual families and their interactions with major social, economic, and political forces. . . . In short, it represents an effort to understand the interrelationship between individual time, family time, and historical time."[37] For this volume, the broader canvas is a dramatic period in the Pacific Northwest: British and American imperialism, the American annexation of the southern portion of the Oregon Country, the intensification of the sectional crisis, and the racialization of Pacific Northwest society. By recounting the history of French Prairie, I have endeavored to connect personal and local realities in the Willamette Valley to larger regional, national, and continental developments. In addition to my interest in the Trans-Mississippi West, I aim to connect French Prairie to the larger history of French-speaking peoples in American history, an area of inquiry that is ripe for further exploration.

In an attempt to overcome limitations in the historical record, I have mined the well-known sources produced by literate English speakers in the 1800s as well as French-language sources recorded by the first group of French Canadian Catholic missionaries in Oregon. These sources are primarily the letters and reports of Father Francis Norbert Blanchet, who later became the first Catholic archbishop in Oregon. The various *Catholic Church Records of the Pacific Northwest*, a lifelong project of the late Harriet Munnick, have also provided important genealogical information. I was also able to locate some limited accounts produced by French-Indian settlers either through dictations to or interviews with English speakers. Although the French Prairie folks were largely illiterate for two to three generations, they were nevertheless a determined and legal-minded group. As a result, they left some documents in the archives of the provisional, territorial, and federal governments.

This study covers the forty-seven years from 1812, the date of the first direct contact between Kalapuyans and Euro-Americans, to 1859, the date Oregon achieved statehood on the eve of the Civil War. Chapter 1 outlines the economy and society of the Kalapuyans and examines the initial years of Native-newcomer relations in the Willamette Valley under the trapping and trading expeditions of the PFC and the NWC. Chapter 2 chronicles the French-Indian families' agrarian colonization of the Willamette Valley and the devastating impact of the "intermittent fever" on the Kalapuyans during the 1830s. Chapter 3 demonstrates the community initiatives that bound the French-Indian families to the initial wave of American Methodist missionaries in the mid-1830s. Chapter 4 traces the establishment of the first Catholic mission in French Prairie and the rise of sectarian tensions between American Protestant and French Canadian Catholic missionaries. Chapter 5 considers political initiatives leading to the formation of the Oregon Provisional Government in the context of competing British and American territorial claims over Oregon in the 1840s. Chapter 6 charts the tensions over ethnic and national loyalties following the Whitman Mission incident and the Cayuse War in the late 1840s and the tightening of Anglo settler colonialism during the 1850s.

Notwithstanding the powerful force of Oregon's founding mythology, the Willamette Valley was not an empty Eden awaiting settlement by hardy American pioneers. It was instead one of the early sites of extensive and continuous intercultural contact. From this perspective, Saint Amant's image of French Prairie as a "hearth of the crossed races" might suggest an alternative vision of early Oregon history. Rather than erasing the complexity of intercultural relations, we might conceive of French Prairie as a contact zone where people of differing ethnicities—sometimes bound by common interests, sometimes in conflict over those same interests—attempted to ford the cultural divide with varying degrees of success. The French-Indian couples who resettled the Kalapuyans' homeland were active participants in the encounter between two cultures, Euro-American and Native American, which was at times intimate, at times violent. Though the bicultural French-Indian families did seek a middle course in their relations with all their various neighbors, their very presence ultimately contributed to the Anglo-American colonization of the Pacific Northwest.

By establishing farming and husbandry operations in the Willamette Valley, the French-Indian families initiated processes of social and ecological change that enhanced the reputation of the Willamette Valley as a destination of choice for Oregon Trail pioneers. Upon the arrival of the American emigrants en masse, the social space for the people of the "crossed races" diminished considerably as the Anglo settlers instituted systems of racial separation. Although the French-Indian families did not develop a distinct Métis identity in the compressed colonial period from 1812 to 1859, they—like their Native kin—did not disappear from the social landscape. Instead they persisted and adapted to changing circumstances using a variety of tools and strategies at their disposal. In exploring the history of French Prairie, *At the Hearth of the Crossed Races* adds another chapter to the Oregon story, complicating and deepening our understanding of the peoples who forged the Pacific Northwest in the nineteenth century.

CHAPTER 1 ❋ Native–Fur Trader Relations
in the Willamette Valley

In late November 1812, employees of John Jacob Astor's Pacific Fur Company (PFC) set to work constructing the company's first inland post in the Willamette Valley. Clerks William Wallace and John Halsey located the post, later named Wallace House, on an upland prairie approximately fifty miles from the mouth of the Willamette River. Situated on the eastern bank, Wallace House lay near the territorial line between the Ahantchuyuk and Santiam Kalapuyans and a few miles south of the area that would later be known as French Prairie.[1] The PFC partners intended the post to serve as a winter base for company employees to collect furs and procure needed venison, thereby reducing the number of mouths to feed at the central depot of Fort Astoria. In addition to Wallace and Halsey, the first group at Fort Wallace included twelve laborers and three hunters: John Day, Ignace Shonowane (Iroquois) and his family, and Pierre Dorion Jr. (French-Sioux) and Marie L'Aguivoise (Iowa) and their young son Paul.[2] In February 1813, a second party, consisting of clerks John Reed, Alfred Seton, and Thomas McKay, two trappers, and thirteen more laborers departed for the Willamette Valley.[3] Over the winter and spring (1812–1813), the Astorians trapped beaver, hunted wild game, and traded with local Kalapuyans for additional foodstuffs.

Wallace and Halsey's decision to situate this first Willamette Valley post in the upper valley within the territory of two Central Kalapuyan groups was not a haphazard decision. Earlier in the spring of 1812, PFC partner Donald McKenzie had completed the first reconnoitering trip into the valley, and he had noted the location and activities of the Kalapuyans as well as the valley's geography, hydrology, and natural resources. The territories of the Santiam and Ahantchuyuk on the eastern bank were noteworthy because they provided relatively easy access to the Willamette River and encompassed more open prairie lands with fewer forested hills than other areas. In addition, the Central Kalapuyan lands were located within a reasonable distance of Fort Astoria along the Willamette and Columbia Rivers. For these reasons, the homeland of the Central Kalapuyans, especially the Ahantchuyuk, became a site of intercultural contact between the indigenous inhabitants and the fur traders, the advance guard for American and British mercantile interests on the Northwest Coast in the early 1800s. The area later became the locale for a hybrid community of French-Indian families born of this commercial enterprise. The first decade of Native–fur trader relations in the Willamette Valley involved tension, conflict, and misunderstanding, and although the Kalapuyans and the small group of Euro-Americans did not seek close or intimate connections with each other during the initial contact period, they reached a measure of coexistence by the end of 1810s.

Situated between the Coast Range to the west and the Cascade Mountains to the east, the Willamette Valley is the largest valley in western Oregon. It is roughly 110 miles long, varies in width from 20 to 30 miles, and covers approximately 3,500 square miles. At several locations, minor hill chains (e.g., Eola Hills, Waldo Hills) rise several hundred feet above a valley floor marked by relatively low relief.[4] Flowing north, the Willamette River is a major tributary of the Columbia River, and the Willamette River Basin comprises roughly 11,500 square miles. The Willamette slowly meanders its way back and forth over a broad alluvial flood-plain, fed by numerous smaller tributaries, streams, and wetlands.[5] In the early nineteenth century, the river featured an extensive, multiple-channel flow, whereas today the river tends to follow a smaller single channel.[6] The valley soils include gravel and sand, significant sections of adobe clay, and large sections of silts and alluvium, which, though lacking significant lime deposits, are rich in humus.[7] The central feature separating the lower Willamette Valley from its upper portion is the large lava sill that forms Willamette Falls at present-day Oregon City.

The Willamette Valley's proximity to the Pacific Coast and its location midway between the equator and the North Pole affords it a relatively mild climate. To the north lies the region of the stormy and cool North Pacific westerlies and to the south the warm, stable air of the subtropics. In the crucible between these two atmospheric systems, the valley receives wet winters and relatively dry sum-mers. The often remarked climatic feature is the annual rainfall, between thirty and sixty inches per year in the valley, and double that in the Coast Range and Cascades.[8] Due to heavy rainfall and mild temperatures, the Willamette Valley has long had a large and diverse biomass. At the turn of the nineteenth century, the upper section of valley comprised several microenvironments, or ecological niches.[9] The largest of these was the oak savannah–woodlands complex, which consisted of wet lowland prairies, drier upland prairies, oak openings, and occa-sional oak forests. Two types of perennial grasses dominated the prairies: *Festuca rubra* and *Deschampsia cespitosa*. In the oak openings and oak forests, Oregon white oak was the prevailing species, while Douglas fir, alder, and laurel were also present in scattered groups or as isolated trees. Understory plants included a collection of grasses, forbs, shrubs, ferns, and berries.

A second microenvironment was the wetland, including marshes, sloughs and swales, and larger inland bodies such as Lake Labish and Wapato Lake (both now drained), all created as a result of low elevations, high water tables, and seasonal flooding. These wetlands were home to the *wapato*, a bulbous marsh herb, while the wet lowland prairies were home to the bulbous camas lily.[10] A third micro-environment consisted of the gallery forests located along the Willamette's tributaries and streams. The bottomland timber included Oregon white ash, bigleaf maple, black cottonwood, western redcedar, and Douglas fir. Secondary species were oak, laurel, alder, cherry, and willow. Salmonberry, red elderberry, hardhack, ninebark, cascara, rose, and Oregon grape made up the understory vegetation in these bottomlands.[11] A final ecological niche was the coniferous forestland of the foothills and mountains of the Coast Range and Cascades Mountains. Due to the higher elevations, Douglas fir was the prevailing arbor species, alongside the secondary presence of bigleaf maple, hemlock, dogwood, vine maple, oak, laurel, and cedar, and understory plants included various berries and the Oregon grape.

Anthropologists have recognized the term "Kalapuyan" as a general ethnic identifier for the upwards of twenty culturally and linguistically related groups that originally inhabited the upper Willamette Valley in the early 1800s (see map 1).[12] At that time, the Kalapuyans likely comprised three related language divisions: North, Central, and Southern (table 1).[13] Robert Boyd has estimated that between 1805 and the late 1820s, the total Kalapuyan population (including the Yoncalla of the Umpqua River watershed) ranged between 8,780 and 9,200.[14] Henry Zenk's analysis of the limited ethnographic data suggests that the Kalapuyans recognized collective entities larger than the single village. Although Kalapuyan hamlets were not consolidated into a tight tribal political structure, they likely retained a collective identity, based on the social, cultural, and economic connections between villages in a local territory.[15] The surviving documentation on the better-known group names (Tualatin, Yamhill, and Santiam) refers to villages that shared a common culture and a common dialect.[16] These Kalapuyan groupings, though not strongly hierarchical in nature, did participate in a larger multivillage political culture, with individual villages retaining access rights to specific resources in specific locations and shared access rights to other "productive locales" within a larger common territory.[17]

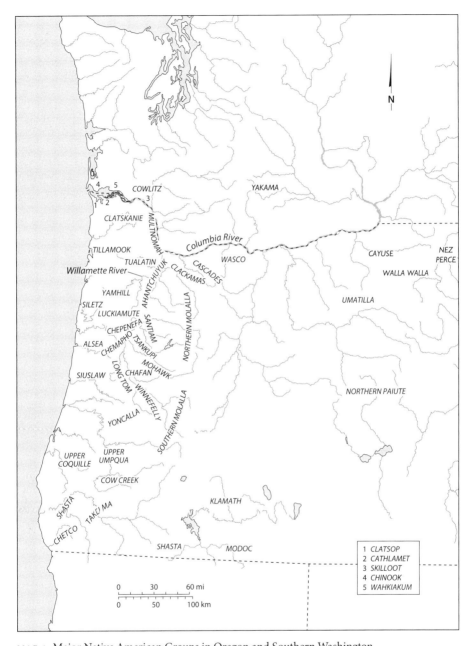

MAP 1. Major Native American Groups in Oregon and Southern Washington.
Map by Bill Nelson.

TABLE 1. Kalapuyan group divisions

Group	Historical variations	Watershed/location
Northern Kalapuyan		
Tualatin	Atfalati, Twalaty	Tualatin River
Yamhill	Yamel	Yamhill River
Central Kalapuyan		
Ahantchuyuk	Pudding River, French Prairie	Pudding River
Luckiamute	Alakemayuk	Luckiamute River
Santiam	Ahalpam, halpam	Santiam River
Chepenefa	Mary's River	Mary's River
Chemapho	Muddy Creek	Muddy Creek
Tsankupi		Calapooia River (Brownsville)
Tcanschifin		McKenzie-Willamette Confluence
Mohawk		Mohawk River, McKenzie River
Chelamela	Long Tom	Long Tom River
Winnefelly		Coast Fork, Willamette River
		Middle Fork, Willamette River
Southern Kalapuyan		
Yoncalla	Ayankeld	Elk Creek
		Calapooya Creek

SOURCES: Beckham, *Indians*; Collins, "Position;" Jacobs, *Kalapuya*; Mackey, *Kalapuyans*;
Zenk, "Contributions;" Zenk, "Kalapuyans."

Historical and ethnographic sources indicate that "Ahantchuyuk" was the name of the Central Kalapuyan group that lived in the Pudding River watershed, an eastern tributary of the Willamette River, in the early 1800s. The name literally translated means "the ones belonging behind, away."[18] Their territory roughly corresponded with the toponym "French Prairie," which is bounded on the north and west by the Willamette River, the Pudding River on the east, and the marshy Lake Labiche to the south (now drained). Synonyms of the name were "Hanchoiks" and "Hanshoke." Anglo-Americans referred to the Ahantchuyuk as the "Pudding River Indians" or "French Prairie Indians." It is also possible that the place name "Champoeg," which may be based on the Kalapuyan term *campuik*, was the name of an Ahantchuyuk village originally located near the later French-Indian hamlet of Champoeg.[19] The original Champoeg may well have been a local trading center for the various Kalapuyan tribes. Historically it was as a useful landing for river traffic because of the break in the dense gallery forests that lined the Willamette River. The Ahantchuyuk's neighbors included both Kalapuyans and non-Kalapuyans. To the east were the Molalla, a Penutian-speaking group, who occupied the foothills and both the western and eastern slopes of the Cascades. To the northeast, Upper Chinookan peoples occupied the lower Willamette Valley, beginning with the coveted salmon fishing grounds at Willamette Falls. North and west across the Willamette was Tualatin territory, and due west across the river lived the Yamhill. Due south of the Ahantchuyuk lived the Santiam Kalapuyans.[20]

In the early 1800s, Kalapuyan peoples dwelt in autonomous villages, each with its own headman.[21] A headman's position was based on wealth (rather than on heredity), and additional community leaders would include shamans and other members of wealthy families.[22] In contrast to the hereditary caste system of the Chinookan peoples of the lower Columbia, Kalapuyan society was apparently less stratified. The main cleavage in Kalapuyan society was that between freeborn villagers and enslaved foreigners. Within the ranks of the freeborn were the head-men and their families, respectable commoners, shamans, and the poorer people of the hamlet. Wealth was not an absolute, as one might gain or lose wealth within the community. Thus, there was a possibility for social mobility.[23]

Slavery appears to have been more common among the Northern Kalapuyans, particularly the Tualatin, than among the Central and Southern groups. This may have been a historical development resulting from the cross-cultural relations between the Northern Kalapuyans and their Chinookan neighbors, as there is evidence of both kinship and trade connections with the Upper Chinookans of the lower Willamette Valley.[24] The Tualatin supplied the Chinookan peoples, who relied heavily on slave labor, with slaves from both inside and outside the Willamette Valley. Slave trading was thus a distinctive component of the Tualatin economy. Since the Tualatin acquired slaves through kidnapping as well through trade, they apparently preyed upon the Central and Southern Kalapuyans.[25] In Kalapuyan society, as in other aboriginal societies in the Pacific Northwest, slavery was a hereditary social status whereby the descendants of foreign captives were also slaves.[26] In keeping with the more flexible Kalapuyan social structure, however, the status of the slave class was not quite equivalent to that of the Kalapuyans' Chinookan neighbors, for occasionally marriages did occur between freeborn and slave, which thereby freed the slave.[27]

Ethnographic information suggests the Kalapuyan practiced patrilocal residence and exogamy and had a preference for polygyny. Kalapuyan men married women from nearby villages and neighboring Kalapuyan and Chinookan groups. The Kalapuyans viewed marriage as an exchange between families, the groom's family securing the prospective wife with gifts to the woman's family.[28] As a result, a father with several daughters might increase his wealth through the marriage of his female offspring. In the case of the death of a husband, the husband's family held possessory rights over the widow, which could be acquired through the exchange of gifts.[29] During the early contact period, the articles used in marriage exchanges included slaves and dentalia.[30] Like other indigenous societies throughout the Northwest Coast, kinship and marriage alliances structured social, economic, and diplomatic relationships in the Willamette Valley.

In the early 1800s, the Kalapuyans' economy—tied to their village-based conceptions of territory and ethnic identity—involved three central activities: a subsistence round based on a gendered division of labor, the use of fire for resource management, and participation in regional exchange networks. Taken as a whole, the cultural, economic, and resource management practices of the Kalapuyans allowed them to maintain relatively sustainable relationships with the valley's flora and fauna.[31] As complex hunter-gatherers, they based their seasonal round on the exploitation of various resources within the riverine, lowland, and upland areas of their territories. The Kalapuyans' resource base was highly diversified as a result of the great variety of animal and plant life in the Willamette Valley. As Henry Zenk has noted, the "regional distinctiveness of Kalapuyan subsistence" distinguished them from their Chinookan neighbors to the north, who relied more heavily on the regional trade and on the salmon runs of the Columbia River and the Willamette River below Willamette Falls.[32]

The Kalapuyans' subsistence calendar consisted of two cycles: one spent in the permanent winter villages and a second spent in various temporary harvesting camps over the spring, summer, and early fall.[33] During the rainy winter months, they survived primarily on preserved food and wild game; however, because winter hunting might not bring in enough calories to offset any drop in food stores, the late winter could be a time of hunger. During the warmer, drier months from March through October, Kalapuyan women and children, working in groups, harvested an impressive array of nutrition-rich foods in several different ecological niches.[34] They migrated to the wetlands and lowlands to harvest camas and *wapato,* to the drier oak savannah and prairies to harvest tarweed seeds, hazelnuts, and acorns, and to the foothill forests of the Coast Range or the Cascades to harvest berries.[35]

During the spring, summer, and early fall, the Willamette Valley Natives also added insects, waterfowl, and aquatic sources to their diet. The fall was an especially important time for men and boys to engage in small- and large-scale hunts of deer and elk, as well as smaller animals. The women processed both the wild game and the animal hides for local use and intertribal trade.[36] For the

Kalapuyans, successful food production relied on skilled and knowledgeable individuals, cooperative work parties, some level of processing, and elaborate storage techniques.[37] Following the completion of the harvest season in the late fall, the Kalapuyans returned to their permanent winter village sites, located along riverbanks or the confluences of tributary rivers and streams.[38]

Environmental resource management was another major component of the indigenous economy in the Willamette Valley. The Kalapuyans maintained the oak savannah–open woodlands complex of the upper valley through controlled prairie fires.[39] Like other Native groups in the Pacific Northwest, the Kalapuyans used regular, managed fires to aid the growth of key plants, roots, and berries and to maintain desired animal habitats. Robert Boyd, the most well-versed researcher in Kalapuyan burning practices, concluded that "with control over and knowledge of the ecosystemic effects of fire, the Indians established an important symbiotic relationship with their environment."[40] As reconstructed by Boyd, the Kalapuyans' annual burning schedule corresponded to their subsistence round. Over the late spring and early summer, they were busy at wetland and lowland prairie sites, harvesting and processing camas and *wapato*. In July and August, they lit occasional fires in conjunction with gathering local food sources on the dry prairies, such as grass seeds, sunflower seeds, hazelnuts, and blackberries. During the closing weeks of the summer, the Kalapuyans would use fire as a means for harvesting tarweed and insects on the high prairies. October was the month for burning the oak openings after the gathering of acorns. The final prairie fires were the late autumn events meant to drive out large game for the communal hunt. With a stock of dried deer and elk meat, the Kalapuyans would return to their riverine villages to wait out the wet valley winters.[41]

While the Kalapuyans' complex subsistence round and their use of fire for resource management remained central components of their economy through the early 1800s, a third element, participation in the regional aboriginal exchange network, introduced them to broader continental changes occurring as a result of European and American imperialism and commercial expansion. As the Northern and Central Kalapuyans occupied the large upper portion of the Willamette Valley, their primary social and economic ties were to the region Yvonne Hajda has described as the "Greater Lower Columbia." This part of the Northwest Coast included Upper and Lower Chinookan, Salish, and Athapaskan communities on both sides of the Columbia River and its lower tributaries from The Dalles to the river's mouth, the Upper Chinookan and Kalapuyan areas of the Willamette Valley, and the various coastal groups from the Quinault River in the north to the Alsea River in the south. All of these communities were connected to some degree to the ancient Pacific-Plateau trade corridor along the great river.[42]

In the late 1700s, the Chinookan peoples who occupied strategic fishing and navigational sites along the Columbia and the lower Willamette played a central role in the flow of goods between the Plateau, the lower Columbia, and more distant regions to the north such as Vancouver Island. European goods arrived in the lower Columbia region during the eighteenth century via the aboriginal trade networks as Europeans and Americans expanded their exploratory, commercial, and colonizing activities on the Northwest Coast and the interior regions of North America.[43] The Chinook proper, who lived on the north side of the Columbia River estuary, took a leading role in the maritime fur trade in the lower Columbia once it debuted in the 1790s. The maritime fur trade became integrated into the existing regional exchange system and afforded coastal groups better access to European goods than those they had previously acquired through the long-distance Plateau-Plains network. It was this prioritization of trade that distinguished the Columbia River Chinookans from the inland Kalapuyans, whose economy relied more on seasonal hunting, gathering, and the firing of the oak prairies than on the regional trade.

One important product that linked the Chinook proper, other Chinookan groups, and the Kalapuyans of the Willamette Valley was the elkskin cuirasses known as *clemals* by the Chinookans. The Chinook obtained the elkskins from their immediate neighbors in the lower Columbia estuary and from peoples in the interior, including the Kalapuyans. The *clemals* were useful to the Chinook themselves, and they were also very valuable as trade items, sought by Northwest Coast groups such as the Haida and the Tlingit, frequently engaged in intertribal warfare.[44] Though the Columbia River peoples also exchanged their surplus salmon for other foodstuffs harvested by the interior peoples, a major focus was the acquisition of valuables, such as slaves and dentalia. These valuables, in addition to resource use rights and ceremonial privileges, were the regional marks of status and wealth.[45] To ensure strong trade links, which were essential to the maintenance of the socioeconomic system, tribal members often married outside their communities. Thus, while the peoples of the lower Columbia region lived in a village-centered world, they maintained marriage ties beyond their local communities. Such regional kinship ties, characteristic of chiefly and upper-class families throughout the Northwest Coast, widened a family's sphere of influence, giving its access to additional prestige goods and resource use rights.[46]

When American maritime fur traders first arrived at the mouth of the Columbia and made contact with the Lower Chinookans in May 1792, the newcomers tapped into the long-standing Columbia River trading system. From 1792 through the spring of 1811, contact between Euro-Americans and Natives of the lower Columbia was concentrated in the lower Columbia River estuary. British and American traders conducted trades from canoes, aboard ships, and in the local villages. By virtue of the Chinookans' geographic location at the mouth of the Columbia, their riverine culture, and their strong motivation to increase their wealth through the prestige exchange economy, they became middlemen in the regional maritime fur trade. The Lower Chinookans, especially the Chinook proper and the Clatsop, maintained a high degree of control over the flow of European goods along the Pacific-Plateau corridor.[47] The Chinookans' middle-man status was incumbent on their controlling access to the traders, and they proved quite tenacious in guarding their strategic position. Tensions that developed during the winter stay of the Lewis and Clark expedition at Fort Clatsop (1805–1806) and the failure of the Winship brothers to establish the first permanent Euro-American fur trade post on the Columbia (1809–1810) evinced the Lower Chinookans' determination and ability to control trade relations between their interior Native partners and these newcomers.[48]

❋   In the spring of 1811, the *Tonquin*, an American trading vessel, arrived at the mouth of the Columbia, bringing the first contingent of Astorians to attempt a permanent fur trade outpost in the lower Columbia.[49] After spending several weeks crossing the Columbia bar and searching for a post site, the partners aboard the *Tonquin* (Alexander McKay, Duncan McDougall, and Robert and David Stuart) settled on a site on the south shore of the estuary near Point George (present-day Smith Point), located in the territory of the Clatsop. The Astorians embarked at the site on April 12, 1811, and the next day began construction of Fort Astoria.[50] While the laborers and clerks built the fort, the partners set to work cementing trade relationships with the nearby Clatsop, the Chinook proper on the north shore, and with various Upper Chinookan groups living several miles farther upstream.[51] In keeping with the Pacific Fur Company's (PFC) strategy of establishing trading posts farther inland, several parties of Astorians set out on exploratory trips along the Columbia River and its tributaries over the course of the next year. The first group of reinforcements arrived overland, reaching Fort Astoria between January and February 1812, after an arduous transcontinental journey. A third group arrived aboard the *Beaver* in May 1812, bringing the total PFC contingent to some 126 men.

   Although an American-owned company, the PFC's labor force resembled that of other prominent fur trade firms, notably the North West Company (NWC) and the Hudson's Bay Company (HBC), which organized its employees into a

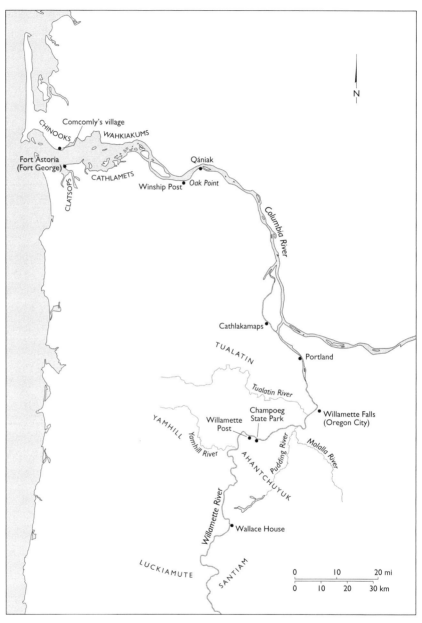

N

Comcomly's village

CHINOOKS
WAHKIAKUMS

Qániak

Fort Astoria
(Fort George)

CATHLAMETS

CLATSOPS

Winship Post   Oak Point

Columbia River

Cathlakamaps

TUALATIN

Portland

Tualatin River

Champoeg
State Park

Willamette
Post

Willamette Falls
(Oregon City)

YAMHILL

Yamhill River

Pudding River

Molalla River

AHANTCHUYUK

Willamette River

Wallace House

LUCKIAMUTE
SANTIAM

0		10		20 mi
0	10	20	30 km

MAP 2. Lower Willamette Valley and the Fur Trade, 1812–1820s. Map by Bill Nelson.
Courtesy of the *Pacific Northwest Quarterly*.

military-style hierarchy based on ethnicity, nationality, and class.[52] The PFC's managerial or officer class of partners and clerks included a small number of Americans and a majority of Canadian residents, mainly educated emigrants originally from Scotland and England. Many of the Canadian partners and clerks were veterans of the Montreal-based fur trade. These officers supervised a multiethnic laboring class comprising French Canadians originally from Lower Canada, Hawaiians recruited in the Hawaiian Islands, and a few Americans (see appendix 1). The multiethnic character of the fur trade labor force, dominated by an Anglo-Celtic officer class, continued under the NWC when it assumed control of fur trade operations in the Columbia River Basin in the fall of 1813. A number of eastern Natives (Iroquois, Abenaki, Nipissing) and Métis (of French-Canadian and Indian ancestry) also worked as hunters and trappers for the NWC in the Columbia region (see appendix 3).[53]

As the Lower Chinookan and Euro-American communities adapted to one another during the initial decade of PFC and NWC operations, intercultural relations resembled established patterns for the North American fur trade, with some regional variation.[54] Commercial and sexual relations between Native women and Euro-American men, initiated in the 1790s with the maritime fur trade, continued with the PFC and the NWC as the newcomers sought access to the kinship networks of the Greater Lower Columbia exchange economy. In the lower Columbia, Chinookan women established business partnerships and personal relationships (short and long term) with the fur traders in order to gain access to trade goods and to enhance their own wealth and prestige and that of their families. Freeborn Chinookan women and men also prostituted foreign-born female slaves they owned in exchange for the European goods.[55] As in other parts of North America, the labor and the diplomatic skills of Native women were crucial for the operation of the trade. They managed resources, processed animal pelts, and produced essential foodstuffs, clothing, and other materials. Perhaps most importantly, Native women worked as cultural mediators directly involved in trade negotiations between fur traders and local indigenous groups.[56] The trade in the lower Columbia Basin also contributed to the development of Chinook Jargon (Chinuk Wawa), which became the regional lingua franca and a mother tongue for both Indian groups and mixed-race communities during the early 1800s.[57]

After a year in the lower Columbia, the PFC partners decided to venture into the Willamette Valley (see appendix 2). Donald McKenzie set out for the Willamette Valley on March 31, 1812, with clerk William Wallace Matthews and six laborers in two canoes.[58] After portaging Willamette Falls, the expedition spent over a month exploring the valley, ranging more than one hundred miles south from the mouth of the Willamette River to its upper forks. This party was well armed to resist possible attacks from the Natives; however, no conflicts were recorded in the valley above Willamette Falls.[59] William Wallace Matthews later recalled that the McKenzie party was the first group of Euro-Americans the Indians of the Willamette Valley had ever encountered, and he described the Kalapuyans as timid and friendly in their dealings with the Astorians. McKenzie reported to his fellow PFC officers that the Kalapuyans' "behaviour to him was respectful and obliging in the extreme."[60] When McKenzie's party returned to Fort Astoria on May 11, 1812, he gave a "favourable" account of the valley, noting that "game, beaver, and fish abound there."[61]

Although there is apparently no surviving account of the Astorians' later residence in the Willamette Valley during the winter of 1812–1813, the Astoria logbook does record a dramatic attempt by the Chinook headman, Comcomly, to influence the Astorians' intercourse with the Kalapuyans. Early in the forenoon on February 13, 1813, Comcomly crossed the Columbia River in a small canoe, bringing a few eulachon fish for trade. However, as PFC partner Duncan McDougall noted in the post journal, the real reason for his visit was to communicate "a most sorrowful account concerning Messr. Wallace, Halsey & party whom he says are all destroyed by the natives inhabiting that part of the country where they had settled themselves."[62] According to Comcomly, he was simply repeating a story transmitted by the Upper Chinookan Cathlakamaps (or Cathlahcumpus), whose village was located on the southern bank of Multnomah Channel near the channel's entry into the Willamette River.

The Kalapuyans in Comcomly's tale are particularly treacherous. They decide to rid themselves of the Astorians soon after the newcomers' arrival in the Willamette Valley, accomplishing their objective through duplicity. They appear friendly, offering the Astorians advice on where to search for the coveted beaver. Once the Astorians are isolated from each other at different trapping locations, the Kalapuyans ambush them in small groups. Comcomly, "with much earnestness," assured those at Fort Astoria that his account was true. He even emphasized his own sorrow at this sad tale, insisting that the news of the disaster, coupled with the recent death of a prominent relative, had "kept him crying for days."[63]

Later that day, a Clatsop man, who had previously worked for the Astorians as an interpreter, visited Fort Astoria. He, however, presented a rather different version of the fate of the Wallace and Halsey party. On this man's recent trip down the Columbia, he had not heard that the Willamette Valley party had been harmed, but that some unnamed Natives had formulated plans to "cut them off." The Clatsop man apparently did not want to contradict Comcomly, so he added that the Chinook headman's accounts "were undoubtedly true and everything would take place as he had mentioned."[64]

Alarmed at possible violence against the Wallace and Halsey party, McDougall dispatched a messenger to clerk Gabriel Franchère and his fishing party encamped at Oak Point, near the Upper Chinookan village of Qániak, located on the south shore of the Columbia. McDougall ordered Franchère to visit the Cathlakamaps farther upstream and ascertain the accuracy of Comcomly's information. If there was truth to Concomly's story, Franchère was to enlist the support of the headman Casino to send some of his villagers to warn the Reed and Seton party, which had set out for the Willamette Valley on February 2, 1813.[65] After contacting Casino, Franchère sent word back to Fort Astoria that Comcomly's tale about violence in the Willamette Valley was unfounded, "only a fabrication of some of the Indians."[66] Franchère himself makes no reference to this incident in his narrative, noting that the reason for his trip upstream on February 13 was to procure sturgeon for Astoria.[67]

On February 27, 1813, a fortnight after his previous visit, Comcomly returned to Fort Astoria with further news of the Willamette Valley expeditions. It seems that his original information had been incorrect, and so he related a second version of the Astorians' encounter with a group of Kalapuyans near the Astorians' base camp, this one replete with dramatic elements, including thievery, cross-cultural conflict, intertribal negotiations, and gift giving. The flavor of Comcomly's storytelling can be seen as filtered through the words of Duncan McDougall:

> During their absence the natives near at hand . . . (whom he denominated Calapoyas) visited the place and finding only those two to guard it, rob'd and took away all the principal goods . . . without offering any violence to the 2 S. Islanders, who probably being overpowered in numbers made no resistance. On the return of Wallace & party he, with most of his number, repaired immediately to the lodges of the Indians in order to secure the goods, who, instead of offering to return them, were all assembled with Bows & arrows ready for an assault. . . . [T]he whites proceeded instantly amongst them, seized some and broke their bows or cut the strings. . . . Wallace's party it appeared had taken the precaution to load their Muskets with Powder only, and on perceiving the extremity to which they were reduced fired among the Indians which instantly frightened & dispersed them, and greater part of the goods were obtained.[68]

According to Comcomly, the Cathlakamaps headman Casino responded to this confrontation by immediately traveling upstream to the mid-Willamette Valley to "harangue" the Kalapuyans about the "great impropriety" of their conduct toward the Astorians and to warn the Kalapuyans about the consequences of such bad behavior. Following Casino's warning, he supposedly negotiated a settlement between the Kalapuyans and the Astorians, and Wallace rewarded Casino for his diplomatic effort with a series of gifts (blue cloth, wool hats, and blankets).[69]

In response to this latest report from Comcomly, on March 1, 1813, McDougall sent three men to recontact Gabriel Franchère at Oak Point (Qániak). They were to instruct him to make a second inquiry among the Cathlakamaps about the veracity of Comcomly's stories and, if necessary, to ask the headman Casino to send a party for some written word from William Wallace.[70] Franchère arrived back at Fort Astoria on March 8. He had visited the Cathlakamaps the previous week and reported that the "story last received from Comcomly proves wholly without foundation." In fact, Casino knew nothing about the story. Rather than hold Comcomly responsible for the fabrication, McDougall attributed the deception to "some artful Indians" who wished to disrupt the close relations between the Euro-Americans and the Chinook.[71]

On March 18, 1813, John Reed, Alfred Seton, and the other members of their party returned to Astoria from Wallace House. They confirmed that the stories about conflict with the Kalapuyans were quite untrue. In fact, "They live upon very amicable terms with the natives, who visit them daily & trade roots (their only article of trade) for *meat*. Indeed, they seem so far from having a wish to pillage their goods that they seemed to look with more desire upon the contents of the provision store than that of the goods, were the Bales still remain in the same state as when they took them in."[72]

The fictitious Kalapuyans in Comcomly's story are ignorant, duplicitous, violent, and above all, desirous of European trade goods and technology. In contrast, the documented encounters between the Kalapuyans and the Astorians during the winter of 1812–1813 indicate that the Kalapuyans remained quite comfortable with their own technology and products, exhibiting a limited interest in European trade goods. Some twenty years of indirect contact following the rise of the maritime fur trade did not appear to have greatly altered the material culture of the Kalapuyans.[73] In addition, because the Astorians met the Kalapuyans during the long winter months when they would most likely face food shortages, it is not surprising that the Natives' main interest was securing additional foodstuffs.

Perhaps more importantly, the Kalapuyans interest in trading "roots" for "meat" as reported by John Reed and Alfred Seton suggests that the hunting activities of the Astorians were having a noticeable impact on the availability of wild game.[74]

In light of the fictitious nature of Comcomly's tales and the discrepancy between his depiction of the Kalapuyans and the Astorians' experiences in the Willamette Valley, what explains Comcomly's ruse? Comcomly's words should be read as more than a mere warning to the Astorians. Since the late eighteenth century, Lower Chinookans at the mouth of the Columbia River, including Comcomly and his people, the Chinook proper, had played a prominent role as middlemen in the maritime fur trade along the Columbia River. Utilizing the aboriginal trade networks that extended inland to the Plateau region, Comcomly and the Chinook had increased their wealth, power, and prestige in the Columbia country. The Astorians' strategy of establishing inland posts to trade directly with Native groups—which would effectively bypass the Chinook middlemen—was therefore a direct threat to Comcomly's economic and social position.[75] Thus, Comcomly's stories demonstrate that he sought to continue to monopolize the Columbia River trade.

In response to the Astorians' threat to trump Comcomly's control of trade networks to the Willamette Valley, Comcomly sought to play upon the Astorians' fears of being attacked by poorly known Natives. His tales are in fact more reflective of Euro-American encounters with Upper Chinookan groups in the Columbia River corridor from The Dalles to the Cascades.[76] Beginning with the Lewis and Clark expedition in 1805–1806 and continuing with the PFC, relations between the newcomers and the Native peoples along this stretch of the river were often fraught with tension, violence, and "thievery." The basis for this mutual misunderstanding was the Euro-Americans' unfamiliarity with the riverine Indians' customs of gift exchange, tribute, and established kinship ties that afforded distant and neighboring groups access rights to the Columbia River corridor.[77]

For the Upper Chinookans living along the river from the Cascades and the Dalles, these traditions were not only important social and cultural practices, they were also essential to their economy by providing them with goods, services, marriage partners, and slaves via the great trade that flowed to the lower Columbia from the Plateau and vice versa. Like the Lower Chinookans at the river's mouth, the Upper Chinookans exploited their geographic position to their advantage. However, the Euro-Americans—first the Lewis and Clark expedition and later the Astorians—understood waterways as open transportation routes in keeping with customary Western European legal principles. They did not acknowledge local indigenous notions of territorial rights and the need to exchange gifts or establish kinship ties in order to have access rights through a group's territory, especially when that territory included an important waterway.[78]

In the second, modified tale, Comcomly portrayed the Kalapuyans as perhaps slightly less violent but still quite ignorant of how to cultivate the proper relations with "the whites." As a result, the Cathlakamaps headman Casino journeyed to the upper Willamette Valley to instruct the Kalapuyans on proper fur trade etiquette and arrange a peace between the Natives and newcomers. In both cases, Comcomly employed storytelling to educate the Astorians on the need to cultivate trade relations using the established aboriginal trade and kinship links. If not, the Astorians would run the risk of conflicts with the less savvy Natives of the Willamette Valley, much like the fur traders had encountered in the Columbia River corridor. This interpretation of Comcomly's ruse is in keeping with the lower Columbian cultural norms and geopolitics of the early nineteenth century, as well as with Comcomly's own character as a shrewd political leader ever vigilant about safeguarding his own interests and those of his people.[79] Comcomly sought to control the flow of furs and goods in the region, a clear contrast to the Astorians' aim of cultivating direct trade links with the Kalapuyans, who dwelt in a valley capable of delivering valuable pelts and resources for PFC operations.

Ultimately, Comcomly's diplomatic ruse did not prevent the Astorians from establishing direct contact with interior Native groups. This was a result of the fur traders' determination to implement the logistical strategy long practiced by French colonial coureurs de bois and Montreal-based fur traders, which entailed collecting furs at interior posts and then transporting those pelts to a central depot (here, Fort Astoria) using a brigade system. Despite McDougall's alarm over the possibility of armed resistance, the fur trade enterprise proceeded in the Willamette Valley. The Chinookans were not able to seriously disrupt fur trade activity in the inland valley. However, this episode also suggests that the position of the fur trade colonizers—a small contingent of well-armed men within a largely aboriginal world—was not entirely secure.

Upon their return to Fort Astoria in March 1813, clerks John Reed and Alfred Seton reported that the parties sent to the Willamette Valley to forage for their own food did quite well there because of the availability of wild game. The experienced hunters in their group were able to provide a continual supply of meat for all the men.[80] On June 2, 1813, William Wallace and John Halsey returned to Fort Astoria with their party consisting of twenty-six people, including the laborers and the hunters and their families.[81] The fur traders and the hunters' families had spent over seven months in the Willamette Valley trapping, hunting, and preparing the animal resources, and they returned with nineteen bales of dried meat and seventeen packs of beaver pelts (roughly forty-five pelts per pack). The PFC inventory for the trapping expedition records this as 621 beaver skins, 7 land otter pelts, and 154 beaver skins from the freemen Alexander Carson and Pierre Delaunay.[82] William Wallace reported that he had led exploring parties to the southern tip of the Willamette Valley, nearly to the source of the river, and that beaver were abundant throughout the valley.

While the surviving historical record provides little insight into the fur trade laborers' initial impressions of the Kalapuyans, the attitudes of the PFC's officer class are most clearly articulated in the reports of clerk William Wallace and the narrative of clerk Alexander Ross. Both men perceived the Kalapuyans through the lens of Euro-American cultural values. As hunter-gatherers inhabiting an inland valley teeming with wildlife and various natural resources, the Kalapuyans appeared less advanced, less productive, and less wealthy than the mounted hunters of the Plateau and Plains.[83] The Astorian officer class was particularly annoyed at the Kalapuyans' apparent disinterest in hunting beaver in exchange for European goods. William Wallace referred to the Indians of the Willamette Valley as a "set of poverty-strick beings, totally ignorant of hunting Furs and scarce capable of procuring their own subsistence."[84]

In his first memoir written during the 1840s, Alexander Ross devoted a short passage to the first encounters between the Astorians and the Kalapuyans of the Willamette Valley, classifying them as the "great nation" of the "Col-lap-poh-yea-ass." Like Wallace, Ross saw the Kalapuyans as exceedingly poor in a land rich in natural and animal resources. He described them as an "indolent and sluggish race."[85] Ross associated their apparent lack of productivity to their "minimal" needs.[86] He expressed annoyance at the Kalapuyans' behavior in response to the Astorian hunting parties. Rather than leave the Astorians to their prey, the Natives immediately responded to the sound of gunfire, following the "sound like a swarm of bees, and feast and gormandize on the offal of the game, like so many vultures round a dead carcass."[87] Ross penned these words some three decades after he first encountered the Willamette Valley Natives. His negative characterization of the Kalapuyans stemmed from a general dislike of Indian peoples and his later life experiences, including his ill-fated leadership of the multiracial Snake Country trapping party, his dismissal from the HBC in the 1820s, and his efforts to integrate his mixed-race children into the increasingly racialized society of the Red River colony (present-day Winnipeg). And like a number of the

fur trade officers who made strategic alliances with important fur trade partners, Ross established a long-lasting country marriage—with Sally, an Okanagan
woman from the Columbia Plateau.[88]

At this point in their relations with the Kalapuyans, the fur traders considered
neither local protocols with regard to hunting and trapping, which required kin
(marriage) relations with the Kalapuyans, nor weighed the impact of their activities on the Natives' local resources.[89] Since the Willamette Valley Natives depended
more heavily on wild game than their Chinookan neighbors to the north, the
depletion of such resources was a serious cause for concern and tension between
the Natives and newcomers.[90] As previously noted, ethnographic sources indicate
that the Kalapuyan groups had demarcated territories. The arrogance of the fur
traders and their disregard for Native territoriality obviously upset the Kalapuyans.
Reported "thefts" of beaver and wild game carcasses also likely stemmed from additional local Native concerns. Since the fur traders were guests in the Willamette
Valley, the Kalapuyans would have expected the outsiders to share some of the
local animals they had hunted and trapped.[91] Finally, since the Kalapuyans supplied elkskins to the Chinook for the Northwest Coast trade in *clemals,* the fur
traders' hunting activities would have placed strains on the Kalapuyans' own
regional trade activities. The fur traders' behavior in the Willamette Valley ultimately caused resentment among the Kalapuyans because, from the Natives' perspective, the Euro-Americans appeared rude, arrogant, and selfish.

❉   Over the summer of 1813, the activities of the Astorians quickened in antici-
pation of sending an overland party eastward to update John Jacob Astor in New
York. As a result, several trading parties were sent out to various Native trade
marts to gather the needed food stores for the overland journey, this in addition to
keeping a supply of food and furs flowing into Astoria. Several additional groups
were dispatched throughout the summer on short forays to the Willamette Valley.
On October 10, 1813, a group of Astorians set off up the Columbia River, but along
the way they met a large contingent of traders from the Montreal-based NWC,
and the Astorians, along with the Northwesters, returned to Astoria to determine
the fate of the PFC.[92]

Several months earlier in July 1813, the four PFC partners present at Astoria—
Duncan McDougall, Donald McKenzie, John Clarke, and David Stuart—had
agreed to dissolve the company as a result of the logistical problems created by
the War of 1812. Their decision stemmed from the inability of Astor to resupply
Astoria following the British naval blockade of American ports during the war,
the strong regional presence of the NWC, and the military backing the NWC

FIGURE 1. Costume of a Callapuya Indian, 1845. SOURCE: Charles Wilkes, *Narrative of the US Exploring Expedition* (1845). Courtesy of the Oregon Historical Society, OrHi 104921.

received from the British government in the Pacific Northwest.[93] On October 16, 1813, all the surviving partners, including Wilson Price Hunt, signed an agreement with the NWC representatives, thereby selling the PFC and its assets to the Canadian company. All the employees were released from their contracts and given the option to enlist with the NWC. The returning Astorians left the Columbia with either Wilson Price Hunt aboard the *Pedlar* in March 1814 or with the NWC brigade, which departed for the East in April 1814.[94]

Several groups of fur traders spent the winter of 1813–1814 in the Willamette Valley. These groups included former Astorians awaiting passage home, NWC personnel, and free trappers. Among those who elected to trap for the NWC in the Willamette Valley were Joseph Saint Amant, Etienne Lucier, François Martial, Jacques Harteau, John Day, Moses Flanagan, Micajah Baker, Richard Milligan, Alexander Carson, and William Cannon. The free trappers departed for the Willamette in two parties on October 17 and October 19, 1813.[95] The first group of Northwesters to pass the winter in the Willamette Valley, headed by clerk William Henry, arrived there in mid-November. At that time, William Henry sent word to the partners at Fort George that there was "something bad in agitation among the Natives" of the Willamette Valley. However, due to communication problems between the Northwesters and the unnamed Kalapuyans, William Henry did not determine the exact nature of the problem. In response, the NWC partners, including the recently arrived Alexander Henry the Younger (William's uncle) and Alexander Stewart, dispatched clerk William Wallace and ten men as rein-forcements to William Henry's party.[96]

Rather than reoccupy Wallace House, William Henry's party established itself near the Ahantchuyuk village of Champoeg (see map 2).[97] The group included William Henry's Indian wife and child and twenty-nine men "composed of div-ers [*sic*] nations & languages": six Hawaiians, four Iroquois, one Mississauga, one Nipissing, sixteen French Canadians, and one American, Alfred Seton. The next day, the party began erecting a post, designated "Fort Calipuyaw" (Fort Kalapuya) in Seton's journal. A little over a week later, Seton noted that William Henry was busy "trading some roots with the Calipuyaws along side of me, for Beads, who not thinking the quantity s[ufficient]t, are loudly asking for [more]."[98] This brief description from Seton suggests that the Kalapuyans intended to dictate the terms of trade within their territory, much to the consternation of the fur traders.

The first recorded armed conflict between the fur traders and a Kalapuyan group occurred soon afterward, in mid-December 1813. A group of trappers got into a melee with a group of unnamed Kalapuyans somewhere farther upriver on the Willamette. They arrived at Fort Kalapuya on December 19 and reported that the Indians had fired their arrows at a smaller party of three men, though none of the trappers was harmed. Rather than return fire and "laying the Indians dead at their feet," the trappers hastily retreated in their canoes downriver, "which when the Natives saw, they justly concluded the White Men were afraid of them."[99]

As recounted by Alfred Seton (the only source of this event), the trappers pre-sented themselves as victims of Kalapuyan aggression. Unfortunately, the full text of the introductory sentence for this passage is not available due to damage in the original manuscript. The first portion of the sentence suggests that trappers believed that the unnamed Kalapuyans had treated the trappers improperly: "the reason of the h[urry]ing down was on acct. of the Indians, who [had] behaved to them . . . [text damaged]." The trappers ostensibly hurried away, avoiding a confrontation because, being a party of three, they would have been greatly out-numbered. Clearly though, the trappers had considered returning fire and would have regarded the killing of their attackers as a justifiable course of action. Their flight response was one directed by prudence rather than any ethical or diplo-matic concerns.

On December 25, 1813, clerk Thomas McKay, freeman Registe Belair, and a third man arrived at Astoria from the Willamette Valley bearing letters from William Henry. Henry's reports about the Kalapuyans may explain some of the tension between the two parties. Alexander Henry, paraphrasing his nephew's letter, wrote, "Intelligence from that quarter is [that] beaver are numerous, but the Natives, who are also very numerous, will not hunt them; their sole employment is digging Roots, Cammass, Wapatoes & c. and stealing the Beavers that are caught in traps when opportunity offers."[100] Additionally, Henry relayed his annoyance at the Kalapuyans' "theft" of deer killed by the Northwesters, the Indians having been attracted to the sound of the newcomers' guns. He also reported that the Natives "are exceedingly fond of Meat and will barter everything they have for it. They prefer it to any of our Goods."[101]

The tensions between the two groups flowed from differing cultural perceptions about land and resources. The centuries-old European notion of the Doctrine of Discovery, by which newly arrived Europeans claimed superior and unilateral property rights to Native lands, framed the fur traders' perceptions of the Willamette Valley and the Kalapuyans' actions.[102] Like the Astorians before him, William Henry viewed the Willamette Valley as a vast commons open for the use and exploitation of the Euro-Americans.[103] He neither recognized the Kalapuyans' prior rights to the wild game resources in their territories nor that the "theft" of deer and beaver carcasses may have been a stratagem employed by the Kalapuyans to force the foreigners to respect those rights. The Willamette Valley Natives perceived the fur traders as interlopers because the newcomers had not established kin relations with the Kalapuyans, the customary means for gaining resource use rights in a territory.[104]

The Northwesters took Kalapuyan cultural values and territorial claims lightly due to the Euro-Americans' sense of ethnic and military superiority. Clearly, the company officers did not feel it necessary to ally themselves through marriage to the Kalapuyans, as had Duncan McDougall when he agreed to wed Illche ("Moon Girl"), the daughter of Chinook headman Comcomly. As for the Kalapuyans, their energies were oriented primarily toward their complex subsistence round in the resource-rich Willamette Valley. The fur trade was of limited interest to the Kalapuyans (a stark contrast with the priorities of the Lower Chinookans), which explains why the Kalapuyans, for their part, did not establish close marriage ties with the fur traders.[105] Additionally, unlike the Kalapuyans—whose labor-intensive activities managing the oak savannah of the Willamette Valley were not readily apparent to the Euro-Americans—the fur traders associated property and resource use rights with agriculture and the production of marketable commodities such as furs. Although the fur traders begrudgingly acknowledged the influence of Chinookan leaders such as Comcomly, the Euro-Americans overlooked the role of the Kalapuyans in existing regional trade networks, especially with regard to the supply of elkskins to the Lower Chinookans.

Of all the documentary sources for the NWC period in the Willamette Valley (1813–1822), the journal of Alexander Henry the Younger provides the most detailed information on relations between the Euro-Americans and the Kalapuyans. Alexander Henry, with William Wallace Matthews, led a party to the Willamette Valley, which departed Fort George on January 22, 1814, and arrived a day later on January 23. They passed three days in the vicinity of Fort Kalapuya (later known as Willamette Post) before departing on January 26. On their way to the upper Willamette on January 23, Alexander Henry's party had their first recorded encounter with a group of Yamhill Kalapuyans.

After portaging the falls, Henry's party met the Yamhill, who were en route to trade camas with the local Clowewalla Upper Chinookans of Willamette Falls. While Henry described the Clowewalla as "tolerably disposed towards the Whites," the fur trader developed an instant dislike for the Yamhill, characterizing them as "the most miserable and rascally looking tribe I have seen on this side of the mountains."[106] Henry's poor opinion of the Yamhill stemmed from his own physical aversion to their appearance and comportment. Although Henry was an experienced trader and close observer of Indian lifeways, his own fastidious, self-possessed character often led him to criticize both Natives and lower-class laborers who did not meet his high standards of personal hygiene, social decorum, or self-control.[107] Writing in his journal for himself and his NWC colleagues, Henry noted that four of the seven Yamhill "had some defect in his [sic] eyes" and they were scantily clad only in deerskin robes, with "a small round bonnet of wattap [wapato] on their heads, with a sharp point on the top about three inches high."[108]

Henry described the Kalapuyans as "a wandering race, who have neither horses nor homes, and live in the open air in fine weather and under the shelter of large spreading pines and cedars during foul weather."[109] In comparison with the Plateau peoples, Willamette Valley Natives owned few horses; they were "too wretchedly poor to have anything." Henry concluded that the Plateau peoples lived better because they had horses and were "well provided with everything necessary for a Savage life." Henry was impressed with not only the animal husbandry and technology of the Plateau peoples, but also with their appearance, for he referred to them as "well dressed in leather shirts and leggings garnished with porcupine quills."[110]

Alexander Henry's repugnance toward the Yamhill in particular and the Kalapuyans in general is emblematic of the attitudes of the fur trade officers and reflects the high value Western Europeans—especially those from the British Isles—placed on horse cultures. As Elizabeth Vibert has demonstrated with regard to fur trader–Native relations in the Plateau region, the English-Scots officers held to distinctive notions about Euro-American superiority and social organization that colored the ways in which they perceived the various Native groups. When the officers recorded their encounters with Indians of the Plateau, they portrayed the regional mounted buffalo hunters as industrious and commendable, a departure from the long-standing archetype in both colonial and fur trade literature that depicted Indians as lazy, weak, and unproductive.[111] In contrast to the mounted Plateau groups that Henry held in some regard, his perception of the Kalapuyans corresponded to the stereotypical view that hunter-gathers who range over a wide area are not industrious. It is this view that later led Henry to misconstrue the attitudes and actions of the Willamette Valley Natives.

The first meeting between the Yamhill and Henry's party was not cordial. After speaking with three Clowewalla men who had brought provisions to trade with the Northwesters, one of the Yamhill women "set up a lamentable yell in crying and bawling," and the rest quickly took up their loads and departed. Henry reported that the Yamhill men "eyed" the Northwester "narrowly" after speaking with the Clowewalla. Henry did not determine the reason for the Yamhill's reactions, but he surmised that it may have been linked to the death of an old Clowewalla chief, or perhaps the news of the deaths of the several Columbia River Chinookans killed by a party of Northwesters a few days earlier. Henry and his party, worried about trouble, quickly departed without incident.[112] Later, on his return trip to Fort George, Henry received some secondhand information from the Clowewalla that would indicate a growing distrust of the foreigners on the part of the Yamhill. While stopped at Willamette Falls on his return trip to Fort George on January 26, 1814, Henry noted that the "Yam he las, it seems had told the Indians here of their intention in sending our people from the River." When the Clowewalla asked the Northwesters if this were true, if they intended to vacate the Willamette Valley, Henry told them that they would not be leaving the valley in the face of this threat.[113]

Once established at the NWC post at Champoeg, Henry set about establishing trade relations with the local Kalapuyans. Like fur traders before him, he looked upon his experiences in the valley with some disappointment. Henry reckoned the Kalapuyans did not know the value of trade goods, not recognizing that they might be shrewd traders like their Chinookan relatives in the lower Columbia. In his journal he noted his frustration with a headman who was amenable to Henry's offer to buy the man's horse. However, after Henry learned the headman's price of ten blankets, which Henry saw as exorbitant, he withdrew his offer. He also remarked that the Kalapuyans "have no idea of the value of our goods, and seem to care little about anything further than a few blue beads."[114] Yet, he later wrote that the Kalapuyans preferred deer flesh to any other item.[115] Henry's negative reaction—that is, blaming the Natives for their hard bargaining—stemmed from the fact that he did not come prepared for the local trade. Henry was also annoyed that the Kalapuyans could not be persuaded to hunt beaver, which were abundant throughout the Willamette Valley: "small lakes and ponds we found swarming with beaver still they will not attempt to kill them."[116]

The Kalapuyans were disinclined to trap beaver because such an activity neither fit into their complex subsistence round nor meshed with their long-standing exchange practices within the lower Columbia region. Since the Kalapuyans demonstrated a limited passion for European goods—blue beads—in this initial contact period, they had little need to rearrange their subsistence round to trap beaver. Additionally, as they were less trade oriented than the Chinook, the Kalapuyans did not initially express a desire for close trade relations with these outsiders. Other motivations for the Kalapuyans' indifference stemmed from their previous encounters with fur traders. Given the Euro-Americans' behavior since 1812, the Kalapuyans were understandably distrustful of the newcomers. The Natives may have wanted to retain their autonomy rather than have their economic activities too closely tied with fur traders. Perhaps, like the indigenous groups of southern Oregon, the Kalapuyans believed that maintaining their independence, autonomy, and separation (and sustaining the Willamette Valley environment) was more important than having close trade links with the Euro-Americans.[117]

Trade between the Northwesters and the Kalapuyans remained a modest affair in 1814. Henry noted that the Kalapuyans usually came in small trading parties of two or three families to Fort Kalapuya (Willamette Post). In their relations with the Kalapuyans, the Northwesters conducted trade outside the small post. Given the size of the outpost, this may have been a logistical necessity; alternatively, it may have been a response to safety concerns. Indeed, Henry reported that on January 25, 1814, three freemen formerly of the PFC—likely Milligan, Flanagan, and Baker—returned to the Willamette post and reported adversely on the behavior of the Kalapuyans in the valley: a group of Kalapuyans had wanted to "steal" the freemen's property. However, Alexander Henry concluded that the Natives' fear of the Euro-Americans' guns led them to "act in a more clandestine manner and [prevented] them using open violence to pillage."[118] Though the fur traders may have held a technological advantage thanks to their firearms, they remained outnumbered by several thousand Kalapuyans within the inland valley, and they were a long day's journey from reinforcement at the main post at Fort George (formerly Fort Astoria).

Alexander Henry's party returned to Fort George, while a group headed by clerks William Wallace and Thomas McKay, which included a number of laborers and freemen, remained in the Willamette Valley. When the Wallace and McKay party finally arrived back at Fort George on March 25, 1814, they reported a modification in the attitude of the Kalapuyans. The Willamette Valley Indians seemed "much more reconciled" to the presence of the Northwesters. They expressed regret at the Northwesters' departure and asked them to return again to the Willamette Valley. A local Ahantchuyuk leader, possibly the headman of the village of Champoeg, agreed to take the Willamette Post under his charge, including the four horses and two hogs left there. This headman apparently wished to maintain positive relations with the Northwesters, as Henry wrote he was "well inclined toward" the Northwesters. A few days before the departure of the Wallace and McKay party, a group of thirty Yamhill visited the Willamette Post to trade a large quantity of baked camas. They also urged the Northwesters to return to the Willamette Valley.[119]

Although the Northwesters continued to hunt, trap, and trade in the Willamette Valley, we do not have a clear picture of the developing relations between the Kalapuyans and the fur traders in the years immediately after 1814. This is due to a lack of contemporary sources. Tragically, Alexander Henry's journal ends in May 1814, following his death from drowning at the mouth of the Columbia. Following the amalgamation of the NWC and the HBC in 1821, many NWC documents from the Columbia Department were lost or destroyed, including those covering the Willamette Valley (and the wider Fort George district).

The only other extant documentary sources that shed some light on fur trader–Kalapuyan relations in the Willamette for the remainder of the NWC period (1814–1822) include the narrative of clerk Alexander Ross, *Fur Hunters of the Far West,* originally published in 1855, and to a lesser extent the memoranda book of James Keith, the NWC partner in charge of Fort George.[120] In *Fur Hunters of the Far West,* Ross recounts a hitherto unexamined account of fur trader–Native violence followed by negotiations in and around Willamette Falls in 1816–1817. Ross's rather fanciful narrative is a problematic source, due to its late publication date, the dictates of Victorian travel literature, the fur trader's personal prejudices, and his desire to cast his fur trade service in a positive, even heroic, light. When compared against the limited statistical data in Keith's memoranda book, Ross's account of the confrontation and parlay at Willamette Falls appears plausible, if rather less dramatic than he would have his readers believe.

Ross spent most of his years on the Columbia in the interior of the Plateau region; however, from the summer of 1816 through fall of 1817, he served as assistant to James Keith at Fort George.[121] For this period, Ross recounts a series of problems with Natives controlling access to the Willamette Valley. Although he does not clearly identify the Indian group, it appears that the Clowewalla Upper Chinookans at Willamette Falls, possibly in alliance with some Kalapuyan groups,

TABLE 2. Abstract and comparative statement of Indian trade and trapper hunts at Fort George

Outfit	Apparent Indian trade	Trappers' hunts	Totals
1814	1,741	578	2,319
1815	2,599	1,800	4,217
1816	3,096	897	4,240
1817	2,595	2,295	4,864
1818	2,527	1,507	4,002
1819	3,163	2,556	6,022
1820	3,337	2,933	6,500

SOURCE: Memoranda Book of James Keith, 60.

TABLE 3. NWC returns for Columbia Region, 1814–1821

Outfit	Interior	Fort George	Totals
1814	4,192	2,319	6,511
1815	5,285	4,217	9,502
1816	5,665	4,240	9,905
1817	6,672	4,864	11,536
1818	8,668	4,002	12,670
1819	9,940	6,022 + 158	16,120
1820	7,808	6,500	14,308
1821	11,772	5,593	17,364

NOTE: Outfit 1821 returns included 669 from 1819 and 1820 Snake Parties, brought out in 1821.

SOURCE: Memoranda Book of James Keith, 30, 60–61.

attempted to block the Northwesters' access to the valley. The data on fur returns from Keith's memoranda book indicate that these events may have adversely affected the fur trade, because there was a drop-off in trapping returns for the Willamette Valley for Outfit 1816 (1816–1817) (tables 2 and 3).

For Outfit 1816, the NWC was able to make up of the difference by acquiring more pelts through trade with other regional Native groups. However, there was a loss of some nine hundred furs as compared with the year before. Thus, while Ross may have overstated the drama of the conflict at Willamette Falls to make it more interesting to his Victorian readers, the loss was notable. In Ross's account, James Keith was determined to find a solution to the Willamette Valley problem. Keith, who would have wanted to maintain access to the valley while also smoothing relations with the valley's indigenous population, decided upon negotiation rather than a punitive approach.[122]

After a series of discussions at Willamette Falls between Ross and a group of Upper Chinookans, the headmen agreed to an oral treaty with the Northwesters. According to Ross—the lone source for these events—this agreement recognized that the Willamette River would remain open and that the Euro-Americans would be allowed to move freely to and from the Willamette Valley. In the case of misunderstanding or conflict between the Natives and the fur traders, each party would seek redress for their grievances through the proper channels, whether that be with the partners at Fort George or the appropriate village headmen.

In the negotiations at Willamette Falls, the assembled local Native groups retained the upper hand due to their superior numbers and advantageous geographic position. The Northwesters had to negotiate with the Indians on their terms because the fur traders could neither circumvent the Willamette Falls at that time nor mount a large enough demographic presence to force Native concessions. In 1816, the total NWC personnel contingent for the entire Columbia River region came to 156, which rose to 223 in 1817 (see appendix 3). Because the Native people of the lower Columbia region lived in villages of no more than several score, the Clowewalla Chinookans at Willamette Falls likely needed the support of some Northern and Central Kalapuyan groups from above the falls as well as the Clackamas Chinookans from a few miles downriver. Given this alliance, which would have been strongest during the spring and fall salmon fishing seasons, the assembled groups effectively dictated the form and content of the negotiations, even forcing Ross to wait before beginning the parlay. By eventually reopening the Willamette River to the Northwesters, the allied Native groups signaled the importance of trade relations with the newcomers. However, the Natives demonstrated a determination to dictate the terms of those continued relations. The plausible alliance between the Upper Chinookans and the Northern and Central Kalapuyans in the Willamette Valley demonstrates how long-standing kinships ties and regional geopolitics could be employed against the first wave of landed Euro-American colonizers in the lower Columbia country.

In his conclusion to the passage on the peace negotiations, Ross wrote that "truth compels us to acknowledge that the Indians faithfully and zealously observed their part of their treaty for many years afterwards."[123] In this sense, Ross humanizes the Willamette Valley peoples to some degree. Indeed, his tale of the 1817 oral treaty ends on a positive note, with both Natives and newcomers gaining their objectives while successfully reaching across the cultural divide. And in keeping with Ross's own personality and the dictates of Victorian travel literature, he portrays himself as the ultimate hero of the affair, noting that partner James Keith remarked to him, "Your success removes my anxiety; and is calculated not only to restore peace in the Wallamitte, but throughout the whole neighbouring tribes."[124] Given Alexander Ross's weak command authority leading the Snake Country party of 1824, his characterization of Keith's laudatory remarks are best viewed with a healthy dose of skepticism.[125]

✳ During the initial years of direct contact between Euro-American fur traders and Kalapuyans in the Willamette Valley, relations between the Natives and newcomers were shaped by conflicting notions of territoriality and the exploitation of natural resources, as well as by aboriginal geopolitics in the lower Columbia region. Initially, Comcomly and the Chinook, dwelling at the mouth of the Columbia, sought to control trade relations with the Kalapuyans as the PFC expanded its fur trade network into the interior. In this sense, Comcomly, like other Native leaders on the Pacific Slope, intended to incorporate the traders into existing geopolitical structures. Although Comcomly did not prevent the PFC from penetrating into the Willamette Valley, the Chinook headman's warnings about Indian reprisals, delivered in story form, alarmed PFC officials and illustrated their vulnerability within the Columbia River region. Comcomly's political posturing also highlights the differing responses of the Kalapuyans and the Chinookans to the overland fur trade.

Rather than embrace the trade and cultivate close economic, diplomatic, and marriage ties with the Euro-Americans as had the Lower Chinookans, the Kalapuyans of the Willamette Valley were guarded, choosing limited contacts with the newcomers. The Kalapuyans were selective traders so as not to alter their complex seasonal round toward the commercial (and resource extractive) activity of fur trapping. They exchanged their surplus subsistence goods (*wapato* and camas) for prestige items such as blue beads and for extra meat during the lean winter months. The existing ethnographic and documentary record suggests that the fur traders' cultural arrogance and lack of respect for Kalapuyan territoriality and resource use protocols not only upset the Willamette Valley peoples but also negatively affected the availability of wild game resources. For this reason, the Natives engaged in acts of small-scale resistance in response to the newcomers' hunting and trapping activities in the Willamette Valley.

The Kalapuyans' efforts to assert control over trapping and trading within their territories annoyed the fur traders, who misread the Kalapuyans' complex reactions during the early 1810s. Initially unable, or perhaps unwilling, to expel the fur traders from the Willamette Valley, the Kalapuyans eventually sought trade relations with the outsiders because trade was the primary geopolitical structure of the lower Columbia region. Although the Northern and Central Kalapuyans remained wary of the fur traders, these groups also knew that their Chinookan neighbors to the North and the equestrian peoples of the Plateau sought to benefit from the expanding trade in the Columbia region. Thus, following an early period of adjustment, the Willamette Valley Kalapuyans eventually chose direct though somewhat circumscribed relations with the fur traders by the summer of 1814. Following a plausible confrontation at Willamette Falls in 1816–1817, likely spearheaded by the resident Upper Chinookans, the Northwesters and the Kalapuyans appear to have reached a measured coexistence by the end of the decade.

During the first decade of Native-newcomer contact, the accessible territory of the Ahantchuyuk became an important locale for trade relations, with the village of Champoeg and the nearby Willamette Post serving as base of operations for trapping, hunting, and trading throughout the valley. For the next several years, NWC trappers and freemen continued to trap and hunt in the Willamette Valley on a seasonal basis. In a letter to Wilson Price Hunt dated April 20, 1821, NWC agent Donald Mackenzie reported that "some of the former [PFC] hands are in the country still. For instance [Joseph] St. Amand—[Alexander] Carson—[William] Cannon [Etienne] Lucier & [Joseph] Gervais are trapping in the river Walamet as usual."[126] During the 1820s, fur trade laborers' established long-term partnerships with Native women from various parts of the Pacific Northwest. Upon their retirement from the fur trade, these French-Indian couples would view the land of the Ahantchuyuk as an appealing site for a permanent settlement to raise their children.

CHAPTER 2 ❋ Agrarian Colonization
and the Intermittent Fever

In summer of 1825, Agathe Dupati McKay was born to Marguerite, a Kalapuyan woman, and the French-Algonquin free trapper Jean Baptiste Desportes McKay dit Dupati, a former NWC voyageur.[1] The family of Marguerite and Jean Baptiste continued to grow, and within five years they were living permanently in the territory of the Ahantchuyuk Kalapuyans with Dupati's other wife, Catherine Chehalis, and their daughter, Marie Lisette.[2] The presence and persistence of Jean Baptiste Dupati's growing families mirrored changing historical realities in that portion of the Willamette Valley that would later become known as French Prairie. In the decade from 1823 to 1833, two historic developments—agrarian colonization and the appearance of what became known as the "intermittent fever"—initiated a long-term process of social change that began to marginalize the Kalapuyans within their homeland.

During the first decade of fur trader–Kalapuyan encounters (1812–1822), the Natives and newcomers had reached a measured accommodation in the context of the fur traders' claim on the game and fur-bearing animals of the Willamette. Over the ensuing decade, parties of fur traders continued to hunt, trap, and trade throughout the valley as Euro-Americans recorded no major intercultural conflicts after 1817. By the late 1820s, a growing attachment to the Willamette Valley— with its rich resource base, moderate climate, and natural beauty—motivated a small group of former fur trade laborers to establish an agrarian colony in and around the territory of the Ahantchuyuk Kalapuyans. Several factors contributed to the laborers' colonization efforts in the valley. First, the settlers had developed economic and social ties with the local Kalapuyans over the preceding years. Second, although the majority of the early settlers did not have direct family connections to the local Kalapuyans, most had established long-term relationships *à la façon du pays* (after the customs of the country) with women from the larger Columbia River watershed. Third, despite HBC policies in place designed to prevent retired servants from settling south of the Columbia River, the Willamette settlers were able to reach a mutually agreeable arrangement with Chief Factor John McLoughlin. He extended them credit and supplies, and he allowed them to repay their accounts with the wheat grown on their farms.

Finally, and most tragically, just as the French-Indian families began to colonize the territory of the Ahantchuyuk, "intermittent fever"—a disease previously unknown on the Northwest Coast—struck the Willamette Valley. Subsequent annual epidemics decimated the Kalapuyans, who suffered an estimated 92 percent population decrease from 1830 through 1841. The historical record demonstrates that the French-Indian settler families were not the cause of this scourge, yet they were initially its chief beneficiaries. In response to the dramatic decline in their population, the Kalapuyans regrouped and constructed new families and communities within the Willamette Valley, though on a smaller scale than in previous decades. At the time, the number and size of the French-Indian settler families steadily increased, and a bicultural colony began to take root. The early 1830s marked the beginning of a considerable demographic shift in the Willamette Valley, one which would have an important impact on the indigenous Kalapuyans and also on the history, culture, and identity of the French-Indian settler families. Unlike other mixed-raced fur trade communities that maintained close links with their nearby Native kin for several generations and progressively developed distinct Métis cultures and identities, the French-Indian colonists in French Prairie ultimately followed a different path.[3]

✳ Following a protracted and sometimes bitter trade war, the Montreal-based NWC and the London-based HBC merged into one venture in 1821. With the signing of the poll deed, the HBC essentially took over NWC operations, and the new company gained a monopoly over the fur trade in British North America, including the disputed Oregon Country west of the Rocky Mountains.[4] The British mercantile enterprise became the de facto colonial administrator in the vast region after Spain relinquished her claims north of the 42nd parallel (1819), and Russia agreed to 54 degrees 40 minutes as the southern boundary of her North American colony (1824). Although the Convention of 1818 recognized a joint British-American occupancy policy for the Oregon Country, the American presence in the region was negligible until the 1830s.

When the HBC inherited NWC operations in the Oregon Country (known as the Columbia Department), it gained two rather distinct regions. The northern New Caledonia district—present-day north-central British Columbia—was rich in high-quality furs, and its proximity to northern supply routes made it accessible through the York Factory express system. The Columbia district to the south produced lower-quality furs, and provisioning the region by sea entailed higher costs because of the need to add ships to the company's maritime fleet.[5] In addition, the Oregon Country remained a disputed region between the United States and Great Britain.[6] After the HBC directors in London considered abandoning the Columbia, North American governor George Simpson convinced the directors to retain the southern district as a buffer zone against American trappers venturing into the Columbia region from the Missouri and Platte River watersheds. HBC officials supported the decision to retain this region for several additional reasons: to ensure the presence of British ships in the North Pacific, to contain the Russian presence in Alaska, to challenge American maritime traders along the coast, and to develop supplemental products for markets in the Pacific.[7]

In order to harmonize the consolidation of the old NWC operations in the Oregon Country, Governor Simpson made two voyages to the region during the 1820s. As a result of these visits, Simpson instituted a series of structural changes to HBC operations on the Pacific Slope. Accompanied on the first voyage by the new chief factor, John McLoughlin, Simpson ordered the construction of a new regional headquarters on the lower Columbia River. Fort Vancouver was established about one hundred miles upriver from Fort George on the north bank of the Columbia in Upper Chinookan territory. This new locale would ensure the HBC an outpost on the Northwest Coast in the event that the area south of the Columbia River came under American control. Simpson also pushed for the expansion of the fur trade into previously undeveloped corners of New Caledonia and southern regions of British North America bordering the United States.[8]

After his 1824–1825 visit, Simpson determined that the Snake Country, encompassing parts of the Plateau and Great Basin, should be trapped out of fur-bearing animals as soon as possible. The major reason was to stymie the advance of American trappers into the Pacific Northwest while protecting British territorial interests north of the Columbia River.[9] The HBC fur-trapping expeditions that spread across the Plateau and Great Basin during the 1820s and 1830s appeared to fulfill Simpson's original mission. The Snake Country parties increased Euro-Americans' geographic knowledge, brought additional Native groups into contact with the fur traders, and continued the expansion of mercantile capitalism in the Far West.[10] The "fur desertification" policy carried out by the Snake Country parties also had a very serious and long-lasting environmental impact that negatively affected the region's indigenous populations. The destruction of the beaver population and the expedition's competition for scarce resources in the arid region increased tensions (and clashes) between the fur traders and the Natives and added fuel to the sometimes volatile relationships between Indian peoples in the Plateau and Great Basin.[11]

Peter Skene Ogden (Anglo-Canadian), a highly competitive, sometimes ruthless trader, led the HBC's Snake Party from 1824 through 1830. During his tenure, Ogden explored several regions unknown to Euro-Americans, including southern Oregon, northern California, and northern Utah.[12] Beginning in 1826, Alexander Roderick McLeod (Scottish), John Work (Irish), Michel Laframboise (French Canadian), and Thomas McKay (Anglo-Indian) led various exploratory and trapping parties to the Oregon coast and the Umpqua region of southern Oregon and later to California's Sacramento River Valley, then known as the Bonaventura. The coastal, Umpqua, and Southern (Bonaventura) Parties regularly passed through the Willamette Valley on their way south.[13]

The fur-trapping brigades were among the most physically and psychologically taxing undertakings of the HBC in the Columbia Department. In addition to chief traders, clerks, and higher-ranking laborers, the fur-trapping parties comprised company servants, freemen, and their wives and children. Of the 145 documented freemen who were employed by the NWC and the HBC for the Snake Country expeditions between 1818 and 1845, 40 percent were French Canadians, 25 percent Iroquois, 17 percent Métis, 8 percent Western Indians, 5 percent Eastern Indians, and 4 percent Americans.[14] This ethnic mix in the Snake Country groups mirrored demographic realities in the larger British North American fur trade through 1840, at which time the percentage of French Canadian laborers began a marked decline and the number of Native (Métis and Indian) laborers began a steady increase.[15] The structure and function of the brigades resembled the larger fur trade, with a clear command structure and division of labor. As in other regions, the men's Indian and *métis* wives performed essential functions on the expeditions, including processing and dressing the pelts, gathering and preparing foodstuffs, and producing supplies, implements, moccasins, and clothing.[16]

During the NWC's tenure in the lower Columbia region, Kalapuyans in the Willamette Valley became accustomed to small groups of Euro-Americans moving about their territories for trapping, provisioning, and trading, and after 1824 the Kalapuyans witnessed the increased presence of HBC expeditions passing through the valley on their way to and from southern Oregon and California. Following the expansionist efforts of the HBC in the Oregon Country, the Ahantchuyuk village site at Champoeg, known to the English speakers as Sandy Encampment and to the French speakers as Campement de sable, served as one of the staging areas for the expeditions to the coast, the Umpqua region, and California.[17] The HBC expeditions included both mounted and canoe parties that traveled from Fort Vancouver to Willamette Falls and Champoeg. For the journey southward, the groups would then obtain additional horses at either site from local Indians or resident freemen. When not traveling with the fur brigades or trapping in other parts of the Willamette Valley, the freemen and their families would often camp in and around the territory of the Ahantchuyuk.[18] For example, in mid-May 1826, Willamette freeman Etienne Lucier, then living on a semipermanent basis with his family near Champoeg, sold a total of twelve horses to Alexander McLeod and his coastal survey party who were encamped at Willamette Post (the old NWC post of Fort Kalapuya).[19]

Although the historical record on Kalapuyan–Euro-American relations from 1823 through 1833 remains fragmentary—a period marking the arrival of the HBC and the initial onset of the intermittent fever—the available evidence from the journals and memoirs of fur trappers, travelers, and later settlers suggests that these relations were relatively stable. In contrast to other regions in the Columbia Department (where Chief Factor John McLoughlin ordered punitive actions against specific Native groups), there were no recorded conflicts between the Kalapuyan groups and HBC personnel, free trappers, or the occasional American trapping party.[20] This suggests that the plausible oral treaty reached between the NWC and the Indians at Willamette Falls in 1817 continued to regulate relations between the fur trappers and the Kalapuyans and Upper Chinookans of the Willamette Valley. The working relationship appears to have been based on several factors: the long-standing nature of intercultural relations in the valley, the Kalapuyans' modest adaptation to the economics of the fur trade, their willingness to continue to trade with the foreigners and treat them as guests in the Willamette Valley, the fact that the valley was not a prime region for furs in the Columbia Department by the 1820s and 1830s, some stability in the use and harvesting of natural resources, and kinship relations between the freemen and the Native groups of the larger Columbia River region.

Passages in the journals of fur traders Alexander McLeod, Peter Skene Ogden, and the Scottish botanist David Douglas indicate that the Kalapuyans of the Willamette Valley and the Umpqua watershed sought economically advantageous relations with the Euro-Americans. The various Kalapuyan bands would trade foodstuffs and animal pelts for European goods when the outsiders passed through a group's territory. Both the fur traders and Douglas complained about Kalapuyan efforts to control the parameters of trade in the Willamette Valley.

When Douglas attempted to purchase the animal skin garment of a Kalapuyan child, he ultimately decided against the trade because the child's parent(s) placed "too great a value" on the garment.[21] The Willamette Valley Kalapuyans also occasionally worked as guides and canoe men on HBC brigades descending and ascending the Willamette River, and they often received foodstuffs in exchange for their labor.[22] Thus, some Kalapuyans became actively engaged in economic relations with the fur trappers and negotiated the terms of those interactions. The Kalapuyans' motivation for engaging in these types of exchanges was most likely a desire to supplement their traditional technology and economic activities, as they had since their initial contact with Euro-American fur traders in the 1810s.[23] The available information on Kalapuyan labor under the HBC reflects the general regional trends on indigenous labor in the Columbia Department outlined by Richard Mackie. He noted that after 1821, Native trade and labor in the Northwest for the HBC followed existing patterns within the indigenous economies.[24]

The Kalapuyans also occasionally provided food and shelter to the foreigners and lent them canoes when the outsiders' horses were lost, lame, or worn out from travel. On a trip to the Upper Umpqua watershed in October 1826, David Douglas slipped and fell down a ravine while trying to capture an elk. Injured in the chest, he wrote, "I find now, 5 p.m., a severe pain in my chest. Six Indians of the Calapooie tribe assisted me to my camp, and as it would be very imprudent to undertake any journey as I am, I resolved to return to the camp and asked them to saddle my horse and place the things on it, which they readily did. It gave me more pleasure than I can well describe to think I had wherewith for them to eat, and after expressing my gratitude in the best way I could, one came to lead the horse while I crept along by the help of a stick and my gun."[25]

The hospitality and humanitarian aid Douglas received from various Kalapuyan groups was consistent throughout his travels in the region during the mid-1820s. These decisions to provide support to fur traders and the occasional lost traveler suggest that the Kalapuyans viewed these foreigners as guests in the Willamette Valley. As long as the newcomers respected Kalapuyan protocols and customs, the Indians provided assistance and security for visitors and colonists in the valley.[26]

Kinship was another component that structured intercultural relations in the Willamette Valley in the years prior to permanent agrarian settlement. For the fur trappers, marriage ties with regional Native women provided access to sexual partners and productive labor and cemented the very social and economic ties needed to ensure the success of the fur trappers' livelihood. For regional Indian families, marriage ties were a political institution, providing access to European goods, thereby enhancing a family's social rank and economic position.[27] In the tension between the larger economic structure of the fur trade and women's agency, these alliances could also provide Indian women with a new means to realize social and personal ambitions somewhat distinct from those of their male relatives.[28]

Aside from the relationship between Jean Baptiste Desportes McKay and Marguerite Kalapuya, there is no documentary evidence for formal marriage alliances between the Kalapuyans of the Willamette Valley and the French Canadian settlers during the 1820s.[29] Nonetheless, data compiled from the Catholic Church records in the late 1830s demonstrate that of the original ten French-Indian settler families, eight of the eleven women were natives of the lower Columbia River region (tables 4 and 5). These families included Desportes McKay and his two wives; Marguerite Kalapuya and Catherine Chehalis; Joseph Gervais and Yiamust Clatsop; Jean Baptiste Perrault and Angele Chehalis; Louis Labonté I and Kilakotah Clatstop; Amable Arquette and Marguerite Chinook; Pierre Dépôt and Marguerite Clackamas; and Pierre Bellique and Genevieve St. Martin (French-Chinook). Lisette Shushuwap, wife of Joseph Delard, and Marie Okanagan, wife of Andre Picard, were natives of the northern Plateau region (encompassing present-day northeastern Washington state and southeastern British Columbia).

Etienne Lucier's wife Josette Nouette appears to have been a native of the northern tip of Vancouver Island from the Kwakwaka'wakw (Kwakiutl) village of Nahwitti at Cape Sutil, a well-known port of call for maritime fur traders.[30] Given Josette Nouette's background, she was likely a former slave initially sold via

TABLE 4. Willamette Valley settlers, 1830–1833

Freeman	Home parish	Wife	Wife's ethnicity	Date established
1. J. B. Desportes McKay	[Temiscaming, LC]?	1 Marguerite	Kalapuyan	1831
		2 Catherine	Chehalis	
2. Joseph Gervais	Maskinongé, LC	Yiamust	Clatsop	1832
3. Etienne Lucier	St. Edouard, LC	Josette	Kwakwaka'wakw*	1832
4. Joseph Delard	Sorel, LC	Lisette	Shushuwap	1832
5. J. B. Perrault	St. Antoine, LC	Angele	Chehalis	1832
6. Louis Labonté I	Laprairie, LC	Kilakotah	Clatsop	1832
7. Amable Arquette	St. Laurent, LC	Marguerite	Chinook	1833
8. Pierre Bellique	L'Asumption, LC	Genevieve	French-Chinook	1833
9. Pierre Dépôt	St. Roch, LC	Marguerite	Clackamas	1833
10. Andre Picard	St. Thomas, LC	Marie	Okanagan	1833

NOTES: LC=Lower Canada (Quebec). *Josette Nouette appears to have been a native of Vancouver Island.
SOURCES: Munnick, *CCRPNW-SP, CCRPNW-V*; Lyman, "Labonte"; McKay, *St. Paul*; Slacum, "Slacum's Report."

the Columbia River slave trade network, which brought slaves from Vancouver Island and the Olympic Peninsula into the lower Columbia region.[31] Although the kin relations between the Kalapuyans and the wives of the French Canadians were of a more secondary or tertiary nature (and some, like Josette Nouette, may have originally been foreign slaves), the French-Indian families did share some cultural affiliations with the Willamette Valley peoples because the majority of the women were natives of the larger Columbia River watershed. Of particular note is the prevalence of the daughters of Coboway, a Clatsop headman. Both Yiamust and Kilakotah married French Canadians and were living in the Willamette Valley by the early 1830s.

Lacking additional sources on the aforementioned Indian women who resettled the Willamette Valley with their husbands and children, the role of women in Chinookan society and the personal history of another Coboway daughter, Celiast, suggest that the agency of the Native wives of the male settlers should not be overlooked. While Chinookan women usually did not serve as community leaders per se, they provided essential labor and played important trade roles within both the regional aboriginal economy and the fur trade economy. For example, Celiast Clatsop, who was originally married to French Canadian laborer Basil Poirer, eventually left this first husband in the early 1830s while living at Fort Vancouver. She subsequently entered a lifelong relationship with American Solomon Smith, a literate individual of higher social standing. Smith had come West with the fur trade expedition of New Englander Nathaniel Wyeth in 1832 and then taught at Fort Vancouver, where he likely met Celiast. By 1834, the

TABLE 5. Willamette Valley settler data, 1830–1833

Male settlers from Lower Canada	9 of 10
Other: French-Algonquin	1 of 10
Female settlers from lower Columbia	8 of 11
Female settlers from northern Plateau	2 of 11
Other: 1 from Vancouver Island	1 of 11
Male settlers originally with PFC	3 of 10
Male settlers originally with NWC	4 of 10
Male settlers originally with HBC	3 of 10
Average age of male settlers in 1830	40 yrs

NOTE: J. B. Desportes McKay had at least two wives in 1830.

SOURCES: Munnick, *CCRPNW-SP, CCRPNW-V*; Lyman, "Labonte"; McKay, *St. Paul*; Slacum, "Slacum's Report."

couple was living with Celiast's sister Yiamust and brother-in-law Joseph Gervais in French Prairie.[32]

David Peterson del Mar's case study of Celiast's personal history demonstrates that in the midst of social and cultural changes brought on by the fur trade and later Euro-American settlement, this Clatsop woman clearly sought to control the direction of her own life and ensure the welfare of herself and her family. Her example suggests that while we do not have direct evidence of the role of Native women in the very earliest settlement of the Willamette Valley, we can infer a degree of agency to this group of women. It was essential for these women to maintain positive social and economic relations with the Kalapuyans when their French-Indian families lived seasonally in the Willamette Valley during the 1820s and also when they began to establish a permanent agrarian settlement there in about 1830. These Indian women were familiar with the regional trade language, Chinook Jargon, and drew on any existing extended kin relations as well as their own knowledge of regional trading practices to ensure stable relations with the Kalapuyans. From this perspective, they played a role as cultural mediators, negotiating exchanges between the Kalapuyans and other regional groups, including their own direct relatives in the lower Columbia River basin.[33]

The Willamette freemen—the independent trappers and hunters who contracted with the Hudson's Bay Company after 1822—were primarily French Canadians, their numbers supplemented by a small number of Americans, French-Indian mixed-bloods, and francophone Iroquois. Most had originally come to the Oregon Country as voyageurs and hunters with either the PFC or the NWC. Some trapped independently of the HBC, while others joined the various annual trapping and exploring expeditions, including the Snake, Umpqua, and Southern (or Bonaventura) Parties. When not moving about the Willamette Valley and other parts of the Oregon Country, these free trappers and hunters were seasonal inhabitants of the upper Willamette Valley, especially the Ahantchuyuk's territory.[34]

Born during the period from the late 1770s through the 1790s, these freemen had pursued the physically demanding life of the fur trapper for fifteen to twenty years by the late 1820s and so began to consider retiring with their wives and children, who had shared the trials of the trapping life. Facing the possibility of leaving the fur trade, the men and their families had several options. They might return to the fur trappers' place of origin, be it French Canada, Red River, or the Iroquois settlements in Lower Canada. They might also join their wives' native communities in the western regions. The bicultural families could also choose to live permanently near one of the fur trade posts. And finally, there was the option of establishing an agrarian settlement in the Oregon Country.[35]

The memoirs of Louis Labonté II, son of Astorian Louis Labonté and Kilakotah Clatsop, suggest that the longtime freemen, especially the Astorians, had formed a bond of camaraderie that may have played a role in their decision to retire to the Willamette Valley.[36] Although the historical record has long overlooked the role of the freemen's Indian wives in the decision-making process, there is evidence suggesting that the women also wanted to settle permanently in the valley. In 1838, HBC clerk Francis Ermatinger wrote his brother Edward that Josette Legacé, the *métis* wife of Chief Trader John Work, wished to settle with her husband and children in the Willamette Valley.[37]

It is perhaps best to view the reasons of the fur trappers and their spouses for settling in the Willamette Valley as a set of complex motives grounded in their own historical experiences and the regional culture and environment.[38] For the bicultural French-Indian couples, the territory of the Ahantchuyuk Kalapuyans would have been particularly attractive. The Champoeg was an important and longtime transfer point in the region's existing transportation system, providing water access to the Willamette River and Fort Vancouver as well as the upper Willamette Valley. In addition, the French-Indian families recognized the value of the natural resources of the area. Like other parts of the Willamette Valley that had been managed and utilized by the Kalapuyans for centuries, this territory contained a variety of useful ecozones. The open prairie land was ideal for cultivation and grazing, as it demanded less labor in clearing than forested sites. The other areas—bottomland forests, oak openings, wetlands, wet lowland prairies, and forest foothills—supplied the Native women with useful plants and roots such as *wapato*, camas, and berries, afforded the settlers additional food sources in the wild game and fowl, and also provided access to timber for construction and fuel. Another attraction for the prospective settlers was the mild climate, a contrast to the regions farther north in British North America, and to the arid Plateau east of the Cascades. In seeking to settle in Ahantchuyuk territory, the French-Indian families thus chose an environment that was highly desirable in terms of the regional subsistence practices of the Native women *and* the agrarian culture of the French Canadians.[39]

Nine of the ten original Willamette Valley male settlers were natives of Lower Canada. Theirs was a society with deep roots in the agrarian peasant cultures of Western Europe. The French Canadians composing the largest group of fur trade laborers during the height of the North American fur trade (1770s–1840s) hailed from agricultural communities in the St. Lawrence Valley. Those French Canadians who eventually settled in the Willamette Valley resembled the typical new recruit of this period. When they entered the fur trade in the early nineteenth century, they were young men in their teens or early twenties, mostly from landowning peasant families.[40] At the time, Lower Canada was a precapitalist agrarian society, and although the peasants, or *habitants*, labored under a seigneurial system that supported a landed gentry, the *habitants* formed an independent class that pursued self-sufficiency based on husbandry and subsistence agriculture.

The French Canadian voyageurs who resettled the Willamette Valley were the descendants of French colonists who had themselves colonized and transformed the landscapes of the St. Lawrence Valley, including clearing the land of large forest tracts. The Willamette settlers' *habitant* culture led them to value open prairie lands that would also provide sufficient timber, water, and river frontage.[41] When the French Canadians established farms in Ahantchuyuk territory, they claimed long rectangular lots that tended to be set at right angles to nearby rivers and streams. These claims in French Prairie were comparable to the *longlots* found in Lower Canada and in other North American regions colonized by francophones, such as those in the Mississippi Valley, Louisiana, and the Red River colony in Manitoba.[42] Although very little is known about the earliest homes in French Prairie, David Brauner has summarized the available evidence based on his long years of archaeological research in the area:

> Little detail about the pre-1829 settlement exists in the literature. We can assume that occupation of a year or more at one location required the erection of a single log cabin, probably employing the *piece sur piece* building technique typically associated with French-Canadian construction. Less elaborate long buildings suitable for short-term occupation, storage, or some other function may also have been associated with these isolated cabin sites. Hand wrought square nails were manufactured at Fort Vancouver in small quantities, but were probably not used in the Willamette Valley before the early 1830s. Window glass was not used in regional construction until the mid-1830s. Brick was similarly not used in the Willamette Valley until the late 1830s.[43]

From an economic standpoint, by establishing farming operations in the Willamette Valley the Willamette freemen chose an option in keeping with agrarian traditions in Lower Canada, while they also distanced themselves from the legal strictures and the rents, various fees, and compulsory workdays (*corvées*) associated with French Canada's long-standing seigneurial system.[44] Allan Greer's research on the Lower Richelieu Valley from 1740 to 1840 demonstrates that the region's peasant families relied on both credit mechanisms and wage labor in the fur trade to support their farming economy.[45] By using any savings they had accumulated with the HBC and by drawing on credit accounts with the company's store at Fort Vancouver, the settlers were able to replicate to some degree the social and economic institutions they had known in Lower Canada but without the tax and rent burdens associated with seigeurialism. Retiring to a farm after years in the fur trade was a choice that would not have been unusual at the time. The uncommon element was the men's decision to set up farming operations over a day's journey from the nearest post, Fort Vancouver, and in a locality that even then HBC officials feared might eventually come under American control. However, as John Hussey noted, the territory of the Ahantchuyuk, and Champoeg in particular, served as an important transport hub by providing easy access to the Willamette River and a transit point for fur trappers to pick up horses on their way south.[46] From this perspective, the French-Indian couples located their homesteads within a reasonable distance of Fort Vancouver to obtain supplies and assistance but far enough away to create a settlement at a remove from the HBC and British authority.[47]

Chief Trader Alexander McLeod's comments about the Willamette freemen, recorded in September 1828, provide some of the best evidence of the French-Indian families' motivations for settling permanently in the upper Willamette Valley. At the time, McLeod expressed his frustration that the freemen were loath to join his expedition to the Umpqua country in southern Oregon.[48] He described several reasons for their reluctance to leave the Willamette Valley. First, the Umpqua expedition was less of an economic incentive because the freemen had strong ties with the Kalapuyans, "the Indians from whom they have obtained Furs." Second, McLeod claimed the freemen lacked an entrepreneurial spirit, implying that they were usually satisfied with the few material possessions they owned. McLeod also remarked on the freemen's attachment to the Willamette Valley, observing that "nothing short of decisive measures will ever make them leave their favorite country (Wullamette) should they for instance be disposed to remain."[49]

Another reason for the freemen's reluctance to leave the Willamette Valley was their attachment to their families. During his 1824–1825 trip to the Columbia Department, George Simpson talked to the freemen about joining the HBC expeditions to the Umpqua River, noting that "they are rather shy on account of their families and the hostile character of the Natives."[50] The freemen's fears for the safety of their families may have been a response to the conflictual relations between fur traders and Indians in southern Oregon and the Umpqua River region.[51] It is clear in Alexander McLeod's comments that the French-Indian families shared a sociocultural orientation that differed significantly from that of the HBC's officer class. These families lived among thousands of Native people in an appealing locale, the Willamette Valley, that was within a few days' journey of the women's maternal relations and the fur trade posts. The French Canadian men were particularly concerned about the welfare of their growing families, and with their wives they pursued a mixed economy based on agrarianism, hunting, gathering, and trading.[52] The families' attention to kin and to place is unsurprising given that such values were fundamental to the culture and community life of both the Native women of the Northwest and the French Canadian men from the rural parishes of Lower Canada.[53] In contrast, Chief Trader McLeod prized values associated with both the master-servant culture of precapitalist Great Britain and the culture of mercantile capitalism: deference to one's social superiors, a sober work ethic, entrepreneurialism, an accumulation of capital, and a commitment to the civilized life modeled by the Anglo-Scottish officer class.[54]

The views of the HBC officers—also reflected in a later memoir by Chief Factor John McLoughlin—held out an either/or future for the French-Indian families in terms of their ethnic and cultural affiliations: the bicultural children were to be raised either as Indians or as whites. McLoughlin felt that "half-breeds" raised as Indians would prove "a thorn in the side of the whites."[55] As he remembered his words some twenty years later, McLoughlin had urged the fur trappers to settle in the Willamette Valley, believing that the establishment of a colony geographically separated from the families' Indian relatives would not only ensure that the children would be "brought to cultivate the ground and imbued with the feelings and sympathies of the whites," but that "their mothers would serve as hostages for the good behavior of their relatives in the interior."[56] McLoughlin's perspective combined Anglo notions about a racial hierarchy, colonial ambitions for racial assimilation (in contrast to later American settler notions of racial elimination), and practical concerns about ensuring stable Native–Euro-American relations.

John McLoughlin's version of events, penned in the early 1850s, in fact departs from McLeod's 1828 characterizations of the freemen. McLeod observed that the freeman were quite attached to the Willamette Valley and preferred to remain there whenever possible. However, McLoughlin later wrote that "many of the Canadians objected to go to the Willamette, because it was to become American territory," the reason for their concern being whether they would "not have the same advantages as American citizens." McLoughlin claims he convinced the Canadians that the Willamette Valley was "the best and only place adapted to form a settlement" due to the fertility of the soil and the access to the waterways, and the American government would treat them properly if they were honest men.[57] Given the historical evidence and the historical realities of the 1820s, McLoughlin's later recollections constitute a case of historical revisionism, one that would appeal to the eventual American victors in the struggle for control of Oregon. A more likely scenario is that the French-Indian families were intent on settling in the Willamette Valley because of the benefits the area offered them. Although the French Canadian men may have felt little loyalty to the British crown or the HBC (both of which treated them as second-class citizens), they would have been concerned about their property rights once the international border question was finally settled. Indeed, the French Canadians expressed concern about the legality of their land claims to New England entrepreneur Nathaniel Wyeth in 1833 and to William A. Slacum, who visited the Oregon Country at the request of the American government in 1836. As British subjects, the Canadians were worried that the United States would not honor their preemptive claims.[58]

In addition to their concerns about the larger geopolitical situation, the French-Indian couples had two more additional concerns related to their desire to reside permanently in the Willamette Valley: reaching an agreement with the local Kalapuyans on whose land they wished to settle and securing the support of John McLoughlin, from whom they would need credit, supplies, and—most importantly—livestock. Here the fur trappers had to negotiate with both the aboriginal inhabitants and the local Euro-American colonial power in order to find their own place in the region. Although the freemen had camped seasonally in the Willamette Valley for more than fifteen years by the mid-1820s, it appears that year-round occupation of the land based on agriculture and animal husbandry began only between 1828 and 1830. When French-Indian families—such as those of Etienne Lucier and Josette Nouette, Joseph Gervais and Yiamust Clatsop, Louis Labonté and Kilakotah Clatsop, and Jean-Baptiste Desportes McKay and his two wives, Marguerite Kalapuya and Catherine Chehalis—decided to establish farms in the Willamette Valley, they chose the territory of the Ahantchuyuk.[59]

Because these men and their families apparently settled permanently in this area prior to the intermittent fever epidemic of 1831, they likely obtained the approval of the Ahantchuyuk.[60] Prior to the epidemic, the Ahantchuyuk population numbered about five hundred, sufficiently numerous to resist unwanted intrusions on their lands.[61] Given this historical reality, what motivated this group of Kalapuyans to allow this handful of early French-Indian families to settle in their territory? Unfortunately, it is not possible to answer this question with any degree of certainty because there is no direct evidence from the limited existing Kalapuyan sources. However, that such permission was probably given can be deduced from an examination of Kalapuyan and regional aboriginal cultural logic and from known historical realities of the time.

From a Kalapuyan perspective, permitting these few families to settle in the Ahantchuyuk territory was seen as a way to further incorporate the newcomers into aboriginal systems of trade and kinship, ties that had developed with the newcomers over the previous fifteen years. This practice was in keeping with pre-contact patterns of social, economic, and kinship relations in the Columbia River region. In fact, maintaining social and economic ties through bicultural families was common practice within the larger North American fur trade. Within the Columbia District, fur trader officers and laborers regularly intermarried with aboriginal groups living near fur trade posts such as Fort George, Fort Langley, Fort Nez Percés, Fort Vancouver, and Cowlitz Prairie.[62]

The memoirs of Louis Labonté II, who lived with his family at the Gervais farm near the Ahantchuyuk village of Chemaway from 1831 to 1834, provide the only recorded firsthand account of the relations between the French-Indian families and the Ahantchuyuk Kalapuyans in the early 1830s. His memoirs speak of lively social relations between the indigenous people and the newcomers. Labonté recalled that the children living in the upper Willamette Valley, both Kalapuyan and French-Indian, played together. One of the local youths' favorite sports was diving off a bluff at Champoeg.[63] Although the French-Indian families and the Kalapuyans probably communicated largely in Chinook Jargon, Labonté provides evidence that the young children of the fur-trapping families did learn some Central Kalapuyan words and phrases from their Kalapuyan playmates. Labonté also recalled hunting deer alongside the Kalapuyans, who would don the head of a deer and skillfully act the part of a young buck in order to gain closer proximity to their prey. While the Kalapuyans employed bow and arrow in the hunt, the "young Labonte always used a gun at this sport."[64]

The French-Indian families also appear to have been privileged to attend weddings of the Ahantchuyuk. Labonté's memoirs describe in detail the wedding ceremony of the local Kalapuyans, including the exchange of gifts that solemnized the marriage between two families and between tribal groups if the newlyweds were from highborn members of different tribes. Labonté also recalled the impact of nearly twenty years of trade with the Euro-American fur traders. While wedding gifts included traditional items such as slaves, dentalia shells, and tobacco, they also gave goods of European manufacture such as blankets, guns, kettles, powder, and knives.[65]

In the Willamette freemen's initial efforts to negotiate the support of John McLoughlin and the HBC for their project to settle in the Willamette Valley, they initially faced opposition. In 1828, two fur trappers approached McLoughlin asking for his support in their desire to establish farms in the Willamette Valley. One of the two was Etienne Lucier and the other was either Joseph Gervais or Jean Baptiste Desportes McKay. That year, McLoughlin refused to support the men's project.[66] McLoughlin's refusal was due to the policy of the HBC, which discouraged settlement in the country and required employees who signed contracts to return to their place of engagement. It was also likely based on his concern that a French-Indian settlement in the Willamette might develop independently of the HBC, because the region south of the Columbia might become American territory when the international boundary was finally determined.

Accordingly, that first year in 1828, McLoughlin refused to give Etienne Lucier the needed implements to establish a farm, though he did grant Lucier and his family passage to Canada on the overland express. However, the party the Luciers joined was unable to cross the Rocky Mountains, and so they returned to Fort Vancouver. McLoughlin instructed Lucier and his family to join the Southern Party under the command of Chief Trader Alexander McLeod. At the time, McLoughlin wrote that he hoped "we would find a place Where we could Employ our Willamette freemen so as to remove them from a place where they were anxious to begin to farm."[67] One fur trapper, the former Astorian Louis Labonté, in fact returned to Canada and received his papers of official discharge. He made his way back to Oregon in 1830 and then brought his family to stay with Joseph Gervais and his family near Chemaway in 1831.[68]

By the fall of 1829, it appears that John McLoughlin had changed his mind about opposing the free trappers' desire to settle in the Willamette Valley. His letter to the HBC governor and committee in 1836 indicates that the main reason for his abandoning his earlier position was strategic. In 1827 and 1829–1830, the *Owhyhee*, a Boston ship captained by John Dominis, plied the waters of the North Pacific Coast, including the Columbia River. When Dominis announced that he would return again in 1831, McLoughlin became worried that if the HBC did not accommodate the wishes of the Willamette freemen, they would trade their furs with the Americans.[69] Since the strategy of the HBC was to protect its trade monopoly in North America, McLoughlin was determined to prevent American competitors from "getting a footing in the country."[70] McLoughlin then drew up an arrangement that would provide the freemen with the supplies they needed and ensure the colony's economic reliance on the HBC.[71]

McLoughlin agreed to support the freemen's settlement by keeping them on the books as free trappers. He loaned each family seed, farm implements, foodstuffs, and necessary household furniture on credit, the balance to be paid when the wheat crop came in.[72] He also loaned two cows to each male settler. In his memoirs, McLoughlin presented this policy as a conservative one that provided an equal footing to all settlers because it gave both the poor and wealthier settlers access to cattle.[73] However, McLoughlin's actions must also be viewed in light of his commitment to the HBC's trade monopoly in the Columbia region. He sought to prevent the Willamette settlers from becoming economically independent of the HBC by developing an alternative livestock market. McLoughlin apparently offered a double outfit to those willing to settle north of the Columbia River in Cowlitz Valley, but the "beauty and fertility" of the Willamette Valley motivated most to settle there.[74]

In his memoir dating from the 1850s, McLoughlin presents himself as a venerable paterfamilias directing the settlement plans of French Canadian, French-Indian, and Iroquois trappers, who needed guidance. In his eyes, to prevent the fur trappers from abandoning their farming settlement at "the least difficulty," McLoughlin required that the men have fifty pounds sterling (£50) to supply their families with clothing and implements before he would allow them to settle. McLoughlin reasoned that given their investment, the men would have to persevere despite the difficulties. McLoughlin credited this policy with the success of the settlement.[75] Here McLoughlin demonstrates a view held by many officers and educated observers of the day—that the French Canadian, French-Indian, and Native trappers lacked the industry and work ethic that was required to make them successful yeoman farmers. This is an interesting take on the settlement, for only the free trappers would likely have accumulated any savings. HBC laborers earned between £17 and £19 annually, which afforded them little opportunity to save money.[76]

Louis Labonté II identified former Astorians Joseph Gervais, Etienne Lucier, Louis Labonté I, William Cannon, Alexander Carson, and Jean Baptiste Dubreuil as the first free trappers to initiate settlement in the Willamette Valley, with Gervais as the first and Lucier the second.[77] Pierre Bellique and Genevieve St. Martin were also among the earliest settlers by about 1833. In his interview with Labonté, Horace S. Lyman raised the question as to whether some of the freemen's employment with an American company led them to be more independent—more inclined to look to their own fortunes, in contrast to HBC laborers. Lyman's suggestion that an American spirit of independence influenced the free trappers appears somewhat far-fetched given the limited two-year tenure of the Pacific Fur Company (PFC). It seems more likely that the freemen's *shared history* in the lower Columbia region over the 1810s and 1820s created bonds between the men and their families. Labonté II recalled that the Willamette freemen "formed a little company of comrades and became the first group of independent Oregon people."[78] Louis Labonté I and Joseph Gervais were in fact brothers-in-law, related by marriage through their wives, sisters Kilakotah and Yiamust Clatstop.

Historical sources dating from the 1830s and 1840s indicate that the families of Jean Baptiste Desportes McKay, Etienne Lucier, and Pierre Bellique took up claims fronting the Willamette River in the Champoeg area.[79] Amable Arquette and his wife Marguerite Chinook located their farm a few miles east of Champoeg, outside present-day Butteville. Jean Baptiste Perrault and his wife Angele Chehalis moved to the west side of the Willamette River near the confluence of the Yamhill River. Joseph Gervais and Yiamust Clatsop staked a claim at "Chemaway, a point on the back of the Willamette River about two and half miles south from Fairfield."[80] Following Louis Labonté's retirement from the HBC in 1828, he returned to Lower Canada as per the requirements of his contract and then rejoined his family in the Columbia region. Labonté, Kilakotah Clatsop, and their children first lived with Joseph Gervais and Kilakotah's sister Yiamust for several years in the early 1830s. In 1834 Labonté moved the family to Thomas McKay's farm on Scappoose Plains (Scappoose, Oregon) near the lower Willamette's Multnomah Channel. After two years as foreman for McKay, Labonté and his family finally settled on a riverfront site on the west side of the upper Willamette River, located across the Yamhill River from the Perrault homestead.[81]

Curiously, in the published account of Labonte II's memoirs, there is no reference to Jean Baptiste Desportes McKay and his families, who were some of the first non-Kalapuyan settlers in the Willamette Valley. McLoughlin also disregarded Desportes McKay in his official and personal accounts of the French-Indian colony. These omissions may have been the result of a desire to expunge a less than "respectable" character and his families from the official history. Not only was Desportes McKay a "halfbreed" of French-Algonquin descent, but throughout the 1820s and 1830s he had at least two Indian wives and apparently owned several Indian slaves. Recognizing a slave-owning, mixed-blood polygamist as a founding father of the Willamette Valley settlement may well have proved too controversial for McLoughlin in the 1850s and for Horace Lyman, the American journalist who interviewed Louis Labonté II in the 1890s.[82]

In March 1833, John Ball, an American who had come west with Nathaniel Wyeth's first overland expedition, arrived to try his hand at farming. That summer, he was joined by John Sinclair, another member of the Wyeth party.[83] Ball built a modest establishment, remaining in Champoeg through September 1833.

FIGURE 2. Valley of the Willamette. SOURCE: Henry Warre, *Sketches in North America and the Oregon Territory* (1848). Courtesy of the Oregon Historical Society, OrHi 49030.

His letters and journal, later published by his daughters, provide some details on the small French-Indian settlement at Champoeg. Ball remarked on the valley's unique environment, noting the vitality of both indigenous plants and introduced crops such as peas, barley, and winter wheat. Hogs, horses, and cattle also thrived, deer and elk were plentiful, and the settlers could easily obtain salmon at Willamette Falls. In this early period, the French-Indian economy relied on a combination of Lower Canadian agricultural and husbandry practices, fur trapping, hunting, trading, and the productive work of Native women engaged in traditional subsistence activities. The agrarian colonization of the local landscape by the freemen and their families hastened a process that had begun with the introduction of horses to the Willamette Valley in the 1810s. These French-Indian families introduced livestock, cropping, deforestation, and an agricultural system that began a major transformation of the landscape.[84]

John Ball's comments about the settlers' adoption of local Native customs also indicate the role of the French Canadians' Indian wives in influencing early French Prairie society. In addition to their productive work, the women drew on their Native cultures to shape the settlement's trade relations, material culture, and social life. Louis Labonté II's familiarity with Chinook Jargon demonstrates that the women also taught their children to speak the region's lingua franca.[85] Ball specifically mentions Desportes McKay, whom he noted had at least two, perhaps three wives and a total of seven children. Ball also reported the presence of "five or six slaves and two or three hired Indians, besides cats and dogs without number."[86] John Ball's observations about the Desportes McKay household suggest that during the 1820s and 1830s, some French-Indian families in the Willamette Valley followed the regional practice of owning Indian slaves and utilizing their labor.[87]

Despite Ball's high hopes, his months in the Willamette Valley were disappointing on the whole. With the onset of the intermittent fever in the summer months of 1833, both Ball and Sinclair were incapacitated for days at a time. Most vexing to Ball was the state of the little colony itself. As a New Englander and a graduate of Dartmouth College, Ball found his interactions with the French-Indian families and the local Indians tiresome and irritating. He could not abide the "intrusion of those I did not wish" nor the lifeways of the French Canadians, "who adopted, in many ways, the customs of the natives." Ultimately, Ball became lonely and bored in the Willamette settlement for lack of educated, sophisticated neighbors. "Completely discouraged," John Ball and John Sinclair left the farm at Champoeg on September 20, 1833, and returned to the United States by boat.[88]

❋   In July 1831, the intermittent fever first descended upon the Kalapuyans of the Willamette Valley. The disease had made its initial appearance in the lower Columbia region one year earlier in July 1830. Also known as *la fièvre tremblante* (trembling fever) to the French Canadians and "fever and ague" to the Americans, the disease had been seen in other parts of North America following European colonization, but it was then new to the Pacific Northwest.[89] The intermittent fever spread throughout the lower Columbia and lower Willamette regions over the summer and fall of 1830. Winter halted its progress, but it reappeared again in the summer of 1831, this time reaching the Willamette Valley above Willamette Falls. By 1833 the fever had spread as far south as California's Sacramento Valley, likely transmitted by the HBC trapping brigades.

The first three years of the epidemic, from 1830 through 1833, were the most deadly, with the disease becoming endemic to western Oregon and western Washington thereafter. Robert Boyd, who completed the most comprehensive study to date on the intermittent fever epidemics of the 1830s, concluded that these attacks "probably constitute the single most important epidemiological event in the recorded history of what would eventually become the state of

Oregon."[90] Although the lower Columbia had experienced disease outbreaks on various scales during the late 1700s and early 1800s (venereal disease and smallpox being the most prominent), the intermittent fever marked a demographic turning point for the region's indigenous peoples.

Earlier scholars speculated about the identity of the intermittent fever; researchers now tend to view the epidemiological characteristic of the disease as most likely associated with malaria.[91] The evocative names "intermittent fever," "*fièvre tremblante*," and "fever and ague" correspond with the symptoms of malaria, which include fever, chills, periods of shaking or trembling, soreness and pain in the limbs, and an overall feeling of bodily weakness.[92] Another important characteristic of the disease was a tendency for it to reappear in convalescent victims. John Townsend, an American doctor present at Fort Vancouver in 1834, provided a clinical observation of the disease, noting it attacked liver function in the early stages, which he viewed as a primary reason for the high mortality rate.[93] Both the geographic extension and the seasonal nature of the disease are also indicative of this vectored disease. The intermittent fever appeared during the warmer months and dissipated during the winter. It was most virulent in the lower Columbia and Willamette Valleys, which correspond to the territory of the only known malarial vector in the Pacific Northwest, *Anopheles freenorni*. Finally, the use of quinine, made from the bark of the cinchona tree—used by the HBC to combat intermittent fever—was the preferred form of treatment for malaria in the nineteenth century.[94]

Chief Trader Peter Skene Ogden later wrote that after his absence from Fort Vancouver during the summer of 1830, he returned that fall to find the fort community stricken with the disease. According to Ogden, eighty-one of eighty-two employees at the fort fell ill within twenty days of the first appearance of the disease.[95] In mid-October 1830, John McLoughlin wrote HBC officials that all of the Fort Vancouver personnel were on the convalescent list.[96] Even when company employees survived the disease, they "remained subject to the influence of this pestilential fever."[97] Compounding the physically debilitating nature of the intermittent fever, the enormity of the outbreak left those who were healthy or recovering overwhelmed with nursing the scores who were ill. Despite these difficulties, Ogden attributed the low death rate at the fort to the presence of Western physicians and medicine and the "wise measures" instituted by McLoughlin at Fort Vancouver.[98] Fortunately, the annual supply ship from London arrived in the fall of 1830 and replenished the fort's supply of quinine. By 1833, McLoughlin, a trained physician, developed an additional remedy made from the root of the local Pacific dogwood, though it apparently only relieved the symptoms of the fever.[99]

On October 11, 1830, Chief Factor John McLoughlin wrote to HBC officials that the intermittent fever, "for the first time since the trade of this Department was Established, has appeared at this place and carried off three fourths of the Indn [sic] population in our vicinity."[100] According to Robert Boyd, the first outbreak of intermittent fever extended upriver to The Dalles and downriver to the mouth of the Columbia. It struck the Lower and Upper Chinookan populations of the lower Columbia and the lower Willamette. It likely also attacked the Athapascan-speaking isolate Clatskanie on the southern bank of the Columbia and the villages of the Coast Salish Cowlitz, located up the Cowlitz River on the northern bank of the Columbia.[101]

Although both Indians and Euro-Americans were afflicted with the disease, the death toll in the indigenous communities was much higher due to a combination of factors. One important factor in the high Indian mortality rate was the lack of cultural and medical defenses against previously unknown diseases. Such was the case for the Natives of the lower Columbia and the Willamette Valley in the 1830s.[102] Writings by contemporary observers indicate that the Native people did not have the medical knowledge to fight and treat the disease and followed practices that increased mortality.[103] The most significant counterproductive health-care response of the lower Columbia and Willamette Valley Indians was their recourse to a traditional sweat bath and the subsequent plunge into cold water. Native people customarily engaged in sweat bathing to relieve the symptoms of aches and pain. As contemporary records attest, this traditional practice in fact increased deaths among the Native population because it induced a febrile state, which proved deadly for individuals suffering from malaria.[104]

Peter Skene Ogden wrote that the local Indians did not heed the advice of HBC officials and continued the practice of jumping into cold water to relieve their distress. However, there is a second element to this story: the practice of HBC officials at Fort Vancouver to drive off suffering local Native people because the fort staff was overworked and overburdened by the enormity of the epidemic.[105] The scale of the initial intermittent fever was such that HBC officials focused their energies on caring for company employees and their families. When the fort population was restored to health, John McLoughlin sent HBC men out to assess the situation in the local Native villages.

Given the inability of the HBC to deal with the scale of the intermittent fever in the aboriginal populations and the absence of effective medical countermeasures, entire households and villages were stricken with the disease. Following the first onset of the fever, the responses of populations unfamiliar with the illness increased the death toll. Without quarantine, panic and flight likely spread the intermittent fever from its initial incubation site.[106] Villagers died as a result of abandonment and fatalism and the cessation of subsistence activities and nursing care.[107] In the case of the infants and young children, in addition to the attack on their immune system, the young died from lack of food from nursing mothers, whose ability to produce milk failed when they became ill.[108] As it was, whole villages were depopulated, with only small remnant populations surviving the epidemic. In an account recorded in 1840, French Canadian Catholic missionary Francis Norbert Blanchet noted that the mortality in the villages along the Columbia River was so high that the survivors were unable to bury the bodies. As a result, the Natives burned these abandoned villages in the hope of preventing further spread of the disease.[109] Chief Factor McLoughlin also took the extraordinary measure of ordering interpreter Michel Laframboise to burn an empty village on the western shore of Sauvie Island.[110]

Concerning the origins of the intermittent fever in the lower Columbia country, the Native people firmly believed that an American ship, the *Owyhee*, captained by John Dominis, introduced the disease before leaving the area in July 1830.[111] Robert Boyd, having reviewed the historical evidence, has developed a credible scenario that supports this view. The Boston ship was anchored at St. Helens on the Multnomah Channel from August 4, 1829, to July 21, 1830. In the ship's log, there was a notation that crew member Mr. Jones spent several months at Fort Vancouver recovering from an unidentified illness.[112] Most likely, Mr. Jones or another carrier suffering from a chronic case of malaria was bitten by local anopheline mosquitoes, which in turn infected the local human population. The mosquitoes were breeding in the swampy area around Sauvie Island in the late summer. Since Upper Chinookan women would have been gathering *wapato* bulbs in the waters off the island, they were susceptible to being bitten.

Robert Boyd has provided a likely scenario as to how the disease spread to other populations in succeeding years. The survivors of the first episode retreated to the higher elevations and forested areas away from the lowland village sites or sought refuge with kin relations in villages that were spared from the disease. However, the disease reappeared in the following years because the malarial parasite was present in the blood of those who had survived. In this way, the people living with relatives throughout the Columbia and Willamette Valleys—where the mosquitoes were also present—carried the disease to all of the Chinookan and

Kalapuyan populations.[113] Another element in the spread of intermittent fever was the role of local trading centers as points of disease transfer.[114] Since Willamette Falls and Champoeg were meeting places for Columbia and Willamette River peoples, the northern and central Kalapuyan populations were the first to suffer the disease in the late summer of 1831.

In July 1831, the intermittent fever reappeared at Fort Vancouver. This second wave was worse than the first, and it spread to a larger geographic area.[115] John McLoughlin reported that the disease reached the Kalapuyans of the Willamette Valley by September 9, 1831, and the third year (1832–1833), it continued to ravage the lower Columbia and the upper Willamette Valley.[116] In the fourth year, the intermittent fever appeared in the southernmost section of the Willamette Valley, the upper Umpqua and upper Rogue, the Sacramento and San Joaquin Valleys, and it may have also appeared in southeastern Oregon and the Great Basin.[117] Dr. William Bailey, a settler from 1835, estimated in 1841 that during the height of the epidemic in the Willamette Valley, close to one-fourth of the remaining Kalapuyans died each year. By 1837, William Slacum reported that five to six thousand Kalapuyans had perished.[118]

Like the majority of the HBC employees in the lower Columbia, the French-Indian families settled in the Willamette Valley were undoubtedly affected by the intermittent fever in the 1830s. However, no existing historical sources document the extent of the disease among the settler families. John Ball, who lived nearby the Lucier, Bellique, and Desportes McKay families at Champoeg, described being stricken with the fever and ague in the summer of 1833, but he stressed its impact on the Kalapuyans and Upper Chinookans of the Willamette Valley rather than noting its presence among the French-Indian families.[119] When Chief Trader John Work's Southern Party passed through Champoeg in October of 1833, many if not all the expedition members were sick with the intermittent fever. Work noted the assistance he received from Jean Baptiste Perrault and Jean Baptiste Desportes McKay, yet he made no observations about the impact on the settlement.[120]

Given the persistence of the original settler families through the 1840s, one must conclude that although they became ill with the intermittent fever during the 1830s, many family members did recover. Chief Factor John McLoughlin likely provided assistance to the families if called upon. This conclusion is in keeping with McLoughlin's later assistance given to hundreds of Oregon Trail emigrants in the early 1840s. Indeed, it seems highly uncharacteristic for McLoughlin *not* to have assisted the Willamette settlers. There is one clue that McLoughlin did indeed supply the settlers with medicine to treat the fever. In the summer of 1833,

John Ball dispatched John Sinclair to obtain medicine at Fort Vancouver after both he and Sinclair suffered recurring bouts of the fever and ague.[121] This suggests that the French-Indian settler families had at least one advantage over the local Kalapuyans during the intermittent fever epidemics.

The existing accounts of the early years of the intermittent fever epidemics in the Willamette Valley, historical and mythical in nature, are limited in scope and even smaller in number. However, they do provide a window into the experiences and responses of the Kalapuyans in facing the catastrophe. The only historical account from an aboriginal source survives in the ethnographic texts of Victoria (Victoire) Howard née Wishikin (ca. 1860–1930), who was of Clackamas, Molalla, and Tualatin Kalapuyan ancestry.[122] Over the course of two summers in 1929 and 1930, linguist and ethnographer Melville Jacobs spent several months recording stories, songs, and oral history with Howard, a West Linn resident who had grown up on the Grand Ronde reservation.[123] A story recounted to Howard by her mother-in-law, Wa'susgani, illustrates the experience of the Clackamas Upper Chinookans who lived near the confluence of the Clackamas and Willamette Rivers. It captures the overwhelming devastation of the epidemic on the village level and the common—and often fatal—response of the Native people: "Their village was a large one, but they all got the ague. In each and every house so many of the people were ill now. They said that when they had fever, they would go to the river, they would go drink water, they would go back home, and directly as they were proceeding (back), they would drop right there, they would die. When some of them were feverish, they would run to the river, they would go ashore, they would drop right there, they would die."[124]

During his stay in the territory of the Ahantchuyuk over the spring and summer of 1833, John Ball observed local Kalapuyans "plunging into the water when the fever came on and other improper ways" of responding to the disease and recorded evidence of fatalism among the Kalapuyans, both of which increased the mortality of the local villagers.[125] Ball's account of his encounter with the Clowewalla Chinookans at Willamette Falls in September 1833 illustrates the continuing impact of the intermittent fever: "When I got to the falls an Indian boy of 18 assisted us in carrying our boat. On inquiring of him how his people were, he said that they were sick and dying, and when we came back, as he expected we would, he should be dead. Asking the chief of the band below the falls for two men to row us to the fort [Vancouver], for I was feeble and had with me only my friend Sinclair, he answered that the men were all sick or dead, so he could not supply us. We had to wearily paddle our own canoe."[126]

Victoria Howard also recounted the story of her father-in-law's cousin, Old Wood or K'am'lamayx, an infant at the onset of the intermittent fever. His mother died at the river's edge after seeking water, and he was adopted by some passing Natives, possibly Kalapuyans, who spotted him crawling beside his mother's corpse. He grew to manhood in this foster family before being reunited with his Clackamas kin.[127] As this story illustrates, one of the ramifications of the intermittent fever epidemic in the Willamette Valley was the loss of entire families and whole villages. This was likely accompanied by the reformation of remnant populations, with orphan children being raised by extended kin or foster families.

Robert Boyd has reasoned that another response of the region's Native peoples to infectious disease was to create new myths and rituals to make sense of previously unknown maladies.[128] Because traditional cultural explanations for worldly destruction may not have been able to fully explain the introduction of infectious disease episodes—as traditional medical practice could not adequately respond to the crises—these new myths would offer explanations as well as hope to communities in desperate circumstances by conveying the lessons the survivors had learned through their experiences.

One of the myth texts recounted by Santiam Kalapuyan John Hudson in the early twentieth century points to the fever and ague epidemic.[129] The story of the trickster Coyote and turkey buzzard mentions several key observations about the spread of the disease in the Willamette: news of the disease's presence in neighboring villages, the movement away from low-lying areas to higher elevations, and the knowledge that secondary and tertiary attacks were of a less powerful force.[130] By crafting an adventure story about how Coyote lessened the severity of the disease through the use of his wits, the Santiam Kalapuyans drew on their cultural resources to mount a psychological resistance to the intermittent fever.

In Boyd's analysis of the available population data for the first half of the nineteenth century, as noted earlier, he calculates a 92 percent population loss for the Kalapuyans as a whole over the period from 1830 to 1841. The Kalapuyan population declined from a conservative total of 7,785 for the *whole* of Willamette Valley in 1830 to approximately 600 in 1841. For the lower Columbia region, which included the Chinookans, Clatskanie, and Kalapuyans, the population decline was 88 percent, from 15,545 to 1,932 individuals, over the period 1805–1840.[131] These figures are in keeping with observations from Oregon Trail pioneers of the 1840s and later estimates of Indian population decline.[132] However, the record population total for the Kalapuyans in the early 1840s should be viewed with some skepticism and taken as conservatively low estimates given that the observers were

Euro-American settlers and visitors who would have had incentives—both cultural and practical (i.e., self-serving)—to underestimate the number of Indians living in Oregon in the 1840s.[133]

From 1831 to 1841, the greatest percentage of Kalapuyan mortality was likely due to the annual intermittent fever outbreaks. Additional deaths were the result of additional maladies such as tuberculosis, venereal disease, influenza, and a decrease in fertility rates linked to the effects of malaria.[134] Malaria decreases the fertility in women of childbearing age, causing pernicious anemia, which increases the incidence of miscarriages, premature birth, and stillbirths. The continued attacks of endemic malaria, which lowered the population's resistance to other diseases, further reduced the number of children surviving to adulthood.[135] Under these conditions, even a moderate birthrate would send a population into steady decline, which was the experience of the indigenous population of the lower Columbia and Willamette Valley regions.[136] Given the high mortality rates due to the intermittent fever coupled with additional diseases, chronic ill health, and low birthrates, the 1830s were catastrophic for the Kalapuyans of the Willamette Valley.

Although few details are present in the historical record from the earliest years of the epidemics, observations on the region as a whole give some indication of the social changes affecting the Kalapuyans. Settlers from the late 1830s and early 1840s remarked on the abandoned village sites in the region.[137] One of the major results of the epidemics was the reshaping of smaller communities with refugee and remnant populations, as in periods of warfare or famine. These new villages in the Willamette Valley likely contained people of differing though neighboring languages and dialects.[138] Similarly, some Kalapuyans orphaned due to the epidemics may have asked for shelter among non-Kalapuyan groups, the French-Indian families, and neighboring Molalla and Chinookan villages. The change in settlement patterns also resulted in a disruption of economic activities such as hunting, subsistence rounds, and trading, as well as a disruption of cultural practices and the transfer of traditional knowledge from the elders to the younger generations. Although the surviving Kalapuyans did continue to practice large-scale burning in the Willamette Valley, Euro-American settlers forced a halt to the practice by the late 1840s.[139]

❋ For the Kalapuyans and settlers of the Willamette Valley, the mid-1820s through the early 1830s comprised a period of adaptation and dramatic change.

With the shifts in HBC trapping operations in the Oregon Country, the Kalapuyans responded to the changing times, engaging in occasional labor and coming to the assistance of outside travelers. For their part, the French-Indian families deepened the social and economic bonds they had developed with the Kalapuyans since the 1810s. In the late 1820s, the Ahantchuyuk Kalapuyans accommodated the French-Indians families seeking to resettle permanently in their territory, which also allowed the Ahantchuyuk ongoing access to European trade goods. When unimaginable calamity descended upon the Kalapuyans due to the intermittent fever, altering forever the demographic balance and the social fabric of the Willamette Valley, the surviving Kalapuyans carried on, regrouping into reformulated families and smaller communities.

As scholars have previously noted, the intermittent epidemics of the early 1830s marked a major watershed in the history of the lower Columbia region.[140] For the Kalapuyans of the Willamette Valley, the annual outbreaks of the fever also proved a historic turning point because the heavy population losses they suffered left them less equipped to resist the colonizing efforts of American settlers who began to migrate en masse to the valley within a decade. For the French-Indian families, the dramatic changes in the region's demography meant that, unlike other mixed-race fur trade communities in North America, the French Prairie settlers did not have the opportunity to intermarry and remain closely linked with nearby Native communities over several generations. Indeed, the arrival of American missionaries and settlers in the coming years would set the Willamette Valley on a distinct path in both regional and continental history.

CHAPTER 3 ❋ Methodist Missionaries
and Community Relations

During the early summer months of 1834, the French Canadian male settlers in
the Willamette Valley, likely in consultation with their Indian wives, discussed
the need for religious and educational training for their growing families. By July,
they had decided to send a letter to the nearest Roman Catholic ecclesiastical
seat at the Red River settlement in present-day Manitoba, asking that priests be
sent to their nascent community. Dated July 5, 1834, the Willamette settlers' first
letter to Joseph Provencher, then known as the bishop of Juliopolis, likely did
not reach the Red River colony until the fall or winter of 1834.[1] Having no news
from the bishop by the early spring of 1835, the French Canadians sent a second
letter, repeating their request for priests and "promising to do all in their power
to help them survive." They pledged twenty minots of grain per family to support
the priests, "which the members of the company there saying that they can easily
deliver," as the Willamette Valley was a "beautiful country where one plants and
harvests nearly year-round, and fishing there is in abundance."[2]

The French Canadians' petition for Catholic priests was not to bear fruit until
1838. In a curious turn of events, however, while the French Canadians were busy
drafting their initial letter to Bishop Provencher, the first party of Christian missionaries was already on its way to Oregon. Headed by the Reverend Jason Lee,
a small group of Methodist missionaries joined Nathaniel Wyeth's second expedition to the Pacific Northwest and arrived at Fort Vancouver in mid-September
1834.[3] The Methodists subsequently established their mission in the Willamette
Valley, but hampered by organizational problems, bouts of poor health, and
their own cultural biases, they made no significant attempts to convert local
Kalapuyans during their first three years there.[4]

Jason Lee and his colleagues were, however, more successful in working
with their Catholic French-Indian neighbors, who were their earliest supporters. The French-Indian families proved surprisingly hospitable to the American
Protestants during their early years in the Willamette Valley. The surviving documentary record on intercultural relations in French Prairie for the mid-1830s

illustrates the importance of local Protestant-Catholic initiatives. These cooperative problem-solving efforts demonstrate both the French-Indian settlers' ability to reach across the cultural divide—even in times of tension and conflict—and their own commitment to ethnic, religious, and community solidarity. Because the early French Canadian settlers and their Native wives were nearly universally illiterate and, therefore, left few written records, their role in early Oregon history has long been obscured.[5] However, a fresh examination of the surviving documentary record, including some previously untapped Canadian sources, reveals a complex story in which the French-Indian families in French Prairie, unlettered though they might have been, used all the means at their disposal—including ties with the Methodist missionaries—to advance their own local and community interests within the context of Euro-American colonialism.

❋ The Methodist mission to Oregon developed in response to the journey of a group of Nez Perce (Nimiipuu) and Flathead (Interior Salish) to St. Louis, Missouri, in 1831. The publicity and mythologizing that followed in the wake of the group's visit to St. Louis dovetailed with an evangelizing fervor then permeating American Protestantism. However, the purpose of the group's journey to St. Louis was not to bring about wholesale Christianization or acculturation to the Plateau but rather to provide the Nez Perce and the Flathead with trained religious leaders who might educate the Plateau peoples about Euro-American religion and culture. Nez Perce and Flathead leaders reasoned these religious leaders would afford their people access to both the knowledge and spirit power that the Euro-Americans seemed to have in abundance.[6]

For several decades, the Plateau peoples had experienced the effects of contact with encroaching Euro-Americans, including better access to European trade goods and the deleterious effects of infectious disease epidemics and tribal warfare. In the face of the social, cultural, and economic changes wrought by Euro-American expansion, the Plateau peoples sought guidance in traditional spiritual practices and a new, syncretic religion, which fur trader John McLean referred to as the "Columbia Religion." This new religion combined Native spirituality with elements of Christianity learned from fur traders, Iroquois settled among the Flathead, and from young Natives who had been educated by Protestant missionaries at the Red River colony in Manitoba. Several Plateau groups concluded that they needed more information about the Euro-Americans, their culture, and their religion. They were particularly intrigued by the newcomers' strong spirit power, which seemed to flow from Euro-Americans' religious practices.[7]

In March of 1833, the Methodist *Christian Advocate and Journal* published two letters by William Walker, an Indian agent in Ohio, and Gabriel Disoway, a New York merchant, that furnished readers with an embellished account of the Flathead–Nez Perce delegation to St. Louis in 1831. Walker's initial letter to Disoway crafted an appealing story of how the travelers had come east seeking the Holy Bible and Protestant missionaries for their people, and it included a sketch of an Indian with a stylized "flathead."[8] The Walker and Disoway letters had an electric influence on Methodist readers, prompting a clarion call for missionaries to be sent to Christianize the Indians of the Far West.[9] The Nez Perce–Flathead delegation to St. Louis and the excitement it engendered among American Methodists in the early 1830s coincided with a period of national agitation on the question of the Protestant missionary vocation. Methodism, like the Presbyterian, Baptist, and Congregationalist traditions, rested on a strong evangelical ideology that emphasized the individual conversion experience, revivalism, missionization, the redemptive power of Christ's crucifixion, and the central authority of the Bible.[10] The American Methodists' own evangelical impulse was rooted in two great events in the political and religious history of North America in the late eighteenth century: the American Revolutionary War (1775–1783) and the Second Great Awakening (1795–1810).[11]

The nationalism that emerged following the Revolutionary War offered American Protestants a new ideology linking democratic ideals, political freedom, and Christian liberty. Notions of religious freedom grounded in the separation of church and state coincided with a spirit of revival that became prevalent in the United States beginning in the 1790s and that gave rise to a more democratized American Christianity.[12] The Second Great Awakening was characterized by personal salvation, devotion to God, and a dogged determination to convert the "unchurched." Although the established Protestant sects (Anglicanism, Congregationalism, and Presbyterianism) had led the First Great Awakening in the 1740s, Baptists, Disciples, and Methodists spearheaded this second revivalist movement.[13] Beginning in the late 1700s, evangelical missionaries enthusiastically moved west alongside the American settlers who were streaming into the trans-Appalachia and Midwest regions—with Methodist circuit riders taking a prominent role in the evangelizing effort.[14] Inspired by the evangelical movement, male and female missionaries from New England and New York also set out to Christianize the Indian peoples of the Western regions. Sharing a passionate commitment to spreading the Christian gospel and American institutions, Protestant missionaries and the Protestant press

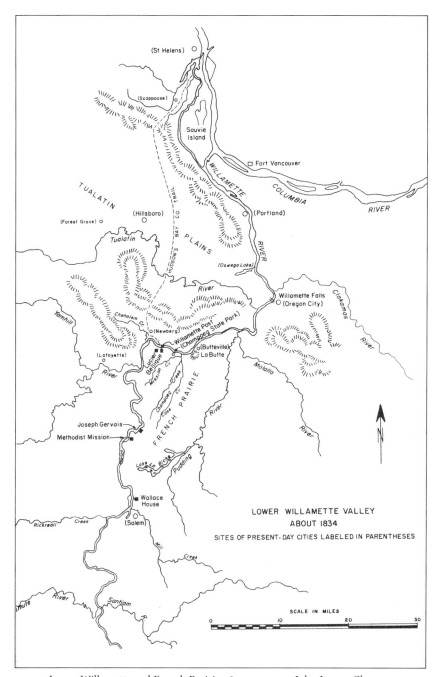

MAP 3. Lower Willamette and French Prairie, 1834. SOURCE: John Jussey, *Champoeg: Place of Transition* (1967). Courtesy of the Oregon Department of Transportation and the Oregon Historical Society.

contributed a religious pillar to Anglo-American settler colonialism on the Western frontiers.[15]

One prominent reader of the *Christian Advocate and Journal* was Wesleyan University President Wilbur Fisk, who urged the Missionary Board of the Methodist Episcopal Church to establish a mission to the Flathead Indians.[16] In late March 1833, board leaders initiated a dialogue with the Methodist bishops on the question of forming the mission. In July 1833, the board approved the idea and named the Reverend Jason Lee, a Canadian-born Methodist minister, as superintendent of the Flathead Mission (later the Oregon Mission). His nephew, the Reverend Daniel Lee, was appointed to the mission in September 1833, and Cyrus Shepard, a schoolteacher and devout Methodist, signed on in December 1833.[17] Jason Lee's organizing efforts over the fall and winter of 1833–1834 coincided with Nathaniel Wyeth's return to Massachusetts from Oregon. Lee subsequently met with Wyeth in Boston, and he agreed to allow the Methodist group to accompany his second expedition.[18] The three missionaries left the northeast in early 1834, making their way to Independence, Missouri. There Jason Lee engaged two laymen, Philip Leget Edwards and Courtney M. Walker, to assist the mission for a period of one year. In late April 1834, the Methodist party finally joined Wyeth at a rendezvous point eight miles upriver from Independence.[19]

During the westward journey, the missionaries met at least twice with mixed Nez Perce and Flathead groups, once toward the end of June and a second time in early July 1833.[20] On both occasions, the Nez Perce–Flathead groups expressed a desire for the Methodists to establish a mission among their people. At the onset of the westward passage, Jason Lee had been open to establishing his mission among these Plateau tribes. However, doubts about the planned Flathead mission crept into Lee's thinking while on the journey. His growing uncertainty appears to have resulted from concerns about the safety of the Plateau region, the geographic isolation of the Flathead territory from fur trade posts, and the Methodists' reaction to both the landscape and the Indians whom they met. Lee himself expressed little confidence that he wanted to remain in the Plateau, an arid environment quite alien to both the New Englanders and the Americans from the Midwestern frontier states.[21] The missionary party finally arrived at Fort Vancouver on September 15, 1834, ten days after Nathaniel Wyeth.

After spending a few days recuperating from their journey, Jason and Daniel Lee set out to search for a location for their mission on September 18, 1834.[22] During their initial sojourn at the fort, Lee decided to locate his mission west of the Cascade Mountains. In his memoir dating from the 1850s, HBC chief factor

John McLoughlin asserted that he advised Jason and Daniel Lee against settling among the Flathead because such a venture would be too dangerous. McLoughlin counseled them to consider the Willamette Valley for the mission site because the valley would provide a prime location to teach the local Indians about the "benefits" of an agrarian lifestyle and, thereby, change their cultural practices, particularly their hunting activities and seasonal migrations. In McLoughlin's view, this approach would ultimately lead to the Natives' Christianization and "civilization."[23] Another advantage to locating in the Willamette Valley was the proximity to the French-Indian settlers established there who would be able to provide assistance to the missionaries.

Jason and Daniel Lee spent September 19 through September 26, 1834, touring the upper Willamette Valley. There the brothers visited the French-Indian families living in Ahantchuyuk Kalapuyan territory, staying with Joseph Gervais and Yiamust Clatsop and their children, who lived on a farm about ten miles southwest of Campement de sable (Champoeg). At the Gervais home, the Lees met Yiamust's sister Celiast and her husband, Solomon Smith, who were living with the Gervais family. Solomon was then serving as a schoolteacher to the local French-Indian children. The other French-Indian families whom the missionaries met at the Gervais farm were happy to see the Lees, and the Gervais family provided the missionaries with food and allowed them to pitch their tent on the Gervais farm. Daniel Lee noted that "at supper we were treated with a fine dish of Canadian soup, excellent pork, and beaver, and bread without bolting, and as fine muskmelons as I ever tasted."[24]

While on this first foray into the Willamette Valley, there is no evidence that Jason and Daniel Lee consulted with the local Ahantchuyuk Kalapuyans about the possibility of establishing a mission in their territory. In fact, when the two men encountered a band of Kalapuyans during their scouting trip, the missionaries demonstrated a marked disinclination to engage the locals or empathize with them: "There are 30 Indians, old and young, a few rods from us, and some of the men are as naked as they were born—a filthy, miserable-looking company, and yet they are quite contented. They subsist mostly on cammas. Probably more than [a few] in this vicinity have fallen a sacrifice to the fever and ague within four years."[25]

Jason Lee's passages in his diary about observing the Kalapuyans but making no mention of speaking with them—even desiring to speak with them—is decidedly odd behavior for a missionary who had traveled more than three thousand miles to convert the Indians of the Far West. It appears from the diary entry that the Lees were not always accompanied by French Canadians from the nearby farms, which would indicate a language barrier existed between the Methodists and the Kalapuyans. Although this might explain why he had no exchanges with these Indians, Lee subsequently made limited efforts to enlist the aid of the French-Indian families in communicating with the Ahantchuyuk.

In explaining why Lee did not solicit the views of the Kalapuyans, it appears likely that he believed the Willamette Valley was open for settlement. He apparently did not consider that the Kalapuyans had title to the local territory, and, therefore, he did not believe it necessary to negotiate with them in order to occupy it. Evidence of this attitude is contained in *Ten Years in Oregon*, the memoir Daniel Lee cowrote with Joseph Frost some ten years later, in which the authors referred to the Willamette Valley as "uninhabited save by a remnant of the Calapooyas."[26] By not engaging in direct talks with the local Kalapuyans— indeed, by not considering such a step necessary—the Methodists bypassed any formal negotiations that would have entailed gaining land concessions from Indian groups to pave the way for Euro-American settlement.[27] This tendency to disregard the Kalapuyans, their territory, and their culture was reminiscent of the earliest contacts between Euro-American fur traders and the Natives during the 1810s. Jason Lee and his colleagues did not prioritize the establishment of stable relations with the local Kalapuyans groups, and this approach to intercultural relations in the valley would progressively intensify as American settler colonialism took root over the next decades.

Despite Jason Lee's lack of engagement with the local Kalapuyans, his decision about where to locate the mission was not an easy one. In his diary, he documented his worries over the momentous decision facing him. He wrote on September 24, 1834, "My mind is yet much exercised in respect to our location. I know not what to do."[28] The source of Lee's distress stemmed from growing realizations about his lack of missionary training and managerial skills and his own limited experience with Indians.[29] In keeping with the spiritual orientation of early nineteenth-century evangelical Methodism and Lee's own devout religious faith, he turned to God for guidance through prayer. Lee also consulted with other members of the party, and upon returning to Fort Vancouver on Saturday, September 27, he finally decided to locate the mission in the Willamette Valley, confirming his decision at Sunday services the next day.

In their narrative on the Methodist mission, Daniel Lee and Joseph Frost outlined four major reasons for Jason Lee's decision to locate the mission in the Willamette Valley. First, subsistence and supply lines were paramount concerns.

The territory of the Flathead was not conducive to Euro-American agrarian culture, and it was too remote to be well supplied by the HBC or by St. Louis-based fur traders. Second, the missionaries felt that the Flathead, or at least those interested in missionization, were too small in number and often at war with the Blackfeet. Third, the Methodists were fearful of being vulnerable to attack by the Blackfeet, who had a fierce reputation for violence against Euro-Americans. Finally, Daniel Lee rationalized that the missionaries would have a larger missionary field with access to more Native peoples in the Willamette Valley, and as they would be better supplied, they would also be better equipped to missionize the Indians.[30]

However, the arguments put forward by Lee and Frost bely a contradiction in the missionaries' reasoning. Throughout their narrative, the authors express an ambivalent attitude toward the Natives' fate. They were sent to convert the Indians and save them from "heathen ways," yet they believed that many, especially the Kalapuyans, were destined to conveniently die off in advance of Anglo-American colonization. The Methodists' ambivalence stemmed in part from their own frustrations that the Oregon Mission did not fit their idealized vision of pious Indian converts who would adopt a settled, civilized (Anglo-American) lifestyle and create "self-supporting Christian communities."[31] It also resulted from the racialism underlying American culture in the antebellum period and from the discourse of the "vanishing Indian" that accompanied America's westward expansion and conveniently exonerated Americans from responsibility for the supposed demise of the region's indigenous inhabitants.[32]

Leaving an ill Cyrus Shepard at Fort Vancouver, Jason and Daniel Lee, Philip Edwards, and Courtney Walker departed for the Willamette Valley on Monday, September 29, 1834. After spending the night aboard Nathaniel Wyeth's supply vessel anchored in the lower Willamette River, the party retrieved their supplies and, with the assistance of some local Upper Chinookans, they headed upriver to establish their mission. [33] On October 6 they arrived at their chosen site not far from the Gervais farm and soon began work on a house structure. The original mission site (also known as Mission Bottom and the Old Mission) was located on the eastern bank of the Willamette River approximately twelve miles upriver from Champoeg on a lowland prairie within the territory of the Ahantchuyuk Kalapuyans (about sixty miles south of Fort Vancouver).[34]

The local Kalapuyan groups, the Ahantchuyuk to the north and the Santiam to the south, apparently did not challenge the Methodists about the location of the mission. While the local bands' numbers had fallen from 150 to 200 to some 30 to 50 individuals by the mid-1830s due to the intermittent fever epidemic, the Kalapuyans still retained a demographic advantage over the Methodists, which would have allowed them to contest the missionaries' presence. However, there is no documentary evidence that the Kalapuyans collectively confronted the Methodists. Based on the two decades of Native-newcomer relations in the Willamette Valley, the Kalapuyans may not have perceived the small group of Methodists as a threat, but rather in a fashion similar to how they viewed the French Canadian fur trappers—as another small group of guests with whom they might occasionally exchange their products or labor for European goods when they were not busy with their complex subsistence round and landscape burning activities. The Kalapuyans occasionally came into contact the Methodists, and like other Native groups across the Pacific Northwest, their limited interest in the religious missionaries was primarily a curiosity about how the newcomers' knowledge and spirit power might supplement their core beliefs. During these transitional years in the Willamette Valley, the Kalapuyans, like several other Indian peoples, did not see the religious practice and culture of the Protestant missionaries to be of any particular benefit to their communities.[35]

Through the months of October and November, as the fall rains turned into winter rains, the Lees and Philip Edwards constructed their first buildings in the valley. Fortunately for the missionaries, they did not work in complete isolation. Beginning in mid-November 1834, they employed Rora, an "old [Sandwich] Islander," and a local Native youth, John Calapooya, to help build the mission's first barn. The employment of Rora and John Calapooya as laborers coincided with the arrival of the Ewing Young party from California. Tennessean Ewing Young led a group of some sixteen American fur trappers and the erstwhile American colonizer Hall Jackson Kelley to Oregon following a decline in Young's financial fortunes in the Spanish colony and considerable legal and financial wrangling with Spanish authorities.[36] In Daniel Lee's history of the Methodist mission, he mentioned that when the mission barn was partially completed, the Methodists realized they would need assistance to finish the structure, and so they called on the French Canadian settlers, who willingly came forward to help their neighbors. The missionaries also hired two Americans who had accompanied Ewing Young's party from California.[37]

For the French Canadians, there were several advantages to the Methodists' presence in the valley. Their initial letters to Bishop Provencher in Red River demonstrated a keen interest in educational and religious training for their families. Upon the Methodists' arrival, French-Indian couples such as Joseph Gervais and Yiamust Clatsop permitted the missionaries to conduct worship services in their homes, and they accepted the missionaries' offer of schooling for their children. Perhaps equally important to the French Canadians was the opportunity for additional socializing. In his diary, Jason Lee expressed annoyance that the French Canadian settlers liked to visit the mission and talk for hours on all manner of subjects in French, which Jason Lee did not well understand.[38] Although Jason Lee was irritated by the garrulous French Canadians and their preference for speaking French, the settlers evinced an ecumenical, community spirit in welcoming the Protestant missionaries to the Willamette Valley.

During the month of November 1834, as the small missionary group and additional laborers finished the log house and the barn that made up the mission's first buildings, three Kalapuyan youths arrived at the establishment. These three, identified as orphans, expressed a desire to reside with the missionaries. First came Sintwa (renamed John March by the missionaries), age ten on November 7, his sister Kyeatah (Lucy Hedding), age twelve on November 16, and Kilapoos (Charles Moorehead), age twelve.[39] In all three instances, the mission scribe wrote that the youths came to the mission of their own volition, and in the case of Kilapoos, he "requested permission to remain in the family." A letter written by Jason Lee to Wilbur Fisk suggests that Sintwa and Kyeatah were Kalapuyans from a nearby community, whose mother had recently passed away.[40] Sintwa may have come ten days before his sister in order to test out the mission while the children's mother was still alive. It is clear that all three took the extraordinary step of seeking refuge not among the local Kalapuyan or Chinookan populations, but with the newly arrived foreigners. This was an unusual development vis-à-vis the Native context, and as such it may indicate the level of social dislocation caused by the ongoing presence of the intermittent fever.

During the period from November 1834 through June 1838, the Methodist mission took in a total of fifty-two individuals, the majority of whom were children, and many of these were orphans (see appendix 4). These individuals' ancestry illustrates the ethnic diversity of the Pacific Northwest, the ethnic mixing that resulted from two decades of fur trading in the region, and the legacy of aboriginal slavery. The children, youths, and few adults who came to the mission included Kalapuyans, Iroquois-Kalapuyans, Iroquois-Chinookans, Upper and Lower Chinookans, Tillamooks, French-Indians, Hawaiian-Indians, Cayuse, Klickitats, Walla Wallas, Shastas, and former Indian slaves of unknown ancestry.[41] Twenty-two of the fifty-two individuals admitted to the mission, or roughly 40 percent of the total, were Natives of the lower Columbia–Willamette region, and among these children fifteen were Kalapuyans from the Willamette Valley.

Another 20 percent were bicultural children from fur trade families. The remaining 40 percent hailed from the coast, the Plateau, the middle Columbia region, and northern California.[42]

The data on the children residing at the mission from 1834 to 1838 indicates that for many children at the mission, illness, disease, and death were serious problems. At least eight of the thirty-two children resident at the mission between November 1834 and December 1836 died within six months to two years of their arrival. Excluding Kokallah, the Tillamook lad who later departed with his father, this leaves a death rate of 25 percent. The sources indicate the children suffered from the effects of the recurrent intermittent fever (malaria), scrofula (tuberculosis of the lung and lymph nodes), influenza (first documented in February 1837), and venereal diseases, which some of the children inherited from their mothers.[43] Given the developing disease ecology that accompanied Euro-American expansionism, the presence of so many diseases at the mission may have been the result of two interrelated developments: the presence of infectious disease among indigenous populations, diseases that the children brought with them, and the introduction of previously unknown illnesses, such as influenza, via regional fur trade networks.

The prevalence of various diseases at the mission, which also regularly struck all of the missionaries, coupled with subsistence tasks and activities related to ministering to the local French-Indian community, often overwhelmed the three missionaries and their lay assistants in the initial years of the mission. The Methodists found themselves with little time or energy to proselytize the local Kalapuyans. In a letter to Wilbur Fisk dated March 15, 1836, Lee admitted as much. He urged the influential Methodist leader to have the missionary board send additional "lay-men to attend to the temporels" so he could "gladly attend to the spirituals."[44] In Lee's view, the labor shortage at the mission could not be solved by recruiting local settlers to become lay workers because in his assessment there was not "a man in this place that can be hired that is fit to be in a mission family."[45]

Here Lee's views on culture, religion, and class colored his attitudes toward the French Canadians—disqualifying them in his eyes for service in the Methodists' missionary project. The French Canadians were not suitable candidates due to their Roman Catholicism, lack of education, illiteracy, poor English skills, and their marriage to Indian women. Rather than seeing the French Canadians' long residence in the region and their wives' ability to speak Chinook Jargon and other indigenous languages as useful assets in the project to communicate with and missionize local Indians, Lee saw only their supposed flaws. Clearly, the French

Canadians and their Native wives did not measure up to the standards of behavior and social decorum prized by white, middle-class Protestants from New England. Lee also asked the influential Wilbur Fisk to have the missionary board send pious families and women to address the practical needs and "civilizing" efforts of the Oregon Mission and to introduce proper Anglo-American gender norms to the Indian women and the Willamette Valley settlement.[46]

The Methodists' disinclination to tap into the social and linguistic connections between the Kalapuyans and the French-Indian community, the poor health of the missionary personnel, and the logistical problems they faced were not the only factors limiting the Americans' efforts among the Kalapuyans. Lee himself expressed disappointment with the local Natives, indicating his own inability to surmount the cultural divide separating the missionaries and the Kalapuyans. In March 1836, Lee characterized the Kalapuyans as "a scattered, periled, and deserted race," and wrote Fisk that "unless the God of heaven undertake their cause, they must perish from off the face of the Earth, and their name be blotted out from under heaven."[47] Lee must have sensed the fatalistic tone this struck, because in the next sentence he expressed hope that God would allow "a remnant" to be saved. Given the Methodists' limited resources, their lack of missionary training, and their ambivalent attitude towards the Kalapuyans, it is not surprising that in these early years, they focused their energies on the mission orphanage and boarding school, the day and Sunday schools for the local French-Indian children, and worship services for the French-Indian families and the small group of Americans who had come to the Willamette Valley with Ewing Young's party.[48]

The surviving documentation produced by the Methodists indicates that despite the cultural, religious, and linguistic divisions separating the American missionaries and the French-Indian settlers, the two groups enjoyed generally friendly relations during the early years of the Protestant mission.[49] The French Canadians and their Native wives opened up their homes, provided food and moral support to the missionaries, and assisted the Americans in construction work when called upon. The French-Indian neighbors continued their support for the Methodist mission by donating labor, attending and hosting services led by Jason and Daniel Lee, and having their children educated by Cyrus Shepard at the mission and later by Philip Edwards in Champoeg. According to HBC officer George Roberts, relations between Jason Lee and his nearest neighbor Joseph Gervais were very friendly. Roberts believed that a "good deal of stuff or kindly contributions of the Eastern People," originally intended for the local Indians, went to Joseph Gervais and his French Canadian neighbors.[50]

The orphaned children admitted to the Methodist mission came not only from lower Columbia Native groups disproportionately affected by the intermittent fever but also from the ranks of former fur trade families. The mission thereby provided the region with a much-needed social service. Here it is important to the note that both the French-Indian families and HBC chief factor John McLoughlin supported this role for the mission. In March of 1836, the leading HBC officers in the region also sent a letter of support and contributed a total of £26 to the mission effort.[51] Françoise Dupati McKay, daughter of Jean Baptiste Desportes McKay (Dupati) and his Kalapuyan wife Marguerite, boarded at the mission for a few years. The French Canadian guardians of Sophie and Angelique Carpentier placed the orphaned sisters in the care of the Methodist missionaries in 1835 and 1837, respectively. Their father, the fur trapper Charles Carpentier, had died in a horse race in the Snake Country in July 1834 while the Snake Party was camped with Wyeth's second expedition and the Methodist missionaries (the whereabouts of the girls' Shoshone mother were not documented).[52] Following the sudden demise of retired Iroquois hunter Louis Shangaretta in the fall of 1835, John McLoughlin appointed Jason Lee executor of the Iroquois' estate, and asked Lee to take Shangretta's orphaned children, Isabel, Joseph, and Nicholas, and his former slaves into the mission (the slaves later left the mission).[53] Marianne Bastien also came to the Methodist mission as a youngster in January 1837, and she remained there until her marriage to Joseph Gingras (French-Okanagan) in the 1840s. Marianne was the daughter of Joseph Bastien, a French Canadian fur trade laborer who had returned to Lower Canada at the end of his three-year contract, and Louise Shasta, who had likely been a slave captured in northern California and traded to the lower Columbia region in the early 1830s.[54]

During the mid-1830s, the Methodists established boarding, day, and Sunday schools at the mission, directed by Cyrus Shepard, and a smaller short-lived school in Champoeg led by Philip Edwards.[55] These Methodist-run schools received the public support of the French-Indian families in French Prairie and followed an earlier informal school headed by Solomon Smith, who had taught the Gervais siblings and nearby children at the Gervais farm prior to the Methodists' arrival. Solomon Smith and Cyrus Shepard had both taught the children of HBC officers and laborers at Fort Vancouver prior to their move to the Willamette Valley. Although the French Canadian men and Native women were themselves illiterate, they clearly recognized the importance of education and literacy for their children. The Methodists, for their part, saw the mission schools as a vehicle to both instruct the mixed-race children in the fundamentals of the

English language and Protestantism and to inculcate in them an appreciation for cleanliness, civilized behavior, and proper gender norms.[56] The Methodists welcomed both children and adults to the Sunday school, and in a letter dated 1835 teacher Cyrus Shepard noted the French-Indian couples' interest in education: "We have a small but flourishing sabbath school, which is exciting an increasing interest. It is composed of mostly half-breeds, with a few Indian youth. Some who attend are married people, and yet commenced by learning their letters. It is truly pleasant to see them coming together, men, women, and children; women bring their children swung over their back on a board, to which they are tied, and which answers the purpose of a cradle."[57]

The surviving documentation from the Methodists attests to their dual focus on Christianizing and "civilizing" the French-Indian children. The missionaries were particularly intent on rescuing the children from what they perceived as the inferior cultures of their parents, particularly that of their Native mothers. In addition to reading, writing, and spiritual instruction in English at the boarding school, boys performed manual and agricultural labor and girls practiced the domestic arts, including the sewing of Euro-American clothing. A description from the Reverend Henry Perkins included in Zachary Mudge's *The Missionary Teacher: A Memoir of Cyrus Shepard* illustrates the racialized perspectives of the Methodist missionaries and provides a glimpse of the lively personalities of the children, which did not always conform to the cultural and gender expectations of the American Protestants, especially their expectation of female submissiveness:

> [Shephard] had under his care twenty-five or thirty of these poor creatures of all classes and descriptions. Of the most of them it might be said they were anything but pretty and anything but interesting. To brother Shepard, however, they appeared like so many angels.... Then there were Angelica and Sophie [Carpentier]. They were indeed somewhat interesting; for they were two half-caste sisters, with sparkling black eyes and long curling hair, and they were so talkative and lively that they would always attract attention. But they were so rude, and it was so hard to teach them anything like propriety, that anybody but brother Shepard would have been quite out of patience with them.[58]

Beginning in 1834, Joseph Gervais and Yiamust Clatsop hosted Sunday services led by Jason Lee at their farm near the mission, and Lee also occasionally preached in the Champoeg settlement. The Methodists continued these meetings in the local community until 1837 when the mission church was finally completed.[59] While the French-Indian families likely saw these religious services as important community gatherings that demonstrated their general support for the

Methodist mission and the educational and social services it offered the settlers, the missionaries viewed the Sunday services as the first step in a long process of leading the mixed-race families to adopt the superior culture, religion, language, and dress of the middle-class Anglo-Americans. However, the language barrier between the Methodists and the French-Indian families remained a significant one during the 1830s. The surviving evidence suggests that the Methodists who settled in the Willamette Valley did not become fluent in French, Chinook Jargon, or any of the regional Native languages, which slowed communications with the local French-Indian adult settlers and noticeably hampered their outreach to the Kalapuyans and other indigenous groups.[60]

The French-Indian settlers' attendance at Sunday services (weather permitting) did nevertheless allow regular interactions between the two groups and thereby facilitated the development of social and kin networks across ethnic, religious, and cultural divisions.[61] The importance of these social connections is evident in the French-Indian support for the Methodists' educational efforts and in their requests to have the Methodist ministers officiate at weddings in the Willamette Valley during the early years of the mission. These weddings featured unions between local Native and *métis* women and American and French-Indian male settlers. Most of the weddings took place in the homes of established families and featured both first- and second-generation settlers, such as Solomon Smith and Celiast Clatsop, who wed in February 1837, and Marie Lisette Dupati McKay, who married the Irishman John Hoard at her father's home near Champoeg in May 1837.[62]

The sources documenting the Methodists' initial years in Oregon illustrate the complexity of the early settler society. In contrast to the ethnic and sectarian conflicts that emerged in the United States between native-born Protestants and immigrant Catholics during the nineteenth century, the French Canadian men and their Native wives in the Willamette Valley demonstrated broad-mindedness toward the newly arrived Protestant missionaries. This is significant given the fact that prior to the Methodists' arrival, the French Canadians had sent petitions to the Roman Catholic bishop at Red River asking for Catholic clergy to be sent to Oregon. Clearly, the concerns and values of these families are evident in their interactions with the Methodists. The settlers were interested in the spiritual and intellectual welfare of their children and the welfare of Native and bicultural orphans in the region. In their eyes, a Protestant mission providing social, educational, and religious services to the community was more important than its denomination. However, given the French Canadians' letters sent to Bishop

Provencher, they were also biding their time until the arrival of French-speaking Catholic missionaries from French Canada.

The French-Indian families' collaboration with the Protestant missionaries during the mid-1830s is an example of the alternative or nontraditional culture of French North American communities born of the fur trade where an official Catholic Church hierarchy was either absent, only present in small numbers, or held limited power. The multicultural world of the fur trade had long exposed French Canadian men and Native and *métis* women to a variety of religious traditions, both European and Indian. This religious and ethnic diversity created an environment in which strict adherence to sectarian and ethnic differences was the exception rather than the norm.[63] Moreover, the survival of the laborers and their families often depended on such flexibility. Equally significant was the fact that the French-Indian families were in a superior position—both demographically and economically—to the Methodist missionaries and the handful of American emigrants living in the Willamette Valley. The French-Indian settlers also had long-standing ties with regional Native communities and with the HBC, which afforded them access to both of these groups. The bicultural families were thus confident enough to work cooperatively with the relatively small number of American Methodists and American settlers on social and economic initiatives of mutual concern. Given their numbers and their mixed economy based on agriculture, trapping, hunting, and gathering, the French-Indian families enjoyed a prominent role in the growing settler community. In this way, the French Prairie settlers continued a social and economic orientation that was inclusive rather than exclusive—they were willing and able to work across both cultural and religious lines for the benefit of their families and their community.

The dynamics of social contact between the French-Indian families and the Methodists during the mid-1830s also raise questions about the attitudes of the Methodists vis-à-vis their Catholic neighbors. Given the sometimes virulent animosity directed at the Catholic Church and American Catholics by American Protestants during the antebellum period, the willingness of the Methodists to work cooperatively with the French-Indian families on religious, educational, and social initiative might seem puzzling.[64] However, when viewed in light of local conditions, the Methodists' actions and attitudes were pragmatic to some extent. Demographic realities shaped social relations in the Willamette Valley during the mid-1830s. The Methodists were initially a small group of five men with no missionary experience and limited resources who were living among a population of Kalapuyans, French-Indian settlers, and former American fur trappers. Had they not demonstrated a willingness to work cooperatively with the settlers, they would likely have found it difficult to persevere in the Willamette Valley on their own. Yet, they too were biding their time, as evident in Jason Lee's request to the missionary board to send reinforcements to the Oregon Mission.

Pragmatic concerns were not the only factors contributing to the Methodists' initial engagement with the French-Indian families. Of equal importance was the missionaries' own evangelical spirituality. All three religious members of the mission—Jason Lee, Daniel Lee, and Cyrus Shepard—were devout Methodists who believed it their Christian duty to minister to the spiritual and educational needs of the settlers (and theoretically the local Indians). Indeed, the Methodists' missionary work was a spiritual quest that might lead to eternal salvation for themselves and their prospective converts.[65] Their writings also demonstrate that they supported the righteousness of the Protestant tradition vis-à-vis Roman Catholicism. This sense of righteousness was not a roadblock to positive social relations in this early period due to the absence of institutional opposition from the Catholic Church.

With no literate, highly educated Catholic clergy in the Oregon Country, there were no direct challenges to the authority or practices of the Methodists, nor little occasion for theological debates to sow discord in the Willamette Valley. This exemption from sectarian strife would last only until the fall of 1838, when French Canadian Catholic missionaries finally arrived in the Columbia region. In the meantime, the French Prairie settlers witnessed an expansion of the Methodist establishment when two groups of reinforcements joined the Willamette Valley mission. The first party, headed by Dr. Elijah White, arrived at Fort Vancouver in late May 1837 and included Dr. White's wife and son, Susan Downing, Anna Marie Pittman, Elvira Johnson, Alanson Beers, and William H. Willson. The second group, led by the Reverend David Leslie, disembarked in early September 1837 and included Leslie's wife and three daughters, Margaret J. Smith (later Margaret Bailey), and the Reverend Henry K. W. Perkins.[66]

❋ The presence of American Methodists in the Willamette Valley during the mid-1830s coincided with the development of several intercommunity initiatives. These initiatives included cooperative efforts that crossed ethnic and sectarian lines as well an intraethnic project pursued by the French-Indian families. The few contemporary observers and historians who noted the participation of French Canadian settlers in these community initiatives focused on the leading roles and the perspectives of American missionaries and settlers and HBC officials in Oregon.[67] However, a closer examination of the surviving historical record suggests that while the French Canadians may have been influenced by both the Methodists and HBC officials, they acted in accordance with their own cultural values and their own interests. Ultimately, the French-Indian families worked cooperatively with the Americans and HBC officials on these additional community initiatives because they sought to maintain healthy social and economic ties with the two groups while also establishing their own institutions. This prioritization of family, community, and local connections parallels the findings of recent publications in Métis studies, Western history, and borderlands scholarship that explore how historical actors—especially mixed-race and nonwhite peoples—have acted in relation to the westward march of the expanding nation-states of North America.[68]

The first community initiative that ranged outside ongoing projects related to religious practice and education was a Methodist-led temperance effort. In the spring of 1836, Ewing Young, who was then settled on a claim across the Willamette River on present-day Chehalem Creek, purchased a large cauldron once belonging to Nathaniel Wyeth's company for the purpose of establishing a whiskey distillery.[69] Young's project eventually came to the attention of the Methodists, who, along with John McLoughlin, led an effort to oppose it. McLoughlin had previously sought to curb the use of alcohol as a trade item in the Columbia Department in keeping with the HBC's 1821 charter. In McLoughlin's 1837 annual report to the HBC governor and committee in London, he notified officials that he had ceased operations at the Fort Vancouver distillery the previous year due to the "bad effects it had on our affairs" and recommended that such a project never be attempted again.[70] According to Elijah White, the New York–born physician who joined the Methodist mission in May 1837, McLoughlin responded to Young's distillery plans by issuing orders that no grains would be ground in the HBC mills for the distilling of liquors.[71]

For his part, Jason Lee conferred with McLoughlin and sought to reenergize the temperance organization, the Oregon Temperance Society, which the Methodists had founded in February 1836.[72] Lee's first step was to confront Ewing directly and ask him to abandon his plans for a distillery. When Ewing declined to accede to Lee's request, apparently for financial reasons, Lee and the other missionaries turned to the larger settler population for support.[73] They organized a temperance society meeting at their mission on January 2, 1837.[74] The outcome of the gathering was the drafting of a petition addressed to Ewing and his business partner, Lawrence Carmichael, outlining the reasons why the settlers believed the two should cease their distillery operations. In comparing the Oregon Temperance

Society petition and the 1837 Willamette Valley census of U.S. envoy William Slacum, there is evidence of overwhelming support for the initiative within the various settler groups. In addition to the four current members of the Methodist mission (Jason and Daniel Lee, Cyrus Shepard, and Phillip Edwards), twelve of the sixteen local English speakers unattached to the Methodist mission signed the petition, fifteen of the eighteen French Canadians affixed their mark, and the retired fur trapper Charlot Iroquois Tsete (listed as Charles Schegete) also made his mark.[75]

Because Ewing Young was a neighbor to the settlers, the temperance society chose a diplomatic response rather than a heavy-handed approach to his distillery plans. In the letter to Young and Carmichael, the petitioners stressed that the presence of alcohol would have a negative effect on the "temporal and spiritual welfare" of both the settler community and the local Indians. They appealed to Young and Carmichael's respect for American jurisprudence, emphasizing that the sale of liquor to Indians was prohibited by U.S. law. The petitioners also stressed that they were "not enemies but friends" of Young and Carmichael.[76] Interestingly, the petition concluded with a passage stating that local settlers who had not joined the temperance society were still encouraged to sign the petition and give a donation to the cause. Finally, they offered to compensate the two men for the monies they had invested in the project, with half of the thirty signatories agreeing to pay a set sum to the temperance effort, ranging from $4 to $8.[77]

Young and Carmichael did not immediately reply to the temperance society petition. However, in the meantime, an unexpected visitor to the Willamette Valley provided a means to resolve the distillery controversy. At midnight on January 12, 1837, William Slacum, the U.S. Navy purser dispatched by Secretary of State John Forsyth to make a survey of the Oregon Country, arrived at the home of Jean Baptiste Desportes McKay near Champoeg. Slacum spent that day meeting Jason Lee and the missionaries, local French-Indian families, and the American settlers, and he had a long talk with Ewing Young. Having been advised of the distillery controversy by HBC officials, Slacum informed Young that he had been authorized by Chief Trader Duncan Finlayson to notify the American that should he "abandon his enterprise of distilling whiskey, he could be permitted to get his necessary supplies from Fort Vancouver, on the same terms as the other men."[78] The naval purser further informed Young that he would assist him by offering the settler a personal loan and passage to California on his ship, the *Loriot*. Such a trip would allow Young to clear himself of allegations of horse thieving leveled by the

Mexican governor of California, charges that had soured his initial relations with the HBC. The next day, January 13, 1837, Young and Carmichael responded favorably to the temperance petition. They agreed to cease the production of ardent spirits "for the present," citing recent "favorable circumstances" that would allow them to "get along without making spirituous liquors."[79]

When Slacum met with French Canadian, British, and American settlers at Champoeg, he extended them an offer of passage to California to purchase livestock in the Mexican territory. As the settlers could not purchase cattle from the HBC—McLoughlin's policy being to loan but not sell its livestock—they signed the articles of agreement for a cattle expedition to California, designated the Willamette Cattle Company. The settlers agreed to raise the necessary funds among themselves and send a contingent of volunteers to California, availing themselves of Slacum's offer of passage on the *Loriot*. The venture was organized as a simple joint stock company whereby the investors contributed funds for the expenses of the trip to California and the purchase of cattle. The investors elected Ewing Young as the expedition leader and Philip Edwards, formerly a lay member of the mission, as company treasurer.[80]

In addition to Slacum and Young, the investors included a number of the American and British settlers living in the Willamette Valley, including Webley Hawkhurst, Calvin Tibbets, William Canning, Lawrence Carmichael, and William Bailey, as well as six well-established French Canadians: Amable Arquette, Pierre Bellique, Pierre Dépôt, Joseph Gervais, Etienne Lucier, and Andre Picard. Slacum loaned Jason Lee $500 for the Methodist mission, and the other investors drew on monies owed them by the HBC.[81] While some nineteenth-century chroniclers argued that the HBC opposed the enterprise, there is no evidence to support such a conclusion.[82] In fact, documents relating to the probate of Ewing Young's estate, published in 1920, attest that McLoughlin invested $558 in the venture and Chief Traders James Douglas and Duncan Finlayson jointly invested $300.[83] At the time, McLoughlin's decision to join the venture rather than oppose it was likely both strategic and economic. A cooperative approach to the settlers' initiative would keep the HBC on good terms with the community while also securing additional cattle for its operations in the Columbia Department.

A party of eleven men departed on the *Loriot* with Slacum on January 18, 1837. After a violent storm at the mouth of the Colombia delayed the ship, Webley Hawkhurst left the party and returned to the Willamette Valley. The ship finally left on February 10, arriving at the Russian outpost of Fort Ross, located north of Bodega Bay, on February 20. The *Loriot* proceeded on to San Francisco with

Edwards and Ewing. After several months of administrative and financial wrangling with Mexican military leaders, civil authorities, and cattle merchants, the Willamette Cattle Company party departed San José in late June 1837. The expedition reached the Willamette Valley in early October 1837 with 630 Spanish cattle and 40 horses following an arduous four-month trip.[84] The cattle were distributed to the investing partners, and William Slacum's share was later sold by his nephew to John McLoughlin. Three additional drives in 1841 and 1843 brought several thousand head of cattle, several hundred sheep, and some two hundred horses to the Willamette Valley, which increased farming and livestock operations, intensified the ecological transformation of western Oregon, and significantly decreased the settlers' dependence on the HBC as a source for domesticated animals.[85]

In the various writings on the Willamette Valley, both nineteenth-century chroniclers and later historians have emphasized the roles of HBC officials, U.S. envoy William Slacum, and the Methodist missionaries in the development of the Oregon Temperance Society and the Willamette Cattle Company.[86] When they have alluded to the participation of the French-Indian settlers in these events, they have conflated the interests of these settlers with those of the HBC or the Methodists, thus intimating that the French Canadians largely followed the advice of their more educated social betters. Robert J. Loewenberg, author of a study on Jason Lee and the Methodist mission, concluded that the HBC was the real power behind the success of the temperance effort against Young. He found that the Willamette Valley settlers acted in accordance with the wishes of HBC officials because the company, as the only source of supplies and foodstuffs in the region, held significant moral authority over the settlers.[87] However, as Daniel Lee recorded the temperance society effort some ten years later, the HBC "seconded" the Methodists' temperance effort. Daniel Lee also believed the Willamette Valley settlers had supported the initiative due to the righteousness of the temperance cause and the moral persuasiveness of the missionaries.[88]

These long-standing interpretations do not fully explain the actions of the French Canadian male settlers, however. They do not address the question of agency—more particularly, why the French Canadians chose to participate in these community initiatives. By reexamining the limited source record on the French-Indian settlers, it is clear that they did not simply act in deference to the wishes of the HBC, the Methodists, or the other American settlers but rather in accordance with the best interests of their own community. Living in a rather isolated settlement in the Willamette Valley, the French-Indian families were somewhat removed from the controversy over "the Oregon Question" of whether or not the Oregon Country would become U.S. or British territory. By their actions, the French Canadian male settlers sought to maintain positive ties with the HBC, the current representative of the British government, the Methodists, and the other American settlers.

As Robert Loewenberg correctly surmised, the French Canadians could not afford to alienate HBC officials due to their economic dependence on the company for supplies in exchange for the grain raised on their farms. This was one factor contributing to their support of John McLoughlin in his opposition to Young's distillery plans. However, six of the well-established French Canadians were also astute enough to seize an attractive economic opportunity in joining the Willamette Cattle Company venture. This entrepreneurial initiative, while not completely at odds with the HBC, was a means by which the French-Indian community could take a step away from the economic control of the British company. In seeking a delicate balance in their relations with the HBC, the French Prairie settlers were not unlike the buffalo-hunting Plains Métis who traded with American interests in the mid-1800s and the Métis freemen of northwestern Saskatchewan who sought self-sufficiency and economic independence in face of HBC efforts to constrain their labor and wages in the late 1800s.[89]

Maintaining positive relations with the Methodists was also a determining factor. The French-Indian families benefited from the religious, social, and educational services offered by the small group of dedicated, educated missionaries. Perhaps most important was the need for the settlers to ensure themselves a stable social and economic position in the event of a future American annexation of the Willamette Valley. Close ties with the Methodists might ensure that end. If the settlers supported the Methodists on the temperance issues, the missionaries might in turn support the French-Indian families should the Americans eventually gain control of the region south of the Columbia River. This issue was a serious concern in the minds of the French Canadians, as demonstrated by their discussion with William Slacum at Champoeg on January 13, 1837. Slacum reported to U.S. officials that the French Canadians were worried about the legal title to their lands in the event of an American annexation of the Willamette Valley.[90] Although unlettered in the formal sense, the French Canadians realized that two national interests were at stake in the Oregon country. Their public support for the temperance effort simultaneously strengthened their ties with the American Methodists and with the HBC, the de facto representative of the British government.

Two additional factors likely played a role in the French Canadians' decision to sign the temperance petition. As a religious leader and an educated man, Jason Lee held a position of moral authority among the French Canadians, and so they would have agreed to consider the Methodists' temperance initiative. William Slacum noted that "every white man" in the Willamette settlement held Jason Lee and his associate missionaries with some regard.[91] This is the same sentiment expressed by naturalist Robert Townsend on the missionaries' overland journey to Oregon in 1834. He observed that although Jason Lee evinced the pious, sometimes self-righteous attitude typical of evangelical Protestant missionaries of the period, he had a gentle way of critiquing the "rough" fur trappers in such a way that they came to respect him.[92]

On the issue of temperance itself, the French Canadians would not have endorsed a complete ban on alcohol but rather the notion that some measure of local regulation was warranted. The consumption of alcohol was not only a component of the Catholic mass in the Canadians' native Lower Canada, but alcohol also was a significant part of the fur trade throughout North America. It played a central role in community events, holidays, and celebrations characteristic of the trade.[93] Yet it could also create grave problems for both Native and fur trader communities, particularly in those areas outside the jurisdiction of the HBC or where HBC trade policies and personnel ration guidelines received short shrift.[94] Not infrequently, Native leaders pushed for a ban on the trade of alcohol. Given the HBC's ongoing problems with American maritime fur traders' use of alcohol on the Northwest Coast and McLoughlin's ending of distillery activities at Fort Vancouver, both the French Canadian male settlers and their Indian wives would have been aware of the potential problem of alcoholism in the Willamette Valley. The physician Elijah White, who joined the Methodist mission in the late 1830s, noted in his memoirs that drunken brawls would sometimes erupt in French Prairie during the Christmas season when the head of each household would receive a "few gallons of liquor." He mentioned one case in which a drunken man nearly beat his wife to death, and she "lay insensible for thirty days."[95]

The petitions sent by the Willamette settlers to the bishop of Red River in 1834 and in 1835 indicate that the French Canadian men—and likely their Indian wives—were keenly interested in the welfare of their families. Having retired from the fur trade to an agrarian community, the couples demonstrated a desire to establish those social institutions not found in the smaller fur trade outposts— namely, schools and churches. While both English and Scots fur trade officers and educated Americans tended to disparage the French Canadians as uneducated, ignorant, and lacking in "moral restraint," the settlers, by their actions, belied such stereotypes.[96] The decision to support the Methodists' temperance society suggests that the French-Indian couples were concerned about social issues that could have a serious impact on the nascent community, namely the problem of alcoholism.

At the same time that the French-Indian families lent their support to the Methodist mission and cooperated in community initiatives such as the temperance movement, they continued to lobby for Catholic missionaries from French Canada. Responding to the settlers' letters from 1834 and 1835, Joseph Provencher "encouraged them to persevere" in the practice of their faith and promised to do all in his power to send clergymen to the small colony as soon as possible. However, he also informed them that he was unable to dispatch priests directly from Red River because none was then available for a new missionary initiative.[97] In the spring of 1836, the French Canadian settlers sent a third letter to Bishop Provencher.[98] As all of the French Canadian settlers at this time were illiterate, they dictated the text to an English speaker, an individual who was himself semi-literate (spelling preserved):

Reverend sir   Willammett March 22th 1836

We recived your kinde letter last fall wich gave us Much pleasure and ease to oure minds for it has bean a Long time since we have heard the Likes of it[.] it has Gave us a new heart since we recived your kinde instructions to us[.] we will do oure Best in deavours to instruct oure fammilies to youre wishes[,] still Living in hope to some Speadet Releafe wich we are Looking for with eager hearts for the day to Come[.] since we Recived youre kinde Letter we have beGun to Build and make some preparations to Recive oure kinde father wich we hope that oure laboure will not be in vain[,] for you know oure sittuwations better than oure selves[.] for Some of us stands in greate Neade of youre Assistance as quick as possible[.] We have nothing to Right to you about the Countrey but that the farms are All in a very thriving state and produces fine Crops[.] We have sent theis few Lines to you hoping that that it will not trouble you to much for Righting So quick to you[.] but the Countrey is setteling Slowley and oure Children are Learning very fast wich make us very eager for youre assistance wich we hope by Gods helpe will be very sone[.] oure prayers will be for his safe Arival[.] We have sent you a list of the families that Are at preasent in the settlement[,] so more preasent[.] from youre humble servants.

	[Mark]	Children
Joseph Jarvay [Joseph Gervais]	X	7
Xaviar Laderout [F. Xavier Laderoute]	X	1
Eken Luceay [Etienne Lucier]	X	6
Peare Belleck [Pierre Bellique]	X	3
Charles Rondo [Charles Rondeau]	X	3

Charles Plant [Charles Plante]	X	4
Pear Depot [Pierre Dépôt]	X	1
Andrey Pecord [Andre Picard]	X	4
Joseph Delar [Joseph Delord]	X	5
Louey Fourcy [Louis Fourcier]	X	3
Lamable Erquet [Amable Arquette]	X	3
Jean Bt Perrault	X	2
Joseph Desport [Joseph Despard]	X	3
Andrey Longten [Andre Longtain]	X	4
John Bt. Desportes [McKay]	X	8
William Johnson	X	2
Charlo Chata [Charlot Iroquois Tsete]	X	
William Mcarity [William McKarty]	X	

The letter was signed by fourteen of the French Canadian men then settled in the Willamette Valley in 1836, the French-Algonquin Jean Baptiste Desportes McKay, and the former Iroquois fur trapper Charlot Iroquois Tsete.[99] Aside from the Irishman William McKarty, who had come to Oregon with the Ewing Young party, the petitioners were all former fur trade laborers and trappers of long residence in the Pacific Northwest who had retired to the Willamette Valley with their wives and children (the Englishman William Johnson was a former laborer for the NWC and the HBC).[100] Although these petitioners were illiterate and uneducated in the formal sense—not unlike the majority of the inhabitants of rural Lower Canada in the early 1800s—they found a means to communicate their needs to the Catholic hierarchy, one that bypassed their former employer, the HBC.[101]

The view that the French Canadians acted in response to McLoughlin's urgings rather than on their own initiative conflates the interests of the HBC chief factor and the settlers, again negating the French Canadians' own agency in the development of historical events.[102] The evidence suggests a more nuanced interpretation, one in which the French Canadian settlers expressed a genuine desire for Catholic clergy, and this desire received support from the highest official in the Columbia Department, John McLoughlin. Francis Norbert Blanchet, the Catholic priest who led the eventual mission to the Columbia in 1838, interpreted the French Canadians' petitions to the Bishop of Red River as an independent initiative. In an 1841 letter to HBC North American governor George Simpson, for example, Blanchet wrote that "in writing these requests to their bishops, at a distance of 20 leagues from their bourgeois, they were not influenced but by the desire of their hearts."[103] Blanchet's assessment was probably correct, although it is important to note that his emphasis on the French settlers' independence would likely have been partially motivated by a desire to convince Governor Simpson of the settlers' devotion to their faith.

The semiliterate nature of the 1836 appeal indicates that the French Canadians would have not received assistance from either the Methodists or HBC officials, as all of these men exhibited a more advanced level of writing skill than indicated by the text. This internal evidence reduces the list of possible writers to a handful of early Anglo-American settlers who enjoyed close relations with the French-Indian families, particularly English speakers who were unfamiliar with French surnames and French pronunciations. The likely candidates are Joseph Gervais' brother-in-law, Solomon Smith, who taught the children of the French-Indian families before the arrival of the Methodists and who was married to Celiast Clatsop, and the American Thomas Jefferson Hubbard, who married a local Native woman, Mary Somamata, at the home of Pierre Bellique in April 1837. Like his fellow Irishman William Johnson, John Hoard, who married Marie Lisette Dupati McKay in May 1837, appears to have been illiterate, so he can be taken off the candidate list.[104]

The settlers' appeals of 1834, 1835, 1836, and a final one in 1837 show a clear, consistent message. They desired social, religious, and educational institutions for their growing colony, preferably directed by Roman Catholic clergy from Quebec. While the French-Indian families welcomed similar opportunities offered by the Methodist missionaries, the French Canadian male settlers, at least, wished to create the central institution in French Canadian rural society: the local parish church. The French Canadians living in the Willamette Valley largely hailed from rural communities throughout Lower Canada, traditional sites for the recruitment of fur trade laborers. In these villages, the local parish provided French Canadian *habitants* with traditional Catholic worship services and sacraments, as well social welfare assistance and some educational opportunities. It was also an important site of community life, where villagers would gather for discussions, debates, and other types of weekly socializing. In this sense, the local parish served a dual purpose as both a religious and a secular institution for rural French Canadians. This attitude, which was somewhat at odds with the views of many French Canadian priests and the more ultramontane French Canadian church hierarchy, stemmed not only from the historical geography of the St. Lawrence region and French Canada's agrarian culture but also from financial considerations. Because villagers supported the operations of their local parishes, they tended to view the parish as a community institution rather than as an extension of the larger Catholic Church. As a result, the parish buildings, including the rectory, might well be used for both regular socializing and special community events.[105]

Given the French Canadians' understanding of village life in Lower Canada, it is not surprising that they would welcome the Methodist missionaries, even to the point of coming by to socialize with Jason Lee on a regular basis. Such behavior was in keeping with their notions about community life. And yet, however much they cooperated with the American Methodists, who practiced a religion different from their own and spoke a foreign tongue, the Methodist mission would never belong to the French-Indian families in the same way that a parish in rural Lower Canada would belong to the local villagers. Thus, the French Canadians' petitions to Bishop Provencher were as much aimed at providing their families with religious and educational opportunities as they were intended to create community institutions that would enrich the social life of the French Prairie settlers.

In response to the settlers' letter of March 1836, Bishop Provencher sent the French Canadians another pastoral letter providing encouragement and support for the small colony. He may have suggested that he would try to visit the Willamette settlement. However, he was not able to offer any information on concrete plans for the future. Church officials in Red River and Quebec were still trying to negotiate the logistics of sending missionaries to the Columbia region. The most important hurdles facing church leaders were gaining approval from the HBC, finding personnel sufficiently trained for the travails of missionary work, and securing the financial resources needed to support the proposed mission.

In the meantime, the French Canadians found the delay vexing. They sent another letter to Joseph Provencher in March 1837, their frustration evident in this fourth and final appeal (spelling preserved):[106]

Reverend Sir   Willammett March 8, 1837

We have taken the Opportunity to Rite to you hoping this Will meate you on youre way to oure Settlement for we are waiting with Greate Angsitty for youre Arivall[,] wich we have beane looking for[,] this sometime since we have the Pleasure of Reciving youre kinde leatter[,] wich Gave us Greate encouragement[.] But we finde the time very long[.] Reverend Sir you will think us very troublesome[.] But we hope you will excuse us for We have much Neede of some Assistance from you[,] *for we have allmost Every Religion but our own[,] wich you know Reverend Sir with oute youre Assistance wen we are surrounded by every One[,] it will be very hard for us to bring Our famelues up to our owne Religion wen theire i[s] so maney others around them[.]* We are bringing oure famelyes up as well as we possible Can[.] But not so well as We would wish[.] We have built a bidend [building] to receve the Reverend Gentlemen that Should please to Come wich will be a hapy Day for us[.] we still remaine youre humble Servants[.]

Willammette Settlers [italics added]

	[Mark]
Peare Belleck [Pierre Bellique]	X
Joseph Desportes [Joseph Despard]	X
Charlo Chayta [Charlot Iroquois Tsete]	X
Andrey Longten [Andre Longtain]	X
John B. Desportes McK [McKay]	X
Atoam Lafourty [Michel Laferté]	X
Jonva [F. Xavier] Laderoute	X
Joseph Jarvay [Joseph Geravis]	X
Charlo Raut [Charles Plante]	X
Charls Rondo [Charles Rondeau]	X
Joseph Delar[d]	X
Louey Labounty [Louis Labonté]	X
Luey Foursey [Louis Forcier]	X
Peare Depo [Pierre Dépôt]	X
Lemob Erquect [Amable Arquette]	X
Eken Lucey [Etienne Lucier]	X

Nearly all of the French Canadian male settlers affixed their marks to this second surviving letter to Bishop Provencher. While a few names are missing from the missive (Andre Picard and Jean Baptiste Perrault), two new settlers, Louis Labonté I and Michel Laferte dit Placide, demonstrated their support for the community effort to bring Catholic clergy to Oregon.[107] The tone of this final letter is more urgent, with the French Canadians referring directly to their concerns about the growing prominence of Protestant missionaries in Oregon. Their concerns may have been magnified by the arrival of a group of American Presbyterian missionaries, headed by Marcus and Narcissa Whitman, at Fort Vancouver in the fall of 1836. Although the Presbyterians decided to establish their missions among the Cayuse and Nez Perce (Nimiipuu) in the Columbia Plateau east of the Cascades Mountains, this letter marks a shift in the French Canadians' attitudes toward Protestant missionaries in the region.

Without institutional support from the Catholic Church, the French Canadians appeared increasingly worried about bringing their families "up to [their] own religion." This ambiguous attitude toward the Protestant missionaries may also indicate growing concerns about the social and political position of the mission-aries vis-à-vis the French Canadian settlers. In such an instance, the presence of an educated Catholic priest would strengthen the standing of the bicultural com-munity, for the settlers would then have an additional community representative to advocate on their behalf. The settlers' determination to establish a parish and make ready for a priest's arrival is evident in their decision to begin construc-tion of a church, despite the lack of a firm commitment from Canadian church officials.

Although the French-Indian families did not leave their own written descrip-tions of French Prairie during the 1830s, sources produced by American observers provide a portrait of the community just prior to the arrival of the first Catholic missionaries and American overland emigrants in the late 1830s and early 1840s. These observers noted current agricultural operations in the Willamette Valley and the great attractiveness of the area for agrarian settlement, while also musing about the decline in the Native population and the possibility of an orderly coloni-zation of Oregon. The Reverend Samuel Parker, a Presbyterian minister who made an exploratory tour of the Oregon Country on behalf of the American Board of Commissioners for Foreign Missions (ABCFM), surveyed the Willamette Valley in the fall of 1835. He visited Champoeg (also known as McKay's Settlement) and the homesteads twelve miles south near the farm of Joseph Gervais and Yiamust Clatsop. In his published travel account, Parker characterized French Prairie as an appealing if somewhat rustic settlement:

> The settlers are mostly Canadian Frenchmen with Indian wives. There are very few Americans. The Frenchmen were laborers belonging to the Hudson's Bay Company, but have left that service, and having families, they have commenced farming in this fertile section of country, which is the best of the Oregon Territory that I have yet seen. It is well diversified with woods and prairies, the soil is rich and sufficiently dry for cultiva-tion, and at the same time well watered with small stream and springs. These hunters, recently turned farmers, cultivate the most common useful productions—wheat of the first quality to as great an extent as their wants require. A small grist mill is just fin-ished, which adds to their comforts. They have a common school in each settlement instructed by American young men who are competent to the business.[108]

In a later passage on the Methodist mission, Parker noted the "very interesting Sabbath school among the half-breed children" and the possible future usefulness of the mission as a whole. However, he also pinpointed "one important desider-atum": the absence of "Christian white women" to "exert an influence over Indian females." Parker was convinced that the "female character must be elevated, and until this is done but little is accomplished."[109] In Parker's view, although the French-Indian families and the Methodist mission were making progress in the areas of education and agriculture, substantive cultural advances would not be made in the Willamette Valley until the Indian and *métis* women adopted Anglo-American gender roles and a commitment to female domesticity.

William Slacum, the American naval officer who visited the Willamette Valley in January 1837, reached conclusions similar to those of Samuel Parker. While Parker focused on the opportunities for religious missions and cultural uplift in the Pacific Northwest, Slacum represented American interests and considered the possibilities for American colonization. His census of the Willamette Valley settlers documented demographic growth shifts in the Willamette Valley during the 1830s (see appendix 5). By 1837, at least eighteen French-Indian families were living in the valley, comprising an estimated population of eighty-five people.[110] Alongside the eighty-five French-Indian settlers and the thirty to fifty Ahantchuyuk Kalapuyans, there were also increased numbers at the Methodist mission, a few other fur trade families, and a diverse group of English-speaking male settlers from the United States, England, and Ireland living in the Willamette Valley in 1837. The other fur trade families included Charlot Iroquois Tsete and Marie Thomas (Iroquois-Upper Chinookan) and their children, and William Johnson, his Native wife Polly, and their two children. Following the arrival of two sets of reinforcements in late 1837, the Methodist mission housed forty-four individuals, including fourteen adult missionaries, four children, and some twenty-six surviving boarders. There were also sixteen other Anglo male settlers in the Willamette Valley, plus Solomon Smith and Celiast Clatsop and their children living at the Gervais farm.[111]

A review of William Slacum's census data on the Willamette Valley settlers also reveals economic developments in French Prairie (table 6). By the late 1830s, the French-Indian families had enclosed an average of 233 acres and were farming an average of 42 acres per family. Their average annual wheat production per family was 551 bushels, of which they sold the surplus to the HBC at Fort Vancouver via the company depots at Champoeg and Willamette Falls.[112] Etienne Lucier and Josette Nouette ran a grist mill in the northern part of French Prairie at Champoeg, and Joseph Gervais and Yiamust Clatsop had installed another mill in the south on their farm near the Methodist mission. The French-Indian families also had important holdings of horses and domestic animals, and they raised oats, peas, and beans and produced apples, pears, and peaches for domestic consumption.[113] The more well-established French Prairie settlers—such as Jean Baptiste Desportes McKay, Joseph Gervais, Etienne Lucier, and Pierre

TABLE 6.   Willamette Valley settler data: William Slacum's census, 1837

Male settlers with French surnames	13*
Average acres enclosed	233 acres
Average acres cultivated	42 acres
Average wheat production	551 bushels
Average number of horses	12
Average number of hogs	28
Average number of houses	2
Male settlers with Anglo surnames	17**
Average acres enclosed	55 acres
Average acres cultivated	14 acres
Average wheat production	122 bushels
Average number of horses	17
Average number of hogs	11
Average number of houses	1

NOTES:

*At least five settlers were not listed in Slacum's census of 1837: Charlot Iroquois Tsete, Joseph Despard, Louis Labonté I, Michel Laferte dit Placide, and Andre Picard.
**Only five of the seventeen men with Anglo surnames had acreages and working farms: Ewing Young, Lawrence Carmichael, William Johnson, James Neil, and Thomas Jefferson Hubbard.

SOURCE: Slacum, "Slacum's Report"; appendix 5 in this volume.

Bellique—were the earliest colonists with the longest tenure in the valley. It was this relative wealth that allowed six of the leading French Canadians to invest with the Willamette Valley Cattle Company and join the intercommunity initiative to bring new domestic stock to the valley that would be free from HBC oversight.[114]

✳ The decade of the 1830s was a transitional one in the Willamette Valley. The Northern and Central Kalapuyan groups—the Tualatin, Yamhill, Ahantchuyuk, and Santiam—experienced a dramatic decline in their overall population and saw an expansion of the French-Indian community in the homeland of the Ahantchuyuk. The new place name of "French Prairie" marked this historic demographic shift. While the smaller Kalapuyan groups retained social, economic, and some kin ties to the bicultural community in their midst, they also witnessed the arrival and colonization of their lands by Euro-Americans who had no long-standing ties with them. Americans from the Ewing Young party claimed lands on the west side of the Willamette River, and American Methodists established a mission south of Champoeg. This new wave of settlers and missionaries added to the social, economic, and ecological processes of Euro-American colonization that had first began with the fur trade in the 1810s. The arrival of the Anglo-Americans also accompanied the beginning of an important economic shift in the Willamette Valley from the mercantile capitalist system of the fur trade to the agrarian economy of early settler colonialism. This new economic system coupled with tremendous population losses due to the intermittent fever began to marginalize the Kalapuyans within their own homeland.

As the French-Indian community grew by both natural increase and the arrival of new retirees and their wives from the fur trade, the bicultural couples focused on the social, economic, and educational needs of their families. Despite their universal illiteracy, they found a means to petition for French Canadian Catholic missionaries, and while the wait for a Catholic priest dragged on year after year, they turned their attention to the American Protestant missionaries who trekked to Oregon in 1834. The attitude of the French-Indian couples toward the Methodists and the few Anglo men who settled nearby during this period was one of accommodation. A willingness among the various settler groups to work together on initiatives allowed for the creation of a common ground in the Willamette Valley during the 1830s. The ability of the French-Indian families, the Methodists, and the handful of Americans to work across ethnic and sectarian lines resulted from a complex set of factors: pragmatism, self-interest, spiritual and cultural traditions, and a mutual need for social and economic development.

Historical sources documenting the intercultural relations between the Americans and the French-Indian families demonstrate a growing sense of community among these earliest settlers. For as much as they aided their Protestant neighbors, they remained determined to establish a local Catholic parish, a social institution that would allow the French Canadian male settlers to recreate elements of their Native culture of Lower Canada. Their yearly petitions to the Catholic bishop at Red River, Joseph Provencher, from 1834 through 1837, demonstrate a growing desire for a French Canadian, Catholic presence in French Prairie. While supporting the Methodists and benefiting from the educational opportunities they offered, the French-Indian families were themselves active agents in colonization of the Willamette Valley, steadily working to advance their family and community interests. Over the 1830s, the French-Indian community continued to grow and improved its economic standing by expanding its agricultural operations, including supporting the entrepreneurial opportunities presented by the creation of the Willamette Cattle Company and its stock drive from California to Oregon.

However much the French-Indian families and their American neighbors were able to find common cause during the 1830s, there were nevertheless hints of divergence and tension. There were in fact two visions for colonial society in the Willamette Valley during this transitional decade. The French-Indian homestead in French Prairie—the "hearth of the crossed races"—represented a relatively inclusive society not unlike other fur trade and Métis communities across North America. Such a worldview allowed for cultural difference, intermarriage between ethnic groups, linguistic and religious diversity, and relatively stable social and economic relations with nearby indigenous communities. A second vision, represented by the Methodist missionaries, stressed a more exclusive colonial society, one in which Protestantism would play the dominant role, Anglo-American behavior, dress, and gender roles would prevail, and "civilized," English-speaking inhabitants would live in orderly agrarian communities. In their published writings, the Methodists and other American visitors to the Pacific Northwest emphasized this more exclusive, ordered society. They portrayed the Willamette Valley as an ideal location for an American settlement, adding their voices to the romanticized image of Oregon in American popular culture. In these embellished accounts of Oregon—really the Willamette Valley—the Indian populations were in decline, and they were ultimately destined to vanish from the landscape, which would leave the country open for Anglo-American colonization.

CHAPTER 4 ✴ Catholic Missionaries and
Community Tensions

On March 16, 1838, a little over a year after the visit of U.S. envoy William Slacum
to the Willamette Valley, a group of settlers met at the Methodist mission to dis-
cuss a petition to the U.S. Congress. The petition, drafted by Phillip Edwards and
supported by Jason Lee, proposed that Congress extend its jurisdiction over the
Oregon Country south of the Columbia River as soon as possible. In his argument for American colonization, Edwards noted the region's agricultural and
commercial advantages, the settlers' dependence on the HBC, and the need for
civil governance and federal control over emigration and Indian affairs. After
some discussion, thirty-six men signed the petition, known as the Edwards
Memorial. The signatories included ten members of the Methodist mission, seventeen Americans, and nine French Canadians.[1] The Edwards Memorial had little
impact on U.S. foreign policy; however, it did signal the beginning of a shift in
the developing political culture of the Willamette Valley, as Protestant missionaries increasingly turned their attention to American colonization in the Oregon
Country.

In the fall of 1838, two Catholic missionaries finally arrived in the Pacific
Northwest in response to the annual requests of the French Canadian settlers.
The presence of the French Canadian priest Francis Norbert Blanchet, who
headed the Catholic mission, altered community relations in the Willamette
Valley. At one level, Blanchet's initial tenure in French Prairie strengthened intra-
community ties by concentrating the settlers' energies on the establishment and
maintenance of a Catholic mission. By baptizing the women and children of the
settlement, solemnizing the settlers' country marriages, and instituting religious
instruction and observance, Blanchet advocated for a community culture distinct from the Methodist mission and from the American settlements located primarily on the western bank of the Willamette River. At the same time, Blanchet's
presence raised some tension within the French Prairie community when he
sought to standardize religious observances and regulate gender relations, sexual

behavior, and marriage practices among French-Indian families accustomed to more autonomy, flexibility, and cultural accommodation.

On a second level, the presence of Catholic religious elite, represented by Father Blanchet, served as a catalyst for sectarian conflict in the Willamette Valley. During the initial years of Blanchet's tenure in French Prairie, a series of inter-community controversies revealed a divergence of interests between the French-Indian families, the Methodists, and the American settlers. Francis N. Blanchet's correspondence offers the best documentation on the perspectives of the French-Indian families concerning the incidents that took place in the late 1830s and early 1840s.[2] They reveal dynamics of conflict, cooperation, and misunderstanding and a struggle to address civil affairs within the context of sectarian and cultural differences between the French Canadians and the Americans. These local conflicts paralleled historical developments in late Jacksonian America and the period of constitutional reform and rebellion in Canada. The first dispute concerned tensions that developed over the Farnham Memorial of 1839; the second incident stemmed from a controversy over the funeral of Cyrus Shepard early in 1840; and the final conflict involved problems with the Methodist missionary doctor Elijah White for several months in 1840. Although the French Prairie families had resettled a hinterland on the far western frontier of the United States and Canada (British North America), they, like their indigenous Kalapuyan neighbors, nevertheless began to feel the ripple effects of larger continental forces shaping both countries.

✳   During the mid-1830s, Red River Bishop Joseph Provencher was unable to meet the French Prairie settlers' annual requests for Catholic missionaries. However, he did inform his superior, Joseph Signay, archbishop of Quebec, of the settlers' pleas.[3] In his initial letter to Signay, Provencher indicated that in the spring of 1835 he had had a discussion in Red River with the HBC's North American governor, George Simpson, about the feasibility of sending Catholic missionaries to the Columbia Department.[4] Unlike the American Methodists, French Canadian Catholic authorities needed the permission of HBC officials to travel to the Columbia Department because the company was the official representative of the British Crown in the Pacific Northwest and because it provided the only means of overland transportation to the region.[5] Signay did request official approval for an Oregon mission from George Simpson, though Simpson declined Signay's initial requests for policy reasons. The governor was concerned about lending support to a Catholic mission in the Willamette Valley, which HBC officials believed would likely become American territory when the international boundary was finally established. Simpson also wished to avoid sectarian conflicts between Catholic missionaries and the Methodists already established in the valley.[6]

The proposed Catholic mission to Oregon did receive support from the senior HBC official in the Columbia Department, Chief Factor John McLoughlin. In October 1837, McLoughlin responded to Simpson's recommendation that HBC officials in London turn down the request for a Catholic mission by offering a well-reasoned reply to Simpson's position, an unusual step as few men ever directly disagreed with Simpson. McLoughlin argued that rather than create problems for the HBC, Roman Catholic missionaries would enhance the company's position in the region because it would "prevent the American Missionaries acquiring influence over the Canadians." McLoughlin asserted that if the HBC refused this request for priests, the company would injure its relationship with the French Canadian settlers, noting that "the influence of the Company will be much diminished if they hear that you have refused to accommodate with a passage of a Missionary [sic]."[7] In addition—although McLoughlin had been raised as an Anglican by his domineering maternal grandfather, Malcolm Fraser—the chief factor was sympathetic to Roman Catholicism, the religion of his French Canadian and Scottish mother Angelique Fraser and his sister Marie-Louise (Sister St. Henri), who eventually served as mother superior of the Ursuline convent in Quebec City.[8]

Given Simpson's opposition to a Catholic mission in the Columbia Department, McLoughlin's advocacy was crucial.[9] On direction from the HBC's governing board in London, Simpson finally granted permission for the passage of Catholic missionaries to the Columbia Department in February 1838. Simpson informed Archbishop Signay that the missionary priests should be ready to depart with the HBC's overland brigade that was scheduled to leave Lachine, Quebec, in late April 1838. Simpson granted his approval on the condition that Signay agree to establish the Catholic mission on the north side of the Columbia River in the Cowlitz Valley.[10] Governor Simpson believed that locating the Catholic mission near the new company outpost would not only encourage former HBC employees to settle north of the Columbia but also deter potential conflicts between Catholics and Methodists in the Willamette Valley.[11] Signay agreed to these terms and immediately contacted Francis Blanchet and Modeste Demers, the two priests he had provisionally appointed to the mission while the negotiations with the HBC were still under way. Blanchet would serve as vicar general of the Columbia mission,

P. Vander Keene.   Lith. de V.ᵉ Vander Schelden

MISSION Sᵀ PAUL À WALLAMET. *Lettres 1 et XVIII.*

1. *Cathédrale et maison de l'Archevêque.*   4. *Ancienne église.*   7. *Forge.*
2. *Couvent des Sœurs de Notre Dame.*   5. *Résidence Sᵗ. François-Xavier.*   8. *Montagne Hood.*
3. *Collège Sᵗ Joseph.*   6. *Fermes etc.*   9. *Montagne Molélis.*

FIGURE 3. Mission St. Paul à Wallamet. SOURCE: Pierre Jean De Smet, *Oregon Missions and Travels over the Rocky Mountains* (1847). Courtesy of the Oregon Historical Society, OrHi 104933.

the archbishop's official deputy in the newly created ecclesiastical district that encompassed the entire Oregon Country.[12]

Francis Blanchet, age forty-two, had been a priest for nearly twenty years when he received his appointment to the Columbia mission. After an initial assignment to the cathedral of Quebec City, Blanchet was appointed pastor of St. Antoine of Richibucto, a remote Acadian parish in New Brunswick. Blanchet served seven years in the large, isolated parish whose dispersed and diverse parishioners included Acadians, Irish settlers, and the indigenous Mi'kmaq. Following the New Brunswick post, Blanchet spent eleven years as a parish priest in the village of Cedars in the Montreal diocese. Because the village was a departure point for the fur trade brigades heading west, Blanchet became acquainted with the French Canadian voyageurs, who provided a large portion of the HBC workforce during the first half of the nineteenth century. Blanchet was thus a seasoned representative of the Catholic Church upon his appointment to the Columbia mission in 1838. Trained in the conservative yet rigorous Quebec Seminary, he had completed postings in the main provincial cathedral, in a remote frontier church with a multicultural and multilingual flock, and in a settled, more homogeneous

FIGURE 4. Francis Norbert Blanchet (1870s). Courtesy of the Oregon Historical Society, OrHi 52503.

parish. In contrast to Blanchet, Modeste Demers was a young man of twenty-nine at the time of his appointment to the Oregon mission. He had been ordained in 1836 and then spent two years assisting Provencher at the parish of Saint Boniface in Red River.[13] While Demers had far fewer years of experience in the priesthood, he was familiar with the fur trade settlements and the bicultural Métis communities of the Canadian Northwest.

Blanchet departed Montreal on May 3, 1838, with an HBC canoe brigade in the company of Chief Factor James Hargrave.[14] Their first major destination was Red River, some 2,100 miles to the west. After an arduous trek, the party arrived at Red River on June 6, 1838. Blanchet and Demers left Red River in another HBC canoe brigade on July 10, 1838, and the missionaries spent the next five months traversing the Canadian prairies, crossing the Rocky Mountains, and descending the Columbia River before arriving at Fort Vancouver on November 24, 1838.[15]

Throughout the strenuous overland voyage, Blanchet and Demers celebrated mass, baptized scores of children, and performed several marriage ceremonies between company employees and their Native spouses. Blanchet was able to perform the marriages because he had received a papal authorization to grant couples in common law marriages special dispensations from canon law requirements regarding the publication of three wedding banns, the baptism of non-Catholic spouses, and the impediment of "spiritual cognition" (the lack of religious training prior to baptism for adult converts). Blanchet had also received instructions to confirm the mutual consent of both parties before conveying the sacrament of marriage.[16]

When Blanchet and Demers arrived at Fort Vancouver after their long overland journey, they were warmly greeted by Chief Trader James Douglas (Chief Factor McLoughlin was then on leave in Canada and Europe), the fort's resident HBC employees, and a small delegation from the French-Indian settlement in the Willamette Valley. This small group included Pierre Bellique, Joseph Gervais, and Etienne Lucier, three of the leading settlers in French Prairie.[17] In his memoirs published several decades later, Blanchet described a dramatic first Catholic Mass celebrated at Fort Vancouver on Sunday, November 25, 1838. According to Blanchet, the French Canadians at the fort wept tears of joy upon hearing Mass for the first time in "ten, fifteen, and even twenty years."[18] From the missionary's rosy perspective, the French Canadians were delighted to have access to Catholic services and sacraments, especially for their children, and "were willing and ready to obey their pastors faithfully."[19]

Blanchet and Demers began by offering regular Catholic services and sacraments to the residents at Fort Vancouver, including Mass, vespers, the singing of sacred songs, baptisms, and marriages. Focusing their efforts on Kanaka Village, the fur laborers' multiethnic community situated next to Fort Vancouver, Blanchet and Demers instituted a local mission at the fort that lasted for more than four months from mid-November 1838 to mid-April 1839.[20] During that time, Demers ran affairs at Fort Vancouver, while Blanchet made the first of several temporary missionary excursions to the Cowlitz settlement in the Cowlitz River Valley north of Fort Vancouver and to the French-Indian settlement in the Willamette Valley. The Cowlitz mission lasted a short seven days, from December 12 to 18, 1838, while the first Willamette mission (January 5 to February 4, 1839) and the second Willamette mission (May 8 to June 11, 1839) each lasted a month.[21]

✻   In Blanchet's report to Archbishop Signay about his first sojourn in the Willamette Valley, he perceived a sense of joy on the part of the French Canadians and their Indian wives at the arrival of the missionary.[22] Indeed, the first Willamette mission was a community event. Women and children camped near the log church the French Canadians had constructed in 1836 on a prairie south of Champoeg near Fairfield (it was later relocated several miles north to the village of St. Paul).[23] While the women and children remained at the mission site, the men would return to their farms from time to time. During his stay, Blanchet celebrated Mass, taught prayers, songs, and catechism, and performed the sacraments of baptism, marriage, confession, and last rites. The enthusiasm Blanchet expressed in a glowing report to Archbishop Signay suggests that the priest appreciated the warm welcome he received from the settlers, especially their gesture of constructing a chapel prior to his arrival.[24] His long-term goal was to cultivate the religious culture and institutionalized rituals that formed the foundation of French Canadian Catholicism in the early nineteenth century.[25]

During the first Willamette mission, Blanchet's years in New Brunswick proved useful because the community he encountered evinced a syncretic culture. Like their initial time spent at the Methodist mission a few years earlier, the Native and *métis* women and their children camped out in lodges and tents during Blanchet's first visit to French Prairie. However, unlike their experience with the Methodists, the women and older children likely understood some of Blanchet's prayers and sermons because the priest was more attuned to the need for effective communication. Observing that "these women and children did not all understand French . . . and there was a diversity of languages among the women, according to the districts and places from which they came," Blanchet relied on at least two interpreters from the community during the initial Willamette Mission.[26] One translated the priest's French into Chinook Jargon and the other into "Flathead," a Salishan language of the Columbia Plateau. In his description of the First Willamette mission, Blanchet presented a rather encouraging report on the progress of the French-Indian community to his superiors in Quebec, noting that the women and children learned the sign of the cross and several prayers "in their own language," while the French Canadian men "gained strength in their prayers, which most of them retained to a surprising way."[27]

Blanchet was keen to elicit support for regularized Catholic devotional practices common in Lower Canada, such as the recitation of prayers and the singing of canticles. Since the priest's long-term goal was the acculturation of the French-Indian families and their adoption of French Canadian language and culture, Blanchet initiated a program to improve the French skills of the *métis* children, particularly their reading ability. He was concerned about providing French lessons because several of the children had acquired some knowledge of both spoken and written English after receiving instruction from the Methodist missionaries. There was initially only one semiliterate francophone in the community at the time, Pierre Stanislas Jacquet, a former French seaman from Le Havre (Le Havre-de-Grâce) who wed Victoire Chinook during the first Willamette mission in January 1839. Blanchet urged Jacquet to take up the task of teaching the women and children to read the printed prayers and canticles the priest had brought with him from Quebec.[28]

In addition to noting linguistic realities in French Prairie, Blanchet observed that many of the French-Indian families followed the Northwest Coast practice of aboriginal slavery. This suggests that the early economy of the Willamette

Valley settlement relied on Indian slave labor, including the sexual exploitation of female slaves. The slaves may also have served a prestige function for some Native women in French Prairie, as was the case in Indian communities along the Northwest Coast (however, Yvonne Hajda has noted that with the precipitous decline of the indigenous population in the greater Lower Columbia during the 1830s, the distinctiveness of the prestige system began to unravel).[29] The documentation on Native slaves in French Prairie is sparse; however, the records left by Blanchet and others allow a few conclusions. First, some fur trade laborers originally purchased their female partners as slaves. This was perhaps the case with Etienne Lucier, whose wife Josette Nouette was a native of Vancouver Island, and with Joseph Bastien (now returned to Lower Canada), father of the orphaned Marie Anne Bastien boarding at the Methodist mission, whose deceased mother was identified as Louise Shasta. Both Josette and Louise likely arrived in the Columbia region via long-standing aboriginal trade networks.

Second, the written sources indicate that the Indian slaves of the French Prairie families performed essential labor in provisioning, the domestic sphere, agriculture, and transportation, as did the Indian slaves of fur trade laborer families at Fort Vancouver.[30] Blanchet remarked that during the first Willamette mission, the French Canadian men returned to their farms from time to time "to prevent the waste of grain by their hired hands or native slaves."[31] Over the course of Blanchet's first three years in French Prairie (1839–1841), he performed baptisms and administered last rites for at least a dozen Natives living with local French-Indian families who appear to have been their slaves.[32] The Indians, some of whom Blanchet noted to be orphans, ranged in age from nine to fifty, with the majority in their teens and twenties. Most appear to have been natives of the lower Columbia–Willamette Valley region (Chinook, Upper Chinookan, and Kalapuyan). These individuals resided at the farms of Etienne Lucier, Joseph Gervais, Joseph Delard, Baptiste Aubichon, Charles Rondeau, Pierre Bellique, and Louis Labonté I. Willard Rees, an American settler who migrated to Oregon in the 1840s, noted that "Nearly all the early settlers of French Prairie were the owners of a few of these slaves of both sexes; many of them were faithful laborers and the only valley Indians for many years following the early settlement who would condescend to do manual labor. They generally remained with their masters until gathered up upon reservations by authority of the government in 1855–56."[33]

Before returning to Fort Vancouver at the close of the first Willamette mission in early February 1839, Blanchet staked out a large land claim in the valley, which became the mission of St. Paul.[34] Blanchet wanted to establish a permanent mission in the Willamette Valley as requested by the French-Indian community (the priest made no mention of any discussions with the local Ahantchuyuk Kalapuyans about the proposed mission in his surviving correspondence). In staking a land claim for the mission, Blanchet received solid support from Bishop Provencher and from Chief Factor McLoughlin. Provencher advised Blanchet that a mission in the Willamette Valley must not be "put aside" because the Willamette settlers' persistent requests had brought Blanchet to the region.[35] While waiting for approval from the HBC for a permanent mission in the valley, Provencher reasoned Blanchet could reside occasionally at the Willamette mission site and begin supporting the mission through agricultural operations on the land claimed for the church. This was a significant step, as Provencher had urged Blanchet to become as self-supporting as possible.[36]

Fortunately for Blanchet, McLoughlin was on leave that year, and when he met with the governor and committee of the HBC in London, McLoughlin convinced them of the wisdom of approving a French Canadian mission in the Willamette Valley, presumably using the same arguments he had previously made to Governor George Simpson in the fall of 1837.[37] At Fort Vancouver on October 9, 1839, Blanchet received a letter from James Douglas explaining that HBC officials no longer opposed a Catholic mission in the Willamette Valley. The vicar general consequently assigned Demers to the Cowlitz mission and then departed himself for the Willamette Valley the next day. Blanchet and Demers passed the winter of 1839–1840 at their respective missions.[38]

In establishing a permanent mission in the Willamette Valley among the French-Indian families, Blanchet could embark on a more regularized program of evangelization while also stabilizing the position of the Catholic missionaries in the region. Although the missionaries enjoyed the hospitality of HBC officers at Fort Vancouver, a Willamette mission held several distinct advantages. On a practical level, Blanchet's land claim for the mission in French Prairie and its location among the French-Indian families provided direct access to subsistence resources, financial support, and communal labor activities (known as *la corvée* in Quebec).[39] In addition to supplying the labor and materials needed to build and maintain the St. Paul mission church, the French-Indian families also donated a portion of their grain surplus, the common form of currency in the settlement, to the mission collection (known as *le denier du culte*).[40]

Removed from direct dependence on the HBC and located within a supportive community, Blanchet also sought to carve out a sphere of social and political influence within the developing colony.[41] From this perspective, Blanchet might ensure that the local French-Indian families came under the direct influence of the Catholic Church. Blanchet was particularly worried about the friendly relations between the French-Indian families and the Methodist missionaries, whom Blanchet viewed as heretics determined to lure the French Canadians away from the Catholic faith. Blanchet's vision of a robust French Canadian Catholic mission on the far western frontier was influenced by the minority status of Catholics in Canada, evolving notions of French Canadian nationalism that sought to counter assimilationist pressures in Lower Canada, the Tridentine tradition in the Quebec Church (based on the early modern reforms of the Council of Trent), the conservative, ultramontane leanings of the Catholic clergy in Quebec, and the recent failure of the Rebellions of 1837–1838 in Lower Canada.[42]

Blanchet was also concerned about the Methodists spreading heretical teachings among local Native groups. During his early years at St. Paul, Blanchet made several missionizing trips to the Clackamas, Clowewalla, and other Upper Chinookan villages on the lower Willamette, in addition to other efforts outside the Willamette Valley. Because Blanchet focused his energies on the Chinookans and the French-Indian community, his contacts with the small Kalapuyan groups in the valley appear to have been very limited during this period. The priest was often troubled by the thought that in his absence, the French-Indian families in the Willamette Valley would not only renew close ties with the Methodists but also return to social and cultural practices of the multicultural fur trade, which Blanchet deemed improper. In this sense, Blanchet, like the Methodists, experienced a conflict between serving as missionary to the Indians and serving the needs of the French-Indian community.[43]

Upon establishing a permanent mission in the Willamette Valley in the fall of 1839, Blanchet continued his work among the French-Indian population, saying Mass and providing instruction in literacy, church doctrine, prayers, and sacred songs. He also turned his attention to those aspects of community life that he was accustomed to supervising in Lower Canada: social welfare, moral behavior, and social relations. He began accepting orphaned Indian and French-Indian children at the mission, thereby tackling an ongoing community need, one previously handled by the Methodists.[44] Blanchet also purchased a farm next to the St. Paul mission, which he hoped might benefit the local community: "It will serve to generate income for the support of the men, women, children, widows, orphans and all the Natives as for the Canadians."[45]

Bent on a Catholic civilizing mission, Blanchet sought to root out both the religious influence of Protestant missionaries and the cultural influences of the French Canadians' Indian wives in French Prairie. Blanchet was convinced that without some means to support a church-sponsored social welfare program, newly widowed spouses and children would "fall back" into an Indian lifestyle.[46] The priest believed that the fur trade had exposed the French Canadians to "the most seducing temptations and perversions," notably the practice of "country marriages."[47] Blanchet's concerns about sexual impropriety and the supposed negative influence of the Native women upon their husbands and children stemmed from prevailing views within the French Canadian Catholic Church regarding gender, family, and sexuality. The French Canadian clergy prized "an idealized social order" in which the patriarchal family, patterned after the Holy Family, curbed women's inherently disruptive sexuality and devout women dedicated themselves to a vision of femininity based on bodily purity, domesticity, and submission to male authority.[48]

Blanchet and Demers were familiar, however, with the long-established convention of fur trade marriage, *le mariage à la façon du pays*, which involved both short-term liaisons and long-term relationships between fur traders and Native and *métis* women. Moreover, Blanchet had received papal authorizations to grant dispensations for the canon law impediments to the sacrament of marriage. These authorizations gave Blanchet and Demers an initial flexibility that earlier Catholic missionaries in North America had lacked and made it easier for the missionaries to establish stable relations with the French-Indian families in the Willamette River from the onset of the Catholic mission.[49] The long-term goal of the missionaries was to regularize the mixed marriages between the French Canadian men and Native women (i.e., bring the bicultural couples into compliance with canon law), extend the supervisory role of the Church over marriage and family, and inculcate French Canadian devotional practices within the family. These goals were in keeping with the Tridentine model of Catholicism then championed by the French Canadian clergy. Promulgated as a centerpiece of the Counter-Reformation, the Tridentine model of Catholic religious practice stressed institutionalized rituals and confraternities, social conformity, private devotion, moral rectitude, and a clerical authoritarianism focused on the social control of the laity. This early modern Catholicism that emerged following the Council of Trent (1545–1563) was in marked contrast to the earlier medieval model familiar to the lay peasantry that emphasized community ritual, public culture, popular religion, sociability, and a less intrusive clergy.[50]

Upon their arrival in the Pacific Northwest, both Blanchet and Demers informed the French-Indian families in the Columbia region that they should adhere to Catholic Church regulations regarding marriage and sexual relations. Blanchet and Demers insisted that the French Canadian men and their Indian spouses live separately until the missionaries could perform the sacrament of marriage. As the Catholic Church records illustrate, Blanchet and Demers then set to work baptizing the Native spouses of former and current fur trade personnel, along with their French-Indian children. The Vancouver church registry used for the first and second Willamette missions of 1839 documents a willingness of nearly all the Catholic settlers and their Native wives to formalize their marriage bonds in accordance with Church practice, which also entailed baptismal rites for the mothers and children. While Blanchet may have viewed these baptisms and marriages as a clear commitment to religious practice, particularly the Catholic sacraments, the French-Indian couples likely saw these events as important milestones for their families and the community at large. In sharing these public events at the first two Willamette missions, the French Prairie settlers celebrated bonds of kin, culture, and sociability. In addition, several couples that had initially married under the auspices of the Methodists were remarried by Blanchet, which reportedly caused consternation among the American missionaries.[51]

Over the course of the first and second Willamette missions, Blanchet married twenty-seven couples and baptized their children, which suggests an estimated population of about 120 people for the French-Indian community in the summer of 1839 (table 7).[52] These weddings solemnized the existing unions of longtime settlers such as Joseph Gervais and Yiamust Clatsop, Louis Labonté and Kilkatoh Clatsop, Etienne Lucier and Josette Nouette, and Pierre Bellique and Genevieve St. Martin. The marriages also united recent male immigrants and fur trade retirees with local *métis* and Native women, such as John Hoard and Marie Lisette Dupati McKay, Charles Rondeau and Agathe Dupati McKay, Joseph Rivet and Rose Lacourse, and German Horagan and Nancy Kalapuya.[53] The marriage data confirms that although the women of French Prairie were quite ethnically diverse, nearly all were born in the Pacific Northwest: approximately 45 percent of the women were Natives of the lower Columbia and Willamette Valley region, 25 percent hailed from the Plateau, and another 22 percent were *métis* women of French-Indian ancestry. The two women from farther afield were Nicholas Montour's French-Cree wife, Marie Anne Humpherville, and Etienne Lucier's wife, Josette Nouette, a Kwakwaka'wakw woman originally from Vancouver Island.

Like Susan Kardas's review of the marriage records at Fort Vancouver (1830s–1850s), the ethnic origins of the women of French Prairie reflect the history and geography of the fur trade in the Pacific Northwest.[54] The majority of the Indian women came from villages along important fur trade networks in the lower Columbia and Plateau, as did the mothers of the French-Indian women of

TABLE 7. Catholic marriages at the first and second Willamette missions (French Prairie), 1839 (listed in chronological order)

Groom	Groom's ethnicity	Bride	Bride's ethnicity	Children
1. John Hoard	Irish	Marie Lisette Dupati McKay	Métis-Chehalis	
2. Andre Longtain	French Canadian	Nancy Okanagan	Okanagan	3
3. Joseph Despard	French Canadian	Lisette Chinook	Chinook	3
4. Pierre Bellique	French Canadian	Genevieve St. Martin	French-Chinook	3
5. Toussaint Poirier	French Canadian	Catherine Clatsop	Clatsop	3
6. Jean Baptiste Perrault	French Canadian	Angele Chehalis	Chehalis	2
7. Louis Labonté I	French Canadian	Kilkatoh Clatsop	Clatsop	2
8. Hyacinthe Lavigeur	French Canadian	Marguerite Colville	Colville	4
9. Andre Picard	French Canadian	Marie Okanagan	Okanagan	3
10. François Rivet	French Canadian	Therese Flathead	Flathead (Interior Salish)	
11. Antoine Rivet	French-Flathead	Emelie Pend d'Oreille	Pend d'Oreille	3
12. Joseph Rivet	French-Flathead	Rose Lacourse	French-Chinook	
13. Joseph Delard	French Canadian	Lisette Shushwap	Shushwap	3
14. Charles Rondeau	French Canadian	Agathe Dupati McKay	Métis-Kalapuyan	2
15. Etienne Lucier	French Canadian	Josette Nouette	Kwakwaka'wakw	4
16. Pierre Dépôt	French Canadain	Marguerite Clackamas	Clackamas Upper Chinookan	1
17. François Xavier Laderoute	French Canadian	Julie Gervais	French-Chinook	2
18. Joseph Gervais	French Canadian	Yiamust Clatsop	Clatsop	3
19. Amable Arquette	French Canadian	Marguerite Chinook	Chinook	3
20. Louis Forcier	French Canadian	Catherine Canemah	Canemah Upper Chinookan	3
21. Pierre Stanislas Jacquet	French	Victoire Chinook	Chinook	
22. William McCarty	Irish	Charlotte Chehalis	Chehalis	
23. German Horagan	Irish	Nancy Kalapuya	Tutalatin Kalapuyan	1
24. Charlot Iroquois Tsete	Iroquois	Marie Thomas	Iroquois-Dalles Upper Chinookan	
25. Charles Plante	French Canadian	Agathe Cayuse	Cayuse	1
26. Jean Baptiste Aubichon	French Canadian	Marie Chehalis	Chehalis	1
27. Nicholas Montour	French-Indian	Marie Anne Humpherville	French-Cree	1

NOTES: (1) Jean Baptiste Desportes McKay had three young children and two wives: Eugenie (Jane) Wanakske and Marguerite Kalapuya. (2) Charles Rondeau had two children by his first wife. (3) Julie Gervais is not counted as a child of Joseph Gervais and Yiamust Clatsop. (4) Michel Laferte dit Placide and Josephte Nez Perce were married at Fort Vancouver in 1839. They had five children at the time.

SOURCES: Munnick, CCRPNW-V, CCRPNW-SP, CCRPNW-SL; Osborn-Ryan, Cumulative Baptism Index to the CCRPNW; Watson, Lives Lived West of the Divide, 3 vols.

the settlement, such as the Chinook mothers of Genevieve St. Martin and Rose Lacourse. The great majority of the men (70 percent) were French Canadians from Lower Canada. The remaining male heads of household included three Irishmen (11 percent), three French-Indians (11 percent), one Iroquois (3 percent), and one Frenchman (3 percent). Although French Canadian men remained the dominant ethnic group in the community, these marriage statistics underscore the central role of Native and *métis* women in French Prairie. The settlement was matrifocal in a regional sense, as nearly all the men were born in Lower Canada, the Canadian Northwest, or Europe. Marriage to regional Native women and the daughters of the older French-Indian couples afforded the French Canadians and European emigrants access to social and kin networks and to women's economic and reproductive labor in the developing agrarian colony.[55]

In addition to the mixed marriages, Blanchet also faced some instances of polygamy, which, though not the predominant family form in the western fur trade, was not unknown. In such cases, Blanchet insisted that Catholics in the Columbia region separate themselves from any additional wives.[56] He was particularly concerned about men who had left behind a wife in Lower Canada. During Blanchet's second Willamette mission, he encountered vocal resistance from one individual in particular, Jean Baptiste Desportes McKay dit Dupati. Desportes McKay's comportment was especially troublesome for Blanchet because the French-Algonquin proved himself an unapologetic polygamist. At the time, Desportes McKay had at least two female companions—one of whom may have originally held the status of slave—and perhaps a third wife still alive in Canada. The two country wives were Eugenie (Jane) Wanakske, daughter of a Clowewalla headman, and Marguerite, a Kalapuyan woman.

During the summer of 1839, Blanchet attempted to separate Desportes McKay from the two women until such a time as Blanchet could verify that the French-Algonquin's first wife had died and that he had committed himself to a single spouse. Desportes McKay was unresponsive to Blanchet's efforts: he would abandon neither Eugenie nor Marguerite because he had children with both women and because, as he reportedly told Blanchet, "his servant was his."[57] However, Desportes McKay did allow his two young sons, Jean Baptiste and John, to be baptized at the first Willamette mission in January 1839, and he saw his two teen-aged daughters, Agathe and Marie Lisette, baptized and married (his ten-year-old daughter Françoise was apparently still living at the Methodist mission). The former fur trapper did finally marry in the Church in November 1843, when he wed Eugenie (Jane) Wanakske.[58]

In April of 1840, Archbishop Signay advised Blanchet to take a more compassionate approach on the question of country marriages between cradle Catholics and Natives. Signay explained, "If the Indian women [*infidèles*] married according to the custom of the country present themselves to be admitted among the catechumens and believe in good faith that their marriages are valid, you should leave them alone and not demand that they separate. A practice to the contrary could have the effect of making the couples who are genuinely married separate forever."[59]

Although the head of the Catholic mission retained his reproving attitude, he was somewhat more adaptable to existing social conditions among the settler population in the Willamette settlement than the Methodist missionaries. In addition to Blanchet's willingness to marry French-Indian couples on short notice—due to his papal authorizations and his recognition of preexisting common law marriages—the vicar general became proficient in Chinook Jargon, which allowed him to communicate more effectively with the women and children of the French-Indian community.[60] Blanchet also developed a visual teaching tool for Christian evangelization, *l'échelle historique*, later known as the Catholic Ladder, during his second Willamette mission in the summer of 1839. This visual narrative, a type of memory aid, was based on the "sahale stick" ("stick from heaven" in Chinook Jargon), which Blanchet had first used during his mission to Cowlitz Prairie in the spring of 1839. The Catholic Ladder relied on a notation system supplemented with images that represented the history of the world and the development of Christianity. It proved popular with the members of the French-Indian community in the Willamette Valley and later with segments of the region's Indian population interested in the religious traditions of their French Canadian kin relations. Blanchet's Catholic Ladder later also contributed to the increasing acrimony between Catholic and Protestant missionaries in the Pacific Northwest because of its unflattering portrayal of Protestantism as a heretical, withered branch of Christianity (which prompted the Protestant missionaries Henry H. and Eliza Spalding to create a competing Protestant Ladder in the mid-1840s).[61]

While Blanchet made some accommodations to local conditions in the Willamette Valley, he remained focused on moral behavior, regularized religious practice, and acculturation. Particularly distressing to Blanchet was what he viewed as the tendency of French Canadians in the fur trade to adopt Indian cultural practices. In his report on the third Willamette mission (October 10, 1839, to March 19, 1840), he complained that "in the service, there are old servants, single and married, in charge of children who live like savages." Blanchet also wondered "how many Canadian children have been abandoned among the savages by their *malheureux* [unfortunate] fathers?"[62] Blanchet was not only perturbed about what he perceived as a lackadaisical attitude on the part of the French Canadian fathers regarding their Christian duty to educate their children, he was also upset about what he perceived as a laissez-faire attitude on the part of the HBC, believing that the company wanted to relieve itself (*s'en debarrasser*) of any responsibility for retired company laborers and their families.[63] Conveniently forgetting the French Canadians' annual appeals to Bishop Provencher, their support for the welfare of Native and French-Indian orphans, their construction of a church for the community, and their monetary and labor contributions to the mission, Blanchet was critical of the bicultural nature of the French Prairie colony because in his view, the French Canadian men knew better. Blanchet believed that by accommodating the culture of their Native wives and allowing them a measure of authority within the family, the French Canadian men had demonstrated both indifference and a lack of moral rectitude, and as a result they threatened to deprive their wives and children of Christian salvation and the benefits of Western culture.[64]

Not unlike fervent parish priests in Lower Canada and Catholic missionaries in western regions of the United States (and also the Catholic clergy in France), Blanchet encountered a range of attitudes from community members in response to his attempts to inculcate religious practice and regular church attendance in the Willamette Valley.[65] Blanchet trained a few promising *métis* members of the community to instruct the children on religious matters (prayers, songs, and catechism), as well as reading and writing. By 1840 one such lay teacher was Jean Baptiste Jeaudoin, age eighteen, the eldest child of French Canadian laborer Charles Jeaudoin and his late wife (Chinook). After receiving instruction from Blanchet, the young Jeaudoin eagerly began teaching other community members. Blanchet informed his superiors that Jeaudoin would spend his spare time, usually on Sundays, teaching the Catholic Ladder to the local settlers.[66]

The Native women in the French Prairie who participated in the prayers and masses during the early Willamette missions likely reacted to Blanchet's proselytizing in a manner similar to other Indian peoples who had religious encounters with Christian missionaries. Those who responded positively to the Catholic rituals and sacraments did not necessarily abandon their own indigenous spirituality; rather, they saw the Catholic religion as an addition to their existing beliefs and practices.[67] A case that contrasts with the measured response of the Indian women from the Pacific Northwest to Blanchet's preaching was the more enthusiastic reaction of a middle-aged *métis* couple originally from the Canadian

Northwest. During the second Willamette mission in the summer of 1839, Marie Anne Humpherville, age forty-seven, and Nicholas Montour, age fifty-seven, demonstrated enough religious zeal to be mentioned by name in Blanchet's report. Humpherville (French-Cree) and Montour (French-Indian) had recently retired to the Willamette Valley after Montour's long career in the fur trade as a clerk for the NWC and HBC. In their new community, they were eager to learn the Catholic catechism alongside their children. During the mission, Montour assisted with the daily Mass, while Humpherville, "whose faith was intense," made the necessary steps to become a Catholic. After Montour's abjuration of faith and Humpherville's baptism, Blanchet married them at the mission of St. Paul in French Prairie.[68]

Although Blanchet employed a variety of methods in his efforts at social control over the French-Indian community, he recorded some instances of resistance to his actions on the part of Native women in the settlement. In the fall of 1840, Blanchet wrote Modeste Demers about a conflict he had had with Catherine Clatsop, wife of Toussaint Poirer. The couple and their children had settled in the Willamette Valley after Toussaint retired from thirty years in the fur trade as a middleman and cooper with the NWC and HBC. Blanchet harangued Catherine for an unspecified reason. As Catherine did not appreciate the priest's treatment, she insisted that the couple return to her native territory on the south shore of the Columbia River estuary, which they did (they eventually returned to French Prairie sometime later).[69] That same fall, Blanchet also complained about the obstinate nature of Susanne Tawakon (Iroquois-Upper Chinookan), the wife of Willamette mission verger Amable Petit. Accustomed to a degree of autonomy within her family and community, Tawakon preferred to be the "mistress of the household," and she did not appreciate comments about her domestic arrangements, presumably from Blanchet. As a result, Tawakon and Petit returned to Kanaka Village at Fort Vancouver for a time. In keeping with his training in the Tridentine tradition in Quebec and its emphasis on patriarchal control within the family and the Church to curb female sexuality, Blanchet remarked that Susanne Tawakon had "debauched" Amable Petit by pressuring him to turn his back on the mission. However, Petit himself expressed frustration with working conditions at the Willamette mission: shortly before the couple's departure in late August 1840, Petit told Blanchet that he "liked work at Fort Vancouver better than work at the mission."[70] Sometime before January 1842, Petit and Tawakon returned to French Prairie and Petit resumed his duties at the St. Paul mission, witnessing the baptisms, marriages, and burials of community members.

The limited qualitative sources on French Prairie in the late 1830s, combined with the Catholic Church registers kept by Francis N. Blanchet, help illustrate the level of religious devotion and the social dynamics of this bicultural settler community. As demonstrated in the attitudes of *métis* settlers Jean Baptiste Jeaudoin, Nicolas Montour, and Marie Anne Humpherville, religious practice and education could be positive experiences for both men and women, providing both a sense of purpose and a connection to the local community—especially in times of significant social change.[71] Indeed, the willingness of most French-Indian families to solemnize their unions in Church weddings during Blanchet's first Willamette mission suggests that the local church, built by the settlers themselves, became a central gathering place for the community. Located midway between the farms at Champoeg in the northern part of French Prairie and the Gervais farm in the southern section, the St. Paul mission was a social institution that belonged to the French-Indian families—a contrast to the American Methodist mission.

Still, the arrival of Father Blanchet was not without incident for the settlers. The documented resistance of Jean Baptiste Desportes McKay, Catherine Clatsop, and Susanne Tawakon to Blanchet's attempts to regulate gender and sexual relations highlights the limits of Blanchet's authority over the community. Not unlike Catholic parishioners and clergy in Lower Canada and the French-Indian settlements in the Great Lakes and lower Missouri region, Blanchet and the French Prairie settlers sometimes held differing notions about acceptable social behavior, the role of women, marriage practices, and the level of control a clergyman should have over the local community. These tensions flowed from the cultural differences between the French Canadian Catholic missionary and the interethnic families in French Prairie and from the ideological divide between an educated priest committed to a Tridentine model for the Catholic mission in the Pacific Northwest and a frontier community used to traditions of popular religion, indigenous spirituality, sociability, and cultural accommodation. Blanchet was particularly troubled by a social order in which the behavior of Indianized French Canadians and their Native wives did not conform to the Catholic clergyman's notion of an idealized male-dominated hierarchy within the family and the Church. Although Blanchet was able to adapt his approach to local conditions in the short term, he remained committed to establishing a leading role for himself within the community so as to effect the acculturation of the French-Indian families and ensure their commitment to a more orthodox Roman Catholicism. Thus as Mary Wright has noted, Blanchet, like his Protestant counterparts, preached a Christianized social order that began to undermine the Native cultures of the

Pacific Northwest. This colonializing project aimed at gender and family patterns affected indigenous communities throughout the region as well as bicultural settlements such as French Prairie.[72]

✳ The arrival of Blanchet marked a turning point for social relations between the Methodist missionaries and their French-Indian neighbors in the Willamette Valley due to the cultural, political, institutional, and personal differences separating the Methodist and Catholic missionaries, each viewing the other with a strong degree of antipathy, not uncommon for the mid-nineteenth century.[73] For the Methodists, Blanchet was an unwanted interloper and—given their populist, republican traditions and limited theological training—the Methodists chafed under Blanchet's air of moral and intellectual superiority. They viewed him as haughty, dogmatic, antidemocratic, and autocratic. Thus, although the conflict between Blanchet and the Methodists stemmed from differences over theology, religious practice, and politics, it also flowed from a personal struggle for the leadership of the French-Indian community.

In one sense, Blanchet viewed his initial ministry in the Willamette Valley as a defensive action; he challenged the Methodists in order to prevent the French-Indian families from renouncing Catholicism and converting to Protestant heresies. Blanchet was also very critical of the Methodists' lack of intellectual training and doctrinal rigor, their limited knowledge of the history of Christianity, and their poor performance in missionizing the local Indians. Blanchet perceived the American Methodists as particularly arrogant and illiberal. For all their talk of democracy and freedom, he found their conduct hypocritical because they were intolerant of those who differed in matters of opinion and faith.[74] Moreover, as a supporter of the ultramontane tradition in Quebec, Blanchet found their populist traditions especially troubling. In contrast to the Gallicanist tradition within Roman Catholicism, which gave a greater role to national Church leaders and local customs, the ultramontane approach emphasized allegiance to the pope, the chain of hierarchical command, and strict observance of Catholic teachings. The antireligious sentiments of the French Revolution and the social disruptions caused by the Canadian Rebellions of 1837–1838 were striking examples to French Canadian Catholic clergymen about the dangers of overturning the existing social order and traditional forms of representative government—such as the British parliamentary system. From Blanchet's perspective, the correct course of action was to cultivate the cultural values championed by the Roman Catholic Church in Quebec: political and economic conservatism, deference to one's social superiors, agrarianism, confessional schools, and social stability over social change.[75]

The French Canadian clergy's aversion to the hallmarks of antebellum American culture—evangelical Protestantism, democratic politics, commercialization, social egalitarianism, common schools, and intellectual autonomy—placed Blanchet at odds with the American emigrants who began streaming into Oregon in the early 1840s.[76] The emigrants brought their own antipathy to Roman Catholicism and the British Empire, represented by the HBC.[77] The first hint of the cultural divide that started to put pressure on the French-Indian community in the Willamette Valley was the arrival of the bedraggled Peoria Party. The remaining members of this ill-prepared filibustering expedition reached Fort Vancouver in small groups from the fall of 1839 through the summer of 1840 via the overland route that became the Oregon Trail.[78] The Peoria Party, also known as the Oregon Dragoons, were residents of Peoria, Illinois, who had heard Jason Lee lecture about the Methodist mission in Oregon when he and two Indian students, Thomas Adams and William Brooks, stopped in Peoria in the fall of 1838 on their way to New England.

Inspired by descriptions of Oregon gleaned from Lee and his pupil Thomas Adams, who remained in Peoria for several weeks due to ill health, a group of locals headed by Thomas Jefferson Farnham organized the filibustering expedition with the intention of reclaiming the Oregon Country for the United States.[79] Other members of the party included Amos Cook, Francis Fletcher, Joseph Holman, Robert Shortress, and Sidney Smith, all of whom remained in the Pacific Northwest (unlike Farnham, who returned to the United States after some misadventures in Mexican California). The group's aim of securing Oregon for the United States despite the vast distance involved and the de facto colonial rule of the HBC appears fanciful in hindsight, but it did signal the beginning of a new phase of Anglo-American settler colonialism. This new incarnation of "aggressive expansionism," which focused on the Trans-Mississippi West, built on earlier colonizations of the Midwest and on filibustering expeditions to Texas and combined with the anti-British attitudes, racialism, and the economic, political, and technological developments that characterized late Jacksonian America.[80]

While visiting the Willamette Valley in October 1839, Thomas Farnham, an ardent nationalist, talked with local American settlers about "their fatherland" and "the probability that its laws would be extended over them."[81] According to Farnham, the colonists expressed resentment toward the HBC, which they perceived as domineering because of its trade monopoly in the region and its control of civil and judicial affairs.[82] In his travel memoir published in 1843,

Farnham quoted "constantly repeated inquiries" that he heard from his country-men in Oregon: "Why are we left without protection in this part of our country's domain? Why are foreigners permitted to dominate over American citizens, and make us as dependent on them for the clothes we wear, as are their own apprenticed slaves?"[83] Farnham was himself particularly troubled by the bicultural nature of the Willamette Valley settlement and the tendency of local white men, who "in desperation to their lonely lot," took "wives from the Indian tribes around them."[84] He was convinced that American society and governance should be extended over the colony to uplift the moral and social condition of these particular settlers.

A lawyer by training, Farnham collaborated with several Americans in drafting a petition to the U.S. Congress outlining their perceived grievances. Various accounts suggest that William Bailey and two members of the Methodist mission, David Leslie and Elijah White, actively participated in writing the petition and circulating it among the Willamette settlers in late October 1839.[85] Sixty-seven male settlers signed their name (or affixed their mark) to the missive, including the Methodist missionaries, American settlers, European emigrants, and more than two dozen former employees of the HBC. In Farnham's version of events, the British subjects who signed the missive were desirous of becoming American citizens; however, he did note that Blanchet refused to sign the petition.[86] Farnham subsequently sent the document, known as the Farnham Memorial, to Congress from Honolulu, and Senator Lewis Linn of Missouri officially presented it to Congress in early June 1840.

The Farnham Memorial contained arguments supporting the American annexation of the Oregon Country that were present in the Edwards Memorial of 1838. Both documents emphasized that the region was rich in natural resources, strategically located for trade with the Pacific, and that the settlers were in need of formal government in order to protect their lives and their property. The second petition contained a heightened level of nationalist fervor and anti-British sentiment, expressed by the authors' criticism of the British government and its representative, the HBC (Jason Lee and Phillip Edwards had avoided such a direct approach in their petition of 1838). The authors of the Farnham Memorial specifically warned Congress about the British exploring expedition, commanded by Captain Edward Belcher, which had recently surveyed the region, and about the perceived machinations of the British government and the HBC to establish unilateral sovereignty over the Oregon Country north of the Columbia River.[87] The petition's alarmist rhetoric describing intercultural relations and social order in the region mixed anti-Indian and anti-Catholic attitudes with

Anglophobic conspiracy theories.[88] Farnham and his fellow writers depicted the Pacific Northwest as a dangerous region in which the settlers were "exposed to be destroyed by the savages around them, and others that would do them harm." Their request for American rule to be extended over Oregon was urgent because they needed protection against these perceived threats and because their informal "self-constituted tribunals" were insufficient to handle the "crimes of theft, murder, infanticide," which were "increasing among them to an alarming extent."[89]

When news of the Farnham Memorial reached McLoughlin in February 1840, he was distressed by what he perceived as the ungrateful and slanderous accusations penned by American settlers, whom he had consistently assisted (though not completely altruistically).[90] He was also disappointed by the participation of the French Canadians. In his correspondence with McLoughlin regarding the petition, Father Blanchet outlined the French Canadians' predicament. The illiterate French Canadians relied on an oral description of the text and they claimed to have been misled by the Americans. According to the Canadians, the Americans had told them that the Farnham Memorial was a restatement of the Edwards Memorial of 1838, which McLoughlin had not opposed. David Leslie reportedly convinced Charles Rondeau that there would be no harm in signing the petition.[91] However, the Farnham Memorial caused enough tension between the French Canadian settlers and HBC officials to motivate a group of eighteen colonists to dictate a letter to McLoughlin explaining the misunderstanding in March 1840. They emphasized the valuable assistance they had received from the company, which had allowed them to establish farms in the Willamette Valley. McLoughlin's *métis* stepson, Thomas McKay, who maintained a second farm in the Willamette Valley in addition to his primary residence near Scappoose, signed his name and seventeen settlers made their mark, including all of the leading French Canadians.[92]

It is important to consider whether the French Canadians would have had reason to question the motives and testimony of the authors of the Farnham petition. From all accounts, the French Canadian settlers were on positive terms with practically all of the Americans, including the Methodist missionaries. Moreover, the various settler groups had previously cooperated on several community initiatives, the leading Canadian settlers having supported the Edwards Memorial of 1838. Seen from this perspective, the French Canadians likely affixed their marks to the Farnham petition in accordance with their long-standing approach to relations with their American neighbors. The French Canadians were determined to maintain ties with the Americans because the United States might annex the

Oregon Country south of the Columbia River. Since the Edwards Memorial had not harmed their relationship with HBC officials, the French Canadians thought that this new petition would allow them to retain a voice within the developing settler society without adverse consequences. Their support for both the Edwards Memorial and the Farnham Memorial in the late 1830s demonstrated continuity with their earlier cooperative efforts involving the Methodists and other American settlers during the mid-1830s.

The French Canadians continued to seek a middle ground between competing interests in the Willamette Valley. The controversy over the second memorial nevertheless suggests a subtle shift in the political culture in the valley, notably an increasing nationalism among their American neighbors. The French Canadians' letter to McLoughlin was an attempt at damage control; however, the fact that the French Canadians were illiterate in comparison to the Americans put them at a distinct disadvantage. And unlike the French Canadian settlers, many of whom had been away from their homeland for decades, Francis N. Blanchet had departed Lower Canada amid the Rebellions of 1837–1838, whose leaders espoused republican ideals comparable to nationalist and populist groups in the United States. Thus, while the French Canadians in French Prairie offered some support to their American neighbors, Blanchet was much more skeptical of the Americans' motives, which led him to refuse to sign the Farnham Memorial. The deception on the part of the Methodist missionaries in the Farnham affair proved an opening salvo in the simmering discord between American Protestants and French Canadian Catholics in the Willamette Valley.

By the fall of 1839, evidence of another shift in social relations between the valley communities emerged in the letters of Susan (Downing) Shepard, the wife of mission teacher Cyrus Shepard. Her view of the altered social landscape was colored by her own antipathy toward Catholicism, which she shared with the other Methodist missionaries. Writing about a recent Methodist mission meeting in a letter dated September 15, 1839, Shepard noted that it was "quite a rare thing to see the French people out to meeting since [their] priest came here." She believed that Blanchet had "forbidden" the French-Indian families from calling on the Methodist mission because they did not visit the missionaries "as frequently as formerly with there familyes [sic]."[93] Given the previously friendly interactions between the Methodists and the French-Indian families, Shepard viewed the bicultural settlers as "ignorant" because they blindly followed Blanchet's instructions and allowed him to take a leadership role in their community.[94] She was particularly offended by the French-Indians' "foolish" behavior of permitting themselves to be rebaptized and remarried by Blanchet after Jason Lee had previously performed these services. Thus, from the Methodist perspective, the change in relations between the two communities demonstrated that Blanchet, and perhaps the French-Indian families, harbored unneighborly attitudes.

A few months after Shepard made her comments, tensions increased sharply between the two groups. The event that sparked a worsening in intercommunity relations was the death of her husband, Cyrus Shepard. He had long suffered from scrofula (tuberculosis of the lymph glands), and in the spring of 1839 the disease attacked his right knee joint. He suffered in pain throughout the summer. During the fall his condition deteriorated so much that by November, he was being bled on a regular basis to relieve the pressure on the joint. On December 11, 1839, Dr. Elijah White amputated Shepard's leg; however, this failed to stop Shepard's decline, and he passed away on December 31, 1839.[95]

In one of his last letters, addressed to Methodist missionaries stationed at The Dalles (Wascopam) station, Shepard expressed gratitude for the sympathy shown him by the "French, English, Americans . . . [and] poor Indians."[96] Accordingly, the Methodists invited all the Willamette Valley settlers to Shepard's funeral scheduled for early January 1840. Upon receiving an invitation, a representative for the French Canadians approached Father Blanchet about his views on the funeral. Blanchet advised the French Canadians not to attend the funeral service, explaining that it would be improper for the Catholic families to do so because the Methodist missionaries, including Cyrus Shepard, had blackened the name of the Roman Catholic faith with "malicious slander," epitomized in the Methodists' distribution of the popular nativist propaganda, *Awful Disclosures of the Hotel Dieu Nunnery of Montreal* (1836) by Maria Monk.[97] The Methodists' decision to distribute Monk's so-called confessional was perhaps more troubling to Blanchet than it was to the French-Indian families, as it attacked the French Canadian Catholic Church and because they themselves were illiterate and thus unable to read the anti-Catholic tract. Additionally disturbing for Blanchet was Shepard's reported beating of a French-Indian child who had dared to declare that the beating did not stop "him from loving the religion of his deceased father."[98]

Unfortunately for Blanchet, rather than communicate his position directly to the Methodists or negotiate with them about Catholic attendance, he apparently left the matter to the French Canadians. The French Canadian who had sought Blanchet's council informed the Methodists that Blanchet forbade the Catholics from attending the funeral. Given the former neighborly relations between the two communities, the Methodists were offended by Blanchet's actions. The funeral went ahead as scheduled, and in accordance with Blanchet's interdiction, the French Canadians and their families did not attend the service. Blanchet recorded in a letter to his brother Augustin Blanchet that some of the Irish settlers in the valley did attend the funeral—presumably John Hoard, William McCarty, and German Horagan. They reported to Blanchet that during the service, the Methodists severely criticized the Catholics in general and Blanchet in particular.[99]

During the controversy that ensued, Blanchet saw himself as the victim of both the Methodists' ill will and the cowardly demeanor of the French Canadians— from whom he expected deference and obedience. Blanchet wrote to James Douglas at Fort Vancouver, who agreed that the French Canadians should have demonstrated courage and supported their priest.[100] Douglas admitted that he felt "a degree of uneasiness" about the "bad feeling [that] had been excited among the Americans" because of the Canadians' refusal to attend the funeral. He was particularly harsh in his judgment of the "Canadians, who throw odium on their spiritual guide, where in justice they ought to have shielded you from the storm, by declaring with many frankness that they were influenced in that instance by the rites and essential doctrines of their Church. They are indeed devoid of Spirit, pride or self-respect, and must act another part, before they are considered worthy of having you among them."[101]

In his response to Douglas's letter, Blanchet expressed his belief that this misunderstanding between the Methodists and Catholics demonstrated the need for vigilance on his part. He recommitted himself to protecting his "flock" from heretical doctrines. Indeed, Blanchet saw a parallel between the work of the Apostles and his work against the heresy of the Methodists.[102] With hindsight, Blanchet felt that the Methodists should have written him a letter and requested that the Catholic community attend the funeral. This would have allowed Blanchet to explain the situation and perhaps allowed the Catholics to attend the burial service.[103]

Blanchet was particularly insulted by what he perceived as the anti-Catholic chauvinism of the American Methodists. He felt that they did not treat others with respect but demanded that they be so treated. According to Blanchet, they also made public threats against the Catholics and claimed that they would eventually gain the upper hand in the Willamette Valley. These impulses of evangelical Protestantism, Anglo superiority, and populism were the same forces that challenged French Canadians and Catholics in Canada; however, given Blanchet's experience with a conservative French Canadian nationalism led by the hierarchy of the Catholic Church in Quebec, he was not bowed by the Methodists. Rather, he expressed confidence that the American settlers and the Methodists would regret their lack of consideration.[104]

Clearly, in this instance, it was the underlying cultural, political, and religious differences between the two camps that fueled mutual misunderstanding. Blanchet hailed from the hierarchical tradition of the Tridentine Church in which the parish priest held a distinctive leadership role and wielded considerable power within the community. The Americans, who came from a society that valued evangelical traditions, social egalitarianism, and social mobility, had difficulty understanding the priest's authority to instruct the Canadians not to attend the funeral service. Indeed, given the former relations between the two communities, the Methodists would have seen the refusal not as faithfulness to the Catholic Church but as a social snub inspired by a haughty newcomer. It likely never occurred to the Methodists to write Blanchet asking permission for his flock to attend the funeral. They may not have known that French Canadian Church policies at the time strongly discouraged French Canadians from participating in Protestant services. Indeed, this is the most likely scenario because the Catholic members of the local community had attended Methodist services for several years prior to Blanchet's arrival. These cultural differences were compounded by the sectarian hostilities that existed between the Catholic priests and the Methodist missionaries; each camp viewed the other with considerable animus. Both Blanchet and the Methodists had witnessed the popularity of evangelical Protestantism and the emergence of anti-Catholic nativist movements that accompanied increased Catholic immigration and the expansion of the Catholic Church in North America during the early 1800s.[105] While the Methodists embraced these developments, Blanchet sought to protect the nascent Catholic Church and the French-Indian settlers from their influence.

In light of the problems raised by the Shepard funeral, Blanchet came away from the controversy he had provoked with two observations. Despite the cultural and religious differences between the Methodist and French-Indian communities, Blanchet believed that they were all "the children of the same Father, the same God." As such, they should endeavor to live in harmony and peace.[106] In his letter to James Douglas, Blanchet also stated that he would need to press the Methodists to respect the principle of religious freedom and the liberty of the individual conscience. He went so far as to use this argument in support of the notion that husbands did not have authority over the spiritual and religious choices of their wives.[107] Blanchet's views on gender and religion drew on currents in French Canadian Catholicism, which held that men naturally headed hierarchies within the Church, society, and the family, while women filled subordinate though important roles within these various spheres. Since the colonial period, the Catholic Church had recognized social, familial, and religious contributions for women and had sought to nurture the religious lives of women. Committed to a hierarchical organization of religion and society, French Canadian Church leaders believed that the male clergy must supervise and regulate women's spirituality, sexuality, and behavior.[108] Given the dominance of Protestantism in North America and the British Empire, Blanchet's support for the freedom of religion was not an argument for religious pluralism but rather a defensive position affirming the threatened rights of Catholic minorities and the authority of the Catholic clergy in Oregon, which included Blanchet's surveillance of the spiritual and social lives of the women in the French Prairie settlement.

Relations with the Methodists were tested once again in February 1840. On February 1, in response to an invitation to join the Methodists' temperance society, Blanchet wrote a long, detailed letter in French to Elijah White explaining why he would not take part in the movement. The Catholic priest also outlined a series of complaints regarding the Methodists' malfeasance against the French-Indian community in recent months. These included duping the French Canadians into signing the Farnham Memorial, defaming Blanchet, whipping a *métis* orphan of Catholic parents, and professional misconduct on the part of Dr. White. The charges against White were serious, with Blanchet intimating sexual misconduct by White against Julie Gervais (age twenty), the young wife of François Xavier Laderoute (age forty), and the daughter of Laderoute's neighbor Joseph Gervais.[109] Blanchet asserted that White visited the woman and conducted a physical exam without the woman's husband being present. According to the priest, such behavior was not only at odds with French Canadian culture, but it also exposed the young woman to temptation and caused sorrow to her husband.[110]

Blanchet sent a copy of the letter to James Douglas, who responded with concern about Blanchet's lack of moderation in charging Dr. White with a serious moral breach. Douglas warned Blanchet that if proved false, the accusation against Dr. White might "recoil with equal force upon the author of the calumny."[111] Blanchet took Douglas's opinion quite hard, reprimanding himself for a lack of diplomacy in his dealings with the Methodists. Fortunately for Blanchet, since the letter was written in French, White claimed that he did not comprehend the full force of the priest's charges. In White's memoir of his years in Oregon, compiled by Miss J. A. Allen in 1848, he made made no mention of this incident; however, there is some evidence to suggest that White had a penchant for sexual impropriety with women.[112] At his trial before Jason Lee and a group of Methodist leaders in September 1840, White was found guilty of "imprudent conduct," having taken "unwarranted liberties with several females" of the Methodist mission. White was also found guilty of "disobedience to order of the church" and "dishonesty" related to a neglect of his duties at the mission and his appropriation of mission funds for his personal use while Jason Lee was away on his first return trip to the East.[113]

In response to the letter from James Douglas, Blanchet revisited the Laderoute-Gervais farmstead and asked for more detailed information on the charges against Dr. White. The couple gave testimony that suggests two possible scenarios: professional and sexual misconduct on the part of Dr. White or a consensual sexual liaison between Elijah White and Julie Gervais. According to Blanchet, Julie Gervais stated that White's first visit took place at the home of her father, Joseph Gervais. A second visit occurred at the doctor's house, and two additional visits took place at the couple's farm in the absence of her husband. These final two encounters occurred in the farm's granary "despite the repugnance of the female who said that her body remained untouched and she only had a stomach ache."[114] A later visit was canceled after Blanchet forbade it. Because Blanchet mentioned that this alleged misconduct caused "sorrow" to Laderoute and because Julie Gervais protested her innocence despite the fact that two of the visits had occurred in the Laderoute-Gervais granary rather in the couple's home, there may have been some type of sexual liaison between White and Julie Gervais that had come to the attention of her husband, who then reported it to Blanchet.

Given the concerns of James Douglas and Blanchet's own worries, the priest wrote a second letter to Dr. White in which the priest attempted to retract what he had written in his initial letter. Writing in English this time, Blanchet apologized if he had inadvertently injured White's character. After Dr. White asked another missionary, Mr. Willson, to translate the original French letter, this second letter caused friction between Blanchet and White. Dr. White feigned both surprise and anger at the charges, writing that "If it shall appear that Saddy root [Laderoute] has done me injustice, I am sure you will have no objection to his being brought to justice or properly exposed to the publick."[115] Nevertheless, "out of respect" for Blanchet, White agreed to remain silent on the issue for the time being.

Worried that the letter would become public, Blanchet went to see Elijah White to try to resolve the situation. The encounter was an attempt at diplomacy that, according to the account left by Blanchet, illustrates the personalities of both men. Blanchet, who presented himself as both the spiritual leader and civil representative of his community, insisted that even if the relations between Dr. White and Julie Gervais had not involved a criminal act, they did involve imprudence. To avoid future misunderstandings, Blanchet advised White to follow several rules of conduct: if possible he should dispense remedies that would not involve physical exams, and if a physical examination was necessary, the doctor should request the husband's permission and examine the female patient in the presence of her husband.[116] Blanchet recounted that White was surprised that a priest should have become involved in such a matter. The doctor protested his innocence with the argument that he had only acted out of duty and responsibility. He accepted Blanchet's apology and explanation and returned Blanchet's original letter. They shook hands over the matter before Blanchet departed from the Methodist mission.

Although Blanchet had managed to resolve this affair, it was not the last time he would face considerable worry over the conduct of Elijah White. In the meantime, Blanchet and the French-Indian settlers witnessed the enlargement of the Methodist mission in the Pacific Northwest. In early June 1840, Jason Lee, the Indian student Thomas Adams, and a large group of ordained and lay missionaries and their families arrived at Fort Vancouver aboard the *Lausanne*, which had departed New York in early October 1839. Some fifty-two adults and children made up this group, which became known as the "Great Reinforcement" and included ministers, a physician, a mission steward, female teachers, and several skilled laborers to work in farming, carpentry, cabinetry, and blacksmithing. With the added personnel and resources, Jason Lee and his colleagues embarked on an expansion and reorganization program that included new mission stations at Willamette Falls (Oregon City), the Clatsop Plains, and Nisqually on Puget Sound, as well as increased efforts at the Wascopam branch mission at The Dalles. The Methodists also began work on plans to move the Willamette Valley mission from its original site near the river to a new location ten miles south at Chemeketa (Salem), a move which they completed in 1841.[117]

Although the Methodists hoped their increased numbers might lead to greater self-sufficiency, the existing documentary evidence suggests continued reliance on local Indians and settlers in the Willamette Valley, who occasionally provided assistance to the American missionaries more accustomed to life in the towns and cities of the eastern seaboard. In a letter posted in the fall of 1840, Adelia Judson Olley, wife of layman James Olley, recounted the journey of members of the *Lausanne* party from Fort Vancouver to the Willamette mission the previous June.[118] Fur trade laborers and Natives conveyed the Americans in six canoes from

Fort Vancouver, across the Columbia River, and up the Willamette to Willamette Falls. After portaging the falls and camping one night en route, the missionaries continued on by canoe to Champoeg, where they arrived in the evening quite fatigued. However, the settlers at Champoeg had prepared for the group's arrival and were waiting with horses to take them to the Methodist mission. As their progress was apparently slowed by the presence of women and children, "it was resolved by the foremost of [their] party to stop at a Frenchman's house until morning."[119] This was most likely the homestead of Joseph Gervais and his third wife, Marie Angelique Chinook (Gervais's second wife Yiamust Clatsop had died in January 1840). Olley and her companions slept "on the floor of the truly hospitable family who entertained us, and supplied us with all the necessaries in their power," and "after partaking of a plentiful and wholesome breakfast," the Americans set off again and arrived safely at the Methodist mission at noon on June 7, 1840.[120]

This unremarked account of assistance received from local Indians and French-Indian families echoes an earlier adventure of Elijah White, which appears to have taken place in the fall of 1837. After a visit to Fort Vancouver, White set out via canoe for the Methodist mission. The doctor reached Willamette Falls with the canoe brigade, and shortly thereafter he decided to travel alone on horseback across French Prairie in the hopes of reaching the mission in half the time it would normally require using the river route. However, White was soon lost, his horse exhausted, and he spent a night shivering in the woods, afraid of an attack by the wolves roaming the Willamette Valley. The next day as he stood on the bank of the Willamette River, a "canoe rounded a point, came directly towards him, and to his joy, he discovered its occupants to be one of his neighbors Mrs. Bilake [Genevieve St. Martin, wife of Pierre Bellique], a youth named Lucia [Lucier], and an Indian crew."[121] Communicating in broken English and some Chinook Jargon, White learned that St. Martin was returning to French Prairie after having been "absent from home for [a] week." Seeing White's hunger and distress, she saw that he was fed and had him board the canoe for the remainder of the trip to her home in Champoeg. The group arrived at "her residence about midnight, and had hardly stepped inside the door, when she called a slave boy, and commanded him to catch up the race-horse immediately." In the meantime, St. Martin "set before her visitor, milk, pork, potatoes and bread." In White's romanticized account of his encounter with St. Martin, she supposedly said (in Chinook Jargon and broken English): "Mrs. White is not far from frightened to death about you. I have ordered a good horse for you, do not spare him, return to your family as fast as he can carry you." White arrived at the mission about 3:00 a.m., and there "enjoyed the happiness of embracing his family, who had become very much alarmed at his prolong[ed] absence."[122]

Following the return of Jason Lee to Oregon in the summer of 1840, questions emerged about Elijah White's conduct in Lee's absence, which led to a trial before members of the mission and eventually to White's resignation. Upon White's break with Jason Lee and the Methodist mission in September 1840, White asked for Blanchet's permission to hold a meeting to transact some business at the Catholic mission before White and his wife departed for the United States. Blanchet, believing this "business" involved members of the Catholic community, agreed to White's request. Rather than a friendly meeting with the local French-Indian community, White had arranged a public meeting with Jason Lee and members of the Methodist mission, other American settlers, and the French-Indian families.[123] His purpose was to vindicate himself in the eyes of the settlers by having the Americans and Canadian settlers act as judges in his confrontation with Jason Lee.[124]

At the meeting, Dr. White proved to be quite the showman and easily disputed, point by point, the series of accusations that Jason Lee had leveled against White, which were related to White's conduct while Lee was away in the United States from March 1838 to June 1840.[125] As to the contention that White had taken "unwarranted liberties with females" at the mission, White simply dismissed the charge with the response that he had only "embraced one."[126] Blanchet described the encounter as a public humiliation for Jason Lee. In the face of White's oratory, Lee defended himself quite poorly, and as a result White gained the support of the French Canadian settlers. Jason Lee's account of the event supports Blanchet's view that White had planned the meeting to publicly humiliate Lee in response to what White perceived as a grave injustice done to him by Lee and the local Methodist leaders.[127]

While the French Canadian settlers declared they were not competent to judge White, they urged Jason Lee to give White all the documents he would need to clear his name and restore his reputation upon his return to the East. Given the public forum, Lee had little choice but to agree. The French Canadians' support for White rested primarily on the doctor's reputation for generosity among the settlers, as White had not charged them for medical visits.[128] Although Blanchet was initially upset that White had used the Catholic mission for a public meeting to discredit Jason Lee, Blanchet later believed that the confrontation between White and Lee had weakened Lee's influence among the French-Indian settlers.

In a letter to his brother Augustin, Blanchet noted that "in this way were all humiliated[,] the enemies of the Catholic Mission."[129] However, although Dr. and Mrs. White departed Oregon on generally good terms with the French Canadians, the incident had strained relations between the Catholic priest and the remaining Methodist ministers.[130]

❋ As Blanchet's initial wrangles with the Methodists demonstrate, the arrival of French Canadian Catholic missionaries marked a turning point in the Willamette Valley. In some respects, Blanchet's presence among the French-Indian families was a boon for the French Prairie settlement. The families were able to attend Mass in French, solemnize their marriages in the Catholic Church, and officially recognize their children. With the construction of the St. Paul mission, the bicultural families created a gathering place where they might also see their children educated in French, while also regularly socializing with their neighbors. In this sense, the erection of a Catholic mission afforded the French-Indian settlers a sociable place of their own, and—in contrast to the Methodist mission—one that might offer personal opportunities for community members. Moreover, Blanchet's ability to accommodate some local conditions within the Catholic mission—legitimizing country marriages, learning Chinook Jargon, and developing the Catholic Ladder—strengthened the community by recognizing its syncretic culture, at least initially.

Blanchet's arrival was not without conflict, however. The resistance by some settlers to Blanchet's administrative approach and his attempt to regulate the marital practices, behavior, and sexuality of the bicultural settlers, particularly the roles of the Native and *métis* women in the settlement, demonstrated that there were limits to the priest's authority and contrasting views on gender within the French Prairie community. While Blanchet sought to curb the agency and cultural influences of the Native and *métis* wives of the settlers in the hopes of creating a social and religious order more in line with the idealized notions of the French Canadian Catholic clergy, both the men and women of the settlement were measured in their response to the priest's overtures. They clearly supported the new Catholic mission, yet they remained comfortable with their long-term practices of cultural accommodation.

The most significant problems in French Prairie resulted from the cultural, institutional, and political differences between Blanchet and the American Methodist missionaries. As a designated Church leader, Blanchet sought to alter the long-standing social dynamics between the French-Indian families and the Methodists. Schooled in the Tridentine and ultramontane traditions of the French Canadian Catholic Church and supportive of the Church's vision for a conservative political nationalism in Lower Canada, Blanchet was especially wary of American attempts to expose Catholic settlers to Protestant heresies and garner French Canadian support for an American annexation of the Willamette Valley. Moreover, the French Canadians' experience with the controversy over the Farnham Memorial demonstrated that lacking literate, educated individuals, the settlers remained at a disadvantage vis-à-vis their American neighbors, who advocated for the populist and republican structures of Jacksonian democracy and evangelical Protestantism. Blanchet's circumspection proved warranted given the swirl of anti-Indian, anti-Catholic, and anti-British sentiments underlying the Farnham petition.

Both political differences and international tensions over British and American territorial claims in the Oregon Country thus began to impact social relations in the Willamette Valley by the late 1830s. The French Canadian settlers remained determined to safeguard their own interests, namely the welfare of their families and property. Their miscalculation over the Farnham Memorial had temporarily strained their relationships with the HBC and showed their vulnerability between the competing interests of the British company and American settlers bent on the annexation of Oregon by the United States. In the coming years, the French Canadian settlers would draw on their previous experience with the Methodists and American settlers, as well as seek the assistance of the local Catholic leader, Francis Blanchet, in responding to the Oregon Trail emigrants who flooded into the Willamette Valley during the 1840s.

The mass migration of American emigrants to the distant Oregon Country was a movement several decades in the making.[131] In the early decades of the nineteenth century, Americans continued to migrate from the eastern seaboard into the Trans-Appalachian West, the Old Northwest, and the Mississippi Valley. Growing demographic pressures on the land and exhausted soils pushed families and entrepreneurs—both northern and southern—to seek new Indian territories for colonization and exploitation. The 1830s proved too early for large-scale emigration from the Mississippi Valley to the Far West, but by the 1840s the same social and economic forces that had driven Americans into the Midwest led many to set their sights on the distant Oregon Country.[132]

Americans were inspired to migrate to the Far West in part because their conception of Oregon closely resembled the semiforested, mixed landscape of their western European agricultural traditions and those of the Midwest, in contrast to the treeless, dry prairies of the Great Plains, then known as the "Great Western Desert."[133] This vision of Oregon developed over the early decades of the 1800s, influenced by proponents of American territorial expansion and seconded by the correspondence and published writings of Methodist missionaries in western Oregon and Presbyterian missionaries in the Plateau region.[134] These boosters of an Anglo-American conquest of the Far West also operated on received notions about the disappearance and decline of the region's Native peoples, which conveniently dovetailed with American views on the racial superiority of Anglo-Saxon civilization. From the 1830s and through the 1850s, published letters and travel accounts penned by American residents and visitors kept Oregon in the public eye, and the overland journeys of the Whitmans and Spaldings in 1836, the Peoria Party in 1839, and the initial wagon trains of the early 1840s demonstrated to Anglo-Americans that overland migration to the distant Pacific Northwest was possible.[135] As Gray Whaley has argued, the American missionaries who journeyed to Oregon in the 1830s and 1840s laid the groundwork for American settler colonialism in the Pacific Northwest by linking American settlement with a "divinely inspired nationalist mission" and by popularizing "the image that Indians were destined to vanish as a consequence of divinely appointed historical processes."[136]

CHAPTER 5 ❋ American Settlers and
Political Initiatives

> The Canadians on the whole are accustomed to feel that they are inferior to no one,
> except those who have emigrated from France; evidences of this appear constantly even
> over the most trifling incidents. Thus they call the finest domestic duck, French duck;
> shoes made of English leather, French shoes; pounds sterling, louis; Europe, France; and
> all white men, Frenchmen. Even the Indians themselves have been so imbued with this
> deep-rooted tradition that an aged guide, an Iroquois Métis whom we asked where a fine
> gun he was carrying over his shoulder had been made, replied that it had come from *la
> vieille France de Londres* (London in old France). Even Napoleon's name is not unknown,
> several natives having named their children in his honor. The settlers' houses are built
> uniformly of wood, lands under cultivation are enclosed with light fences or hedges. At
> each white settlement has been established a mission which serves as a center for the
> French-Canadian colony.

This passage from the travel memoir of Eugene Duflot de Mofras, who visited
Oregon in the fall of 1841, recounts an attitude of cultural superiority among the
French-Indian settlers of the Willamette Valley.[1] Mofras, a diplomat attached to
the French legation of Mexico, was charged with providing the French Foreign
Ministry with much-needed reconnaissance on political, commercial, and geographic conditions in western Mexico, Baja and Alta California, and the Oregon
Country.[2] Mofras's travel memoir, published in 1844, echoed not only French
ambitions in the Pacific but also nostalgia over lost French possessions in North
America, and he clearly played up the superiority of French culture to his francophone readers in Europe. The image of French Canadian settlers in Oregon as
depicted in this short citation might seem a fanciful tale drawn from the imagination of Mofras.[3] Indeed, when referring to both British pounds and American
dollars, the French Canadians commonly used the old French term "piastre," not
louis as suggested by Mofras.[4]

This portrait of the French Canadian settlers expressing matter-of-fact confidence in their French heritage and culture raises questions about how they

perceived themselves in relation to the Anglo-Americans who migrated to the Pacific Northwest via the Oregon Trail during the 1840s—for the new colonizers brought their own sense of national superiority to the Oregon Country, and they were largely ignorant of the French-Indian settlement that flourished there. American emigrants arriving in the Willamette Valley encountered a heterogeneous colonial society, due in large part to the dynamic community created by the French-Indian families. Their long tenure in the valley had allowed them to develop a unique and privileged position in the region. Relying on a diversified economy, the French-Indian families were able to meet their subsistence needs and supply the HBC with wheat and other grains for export to Russian America. While supportive of the local Catholic mission, the settlers demonstrated a degree of independence in their hospitality to outsiders, their continued relations with the Methodist missionaries, and their lively social life.

Given the French-Indians' economic position and long tenure in the valley, their community demonstrated solidarity in the face of several challenges during the 1840s. The community was strengthened by the arrival of French-speaking reinforcements for the Catholic mission, and as increasingly larger groups of Americans migrated to western Oregon, the French Canadian male settlers proved willing to participate in debates about the future of local governance in the Willamette Valley, though the majority did not initially agree with their Anglo neighbors about the need for a more cumbersome governing structure for the colony. The Americans and the French-Indian families maintained a demographic parity in the valley before the migration of 1843, which marked the beginning of an overall change in the Willamette Valley's colonial society. American settlers and visitors, while welcoming assistance from the French-Indian families, tended to criticize their economic and cultural choices in the valley, including the French-Indians' use of the area's natural resources. At the same time, continuing ecological changes in the Willamette Valley negatively affected the economic and subsistence activities of the Kalapuyans, as did the influx of non-Kalapuyans (large numbers of Americans and a smaller number of French-Indian families) who claimed the Natives' land and resources. As the imperial rivalry between the United State and Great Britain over the Oregon Country intensified during the 1840s, the Anglo-Americans progressively gained ascendancy over social, political, and economic institutions in the settler colony, a dominance that was assured by the Oregon Treaty of 1846. In this crucible of American westward expansion, the bicultural families of French Prairie maintained their long-standing focus on community self-interest as they faced new pressures from both the Anglo-American settlers and the elite francophone missionaries.

✳ The settler population in the Willamette Valley increased steadily in the early 1840s. Initially, small parties of Americans made the overland journey to the Willamette Valley: the yearly migrations numbered 13 in 1840, 24 in 1841, and 125 in 1842.[5] A covered wagon caravan of some twenty-five families sponsored by the HBC also migrated from the company's Red River settlement in the Canadian Northwest in 1841. They were originally sent to farm for the Puget Sound Agricultural Company, an HBC subsidiary, at either Fort Nisqually or the Cowlitz post. As both of these sites were located north of the Columbia River, HBC officials intended to bolster British territorial claims to this area and as well as Puget Sound. By 1842, however, these families began to migrate south to the more attractive Willamette Valley. The group included both Anglo-Indian and French-Indian families. The more numerous English-speaking families tended to settle in the Tualatin Plains, while the French-speaking families joined the French-Indian community on the east bank of the Willamette River.[6]

Although French Canadians retiring from the HBC headed the majority of new French-Indian families resettling in the territory of the Willamette Valley Kalapuyans, a small number of French-speaking emigrants from both the United States and Canada made the trek to the Northwest via the Oregon Trail. The 1842 overland party initially headed by Elijah White included a group of seven French Canadians, most notably François Xavier Matthieu, a former trader with the American Fur Company who later became involved in the formation of the Oregon Provisional Government.[7] Beginning with the party known as the Great Migration of 1843, which included some 875 Americans, the Anglo settler population in Oregon jumped dramatically. Thereafter the annual overland emigration from the United States to Oregon ranged between 1,200 (1846) and 4,000 (1847) individuals per year through 1848. John Unruh estimated that 11,512 Americans trekked to Oregon prior to the California Gold Rush of 1849 (see table 8).[8]

In the summer of 1841, the head of the U.S. Exploring Expedition, Lieutenant Charles Wilkes, recorded a figure of 600 for the entire Kalapuyan population of the upper Willamette Valley and 275 for the Upper Chinookans of the lower Willamette Valley.[9] This suggests that the twelve Kalapuyan groups in the valley may have been reduced to bands of approximately fifty members. A more critical reading of Wilkes's estimation would place the indigenous numbers in the valley closer to 1,000 in the early 1840s.[10] Factors that likely influenced Wilkes's

TABLE 8. American overland emigration
to Oregon, 1840–1848

Year	Yearly Total
1840	13
1841	24
1842	125
1843	875
1844	1,475
1845	2,500
1846	1,200
1847	4,000
1848	1,300
Grand Total	11,512

SOURCE: Unruh, *The Plains Across*, 119.

undercounting of the Native population include the brevity of his stay in the valley, his limited contacts with the Kalapuyans, and his reliance on population numbers supplied by Protestant and Catholic missionaries, who shared the prevalent view of Euro-American racial superiority and the steady decline of indigenous groups in the Pacific Northwest.[11]

The Great Migration of 1843 began to tip the population balance in the Willamette Valley, giving the incoming Americans demographic ascendancy over both the French-Indian families and the Kalapuyans, because these two populations did not experience the same level of increase as the Americans. While the Kalapuyan population for the entire valley ranged between 600 and 1,000 (perhaps 50–100 for the Ahantchuyuk), the French-Indian community in French Prairie included about 60 families in the early 1840s and some 600 men, women, and children by the mid-1840s.[12] Following the arrival of another 1,475 Oregon Trail migrants in 1844 and 2,500 in 1845, the American settler population majority began to dominate the colonial society developing in the Willamette Valley.[13] Lt. Henry H. Warre and Lt. Merwin Vavasour, British army officers who reconnoitered the Pacific Northwest in 1845, concluded that "even in 1844 the citizens of the United States formed a large majority over the only British subjects in the Oregon country."[14]

Documentary accounts of the Willamette Valley from the 1840s present a multilayered portrait of French Prairie, while also revealing much about the literate observers who recorded their impressions of the area. Echoing earlier sources from the 1820s and 1830s, American visitors and settlers noted a backwoods, rustic character to the established Willamette Valley settlements, which included both the French-Indian families and Anglo-Indian families of retired fur traders. Although Anglo-American visitors and emigrants recognized the economic and environmental transformations wrought by the French-Indian families in French Prairie by their agricultural production, stock raising, and orchards, the Americans believed that the French Prairie families (as well as the smaller number of Anglo-Indian families) were not as hardworking, disciplined, or entrepreneurial as their American compatriots back in the United States. American visitors such as Lt. Charles Wilkes concluded that the French Canadians and their bicultural families were satisfied with a modest livelihood, which they achieved based on a moderate level of exertion thanks to the region's salubrious climate. For these elites, the French-Indian families lacked a progressive, entrepreneurial mentality because they appeared uninterested in creating new businesses, increasing their wealth, or improving their crop yields. In Wilkes's published account of the U.S. Exploring Expedition, the lieutenant made a clear distinction between French Canadians and Americans: "In passing through the Willamette, I had a good opportunity of contrasting the settlers of different countries; and while those of French descent appeared the most contented, happy, and comfortable, those of the Anglo-Saxon race show more of the appearance of business, and the 'go-head' principle so much in vogue at home."[15]

In 1845 John Dunn, a former postmaster with the HBC, published an account of his years in the Pacific Northwest that featured a rare description of the dwellings of the Willamette Valley settlers' families (both French-Indian and Anglo-Indian) just prior to the Oregon Trail migrations. As an Englishman sympathetic to the HBC, Dunn saw the influence of his former employer as a key factor in the advancement of the settlement, and he criticized the published accounts of Charles Wilkes and Thomas Jefferson Farnham, whom he charged with promoting the Willamette Valley to induce American emigration. Although Dunn viewed American settlers and visitors as interlopers on the Pacific Slope, he too described the colonial outpost in relation to European standards of civilized society:

The residences show different degrees of comfort, according to the property, the intelligence, and industry of the occupiers; from the rude log-structure, of fifteen to twenty feet square, with mud-chimney—a wooden bench in place of chairs—a bedstead covered with flag-mats—a few pots, and other trifling articles, to the large tolerably well-built, and equipped farm-house; in which the owners enjoy, in rude plenty, the produce of tolerably well-tilled, and well-stocked farms. These spots of cultivated land, of course vary in extent and quality of culture according to the skills and resources of the owners. Some farms consist of thirty acres; some consist of one hundred. The best appointed farms are those of the Company's servants. Mr. M'Kay [Thomas McKay], who has a farm under the Company's sanction, has lately erected a grist-mill. . . . These dwellings do not, properly speaking, constitute a village, but are scattered over a surface of several miles, though some few are clustered together.[16]

The tendency of American visitors to Oregon to depict French Canadians and French-Indians as unprogressive and unambitious is reflective of a stereotype then current among middle- and upper-class Protestants in the United States, which had its origins in the imperial rivalry between England and France in North America, the Seven Years' War, and the Revolutionary War.[17] During the antebellum period, Francis Parkman, among others, articulated this stereotype in his popular travelogue *The Oregon Trail* (1849) and later refined it in his multivolume series, *France and England in North America* (1865–1892). In Parkman's view, Anglo-Americans flourished in North America due to the virile, modern, and dynamic nature of English civilization as compared to the economically and intellectually stunted legacies of French colonial America, particularly medieval-style seigneurialism, Roman Catholicism, and absolutist political traditions. This older view of French colonization and French North Americans, fused with the contemporary dynamics of Anglo-Saxon racialism and American territorial expansion, colored American perceptions of French Prairie and the Willamette Valley during the 1840s.[18]

Another factor that influenced American views of French Prairie settlers flowed from the newcomers' conception of the natural world and their preconceived notions about the Pacific Northwest—namely that the Willamette Valley was a promised land destined for American colonization. In the minds of the incoming Anglo-Americans, only they possessed the superior biological origins, inherent abilities, and correct culture and religion to fully and properly develop the natural resources of the Oregon Country.[19] The incoming American emigrants pursued economic and environmental practices in the Willamette Valley that matched this vision of the Oregon Country—all the while comparing their own practices to those of the French-Indian families and the local Kalapuyans. In this sense the Americans sought to recreate the landscapes of their native communities in the eastern woodlands, areas which had experienced generations of transformation with each new wave of European colonization and that were then in the midst of a market revolution that stressed the commodification of well-managed landscapes.[20] Although the French-Indian settlers were active agents in the HBC's two-tiered commercial system in the Pacific region—comprising a northern interior fur trade and a southern provisioning trade—American settlers and visitors saw a less robust, less energetic colony in French Prairie because it did not exactly match the newcomers' home regions in the Midwest and eastern seaboard.[21]

American visitors and emigrants to Oregon saw proof of the arrested development of the French Prairie community in the French Canadians' long-standing domination by the British. Some vocal American settlers believed that HBC officials kept the French-Indian families in a position of semi-servitude because as holders of a monopoly, the officials could set arbitrary prices for both grain and trade goods that the families were obliged to pay.[22] There is some truth to this observation, since Chief Factor McLoughlin paid the farmers for the grain in a combination of cash and HBC goods only accessible through the company stores at Willamette Falls and Fort Vancouver.[23] However, these viewpoints also attest to the Americans' enthusiasm for Jacksonian democracy, the market revolution then transforming the United States, and their antimonopolistic and anti-British sentiments. In viewing the French-Indian families as largely beholden to the HBC, the Americans failed to appreciate that the company was also dependent on the settlers for grain and other food supplies that the company was contracted to sell to the Russian American Company in Alaska. Indeed, through the mid-1840s, the French Canadian settlers, adapting to new economic opportunities, supplied up to three-fourths of the wheat purchased by the HBC for its operational and contract needs.[24]

An analysis of the agricultural data from Elijah White's 1842 enumeration of Willamette Valley settlers reveals that the French-Indian families held a slight edge over the Anglo-American emigrants with regard to the average improved acreage and the amount of wheat and grain produced per farm, while the American and immigrant farmers on average held somewhat larger cattle herds (see table 9). According to White's census, there were roughly sixty male settlers with French surnames farming land claims and some fifty other land claimants with non-French surnames. The average acreage under improvement for the French-speaking settlers was sixty-five, while the average for the Anglo and immigrant settlers was forty-six. The average annual wheat and grain production of the French settlers was 337 bushels and 166 bushels, respectively, compared to the non-French settlers' 310 bushels and 148 bushels. William Bowen's analysis of wheat crop yield reports from 1846 and 1850 revealed a "remarkable concentration of larger than average production units on French Prairie" through the late 1840s. Bowen found that fifteen of the nineteen farms in Oregon producing more than 1,000 bushels of wheat were located in French Prairie, and taken together the fifteen farms generated some 14 percent of Oregon's entire crop.[25]

TABLE 9. French and Anglo settlers in the Willamette Valley: Elijah White's Census, 1842

Male settlers with French surnames with land claims	60
Average acreage under improvement	65 acres
Average wheat production	337 bushels
Average grain production	166 bushels
Average number of horses	19
Average number of neat stock	18
Male settlers with non-French surnames with land claims	50
Average acreage under improvement	46 acres
Average wheat production	310 bushels
Average grain production	148 bushels
Average number of horses	20
Average number of neat stock	37

NOTE: "Neat" refers to common domestive bovine (cattle).
SOURCE: Elijah White's "Census of Settlers in the Oregon Country, 1842."

The diversified economy of the French-Indian families was a rational economic strategy that resembled the economies of other bicultural Native-European settlements in North America also transitioning from a primary reliance on the fur trade to an expanded engagement with agriculture production and animal husbandry.[26] The French Prairie settlers raised grains, domestic animals, fruits (apples, pears, and peaches) and vegetables (especially peas and beans) for subsistence, barter, and sale at both the local and regional level.[27] They sold their surplus grain to the HBC in exchange for European trade goods and additional foodstuffs. And despite Charles Wilkes's critique of the Willamette Valley settlers, he documented both the superior yield of the valley farms and the very favorable condition for stock raising.[28] The French-Indian families also continued to supplement their wheat production with trade in animal pelts. The availability of wild game in the valley gave the French-Indian families both a ready food source and a product for trade with the HBC. These included the remaining beaver, elk, deer, antelope, bear, wolf, fox, muskrat, and marten populations in the Willamette Valley.[29]

As no official currency was in circulation, the local economy operated on a dual system. By the 1830s, the fur trade value standard of "made beaver" had begun to be replaced by grain as the common unit of exchange.[30] The settlers received credit in bushels for their grain at the HBC store at Fort Vancouver and later Oregon City, in order to obtain manufactured goods. They also shared farm implements, engaged in communal labor at neighboring farms, and bartered goods, services, and foodstuffs with their fellow French Prairie families, local Kalapuyans, and nearby American settlers.[31] Former Methodist missionary Margaret Jewett Bailey, who lived in the Champoeg area with her husband William Bailey, recounted an instance in which two of her neighbors shared ownership of a horse-drawn cart. In another instance, a local "Frenchman" planned to break ground for Margaret's husband and, oblivious to Protestant views of the Sabbath, sent his plow ahead on a Sunday morning.[32] Although the documentary record on French Prairie for the 1840s focuses largely on the economic roles of French Canadian men, it is clear that the Native and *métis* women of the settlement continued to make essential contributions to the family economy through their economic, domestic, and reproductive labor. They were also active in the trade and barter systems, and they were willing to approach local Anglo-American women to obtain desired goods and services. Margaret Bailey regularly faced barter requests from the Native wives of the French Canadian settlers. One neighbor begged Bailey for one of her calico dresses, which she declined to give her; another insisted that Bailey accept a cow in exchange for one of Bailey's silk dresses.[33]

Equally important, marriage to the daughters of established Willamette Valley settlers afforded newly retired French Canadian voyageurs access to social networks, community support, labor resources, land, farm implements, and domestic animals (see tables 10a and 10b).[34] From a total of 104 French-speaking settlers who either registered their land claims with the Oregon Provisional Government (91) or had their farms mentioned in the descriptions of recorded land claims (13), 77 percent were French Canadian, 19 percent French-Indian, 2 percent French American, 1 percent French, and 1 percent Native. Of the 93 confirmed settlers who were married, 47 percent of the wives were *métis* women of French-Indian ancestry, 43 percent were Native, 4 percent were Natives of mixed ancestry (Iroquois, Hawaiian, or Nipissing fathers and regional Indian mothers), 2 percent Anglo-Indian women, 1 percent French Canadian, 1 percent French American, and 1 percent Anglo-American. The ancestry of the settlers' wives reveals that some 53 percent of the women in the French Prairie community were the daughters of fur laborers (French Canadian, Anglo-Celtic, Iroquois, Nipissing, Hawaiian, and American), while 43 percent were Native women almost entirely from key trade areas in the Columbia Plateau and the Northwest Coast (present-day Oregon, Washington, and British Columbia). In contrast to the French Prairie marriage data from about a decade earlier in 1839 (see table 7), the statistics from the late 1840s point to a subtle shift in the choice of marriage partners for the French Canadians retired from the fur trade and their French-Indian sons who were

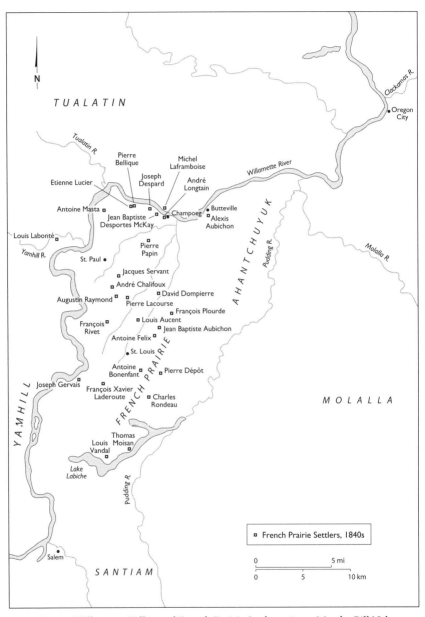

MAP 4. Lower Willamette Valley and French Prairie Settlers, 1840s. Map by Bill Nelson.

starting to come of age and establish households of their own. All but one (Jean Baptiste Dorion) of the nineteen younger French-Indian men married women of a similar background, the mixed-race daughters of fur traders.

The French Prairie settlers further contributed to the development of the settler economy in the Willamette Valley by their support for various enterprises. In the early 1840s, Francis Norbert Blanchet and Modeste Demers obtained a gristmill through the HBC and had it installed at the St. Paul mission with the help of local parishioners (in 1847, Blanchet sold the mill to settlers Miles McDonald and James McKay).[35] Blanchet and the Frenchman Pierre Stanislaus Jacquet also invested in American-led efforts to transport more cattle and horses from Mexican California during the mid-1840s. A number of French Canadians and their sons signed on for the cattle drive from California, and some also worked temporarily tending and herding the animals for the Willamette Cattle Company in the valley.[36] By meeting their needs through a mixed economy based on agricultural production, hunting, trapping, barter, and communal and paid labor, the French-Indian families adapted aspects of their former occupations in the fur trade and their agricultural heritage from Lower Canada.[37] This mixed approach suited the settlers at the time because it allowed them to maximize the use of their local resources while also spreading economic risk.

While the French Prairie families pursued a diversified economy that remained relatively stable through the 1840s, their resettlement of the Ahantchuyuk territory continued to have a detrimental effect on the local Kalapuyans. The major factor affecting the Ahantchuyuk and other Kalapuyan groups was the ongoing ecological transformation of the Willamette Valley that had begun with the introduction of fur trapping in the 1810s and the establishment of Euro-American agriculture and husbandry during the 1820s. The steady rise in the non-Kalapuyan population combined with the increasingly commercialized operations throughout the Willamette Valley accelerated this large-scale environmental modification.[38] The French-Indian settlers and the incoming Americans hunted local game and fowl, plowed prairie land and native grasses, and allowed their farm animals to forage at will on Kalapuyan staples such as camas and *wapato,* and on the valley vegetation once reserved for wild game.[39] By trapping the fur-bearing animals, hunting wild game, and increasing the acreage reserved for stock raising and agriculture, the French Prairie settlers necessarily reduced the Kalapuyans' access to vegetable staples and protein sources for subsistence and traditional materials needed for production, trade, and religious practices.[40] This contraction of the Kalapuyans' territory and resources intensified the disruption to their economy and food supply, which had not recovered from the devastating impact of the intermittent fever epidemics of the 1830s. The combined effect of these changes on the society, economy, health, and spirituality of the Kalapuyans led to increased periods of hunger, susceptibility to introduced diseases, and continued population decline.[41]

Surrounded by a growing settler population, the Kalapuyans were well aware of the emigrants' ecological transformation of the Willamette Valley.[42] Despite vocal opposition from the Americans, small bands of Kalapuyans continued to follow their traditional subsistence rounds and to burn portions of the Willamette Valley on an annual basis as they were able.[43] They also sought assistance and work in the settler communities. This may have been more prevalent in the Ahantchuyuk–French Prairie area, given the long-standing relations between the Kalapuyans and the French-Indian families. French Canadian emigrant François-Xavier Matthieu, who arrived in Oregon in 1842, remembered that Negro slavery "did not make much of stir on French Prairie" in the mid-1800s because there was a pool of low-wage Indian laborers ready to work on local farms or man canoes in the river. According to Matthieu, these Indians worked in exchange for food-stuffs and goods such blankets.[44] However, given the French-Indian families' reliance on aboriginal slave labor, Matthieu's observations, like those of other settlers such as Willard Rees, point to a continued exploitation of Native slaves in French Prairie through the 1840s and early 1850s.[45]

Although the French-Indian settlers left little in the way of written documents, the writings of elites such as Father Blanchet and literate observers from outside the community provide a small window into the settlers' community life during the 1840s. Mofras wrote of the settlers' supposed sense of ethnic superiority, while other observers remarked on the colonists' warmth, openness, and hospitality. For example, John Minto, who arrived in the Willamette Valley in the fall of 1844, recalled that the Canadians "were kindly and hospitable to the incoming Americans but seemed scarcely to understand them."[46] François Xavier Matthieu told interviewer Horace Lyman in the late 1890s that "all the settlers of the Prairie he found to be hospitable in the extreme; they were willing to share with the stranger anything they had."[47] Duflot de Mofras, like Jason Lee several years before, noted the gregarious, sociable attitude of the French Canadians. When Mofras visited the settlement in the fall of 1841, the French Canadians plied the French traveler for information about France. They gave him a warm welcome at their farms, loaned him the "best horses," and supplied him with guides for his exploration of the Willamette Valley.[48] American emigrant Willard Rees, who settled in French Prairie in 1845 after purchasing a farm from a local French Canadian, recalled that "these old Canadian voyageurs were a very kind people;

they dispensed with a liberal hand alike to stranger and friend the rude hospitality of those primitive times, to a degree unknown to the country since the disturbing innovations that swept over their Eden home in 1849–1850, borne from the gold-glittering Sierras of the south."[49]

The observations of Margaret Bailey, which she aired in her autobiographical novel, *The Grains* (1854), point to complexity in the social relations between Anglo-American and French-Indian settlers in the Willamette Valley during the 1840s and early 1850s. As a devout, educated Methodist, Bailey came to Oregon in the late 1830s with idealized notions about proper interpersonal etiquette, religious practice, and gender roles based on the cultural, religious, and racial notions of her upbringing and conversion experience in New England. In her view, Oregon lacked a tidy social order comparable to that of the northeastern United States. While Bailey struggled with her Christian vocation, male authority, an abusive marriage, and the social ostracism that resulted from her own outspokenness, she could be empathetic in her relations with the local Native and *métis* women of French Prairie.[50] Bailey observed some of the hardships that the women and children of French Prairie faced due to domestic violence and alcoholism. At one point during Margaret and William Bailey's fifteen years (1839–1854) in French Prairie, they took in "a little French girl," so severely beaten by her aunt that she had a broken collarbone and contusions on her head as well as "finger and toe nails nearly all torn off."[51] On another occasion, Margaret Bailey received a morning visit from a "half-breed young woman," whom Bailey "much loved," and the young woman's husband. The man was "much intoxicated," and so his "amiable wife tried to hide his shame." Bailey expressed admiration for the woman's patience with her husband and recorded the woman's statement that her husband "never was intoxicated till he went to the infamous John Hoard's [*sic*]" saloon in Champoeg.[52] In another instance, Doctor Bailey was "called to a Frenchman, who in a drunken frolic, set out to run a race with one foot in the stirrup and no bridle on his horse."[53] The man was thrown from the horse and barely survived.

Margaret Bailey also noted the domestic tribulations of Angelique Carpentier, the *métis* orphan who had been raised at the Methodist mission with her sister Sophie following the death of their father in the 1830s. Upon leaving the mission as a teenager in the 1840s, Angelique married a settler of part-Hawaiian ancestry, Peter Anderson, in a civil ceremony and had several children.[54] Bailey received a visit from Angelique in the early 1850s during which the young woman recounted her difficulty caring for her children due to a physical deformity. According to

Bailey, Angelique's right shoulder had grown "very large," but her left shoulder had not grown at all, and she was bent "nearly double." Angelique attributed the condition to her early years at the Methodist mission when she was forced to carry the children of Susan (Downing) Shepard, widow of Cyrus Shepard, "when she was small and not well."[55] Bailey confirmed Angelique's observations about her time at the mission and agreed with her wish to ask Susan Shepard to come care for Angelique's children in her hour of need. Angelique may have lacked family support in the early 1850s because her sister Sophie Carpentier and her brother-in-law, Cesaire Beaudoin, who had married at St. Paul in 1844, were no longer living in French Prairie at the time. Sophie and Cesaire had served as the godparents to Angelique's first child, Louise, in 1846, but they disappeared from Catholic Church records after 1848 and were apparently absent from the baptism of Angelique's son George in 1852.[56]

Although intended as a criticism of her former missionary colleagues, Bailey's description of Angelique Carpentier's domestic trials points to the interconnections between race and gender in French Prairie and the Pacific Northwest during the 1840s and 1850s. While Margaret Bailey had regular contact with local Native and *métis* women married to French Canadians, white settler women did not necessarily share Bailey's attitude of friendliness. On another occasion, Bailey had a visit from Marie Marguerite Chinook, the second wife of Etienne Lucier, who told Bailey that the "wives of the French" said that she was "the only one of the Boston missionary women whom they like," because she was "always the same, kind, pleasant, and social and never too proud to speak to them."[57] Bailey also mentioned one enterprising American woman, who "has been pleased in passing about the country, to accept [Bailey's] hospitality in preference to staying at houses where Indian women are in the head."[58] Margaret Bailey apparently shared some of the racial views of her Anglo-American compatriots, for she remarked that "some French neighbors have bought barouches—undoubtedly their Indian wives will now *out-shine* the white ladies."[59] The ability of the French Canadians to purchase a luxury item such as a barouche—a four-wheeled carriage with a front seat for the driver and central seats that allow two couples to face each other—would have been beyond the means of recently arrived Oregon Trail emigrants focused on obtaining land, shelter, and supplies for farming operations.

The racialized thinking that created tension between Native women and American women are echoed in the memoirs of Martha Ann (Morrison) Minto, who married settler John Minto in 1846. Prior to her marriage, Minto lived with her family in the Clatsop Plains on a farm that her father rented from Solomon Smith and Celiast Clatsop. In an interview from 1878, Minto recalled the hardships and privations her family endured upon their arrival in Oregon and noted what she perceived to be an air of superiority expressed by Celiast Clatsop, whom Minto also saw as particularly strong willed.[60] Similarly, over the winter of 1851–1852, Elizabeth (Miller) Wilson, a recent emigrant from New York State, met John McLoughlin and his French-Ojibway wife Marguerite Wadin McKay. Wilson recalled that McLoughlin was

> chivalrous in his courtesy to women. Though his wife was a half breed of the Objiway nation[,] course, haut, fat, and flabby, he treated her like a princess in public and in private he was as loyal to her as if she was a daughter of the Queen Victoria. In handing her out to dinner he saw that she was assigned a place of honor; that is to say he would suffer no indignity or slight to her. His fine handsome form beside the uncorseted figure of the old Indian woman presented a strange contrast as she waddled beside him like one of another species. His gallantry to her knew no bounds. On state occasions, straight as an arrow, & magnificently appareled, he would stand like a splendid statue while this female aboriginal rolled out before him in plain clothes and no figure whatsoever.[61]

As illustrated in these examples, American women settlers took umbrage at the stance of Native and *métis* women who saw themselves as equal to and even superior to the Anglo emigrants. The American women's desire for social status and for separation from Indian and mixed-race women points to a racialization of the Pacific Northwest during the 1840s and 1850s—a process that turned in part on conceptions of fashion, femininity, domesticity, and social decorum so important to middle-class Protestants.[62] These social and cultural changes taking place in western Oregon reflected the central and interconnected roles of race and gender in the Anglo settler colonization of both the United States and Canada during the 1800s.[63]

Although Margaret Bailey remained on friendly terms with the French-Indian settlers, she found these relationships to be rather challenging at times due to the religious and cultural differences separating the bicultural Catholic families and herself, a devout, middle-class, Anglo-American Protestant from New England. In Bailey's eyes the French Prairie settlers lacked education, sophistication, and an appreciation for her religious principles, and they demonstrated behaviors and attitudes that were morally censurable. She complained that her interactions with her "French" neighbors left her in "want of [C]hristian society." According to Bailey, "the principle ornaments of conversation" in the quarter were "infidelity, blasphemy, worldliness, and all manner of ungodliness."[64] Bailey was particularly annoyed by the settlers' lively social activities on Sunday. Rather than spend the day in prayer or quiet contemplation, the French-Indian settlers were wont to "cart and pack their wheat to mill, go for their flour, trade cattle and horses, gamble, run races, &c., on the Sabbath."[65] Bailey even noted with distress that during the funeral procession to bury Marie Chehalis, wife of François Quesnel, in May 1841, two men left the procession to examine some nearby wheat.[66] She could not understand how the settlers could be so "profane and intemperate" and "not lose their standing in the church!"[67]

Bailey's ingrained anti-Catholic views led her to misperceive the settlers' relationship with both Catholic Church officials and the officers of the HBC. Anglo-American settler Medorem Crawford confirmed that the French-Indian families engaged in social activities such as horse racing that were viewed with disfavor by Chief Factor John McLoughlin at the regional HBC headquarters in Vancouver. Crawford asserted that McLoughlin kept himself informed of the settlers' activities and would reprimand them for their intemperate behavior.[68] So too would the resident Catholic priest, Father Blanchet. His letters from the 1840s contain continued criticism of what Blanchet perceived to be morally disreputable conduct among the French-Indian settlers. When Blanchet traveled to Fort Vancouver to perform funeral services for HBC clerk William Kittson a few days after Christmas in 1841, the Willamette settlers took the opportunity to organize a dancing ball at the farm of Andre Longtain at Champoeg. The event itself was not as troubling to Blanchet as the fact that the French Canadians had invited Protestants and "three men living in concubinage."[69]

Blanchet took the settlers' behavior personally, feeling that it reflected poorly on both himself and the Catholic Church. The priest attributed the settlers' robust social calendar to his frequent absences for missionary activities and to the "work of the demon." He reacted by redoubling his efforts to instruct and supervise the settlers, and he petitioned his superiors in Quebec for additional missionaries to aid him at St. Paul.[70] In an undated letter to Joseph Signay, Bishop of Quebec City, from 1842, Blanchet further elaborated on the settlers' behavior and his efforts to reform the populace: "The disorder reigned in the village of the engagés, the vice showed itself with affront. The fear of God and his judgments . . . with the help of grace and the protection of Marie, patron of the chapel, had begun to be felt. The criminal liaisons were broken or changed into holy alliances. The symbols of the apostles and the ten commandments were explained in a series of evenings."[71]

For Blanchet, the French-Indian families stubbornly clung to attitudes and practices that reflected their history in the fur trade, as well as the independent streak of the Lower Canadian peasantry. Duflot de Mofras, however, viewed Blanchet's role in a more positive light. The Frenchman saw in the settlers a willingness to follow the priest's guidance in the absence of civil authority, noting a "touching incident indicative" of Blanchet's "patriarchal justice." After a community council comprising several French Canadians and presided over by Blanchet found a French Canadian guilty of having stolen the horse of an American, the man received a stiff sentence. He was ordered to return the horse and remain outside the door of the mission church without entering for three months. After the second week, Blanchet allowed the man to rejoin the congregation. Mofras concluded that Blanchet's punishment was so effective because it embodied a type of restorative justice that redeemed the individual while also strengthening the community.[72] The observations of Mofras demonstrate Blanchet's ongoing efforts to mold French Prairie to the idealized social order of the Tridentine tradition in French Canadian Catholicism. Through a public trial combined with a communal punishment involving church attendance and access to the sacraments, the priest sought to ensure that social reconciliation and community inclusion flowed through the authority of the Catholic Church and its representative, Blanchet.[73]

Although Blanchet criticized the morality and social behavior of the French-Indian settlers—including what he perceived as their inconsistent respect for his authority—both he and outside observers remarked on the general community-wide importance of the Catholic mission and the religious practices of its members. The "great dispersion of the dwellings," weather constraints in the winter and fall, the men's intense work schedules in the sowing and harvest seasons, and the long work hours of the women constrained Blanchet's efforts to ensure regular church attendance and religious instruction in the community. Nonetheless, Blanchet reported continued success in the recitation of prayers within the family homes and increased knowledge of the catechism.[74] For her part, Margaret Bailey lamented the fact that by the 1840s, "not one of the Indians, half-breeds, or whites who joined the mission church during the great revival of religion . . . in 1839 or previously to that time, are now members of the Methodist Church."[75] Bailey was further aggrieved that all but one of the Indian and *métis* children who had been educated at the Methodist mission had apparently become Catholics under the influence of Blanchet and the local Catholic settlers. This one exception may have been Angelique Carpentier: although she had her children baptized in the Catholic church, she did not marry in the church and expressed limited interest in organized religion.[76] Aside from outliers such as Angelique Carpentier, the French-Indian families showed their continued support for the local Catholic church by attending Sunday mass as they were able and by donating their labor to the mission farm on a rotating basis. The proceeds from the crops raised on the farm went toward the support of the Church and its social services, which included education and the care of widows and orphans.[77]

✳   With the growth of the settler population in the Pacific Northwest, Father Francis Norbert Blanchet petitioned both Bishop Signay in Quebec City and HBC governor George Simpson in Red River for additional staff for the Columbia mission. In the fall of 1842, French Canadian priests Antoine Langlois and Jean Baptiste Zacharie Bolduc arrived by boat from Boston via the Sandwich Islands (Hawai'i) after having spent nearly a year in transit. They served as deacons for the first High Mass celebrated at St. Paul on September 18, 1842. Shortly thereafter, Blanchet assigned Bolduc to the Cowlitz mission and Langlois to the Willamette Valley, where Langlois also supervised the newly established St. Joseph College for boys at St. Paul.[78]

The Roman Catholic mission in the Pacific Northwest received a group of European reinforcements in 1844 following months of negotiation between Church officials and religious orders in Quebec, the United States, and Europe. These missionaries, headed by the Belgian Jesuit Pierre-Jean DeSmet, included four other Jesuits and six francophone nuns from the Belgian order of Notre Dame de Namur.[79] The group arrived at St. Paul in mid-August 1844 following a long sea voyage aboard the *Indefatigable*. While most of the Jesuits, notably DeSmet, later set out for other missionary fields in the Pacific Northwest, the six sisters of Notre Dame de Namur remained in the area, establishing female academies in St. Paul and later in the burgeoning town of Oregon City. In November 1844, Blanchet received a packet of letters from his superior, the bishop of Quebec, which had been forwarded from Rome. Nearly a year earlier, in December 1843, Pope Gregory XVI had erected a new vicariate apostolic covering the Oregon Country and appointed Blanchet bishop of the new vicariate, which was named after the ancient diocese of Philadelphia (later changed to Drasa).[80]

Like other literate observers, the sisters of Notre Dame de Namur left a written record of their time in French Prairie that reveals as much about the European missionaries as about the French-Indian settlers whom the women sought to inspire to Catholic religious devotion and a healthy respect for French culture. This first group of six nuns in Oregon included Sister Ignace de Loyola (Rosalie Duquenne), Sister Marie Catherine (Marie Therese Cabareaux), Sister Marie Aloysia (Jeannette Chevry), Sister Marie Cornelia (Marie Antoinette Caroline Neujean), Sister Norbertine (Seraphine Verreux), and Sister Marie Albine (Joseph Gobert), with Sister Loyola serving as the superior of the missionary group.[81] The sisters' letters to their superior in Namur, Mother Constantine, shine a light on the role of gender in cultural interactions at the St. Paul mission and offer some additional clues as to the historical experience of the French Prairie families during the 1840s.

The correspondence—in rather effusive terms—attests to the settlers' ongoing support for the Catholic mission and their attendance at major religious observances, which appear as important community events in the sisters' letters. For the missionaries' first feast of the Assumption of the Virgin Mary at St. Paul in August 1844, various families throughout French Prairie made the trek to St. Paul, some having set out from their farms the night before while others brought food provisions to last the entire day. Once arrived, the settlers filed into the church and sat segregated by gender, men to one side and women to the other. Monsignor Blanchet celebrated the Assumption Mass, which featured a children's choir of some twenty youngsters. Following the Mass, the women and children of the parish were particularly interested in chatting with the Belgian nuns and expressing gratitude for their labors at the mission.[82] Native women also assisted in cleaning and preparing the church for special occasions, while their husbands contributed freshly cut branches and garlands of flowers.[83]

From the perspective of the Sisters of Notre Dame de Namur, the women and children of French Prairie were enthusiastic in their response to the nuns' efforts at general religious instruction and the more focused preparations for important milestones such as the sacrament of communion. Over the fall of 1844, as the nuns waited for local workers to finish the construction of their convent and school, the women commenced teaching the women and children of the settlement in the open area. As with Blanchet's early missions in the Willamette Valley, women and children from farms at a considerable distance chose to camp out nearby in order to attend the sisters' catechism lessons. The women brought melons, potatoes, eggs, and butter and shared them among themselves and with the nuns. While the sisters appreciated the friendliness of the French Prairie women, they expressed irritation with the workers building the convent and school because the men insisted on being paid for their work when the nuns had yet to raise any funds from the mission farm or the school.

Eventually several of the nuns pitched in to speed up the construction work, and Sister Loyola negotiated with the workers to complete the convent in time for winter. Once the buildings were completed later in the fall of 1844, the sisters welcomed both day students and boarders to the school, known as Sainte Marie du Willamette.[84] The majority of the girls enrolled at the school in 1850, seventeen out of twenty-one, had parents of French Canadian and Native or *métis* ancestry, while the remaining four pupils had Iroquois fathers and Chinookan mothers. The student body included a mixture of children from prominent French-Indian families, such as Ester Bellique (French-Chinook), Lucie Perrault (French-Chehalis), and Angelique Plamondon (French-Métis/Cree), as well as from more recently arrived families, some of whom later became orphans, such as Marie Adeline Liard and her sister Marguerite (French-Nez Perces), Marie Presse (French-Tlingit), and Marianne Laurent and her sisters Catherine and Cecile (Iroquois-Chinook).[85]

The missionary outlook of the sisters of Notre Dame de Namur combined the evangelicalism of the ultramontane Catholic Church, European racialism, and the domestic ideology that characterized the expansion of Catholic female religious orders in Europe and North America during the 1800s. Having come of age in the aftermath of the anticlericalism and antireligious fervor of the French Revolution and the subsequent revival of French Catholicism, the sisters of Notre Dame de Namur shared an apostolic faith focused on religious education and social welfare, and like Monsignor Blanchet they were committed to a Eurocentric civilizing mission in Oregon.[86] Influenced by the racialist ideology current in Europe and North America, the sisters were particularly focused on rescuing the mixed-race children of French Prairie from the cultural and religious influence of their Indian mothers and the apparently lackadaisical upbringing of their French Canadian fathers. While the Belgian nuns believed the Native women of French Prairie to be "good at heart," they, like the literate Anglo-American women in Oregon, viewed the Indian women and their offspring as uncivilized individuals in need of cultural and spiritual uplift.[87]

As Blanchet had concluded several years earlier, the sisters of Notre Dame de Namur faulted the girls' French Canadian fathers for focusing their energies on their farming operations, which left the education and upbringing of their children to the men's Native wives.[88] The nuns viewed it as their task to correct this error by instructing the girls in the proper role, behavior, and presentation for women as represented by the domestic ideology of French Catholicism in the postrevolutionary period. Although female religious orders in Europe—and particularly in France—sought to expand their activities in social welfare, education, and missionary work, they did not overtly challenge the male-dominated hierarchy of the Roman Catholic Church. As a result, the society and culture that the sisters of Notre Dame de Namur encountered in French Prairie contravened their view of an idealized society that mandated religious devotion and a healthy respect for order, regimentation, and European notions of class, race, and gender.[89]

One of the sisters' first priorities was to educate the *métis* girls, and by extension their Indian mothers, about the importance of cleanliness, domesticity, and good order in the home. The nuns complained in detail about the children's poor hygiene and shoddy clothing, as well as the prevalence of lice. The missionaries banished the lice, made white uniforms for the students, instructed their charges in sewing, needlework, and knitting, and showed the girls how to keep a home neat, tidy, and properly decorated with Catholic icons that would encourage religious devotion within the family.[90] Accustomed to the austerity of Gallic Catholicism, Sister Marie Aloysius wrote to Mother Constantine of the worldly presentation and comportment of the French Prairie girls, who followed the fashions of their Indian mothers: "All the vanity of our little girls consists of adorning their heads with bits of old ribbon, red, yellow, or whatever color. They are quite happy to tie up their hair with a piece of a handkerchief or an apron. Leather is quite expensive here: shoes, such as you will find, are the most beautiful ornament of the women, to which they attach a piece of cloth to serve as a kind of stocking, all of which is covered with beads to form various designs."[91]

Rather than appreciate the handiwork, artistry, and clothing traditions of the Native women of French Prairie, the sisters of Notre Dame de Namur saw evidence of social disorder and a lack of conformity to the middle-class standards of fashion and modesty prevalent in Western Europe. Some of the Catholic Oregon Trail emigrants who settled in French Prairie concurred with the position of the nuns. When Irish-born Hugh Cosgrove and his wife Mary first attended Mass at Saint Paul in 1847, the couple's approach to fashion caused a stir and set Mary Cosgrove on a mission of cultural uplift directed at the women of French Prairie:

> At the meeting, however, where the appearance of strangers caused minute observations, the men all sitting on one side and the women on the other, there were no bonnets—the women wore only a red handkerchief tied over the head; and the latest style bonnets from the east created not only admiration, but much suppressed—though not very well suppressed—merriment in the congregation. On returning home, Mrs. Cosgrove was very dispirited, and exclaimed, "To think that I have brought my family here to raise them in such as place as this!" However, taking up the difficulty in a truly womanly way, she soon had the women of the neighborhood making sun-bonnets, and then instructed them how to weave wheat straw and make chip hats and in course of time they even put on bonnets.[92]

The position of the Catholic nuns and the American Catholic emigrants stood in some contrast to contemporary male observers such as John Minto and Charles Wilkes. In an interview recorded in the late 1800s, Minto recalled that the gaily dressed daughters of the French Prairie settlers were "a sight worth notice as many of them were fine specimens of physical beauty and they sat on horseback as though they were themselves part of the animal they rode."[93] Although Wilkes shared the nuns' view of the superiority of European culture, he did express admiration for the skill, character, and devotion of French Canadians' Native wives:

The ladies of the country [Willamette Valley] are dressed after our own bygone fashions, with the exception of leggings, made of red and blue cloth, richly ornamented. Their feet, which are small and pretty, are covered with worked moccasins. Many of them have a dignified look and carriage: their black eyes and hair, and brown ruddy complexion, combined with a pleasing expression, give them an air of independence and usefulness that one little expects to see. As wives, they are spoken of as most devoted, and many of them have performed deeds in the hour of danger and difficulty, worthy of being recorded. They understand the character of Indians as well.[94]

In a similar vein, the day school students and boarders demonstrated an independent streak in their interactions with the Belgian nuns, which the sisters attributed to the "habitudes sauvages" the children gleaned from their mothers. In response, the sisters emphasized order, discipline, and in some cases corporal punishment for students who demonstrated what the sisters perceived as a disrespectful attitude—likely a lack of deference to the missionaries and the strict educational environment they sought to cultivate.[95]

The letters of the sisters of Notre Dame de Namur to their superior in Belgium, Mother Constantine, attest to the nuns continued devotion to their missionary vocation and their perseverance in overcoming the challenges of life in the Willamette Valley during the 1840s. They were wont to write enthusiastically of the support received from the French Canadians and the men's desire for religious and secular education for their children, especially instruction in reading. Such a position was certainly consistent with the earliest settlers' appeals for French Canadian missionaries in the 1830s. Nevertheless, the nuns' experience in French Prairie during the 1840s was complex. While the French Prairie settlers clearly endorsed the Catholic mission schools in St. Paul, several factors prevented the attainment of the idealized religious community the Belgian nuns so dearly sought. Perhaps most importantly, both class differences and practical considerations impinged on the missionary project. The sisters eventually concluded that as the offspring of farmers and laborers, their charges were most likely destined to become wives and mothers on nearby farms rather than enjoy the life of genteel middle-class ladies. This realization is reflected in the letters to Mother Constantine where the sisters note the need for some families to withdraw their daughters from the school so that they could help their families back on the farm. The sisters also felt that while many children picked up sewing and reading skills fairly quickly, they did not have the aptitude for advanced subjects such as science and mathematics.[96] Finally, in addition to their contributions to the family economy, girls in French Prairie tended to marry as teenagers, which was the case with Nancy Pin, one of the rare students whom the nuns mentioned by name in their published letters.

In the fall of 1845, Nancy Pin and her companions reportedly dictated a short letter to Mother Constantine with the assistance of Sister Loyola. The letter, which follows the syntax of Canadian French, contains greetings of appreciation and a curious reference to the missionaries' need for reinforcements from Belgium:

My Dear Mother,

We are happy to write to you again to wish you a happy New Year and to say that we are content as always with your Sisters, and to thank you again for having sent them. When will the other Sisters come? Too much work for the Sisters here: we all would love to have a little girl from your country; we're not able to learn good manners without seeing her. When will you send her? We all at this town are a little bit good. We all will behave better if you pray for us. Dear Mother, give your blessing to your submissive children.

Nancy Pin and her companions

(dictated but correctly spelled by them)

Nancy Pin, who was then about fifteen years of age, did not complete her education at St. Marie du Willamette. In February 1847 at the age of sixteen or seventeen, she married Gideon Gravelle, a French Canadian then in his mid-twenties who had settled on a farm next to that of Nancy's parents in Yamhill County. Modeste Demers, who officiated their wedding, noted that the spouses could not sign their names to the parish register.[97] It is not surprising that Nancy Pin married as a teenager because she was the eldest daughter of Joseph Pin, a retired French Canadian voyageur, and his wife, Marguerite Pend d'Oreille (Interior Salish), and because this was not an unusual age for brides in French Prairie during the 1840s.[98] The Catholic Church records from the 1840s are replete with marriages between teenage Native and *métis* women and French Canadian settlers who ranged in age from early adulthood to advanced middle age. Indeed, when the Willamette Valley settlers adopted the first Organic Law for Oregon in the summer of 1843, they agreed on regulations that set the age for marriage at sixteen for men and fourteen for the women, provided that individuals under twenty-one received their parents' consent.[99] Nancy and Gideon had their first child in January 1848 and went on to have four more children during their years in French Prairie. The family moved to the French-Indian community of Frenchtown, near Walla Walla, Washington, in the 1860s.[100] The experience of Nancy Pin and her contemporaries underlines the practical considerations, economic responsibilities, and family strategies that restrained the influence of the Sisters of Notre Dame de Namur, as well as the local Catholic male clergy.

As the girls of French Prairie entered their teenage years, they married local settlers and took on essential roles in economic production and social reproduction within their community. Indeed, single male settlers from Lower Canada such as Gideon Gravelle sought marriage alliances with French Prairie families in order to gain access to both female labor and the social networks needed to succeed as a farmer. For the most part, the young women of French Prairie who were fortunate to attend St. Marie du Willamette did not remain for an extended number of years, which was the custom for middle-class girls placed in Catholic female academies in Europe. Thus while the sisters of Notre Dame de Namur sought to bring the local French-Indian families under the authority of the Catholic Church and under the sway of French Catholicism more particularly, their influence was circumscribed during the 1840s. The goals of the Catholic missionary project were to neutralize the autonomy and cultural influence of the Native women of the community as well as the independent streak and folk culture of the French Canadian laborers, yet it is important to take a nuanced view of the process of acculturation to European cultural practices and gender norms prior to the American annexation of Oregon. The French Prairie settlers certainly faced social and cultural pressures from both the increasing Anglo-American population and the Canadian and European missionaries schooled in the superiority of French Catholicism. However, the long-standing nature of the French-Indian community, its economic stability, the inhabitants' reliance on endogamy, and the practical limitations on these outside forces constrained their coercive power during the 1840s.[101]

❋   In the years prior to the Oregon Treaty of 1846, a series of events tested the bicultural community of French Prairie, raising questions about the nature of their relations with the American Methodists and American settlers in the Willamette Valley. While the actions of the American settlers and Methodists have been studied in some depth, the French-Indian perspective on these events has been given less attention.[102] The first event was a controversy over the prosecution of French Canadian Jean Baptiste Perrault for theft in 1841; the second was the attempt at organizing a settler government following the death of American Ewing Young in 1841; and the third was the formation of the provisional government in Oregon during the mid-1840s, a government in which literate, educated Anglo-Americans played a dominant role.

The prosecution of Jean Baptiste Perrault for theft—or more correctly, for retaining lost property—revealed not only ongoing sectarian conflicts between Catholic and Methodist missionaries but, perhaps more importantly, differing notions about civil governance in the settler colony. In early October 1840, a party of Methodist missionaries headed by the Reverends John H. Frost and W. W. Kone was ascending the Willamette River from Mission Bottom to Champoeg when household goods, clothing, and personal items belonging to the Kone family fell into the river after the overturning of a canoe (Frost and Kone were en route to establish a mission in the territory of the Clatsop at the mouth of the Columbia River). A number of the items were later recovered, while others were lost.[103] Some three months later, on January 5, 1841, Joseph Gervais, accompanied by James L. Whitcomb of the Methodist Mission, visited the home of Jean Baptiste Perrault and Angele Chehalis. Jason Lee had asked Gervais to accompany Whitcomb to the Perrault-Chehalis farm because some of the local Kalapuyans had told the Methodists that the Perrault family held *des effets naufragés,* or drowned objects, presumably belonging to the Kones.[104]

Perrault expressed surprise at being accused of possessing the lost Kone belongings and permitted a search of his premises. After the questioning of his wife, Angele Chehalis, and their twenty-year-old daughter, Reine Perrault, the women brought out dresses, linens, and tools for Gervais and Whitcomb to examine. In Father Blanchet's secondhand account of the events, Perrault claimed that the recovery of the objects had occurred without his knowledge, thereby shifting the blame onto his wife and daughter. Gervais and Whitcomb took possession of the items and transported them to the Methodist mission. Upon hearing of the incident from Gervais later than evening, Blanchet penned a letter to Jason Lee, which he sent the next day. Blanchet informed the head of the Methodist Mission that if Perrault were found guilty of retaining lost property, he would have to make a full restitution and express sincere regret for his actions. Blanchet employed a particularly religious argument, making clear that he would hold the man accountable according to Catholic teaching. He invited Lee to come to the Catholic mission to investigate the affair in the interests of rendering justice.[105]

In Lee's response to Blanchet, the Methodist minister agreed that the affair should be thoroughly investigated and a proper resolution agreed upon. Rather than take a direct role himself, he begged off because of illness and expressed confidence that the civil officers selected by the Methodist missionaries in 1839 should handle the investigation: Sheriff James L. Whitcomb and Justice of the

Peace David Leslie. Lee attempted to sidestep Blanchet's authority by suggesting that both he and Blanchet write to John McLoughlin to sound out the chief factor's views on the company's jurisdiction in the case. Lee also explained that Blanchet had not been invited to accompany Gervais and Whitcomb to Perrault's home because Gervais likely did not think it necessary (Blanchet was also saying Mass at the time that Gervais and Whitcomb passed by the Catholic mission).[106]

Following the reception of the letter from Jason Lee, Blanchet organized a public meeting at the Catholic Mission on January 8, 1841, to consider the accusation against Perrault. Although Blanchet invited the Americans to join the meeting, he noted only the presence of James Whitcomb. It is evident in Blanchet's actions and his letters to Lee regarding this controversy that the priest believed it was his responsibility to lead the French-Indian community in prosecuting and punishing Perrault, should the man be found guilty. Blanchet's position stemmed not only from his fears about the Protestant missionaries' efforts to gain influence and converts among the French Canadian Catholics but also from a deep-seated bitterness toward the Methodists and from a very different conception of civil governance. The American Methodists favored the institution of an American-inspired legal system and accompanying political institutions. In contrast, Blanchet maintained the position that since Oregon was not yet American territory, the French-Indian Catholic community could judge and censure its own members. In Blanchet's view, working with civil authorities selected by the Methodists regarding problems within the French-Indian community was not only unnecessary, it was also a threat to community solidarity and Blanchet's own authority. The priest's desire to play a central role in the Perrault affair was consistent with his ongoing efforts to cultivate a well-ordered community in the Tridentine tradition of the Roman Catholic Church.[107]

Contrary to Blanchet's view, the reaction of the French-Indian settlers themselves was not simply one of either following Blanchet or acquiescing to the Methodists. Rather, the settlers expressed a willingness to support a middle course. They would judge and punish Perrault themselves according to their own community standards, and they would also cooperate with the civil authorities selected by the Methodists in order to reach a resolution with the Protestant community—and particularly the Kone family. This middle course is evident in Blanchet's narration of the community's actions during the following days. The French Canadians' decision to pursue collective justice in cooperation with the Methodists was in keeping with local practices in French Canada that had been in place since the French regime. Under both the French and the British, the official legal system was largely an urban phenomenon due to the distances involved, low population density, financial considerations, the limited number of trained personnel, and the desire of rural inhabitants to avoid formal legal proceedings if possible. During the early 1800s, the criminal justice system in the rural areas of Lower Canada combined an overlay of English common law for capital offenses with peasant customs of community regulation (i.e., a reliance on ostracism) and the use of local arbitrators and justices of the peace to handle lesser criminal offenses, personal disputes, affidavits, and licensing matters.[108]

At the public meeting on Friday, January 8, 1841, Blanchet read his initial letter to Jason Lee and Lee's reply regarding the Perrault affair. Immediately thereafter, he turned the meeting over to Whitcomb, in keeping with the wishes of the settlers present. The settlers thereupon agreed that a tribunal should judge the man. Although the community apparently did not conduct an official trial that day, those present seem to have reached a consensus about Perrault's guilt in the case. At the conclusion of the meeting, Whitcomb asked the accused to go to the Methodist mission the following Monday to resolve the matter with the possibility of a formal trial. It is noteworthy that this public meeting illustrated the patriarchal culture of colonial society in both French Prairie and the larger Willamette Valley. Although Jean Baptiste Perrault's wife Angele and adult daughter Reine were clearly complicit in the decision to keep personal items that did not belong to them—perhaps by relying on a "finders keepers" rationale—in the community meeting, Jean Baptiste was held accountable for the conduct of his entire household.

In describing the public meeting to Modeste Demers in a letter dated February 11, 1841, Blanchet wrote that "the people [French-Indian settlers] had the witnesses speak after the public assembly was finished." According to Blanchet, the two Native witnesses, identified as a girl and boy, had been "in the service" of Perrault at the time the Kone belongings were recovered, but they left soon afterward. The two testified that they had found a trunk belonging to the Kones in early October and had brought it to the Perrault-Chehalis home. It contained two "Indian robes," some cotton cloth, some locks and augers, and other tools. Upon arriving home that night, Perrault destroyed the trunk and forbade the Native youths from speaking about the discovery. The two soon left the family's service, and the Natives to whom the young female witness "belonged" decided "to request a reward for what she had found." Blanchet's statement suggests that the youths were likely slaves of local Kalapuyans who had hired them out to the Perrault family. These Kalapuyan owners of the slaves thereupon informed the Methodists of the whereabouts of the Kone possessions, perhaps seeking a reward from the Methodists.[109] In addition to the testimony from the Native youths, some of the French-Indian settlers spoke about gossip circulating in the community that had also raised suspicions about the Perrault-Chehalis family. At the Christmas vigil of 1840, Reine Perrault, the daughter of the accused, had been baptized in one of the lost Kone dresses that had been retailored for the special event.[110]

Although Blanchet attributed Perrault's actions to the man's own weakness and his anxiety about being deported back to Lower Canada by McLoughlin at Fort Vancouver, Blanchet, for his part, was determined to make an example of the French Canadian and his family. Blanchet pushed ahead with a community punishment and sanctioning of Perrault prior to a formal trial at the Methodist mission. Blanchet declared that Perrault and his family would undergo a series of trials requiring penitence and restitution: (1) they were to remain at the doorstep of the mission church for a year rather than hear Mass inside with the rest of the parishioners; (2) Perrault would receive three lashes from his compatriots in the presence of the men, women, and local Indians at the Mass; (3) he must make the rounds of the settlement and ask pardon from each household for his weakness and the scandal he had caused; and (4) he must present himself before the head of the Methodist mission and offer to make reparation for what he had done.

Reading between the lines of Blanchet's correspondence, one wonders whether the priest sought to assert not only his authority but also the patriarchal authority of men over their wives and children with the French-Indian families in French Prairie. Blanchet may even have perceived Jean Baptiste Perrault's inability to control his wife and adult daughter as yet another indication of the independent-minded character of the French Canadians' Indian wives. This reading of the evidence follows efforts of the French Canadian clergy to control and regulate the actions and bodies of female parishioners.[111] After the first Mass at which Blanchet imposed his sentence, Sunday, January 10, 1841, there was an emotional scene when the French Canadian and his family were outside of the church. Everyone cried as Perrault repented and asked forgiveness. He also received "discipline on the part of his compatriots," and his wife and daughter "also received some on the part of the women."[112] Finally, Perrault and his family stood up and were welcomed back into the community with words of admonishment; Blanchet instructed Perrault that he must strive to correct his relationship with the community, with the Church, and with the Methodists.

The next day, Perrault went to the Methodist mission and asked Jason Lee what he should do to make amends, much as he had with the Catholic community.

Lee was surprised, declined to take up the matter, and insisted instead that it be decided through due process of law. As a result, the justice of the peace, David Leslie, took custody of the accused. A jury was selected and witnesses called. In contrast to the public meeting at the Catholic mission, the Indian witnesses did not give testimony. Instead, two white men took the stand, presumably Gervais and Whitcomb. They declared that Perrault had condemned himself when confronted by Whitcomb in January. They declared he was wrong for having kept the objects rather than returning them and for then denying that they were in his home. The jury found Perrault guilty, though the charge was not clear to Blanchet when he recorded the events. In any event, Perrault was fined a total of 82 piastres (or dollars): 25 to the Kones, 25 to aid the building of a jail, and 32 for the costs of the jury. Although Blanchet questioned the proceedings, the French Canadian settlers agreed with the judgment.[113] As with the public meeting in French Prairie, Jean Baptiste Perrault was held responsible for the actions of his entire household. However, in contrast to the prior meeting, the Americans did not countenance allowing the two Indian youths to give testimony, preferring instead to rely on the accounts of local white men. These details demonstrate a difference in the social and political culture of the two communities: while both were patriarchal in nature, the French Canadians were more willing to include local Native people in their deliberations, while the Americans excluded the Indians from participation in the legal proceedings.

A month after the prosecution of Jean Baptiste Perrault, the settler community experienced another serious problem requiring community cooperation on a civil matter. In early February 1841, American Ewing Young, who was then settled along the Yamhill River on the west side of the Willamette River, died, leaving a considerable estate of some seventy-five enclosed acres, a herd of four hundred horses, and six hundred head of cattle. At Young's funeral, ministers from the Methodist mission recommended that the Willamette Valley settlers call a public meeting to "organize a compact to appoint an administrator" for Ewing's estate. The Methodists held an initial, informal meeting soon after the funeral and then a larger public meeting with some of the local settlers on February 17, 1841.[114]

Those present decided to call a larger public meeting for the Willamette Valley settlers for the purpose of organizing committees to draft a constitution, a legal code, and elect several civil authorities, including a governor, a supreme judge with probate powers, justices of the peace, constables, an attorney general, a court clerk, a public recorder, a treasurer, road commissioners, and overseers of the poor.[115] A notice went out to the residents of the valley, including Blanchet, announcing that a second public meeting was scheduled for February 18, 1841, at the Methodist mission. Although Blanchet was opposed to the organization of a formal settler government dominated by Americans, he grudgingly attended the meeting in order to help represent the interests of the French-Indian community (at the time, Blanchet wrote to his colleague Modeste Demers that he went to the meeting expecting to be verbally "attacked" by the Methodists).[116]

In early historical accounts chronicling the development of the Oregon Provisional Government, Anglo-American settlers and writers typically portray the French Canadian participants as an undifferentiated block largely opposed to the formation of a civil compact in keeping with the supposed anti-American views of HBC officials and Father Blanchet. Although scholars have traced this interpretation to William H. Gray's *A History of Oregon, 1792–1849* (1870), they have tended to see the views and actions of Father Blanchet as representative of the French-Indian community as a whole.[117] Such a position overlooks the history of cooperative community efforts and debates in French Prairie—even after the arrival of Blanchet added tensions to the relationship between the French-Indian community and the Methodist missionaries. Although there is no direct evidence from the ordinary French Canadian settlers themselves, their actions noted in the records and memoirs of American settlers, Methodist missionaries, and Father Blanchet reveal a more complex colonial society at the time of the Ewing Young Estate debate. In fact, there were various factors that both linked and separated several factions within the larger settler society, comprising the French-Indian families, the Methodist missionaries and their supporters, and the nonaligned or independent Americans such as Ewing Young.[118]

The February 18 meeting at the Methodist mission opened with tension between the ministers and Blanchet when the priest drew attention to the fact that the French Canadian Catholic settlers were not represented on the committee that had met on February 17 (which he described as the "notification committee"). He questioned the legality of the assembly until it could be "declared competent," apparently by support from the Catholic community as well as the other American settlers. Although Blanchet does not specifically mention whether such public approval was given by those assembled, it apparently was because the meeting proceeded to tackle the probate of Young's estate and the other issues raised by the Methodists. Over the course of the meeting, David Leslie was elected chairman of the committee of the whole, with Sidney Smith and Gustavus Hines as secretaries. The motions of the previous February 17 meeting were reintroduced (Blanchet mentions twelve motions) and debated, as well as a proposal concerning who should serve in the projected civil positions.[119]

According to Blanchet, the original list of individuals the Methodists put forward to fill the civil offices was rejected by the assembly, including a number of nonaligned Americans. As a result, a new list of compromise candidates was drawn up. At that point, Blanchet felt that organizational efforts were moving too fast. In order to have time to consider all the Methodist proposals and to confer with John McLoughlin, Blanchet proposed postponing the election of officers until the first Tuesday in June—except for the positions of sheriff, supreme judge, constable, and the committee members charged with drafting a constitution. According to Blanchet, the nonaligned Americans supported his position and agreed to his proposal in an effort to prevent the Methodist group from dominating all of the administrative positions.[120]

Years later, Methodist missionary Josiah Parrish viewed the situation differently. He did not see a split between the Methodists and nonaligned Americans but rather a near conspiracy by HBC officials, namely McLoughlin, to control the French Canadian settlers through Blanchet. In his 1878 interview with Hubert Bancroft and Asabel Bush, Parrish noted that the "priest I have no doubt was instructed by John McLoughlin to tell them not to participate in this matter. They were of another nation." Parrish also noted that he believed McLoughlin held a threat of expulsion over the French Canadians formerly employed with the company: if they did not behave, he would ship them back to Canada. Thus, as interpreted by Parrish, the French Canadians who had participated in meetings about forming a compact were not free men acting independently of the British company.[121]

In seeking to placate Blanchet and the French Canadians, the Methodist group proposed that Blanchet be the presiding official for the assembly. Blanchet declined in order to retain his ability to address the assembly on his own terms. In his address, the priest noted the progress the assembly had made, but he also drew attention to the civil authority of McLoughlin and questioned whether the actions of the Willamette settlers to create a separate government might be seen as a criticism of the chief factor. David Leslie responded that given the increase in the number of settlers, a more formalized system of government was required to meet the needs of the people. Blanchet voiced his concerns that there was not such a great need, and that he still questioned the authority of the officials who had judged Jean Baptiste Perrault a month before.[122]

The assembly finally agreed on a compromise position. Ira L. Babcock was selected as supreme judge with probate powers; George Le Breton as court clerk and public recorder; William Johnson as high sheriff; and longtime settlers

Xavier Laderoute, Pierre Bellique, and William McCarty as constables. Another group also agreed to serve on a committee to draft a constitution and a legal code. Blanchet would serve as head of the committee, accompanied by Jason Lee, David Dompierre, Gustavus Hines, Andre Chalifoux, Robert Moore, Josiah Parrish, Etienne Lucier, and William Johnson. The assembly agreed to meet at the Catholic mission on the first Tuesday in June to continue the work of the committee.[123]

On June 1, 1841, the settlers met for a second meeting to consider the work of the committee charged with drafting a constitution and legal code. As chairman of the committee, Blanchet reported that the committee had not met to complete the work because of a lack of time and "other reasons." Blanchet took responsibility for this failure and expressed his view that additional work was in fact not needed. Blanchet asked to be excused from his position on the committee, and the assembly agreed. The assembly promptly elected William Bailey to take Blanchet's place and asked the committee to meet in early August to prepare a report for the next assembly meeting, which they scheduled for the first Monday in October. The assembly also agreed to consult with McLoughlin and with U.S. envoy Lieutenant Charles Wilkes for their views on the formation of a civil government in the settlement.[124] Wilkes visited the Willamette settlers a week later, during the middle of June 1841. Afterward, he expressed his view to Blanchet, the Methodists, and the American settlers that a provisional government was not needed at the time due to both the small size of the colony and the diplomatic uncertainty about the future territorial status of Oregon; however, the American settlers interpreted the visit of the U.S. Exploring Expedition as evidence that the United States would work to extend its jurisdiction over the Oregon Country in the near future.[125]

Following the visit of Lieutenant Wilkes in the summer of 1841, efforts to establish a more formal civil government in the Willamette Valley lost momentum. Wilkes's own lack of support for the project, coupled with Blanchet's criticisms and concerns, played a significant role in deflating the movement. Other contributing factors included the tensions between religious and nonreligious factions among the American population and an absence of sustained support from the settlers themselves. This waning of support for an organizing effort was a consequence of timing and community needs. Given the labor and time constraints facing the settlers during the summer and fall harvest seasons, they had more immediate concerns at home. Indeed, since the mid-1830s, public assemblies and cooperative action had been organized in response to specific community needs, such as probating the estate of Ewing Young and the trial of Jean Baptiste Perrault. With the probate judge selected, as well as civil officials to fill law enforcement positions, most settlers did not support the creation of an onerous civil administration that would tax both their labors and property.[126] Efforts by Elijah White, the newly arrived Indian subagent, to revive efforts at organizing a government in 1842 garnered a tepid reception from the Willamette Valley settlers, largely because they perceived White's efforts to be aimed at installing himself as head of the proposed government.[127]

Early in 1843, American settlers interested in renewing efforts to establish a more formal governmental structure set about organizing a series of "wolf meetings" in the Willamette Valley. Historians have linked these efforts to discussions about the need for a local government by members of a debating society that met at the Oregon Lyceum in Oregon City over the winter of 1842–1843.[128] In organizing the wolf meetings, the American settlers articulated a need for coordinated community action in response to predatory attacks on livestock in the Willamette Valley, an argument that resonated with both the Americans and French Canadians because, with the steady expansion of the settler population, predatory attacks on the settlers' livestock had become a major concern. The popularity of this rhetoric of "predatory animals" underscored the incredible ecological transformation of the valley—a transformation that necessitated the destruction of wolves, coyotes, and cougars because they had no value for settlers engaged in farming and animal husbandry for a commercial market.[129]

Over the course of several wolf meetings held in February and March 1843 at the home of Joseph Gervais, at the Methodist Oregon Institute in Salem, and in Oregon City, American and French settlers agreed on a series of measures designed to pay bounties to local farmers and local Kalapuyans for the pelts of wolves, bears, and panthers with the explicit aim of carrying out "a defensive and destructive war against all such animals."[130] In a foreshadowing of the racial regime that the Anglo-Americans would enact in the coming years, the resolution on bounties for the animal pelts specified that while "whites and their descendants" would receive the full bounty for the various pelts, Indians would receive only two-thirds of the bounty amounts enjoyed by whites.[131] In this particular instance, the prominence of the French Canadians ensured that for the time being, their mixed-race children would receive equal treatment with white settlers, unlike their Native relations. Elijah White chaired the final wolf meeting held on March 17, 1843, in Oregon City, which included mostly American settlers. The participants apparently focused their energies on advancing efforts to organize a more formal government. As a result, they called for a large public meeting of the Willamette Valley settlers to be held at Champoeg on May 2, 1843, with "the purpose of taking steps to organize themselves into a civil community, and provide themselves with protection, secured by the enforcement of law and order."[132]

On May 2, 1843, a larger group of some one hundred Americans and French Canadians, about half the male settler population in the Willamette Valley, met at Champoeg to debate the formation of such a government, the writing of a civil code, and the election of civil authorities. After several rounds of discussion and close votes by viva voce, which apparently caused not a small amount of confusion as to what exactly the settlers were to decide, a simple majority of those present voted to support the formation of a community organization. Although there was vocal opposition from most of the French Canadian settlers, as many as seven—Pierre Bellique, François Bernier, David Dompierre, Joseph Gervais, Xavier Laderoute, Etienne Lucier, and François Xavier Matthieu—voted to join with the Americans and form a local government.[133] At additional meetings in June and July, the settlers voted on specific motions for the creation of an Organic Law for the colony, and they selected officers who would oversee the enforcement of the law and the collection of property and poll taxes to provide financial support for the fledgling government.[134]

Several nineteenth-century accounts of the Champoeg meeting—notably the version written by William Gray—emphasize that a "great majority" voted for organization and reduced the number of French Canadians who supported the proposal to just two (Etienne Lucier and François Xavier Matthieu). However, Robert Newell later recalled that "Gervais, Lucier, Bellique, Bernier, Laderoute, Dompierre, and others" supported the initiative, emphasizing that "the motive to organize prevailed by a majority of five; but had the Frenchmen opposed the motion as W. H. Gray says they did, the motion would have been lost."[135] HBC chief factor John McLoughlin, who did not attend any of the meetings that took place in 1843, recalled that as a group the French Canadian settlers declined American offers to "organize a temporary government" in 1842 and 1843 as they were "apprehensive it might interfere with their allegiance."[136] As an officer with the HBC, a de facto representative of the British government in Oregon, and a member of the anglophone elite, McLoughlin interpreted the actions of the French Canadians in 1843 from a nationalistic perspective, though he would later come to revise his own initial position of remaining aloof to American offers to join the provisional government.

FIGURE 5. Inception of the Birth of Oregon. Painting of the Champoeg meeting of 1843 by Theodore Gegoux (dated 1923). Courtesy of Oregon State Parks and Recreation Department. Photograph courtesy of Theodore Gegoux III.

Since the 1800s, historians have tended to reiterate the view that the French Canadians opposed the formation of civil government on May 2, 1843, as a result of their allegiance to British interests, which ostensibly encompassed French Canadian interests.[137] In this they have followed the standard mythology crafted by the American pioneer chroniclers who, unlike the French Canadians, left numerous accounts of their "triumphant" struggle to wrest the Oregon Country from the grip of the British Empire and its oppressive representative in the region, the HBC.[138] Several of the individuals most active in agitating for a provisional government—notably Robert Shortress and William H. Gray—harbored a particularly strong antipathy toward the HBC (which surfaced again in the Shortress Petition to Congress in 1843). From their perspective, opposition to the American settlers' plans coming from former fur trade laborers was suspect. They interpreted the French Canadians' opposition, or lack of support, as a pro-British, anti-American stance. They believed the French Canadians simply followed the instructions they presumably received from John McLoughlin and Francis Norbert Blanchet. There was also a decidedly anti-Catholic position on the part of some of the Americans leading the organizing efforts.[139]

This interpretation is inconsistent with the history of social relations between the French-Indian community and the American settlers. It also overlooks the religious, cultural, and class differences separating the French Canadians from the HBC Anglo-Celtic officer corps and the French Canadians' status as second-class citizens in Canada. Additionally, this interpretation ignores tensions that existed within the French-Indian community itself. It is more accurate to attribute the French Canadians' reluctance to join the local government movement to several factors. Although the documentary record on the French Canadians' position in 1843 is limited, a handful of other sources do provide some additional clues about its nature. François Xavier Matthieu and a few American chroniclers noted that the French Canadians who did support the organization of a provisional government in 1843 were the prominent members of the community. Matthieu was a new arrival, but he had quickly become a prominent figure because he was educated, literate, and familiar with American political culture. Other probable supporters, Gervais, Bellique, Lucier, and Laderoute, were longtime residents with large landholdings. For ten years they had taken a leading role in cooperation with the American Methodists and other settlers on intercommunity projects and issues, such as the trial of Jean Baptiste Perrault. Given the French Canadians' concerns that the Willamette Valley would come under American jurisdiction, which they had expressed to the U.S. envoy William Slacum in the 1830s, they would have been motivated by a cautious desire to continue their cooperation and thereby retain a voice in the developing colonial society.[140]

As for the larger group of Canadians who opposed the 1843 organizing efforts, we can glean a sense of their views from a petition produced in March 1844 by a group who identified themselves as "Canadian citizens, settlers of the Willamette." The signatories—Joseph Gervais, François Rivet, Sidney Smith, Charles Pickett, and S. M. Holderness—prepared the address in collaboration with Father Antoine Langlois, as the original was written in French. The Canadians presented their petition at a meeting of local settlers at Champoeg on March 4, 1844. The tone of the address suggests that the signatories presented themselves as representatives of the larger group of French Canadian settlers. They expressed a willingness to participate in the creation of institutions for the benefit of the community at large, but they preferred a more limited role for the proposed government. They certainly did not want to alienate HBC officials, and they stated explicitly that they would not support any new petitions to the U.S. government because the Oregon boundary question had yet to be resolved. The Canadians also voiced concerns about equitable representation, substantial government expenses requiring a heavy tax burden, bureaucracy, the issuance of land titles that may not be legal when the international boundary was finally established, legal "trickery," and respect for the customs of the French Canadians and the Indians. In this sense, the French Canadians were concerned less with British interests than with protecting their own rights and property in light of assertive posturing of the American settlers. They were also concerned with the well-being of their families, maintaining positive relations with the HBC, and protecting the interests of their local community, which included some consideration for their neighbors, the Kalapuyans.[141]

As evidenced in the Organic Laws of 1844 and 1845—which recognized equal rights for male citizens from the United States and Great Britain and theoretically sanctioned the Northwest Ordinance of 1787, which recognized the preexisting land title of the region's indigenous inhabitants—the French Canadians did eventually reach an agreement with their American neighbors.[142] François Xavier Matthieu remembered that the French Canadians eventually gave their support to the provisional government and noted that he was elected a constable and later a justice of the peace by the majority of the settlers.[143] While the vast majority of the French Canadians were less equipped to serve in the provisional government due to their illiteracy, limited English skills, and lack of education—in comparison to the American settlers—some did contribute to local governance. In 1844, Joseph Gervais, Pierre Bellique, Etienne Lucier, François Bernier, Nicholas Montour, and Louis Pichet served as grand jurors in Champoeg County for the fall 1844 session of the government's circuit court session. In 1845, the French Canadian printer Medard Foisy represented Champoeg County on the provisional government's legislative committee, which was then working on revisions to the Organic Law. The retired HBC tinsmith Adolphe Chamberlain also served on the legislative committee for Champoeg County in 1846 and 1847.[144]

Although a few settlers, such as Joseph Gervais, first refused to pay the provisional government's property and poll taxes, which were initially voluntary, the vast majority of French Canadians, Anglo-Canadians, and Americans were willing to shoulder the tax burden for the new government. So too, a solid majority of the French Canadians later registered their land claims with the Oregon Provisional Government (see table 10a). Some 91 francophone settlers registered their claims in the Willamette Valley between 1845 and 1848 and another 13 prominent French Canadians apparently did not register their farms, but their land was listed in descriptions for neighboring claims (see table 10b). This total of 104 settlers with French surnames included 80 French Canadians, 19 French-Indian sons of French Canadian voyageurs, two Frenchmen, two French Americans, and one Native man, Joseph Brulé (Iroquois-Salish), son of Marguerite

Sooke and stepson of Jean Baptiste Brulé.[145] In 1845, HBC officials John McLoughlin and James Douglas also finally joined the provisional government in order to have a voice in matters affecting the settler community, particularly north of the Columbia, and to protect the financial and property interests of the HBC.[146] Like the French Prairie settlers, McLoughlin and Douglas proved to be more practical than nationalistic in the final instance.

Although the French Canadian settlers were able to have their position as British citizens and their land claims recognized in the Oregon Provisional Government's Organic Law, the law was a reflection of the antebellum political culture of the United States, particularly the Free Soil strain emerging in the North. The Organic Law of 1843 and 1844 outlawed slavery and reserved voting rights for white male inhabitants and their descendants twenty-one years of age.[147] This position mirrored existing statutes in the United States that prioritized the rights and public role of white male citizens and excluded blacks, Indians, and women from participation in civil affairs because the white male citizenry deemed these groups incapable of full inclusion in the body politic. Indeed, the racial and social identity of white male citizens rested on their difference and separation from both nonwhites and women.[148] Although the French Canadians were able to have voting rights written into the Organic Law for their mixed-race sons (as they had with the animal pelt bounty), race remained a potent topic in Oregon's political culture. In the mid-1840s, one event in particular caused panic among white settlers who feared attacks from Indian groups in the Pacific Northwest.

In March 1844, the Comstock incident heightened fears about a possible racial conspiracy between blacks and Indians against white settlers. The incident, which involved a dispute between James Saules, a black man, and Comstock, a Wasco Indian, over the ownership of a horse, resulted in a deadly confrontation between Comstock and his supporters and Saules and several Oregon City residents. Two white settlers died of their wounds, as did Comstock. White residents blamed Saules and another black settler, Winslow Anderson (also known as George Winslow), for the violence. In response to the panic among white settlers following the deadly confrontation at Oregon City, Peter Burnett, a recent emigrant from Missouri, proposed a black exclusion bill before the provisional government's legislative committee in June 1844. As passed, the statute outlawed slavery, required the removal of any slaves brought to Oregon, and provided for the trial and punishment of adult free blacks (men and women) who did not leave Oregon within two to three years of their arrival. Blacks found guilty under the statute would be subject to a whipping of twenty to thirty-nine lashes.[149]

TABLE 10a. Registered land claims of Willamette Valley settlers with French surnames: Oregon Provisional Government, 1845–1849

Name	Ethnicity	Spouse	Ethnicity of spouse	County	Date	Acreage
1. Amable Arquette	French Canadian	Marguerite Chinook	Chinook	Champoeg	1846	640
2. Alexis Aubichon	French Canadian	Marianne Chinook	Chinook	Champoeg	1846	640
3. Jean Baptiste Aubichon	French Canadian	Isabelle	"tribe of the South"	Champoeg	1845	640
4. Pierre Bellique	French Canadian	Genevieve St. Martin	French-Chinook	Champoeg	1846	640
5. Felix Bergevin	French Canadian			Champoeg	1847	640
6. François Bernier	French Canadian	Pelagie Lucier	French-Kwakwaka'wakw	Champoeg	1846	320
7. Louis Boisvert	French Canadian			Champoeg	1846	526
8. Antoine Bonenfant Sr.	French Canadian	Françoise Dupati McKay	Métis-Kalapuyan	Champoeg	1846	640
9. Antoine Bonenfant Jr.	French-Spokane			Champoeg	1848	320
10. Pierre Bonin	French Canadian	Louise Rondeau	French-Walla Walla	Champoeg	1846	640
11. Joseph Bourgeau	French Canadian	Angele Lafantaisie	French-Okanagan	Champoeg	1846	640
12. Silvain Bourgeau	French Canadian	Josette Chinook	Chinook	Champoeg	1848	600
13. Hypolite Brouillet	French Canadian	Angele Gingras	French-Okanagan	Champoeg	1846	640
14. Jean Baptiste Brulé	French Canadian	Marguerite Sooke	Coast Salish	Yamhill	1847	640
15. Joseph Brulé	Iroquois-Salish	Marie Anne Maranda	Iroquois-Kalapuyan	Yamhill	1847	640
16. Andre Chalifoux	French Canadian	Catherine Russie	French Canadian	Champoeg	1846	640
17. Joseph Crochière	French-Cree			Champoeg	1846	640
18. Jean Baptiste Dalcourt	French Canadian	Agathe Cayuse	Cayuse	Champoeg	1847	640
19. Jean Baptise Deguire	French American	Marie Anne Perrault	French-Chinook	Tualatin	1848	640
20. Pierre Delard	French-Shushwap	Josephte Lapierre	French-Okanagan	Champoeg	1846	640
21. Joseph Delard	French Canadian	Marie Toussaint Poirer	French-Clatsop	Champoeg	1846	500
22. Pierre Dépôt	French Canadian	Marguerite Clackamas	Upper Chinookan	Champoeg	1845	640
23. Joseph Despard	French Canadian	Lisette Chinook	Chinook	Champoeg	1848	500
24. David Dompierre	French Canadian	Marguerite Soulière	French-Cree	Champoeg	1846	640
25. Jean Baptiste Dorion	French-Iowa	Josephine Cayuse	Cayuse	Champoeg	1846	640
26. Andre Dubois	French Canadian	Josette Marie Quesnel	French-Chehalis	Champoeg	1846	640
27. Pierre Dubois	French Canadian	Catherine Spokane	Spokane	Champoeg	1846	607
28. Jean Baptiste Dubreuil	French Canadian	Marguerite Chinook	Chinook	Champoeg	1846	640
29. Jean Baptiste Ducharme	French Canadian	Catherine Hu	French-Pend d'Oreille	Champoeg	1846	640
30. Joseph Dupère	French Canadian	Louise Cowlitz	Cowlitz	Champoeg	1846	640

Name	Ethnicity	Spouse	Ethnicity of spouse	County	Date	Acreage
31. François Dupré	French Canadian	Catherine Lafantaisie	French-Okanagan	Champoeg	1847	640
32. Nazaire Dupré	French Canadian	Marguerite Dickerson	Anglo-American	Champoeg	1846	640
33. Edouard Dupuis	French Canadian	Marguerite Chaudière	Colville/Flathead	Champoeg	1846	640
34. Antoine Felix dit Palaquin	French Canadian			Champoeg	1846	640
35. Medard Foisy	French Canadian	Catherine Canemah	Upper Chinookan	Champoeg	1845	500
36. Louis Forcier	French Canadian	Angelique	Lower Umpqua	Polk	1845	640
37. Jean Baptiste Gagnier	French Canadian	Angelique Marcellais	French-Indian	Champoeg	1846	640
38. François Gagnon	French Canadian	Marie	Indian	Champoeg	1846	320
39. Louis Gagnon	French Canadian			Champoeg	1846	507
40. Pierre Gauthier	French-Chinook	Ester Dalcourt	French-Cayuse	Champoeg	1845	"tract"
41. David Gervais	French-Chinook	Marie Anne Toupin	French-Iowa	Champoeg	1846	640
42. Isaac Gervais	French Canadian			Champoeg	1846	640
43. Joseph Gervais	French Canadian	Marie Angelicue	Chinook	Champoeg	1846	640
44. Jean Gingras	French Canadian	Olive Forcier	French-Upper Chinookan	Champoeg	1845	blank
45. Joseph Gingras	French-Okanagan	Marianne Basien	French-Shasta	Champoeg	1845	blank
46. Jean Baptiste Gobin	French Canadian	Marguerite Vernier	French-Iowa	Champoeg	1848	640
47. Gideon Gravelle	French Canadian	Nancy Pin	French-Pend d'Oreille	Yamhill	1845	640
48. Antoine Grégoire	French-Shushwap	Therese Ouvre	French-Nisqually	Champoeg	1845	blank
49. David Grégoire	French-Shushwap			Champoeg	1846	640
50. Felix Grégoire	French-Shushwap			Champoeg	1847	640
51. Paul Guilbeau	French Canadian	Françoise Cayuse	Cayuse	Champoeg	1846	640
52. Stanislaus Jacquet	French	Victoire Chinook	Chinook	Champoeg	1846	640
53. Sigfroid Jobin	French Canadian	Catherine Pepin	French Canadian	Champoeg	1847	640
54. Pierre Lacourse Jr.	French-Chehalis	Victoire McMillan	Scottish-Chinook	Champoeg	1846	640
55. François Xavier Laderoute	French Canadian	Marie Anne Ouvre	French-Nisqually	Champoeg	1848	640
56. Charles Lafantaisie	French-Okanagan	Genevieve Rondeau	French-Métis	Champoeg	1847	640
57. Joseph Laferte (Joachim)	French Canadian	Sophie Aubichcn	French-Chinook	Champoeg	1846	640
58. Michel Laferte dit Placide	French Canadian	Josephte Pend d'Oreille	Pend d'Oreille	Yamhill	1846	640
59. Culbert Lambert dit Robillard	French Canadian	Marie Okanagan	Okanagan	Champoeg	1847	640
60. Louis Laplante	French Canadian	Susanne Dufresne	French-Indian	Champoeg	1847	640
61. Alexis Laprate (Laprade)	French Canadian	Louise Okanagan	Okanagan	Champoeg	1846	640
62. Joseph Laroque (Rochbrune)	French Canadian	Lisette Walla Walla	Walla Walla	Champoeg	1847	330

Name	Ethnicity	Spouse	Ethnicity of spouse	County	Date	Acreage
63. Noel Lavigeur	French-Spokane			Champoeg	1847	640
64. Louis Labonté Jr.	French-Clatsop	Caroline Montour	Métis-Cree	Yamhill	1846	640
65. Hercules Lebrun	French Canadian	Louise Ouvre	French-Nisqually	Champoeg	1847	640
66. François Xavier Liard	French Canadian	Marie Anne Nez Perce	Nez Perce	Champoeg	1847	640
67. Moise Lord	French Canadian	Marianne Sanders	French-Chinook	Champoeg	1847	640
68. Etienne Lucier	French Canadians	Marie Marguerite	Chinook	Champoeg	1846	640
69. Fabien Malouin	French Canadian	Louise Michel	Iroquois-(Chinookan)	Champoeg	1846	640
70. Antoine Masta	French Canadian	Sophie Chinook	Chinook	Champoeg	1846	640
71. Thomas Moisan	French Canadian	Henriette Longtain	French-Okanagan	Champoeg	1846	640
72. George Montour	Métis-Cree	Lisette (Louise) Canote	French-Indian	Champoeg	1848	640
73. Pierre Papin dit Lachance	French Canadian	Susanne Goodriche	American-Chinookan	Champoeg	1847	640
74. Amable Petit	French Canadian	Susanne Tawakon	Iroquois-Chinookan	Champoeg	1845	640
75. Louis Pichet	French Canadian	Marguerite Bercier	French-Indian?	Champoeg	1846	391
76. Joseph Pin	French Canadian	Marguerite	Pend d'Oreille	Yamhill	1845	640
77. Charles Plante (Lapointe)	French Canadian	Pelagie Chinook	Chinook	Champoeg	1848	640
78. André Plourde	French-Métis	Marie Sophie Sanders	French-Chinook	Champoeg	1846	640
79. François Plourde	French Canadian	Susanne Dubois	French-Indian	Champoeg	1846	640
80. Joseph Plouffe dit Carillon	French Canadian	Therese Makaine	Hawaiian-Chehalis	Champoeg	1846	320
81. Jean Pierre Poujade	French	Marie Ann Sable	French American	Champoeg	1848	640
82. Louis Poujade	French American			Champoeg	1847	640
83. Antoine Rivet	French-Flathead	Emelie Pend d'Oreille	Pend d'Oreille	Champoeg	1845	1,280 partnership
84. François Rivet	French Canadian	Therese Flathead	Flathead (Interior Salish)	Champoeg	1845	1,280 partnership
85. Joseph Rivet	French-Flathead	Marie Anne Despard	French-Chinook	Champoeg	1845	640
86. Louis Rondeau	French Canadian	Henriette Yogalta	Uclulet (Nuu-chah-nulth)	Champoeg	1846	640
87. Gideon Senecal	French Canadian	Marie Grenier	French-Spokane	Champoeg	1846	640
88. François Toupin	French-Iowa	Angelique Longtain	French-Okanagan	Champoeg	1846	640
89. Jean Baptiste Toupin	French Canadian	Marie Dorion L'Aguivoise	Iowa	Champoeg	1846	blank
90. Louis A. Vandal (the elder)	French Canadian	Catherine Porteuse	Carrier (Athapaskan)	Champoeg	1846	640
91. Louis B. Vandal (the younger)	French Canadian	Cecile McDonald	Scottish-Indian	Champoeg	1846	640

NOTE: Date and acreage listed are for the first land claim registered with the Oregon Provisional Government.

SOURCES: *Genealogical Material in Oregon Provisional Land Claims, 1845–1849*. Munnick, CCRPNW-V, CCRPNW-SP, CCRPNW-SL; Watson, *Lives Lived West of the Divide*, 3 vols.

TABLE 10b. Willamette valley settlers with French surnames not registered with the Oregon Provisional Government but listed in descriptions of neighboring land claims, 1845–1849

Name	Ethnicity	Spouse	Ethnicity of Spouse	County	Date
1. Louis Aucent	French Canadian	Mary Molalla	Molalla	Champoeg	1846
2. Charles Jeaudoin	French Canadian	Madeleine Servant	French-Okanagan	Champoeg	1846/47
3. Jean Baptiste Jeaudoin	French-Chinook	Isabelle Hubert	French-Spokane	Champoeg	1846/47
4. Louis Labonte Sr.	French Canadian	Kilkatoh Clatsop	Clatsop	Yamhill	1845
5. Pierre Lacourse Sr.	French Canadian	Archange Chehalis	Chehalis	Champoeg	1846
6. Michel Laframboise	French Canadian	Emelie Picard	French-Okanagan	Yamhill	1846
7. Andre Longtain	French Canadian	Nancy Okanagan	Okanagan	Champoeg	1847
8. François Xavier Matthieu	French Canadian	Rose Aucent	French-Cayuse	Champoeg	1846
9. Jean Baptiste Perrault	French Canadian	Angele Chehalis	Chehalis	Champoeg	1845
10. Augustin Raymond	French Canadian	Marie Servant	French-Okanagan	Champoeg	1846
11. Charles Rondeau	French Canadian	Agathe Dupati McKay	Métis-Kalapuyan	Champoeg	1846
12. Jacques Servant	French Canadian	Josette Okanagan	Okanagan	Champoeg	1847
13. Laurent Quintal	French Canadian	Marie Anne Nipissing	Nipissing-(Chinookan?)	Champoeg	1846

NOTE: Date and acreage listed are for the first land claim registered with the Oregon Provisional Government.

SOURCES: *Genealogical Material in Oregon Provisional Land Claims, 1845-1849*; Munnick, *CCRPNW-V, CCRPNW-SP, CCRPNW-SL*; Watson, *Lives Lived West of the Divide*, 3 vols.

The whipping section of the law was deleted in December of 1844 and replaced with a provision that the guilty would be hired out for employment at public auction and their employers charged with removing the individuals from Oregon upon the completion of their work sentence. Although the legislative committee later repealed the exclusion law in July 1845, Quintard Taylor aptly concluded that the law was "more important as a symbol of the evolving attitude toward black migration than as a measure that would immediately eliminate or reduce the 'troublesome' black population."[150] Taken together, the Organic Law and the Black Exclusion Law are further evidence of the racialization of the Pacific Northwest during the 1840s. The Anglo-American emigrants who colonized the region sought to replicate the racial order of their native country, the United States, and in their minds the presence of Native peoples and a possible fifth column—blacks—lurked as probable threats to these ambitions.

✳ During the 1840s, the French-Indian families in French Prairie continued to pursue a middle course in their relationships with their American neighbors. They did so in spite of the anti-Catholic, anti-Indian, and anti-British sentiments among segments of the increasing American population and in the face of an anti-Methodist stance on the part of the Roman Catholic leader, Father Francis Blanchet. At the same time, the agricultural and husbandry operations of the French Prairie settlers, coupled with those of American emigrants, had a negative impact on the Kalapuyans, whose land resources both the French-Indians and the Americans claimed. When visiting the community during this period of the early 1840s, French traveler Eugène Duflot de Mofras wrote of the French Canadians' strong sense of ethnic identity, which appears to have been as robust as that of the incoming American overlanders.

The documentary record of the period attests to the French-Indian settlers' desire to preserve their community and customs while also cooperating with new Catholic missionaries on educational and social welfare projects and with the American settlers on local initiatives, including judiciary cases and debates about the creation of a provisional government. While most of the French Canadians initially voiced their opposition to the proposed government, they later sought to find a compromise with the Americans when faced with their minority status. Seen in this light, the French Canadians' participation in community debates about the formation of a local government—and their early opposition to it—was not so much a nationalistic position as a desire to protect their community interests, cultural practices, legal standing, and property rights. The 1844 address of the Canadian settlers to their Americans neighbors detailed the French-speakers' concerns about what form the provisional government would take, how heavy a tax burden it would impose, and whether it would protect their rights, those of their Indian wives, and those of their bicultural children.

Due to their established presence in the Willamette Valley and their generally positive, long-standing ties with the other various settler groups, the French Canadian male settlers were able to negotiate a relatively favorable position for themselves and their families, as reflected in the provisions of the Organic Laws of 1844 and 1845. Nonetheless, 1843 marked a significant turning point for the French Prairie settlement and for the Oregon Country as a whole. The migration of some 875 American overlanders that year initiated a process of social change in the region. Because of their demographic dominance, the American settlers heightened conflicts with the region's indigenous inhabitants over land and natural resources, hastened the introduction of additional infectious diseases, and began implementing legal statutes and social policies based on prevailing notions of white supremacy. These changes marked the beginning of the end of an earlier heterogeneous and more accommodating colonial society, one in which demographic realities in the Willamette Valley had left no group dominant over the other. The Oregon Treaty of 1846, which saw Great Britain and the United States agree to a compromise of their imperial aims on the Pacific Slope by setting the international boundary at the forty-ninth parallel, formalized the ascendancy of Anglo-Americans in Oregon. Within a decade, the Americans began to actively push for the removal of all Native groups east of the Cascades and thereby forced the French-Indian families to face difficult choices about their allegiances in subsequent violent conflicts between Native peoples and the American settlers.

CHAPTER 6 ❋ Under an Anglo-American Regime

In June 1853, M. J. Cozens, a Catholic bookseller in New York City, issued a pamphlet titled *Protestantism in Oregon: Account of the Murder of Dr. Whitman and the Ungrateful Calumnies of H. H. Spalding, Protestant Missionary*. The pamphlet reprinted a series of articles previously published in a Catholic newspaper, the *New-York Freedman's Journal*, and written by Jean Baptiste Brouillet, a French Canadian priest then serving as vicar general of the Diocese of Nesqually, Washington Territory. Aimed at a largely Catholic readership, the author and publisher of *Protestantism in Oregon* intended the publication to document the facts of the Whitman mission incident of 1847 (also known as the Whitman Massacre) and refute Nativist accusations of a Roman Catholic conspiracy behind the killing of Marcus and Narcissa Whitman and eleven others at the Presbyterian mission. Charges of a Catholic plot against the Protestant missions in the Pacific Northwest had originated in part with Whitman's colleague Henry Spalding, whose life Brouillet had undoubtedly saved in the aftermath of the Cayuse attack on the Whitman mission. Such was the vitriol and enmity with which Spalding wrote of the Catholic clergy—and of Brouillet in particular—that the French Canadian priest felt it necessary to record and later publish his account of the events.[1]

The simmering anti-Catholic sentiment that burst forth in the Pacific Northwest following the Whitman mission incident was one strand in the larger sociocultural transformation of the region during the 1850s. As the United States extended its jurisdiction over this western hinterland in the midst of the nation's sectional crisis, Anglo-American settlers jostled among themselves for political power and wrestled with Native peoples for control over the region's land and resources. To rationalize their actions, the Americans employed a rhetorical arsenal that drew on Anglo-Saxon racialism, white supremacy, Anglophobia, and western expansionism. As scholars have recently demonstrated, the Americans' regime of settler colonialism left little room, both figuratively and literally, for the indigenous inhabitants of the Pacific Northwest. The Anglo-Americans' colonization of the region relied on processes similar to those employed in previous contact zones: cultural violence, religious evangelization, ecological despoliation, armed conflict, dispossession, and forced removal. For the Indian peoples of the region, the decade of the 1850s was a brutal one, as evidenced by the genocidal episodes that erupted in the mining frontiers throughout the Pacific Slope.[2]

Caught within this consolidation of Anglo-American colonialism after the Oregon Treaty of 1846, the French-Indian families of French Prairie witnessed a contraction of their earlier reliance on cross-cultural flexibility as American emigrants continued to stream into the Willamette Valley. These emigrants viewed the French Prairie settlers with a wary eye because of their Catholic religion, their foreign French language and culture, their erstwhile allegiance to Great Britain, and their Indian ancestry and kin links with regional Native groups. The French-Indian families in the Willamette Valley responded in a variety of ways to the reversals of fortune that accompanied Anglo-American settler colonialism. In the late 1840s they supported the Americans' military response to the Whitman mission incident by purchasing war bonds to finance a settler militia and by raising a company of volunteers to participate in the prosecution of the Cayuse War—the first major armed conflict against regional indigenous groups.

In the context of increased tensions between settlers and Indians during the 1850s, many French-Indian couples elected to remain in the Willamette Valley and pursued socioeconomic strategies intended to preserve their household assets and property. At the same time, the mixed-race couples and their children faced a narrowing of their legal and political rights, a situation they contested like many other biracial communities in North America during the 1800s. The French Prairie inhabitants were ultimately unsuccessful in their bid for full citizenship during the mid-1800s due to the increasingly constricted definitions of race in antebellum America. However, their efforts to contest the boundaries of race elucidate social tensions in Oregon during the antebellum years that preceded the state's adoption of a complex miscegenation law after the Civil War.

✳ In the years prior to the Whitman mission incident, the Roman Catholic Church in the Pacific Northwest expanded and reorganized, which added additional stress to an already tense relationship between Catholic and Protestant missionaries in the region. In December 1844, after receiving news of the erection of a new vicariate apostolic in Oregon, bishop-elect Francis Norbert Blanchet departed for his consecration in Quebec and then traveled on to Europe to meet with Church officials, raise funds, and recruit additional missionaries for Oregon. While in Europe, Blanchet presented ambitious plans for an expansion of the Catholic Church in the Pacific Northwest, which included the creation of three new dioceses at Oregon City, Walla Walla, and Vancouver Island. He proposed himself as archbishop of Oregon City, his brother Augustin Magloire Alexandre Blanchet as bishop of Walla Walla, and Modeste Demers as bishop of Vancouver Island. Following the death of Pope Gregory XVI and the Oregon Treaty of 1846, the new pope, Pius IX, endorsed Blanchet's plan, elevated the vicariate to a province, making it the Church's second province in the United States after Baltimore, and recognized Oregon City as the archiepiscopal see of the new province.[3]

In August 1847, F. N. Blanchet returned to Oregon after a six-month voyage aboard *L'Etoile du Matin*. The new archbishop brought with him a large group of reinforcements for the Catholic mission, including seven sisters of Notre Dame de Namur, five secular priests, three Jesuit priests, three lay brothers, two deacons, and an unordained cleric. F. N. Blanchet's brother, Bishop A. M. A Blanchet, traveled overland from Quebec to the Pacific Northwest and arrived at Fort Walla Walla with Father Jean Baptiste Brouillet and a group of Oblate missionaries in September 1847. In late November 1847, A. M. A. Blanchet and Brouillet founded the Catholic mission of St. Anne among the Cayuse on the Umatilla River in eastern Oregon. Although the Whitman mission incident led to the shuttering of the Diocese of Walla Walla and the Cayuse mission, A. M. A. Blanchet and Brouillet regained their footing when Pope Pius IX established the Diocese of Nesqually and transferred both men to the new diocese. The growth of the larger regional Church became a primary focus for F. N. Blanchet upon his return from Europe, and so in December 1848 he relocated from St. Paul in French Prairie to St. John's parish in the growing town of Oregon City.[4]

While the Roman Catholic Church expanded, added new personnel, and erected a conventional hierarchy during the 1840s, Protestant missionary efforts in the Pacific Northwest underwent a number of transitions that had a lasting impact on the region. In 1841, the Methodists relocated their headquarters from the original "mission bottom" on the Willamette River to "mill place" at Chemeketa (present-day Salem), but the larger Oregon mission did not last long after this move. Facing mounting bills, flagging interest in the Oregon mission, demoralization and resignations of missionary personnel, and little evidence of success among the regional Indian tribes, the Mission Board of the Methodist Episcopal Church sent the Rev. George Gary to Oregon in 1844 to resolve the situation (Jason Lee was then en route to the United States, where he died in

1845). Given broad powers by the mission board, Gary liquidated the Methodist mission's movable property, businesses, and landholdings, arranged for the payment of debts, dismissed both employees and clergy, closed the various mission stations, and sold the Indian Manual Labor School to the trustees of the Oregon Institute (forerunner of Willamette University).[5] Although the Methodist mission effectively ceased to exist by 1845, the American settlers formerly associated with the mission continued to play an important role in Oregon politics through the 1840s.

In 1836, two years after the Methodists sent their first group of missionaries to the Pacific Northwest, the American Board of Commissioners for Foreign Mission (AMBFM) organized its own Oregon mission and dispatched the first of several groups to the Plateau region of the Columbia River Basin. This group included Presbyterians Dr. Marcus and Narcissa Whitman, Henry and Eliza Spalding, and William and Mary Gray. The Whitmans established a mission in the territory of the Cayuse at Waiilatpu on the Walla Walla River. The Spaldings located a second mission among the Nez Perces (Nimipuu) at Lapwai, while the Grays served at both mission sites. Additional reinforcements arrived in succeeding years, and they established mission stations at Tshimakain in northeastern Washington and Kamiah in north-central Idaho. These later reinforcements included Asa and Sara Smith, Elkanah and Mary Walker, and Cushing and Myra Eells. The Presbyterian missionaries for the Oregon mission, who hailed from middle-class families in New England and New York, came of age during the early nineteenth century and witnessed the religious revivalism of the Second Great Awakening and their contemporaries' enthusiasm for the larger, worldwide Protestant missionary project aimed at indigenous peoples in the Americas, Asia, Africa, and the Pacific.[6]

The problems that plagued the Presbyterian mission in the Columbia Plateau were not unlike those that had undermined the Methodist enterprise in western Oregon. From the outset, differences in philosophy, personality, and managerial style divided the Presbyterians, and these internal divisions exacerbated the missionaries' individual struggles with isolation, loneliness, limited resources, rustic living conditions, and their own religious vocations. Their greatest challenge was the cultural gulf that separated them from the Native peoples whom they hoped to convert to Christianity. For the Natives of the Plateau who had a genuine interest in learning about the religion, their aim was not to abandon or replace their indigenous spirituality, religious practices, or health care systems but rather to supplement their existing culture with the aspects of Christianity that might prove beneficial. On the other hand, the Presbyterian missionaries came to the region with very distinct notions of their own cultural and religious superiority, which were compounded by their lack of knowledge of the Indian peoples and the intercultural history of the fur trade in the Plateau. The Protestants were equally lacking in the linguistic training needed to communicate effectively in the regional indigenous languages. These deep-seated cultural differences, together with a series of missteps by the Presbyterians, created increasingly strained relations with the Indian tribes, especially the Cayuse in whose territory the Whitmans had established their mission.[7]

During the 1840s, relations between the Whitmans and the Cayuse continued to deteriorate due to the large numbers of Oregon Trail emigrants who traversed the Cayuse territory and relied on the Whitman mission for assistance. The presence of the American overlanders had a deleterious and disruptive effect on the Cayuse because the emigrants despoiled the Natives' land, resources, and water; mistreated individual Indians; and brought new infectious diseases to the Plateau. Equally troubling was Marcus Whitman's effort to promote further American emigration and settlement at the expense of the Cayuse. The situation reached a crisis point in the fall of 1847, when measles struck the Pacific Northwest and had a devastating impact on the Cayuse. Concerned about the apparent malevolent cause of the epidemic, one faction within the Cayuse decided to take decisive action. This faction reacted to the situation in keeping with their shamanistic tradition of *tewatat*, which held healers accountable for the deaths of their patients (i.e., their lives could be forfeit). This decision, combined with the deep-seated resentments that many Cayuse felt toward Marcus and Narcissa Whitman, led to the Cayuse attack on the mission, the killing of the missionaries and eleven others, and the taking of some fifty hostages on November 29 and 30, 1847.[8] Among the hostages was one of the daughters of Henry and Eliza Spalding.

The next day, December 1, 1847, Jean Baptiste Brouillet arrived at the Whitman mission after learning of the killing of the missionaries from a group of Cayuse. Brouillet spoke briefly with the hostages and then buried the dead with the assistance of Joseph Stanfield, a local "Frenchman," who—along with the Anglo-Indian settlers Nicholas Finlay and Joseph Lewis—had been spared by the Cayuse. Brouillet then set out to meet Henry Spalding, who was en route to the Whitman mission. Although a Cayuse warrior had accompanied Brouillet, the priest was able to convince the warrior to consult with his fellow warriors back at the mission as to Spalding's fate. This gave Brouillet time to provide Spalding with some provisions and warn him to flee for his life. Spalding did return safely to Lapwai after a difficult journey, and he and his family received protection from the local Nez Perce as long as war with the American settlers could be avoided. Fearing for his family and his captive daughter, Spalding sent a letter to A. M. A. Blanchet asking that the bishop convey a message to George Abernethy, governor of the Oregon Provisional Government. In his message to Abernethy, Spalding pleaded with the governor to prevent American reprisals against the Cayuse. Spalding also asked for assistance from Blanchet and from the HBC in resolving the current crisis and rescuing both the Spaldings and the captives held by the Cayuse.[9]

Over the course of the next several weeks, A. M. A. Blanchet met with Cayuse leaders several times. At their first meeting, Blanchet expressed "the deep pain and sorrow he felt at the enormous crime" and urged the Cayuse to preserve the lives of the captives. At a later meeting, the Cayuse headmen dictated a letter to Governor Abernethy requesting peace negotiations. HBC Chief Trader Peter Skene Ogden then reached Fort Walla Walla on December 19 and arranged for a larger conference with regional Native leaders, including both the Cayuse and the Nez Perces. At the meeting, Ogden upbraided the headmen for the killings at Waiilatpu and outlined the HBC's position favoring a peaceful solution to the crisis, but he also warned of possible repercussions from the American settlers. Ogden was able to negotiate the release of the hostages and the escort of Spalding and his family to Fort Walla Walla by the Nez Perces. The HBC rescue party departed the fort with the freed captives and the missionaries from Lapwai on January 2 and arrived in Oregon City on January 10, 1848. The group also included A. M. A. Blanchet and two other missionary priests. Although Father Brouillet sought to continue the Catholic mission on the Umatilla River, the hostilities in the ensuing Cayuse War forced him to leave the Plateau a month later in mid-February, 1848. A. M. A. Blanchet and Brouillet and their colleagues from the Diocese of Walla Walla relocated temporarily to the Catholic mission in the Willamette Valley until their appointment to new posts north of the Columbia River.[10]

As the American settlers set about organizing a military response to the Whitman mission incident, a new strain of anti-Catholic Nativism emerged in the Pacific Northwest. The principal author of this campaign was none other than the Presbyterian missionary, Henry Spalding. Upon his arrival in the Willamette Valley in January 1848, Spalding spoke out against the Catholic missionaries in the region, notably A. M. A Blanchet and Jean Baptiste Brouillet, two men who had been instrumental in saving his life and those of his fellow missionaries. The roots of Spalding's anti-Catholic crusade in the aftermath of the Whitman mission killings lay in his own personal history, previous anti-Catholic views, and the larger historical context. Spalding's contemporaries noted his personal insecurity and anxiety due to his illegitimate birth and limited education, as well as his periodic struggles with mental illness. Additionally, strong tensions and a mutual animosity had marked relations between Protestant and Catholic missionaries in the Plateau during the years prior to the Whitman mission incident. Having survived the attack on Presbyterian missionaries, Spalding felt personally betrayed when his letter to A. M. A. Blanchet was printed in the *Oregon Spectator* with other documents related to the tragic incident. He felt a strong sense of shame and humiliation because his request for assistance from the Catholic missionaries and the HBC, together with his plea to Governor Abernethy to avoid retaliation against the Cayuse, appeared to show him as a pitiful figure. Although Spalding's actions were certainly understandable at the time, he never forgave the Catholic clergymen for allowing his letter to A. M. A Blanchet to be published.[11]

As a result, Spalding initiated a campaign to discredit the Catholic missionaries, suggesting that they had engaged in a conspiracy with the Cayuse to destroy the Presbyterian mission project in the Plateau. The apparent evidence for this conspiracy was the fact that the Catholic missionaries—as well as local Catholic settlers and fur traders, including French Canadians and mixed bloods—were unharmed in the attack on the Whitman mission. Spalding also suggested complicity on the part of HBC officers, whose loyalty was also suspect because of their British nationality and their positive relations with the Catholic missionaries. Spalding publicized his charges in a series of articles in the *Oregon American and Evangelical Unionist*, and these accusations found some support among Anglo-American settlers due to both regional conditions in the Pacific Northwest and the rising tide of anti-Catholic Nativism in the United States. In this context, the contention that foreign Catholic missionaries and their French Canadian and mixed-blood adherents had conspired with "hostile" Indians to assassinate Protestant missionaries seemed a plausible theory to some of the Americans. Indeed, in the aftermath of the Whitman mission incident, the Oregon Provisional Government voted on a resolution to expel all Catholic missionaries from Oregon. Although the resolution was defeated, U.S. officials ordered the closing of the Catholic missions on the Plateau. The Nativist rhetoric portraying Catholics, French Canadians, French-Indian mixed bloods, and British settlers as disloyal, internal enemies gained a public airing in the late 1840s, and this explanation for the Whitman mission incident reappeared periodically in succeeding decades, most notably in William Gray's *A History of Oregon* (1870). As Francis Victor Fuller recognized in the later decades, the underlying causes of the Whitman mission killings—the grievances of the Cayuse and the federal government's neglect of Indian affairs—went largely unexamined by the American settlers.[12]

In December 1847, Governor Abernethy sent out a call for an armed response to the Whitman mission incident. The provisional government then approved a bill to raise a regiment of volunteer riflemen in the Willamette Valley and to finance the regiment by means of personal loans from wealthy settlers and $100,000 in war bonds to be purchased by the general populace. In response to these developments, many French-Indian families in French Prairie made a collective decision to side with the Anglo-American community. Their first form of support was financial. F. N. Blanchet raised $159.79 in "contributions des habitants" from French Prairie and purchased an initial bond in January 1848. Blanchet's colleague Jean Baptiste Bolduc collected an additional $300 for the purchase of a second bond in May 1848. Two French Prairie settlers—François Toupin, son of the French Canadian Jean Baptiste Toupin and Marie L'Aguivoise (Iowa), and Amable Arquette, a French Canadian—purchased individual bonds for $30 and $31, respectively, in January and March 1848. These individual amounts were comparable to those of American farmers in the Willamette Valley, who generally purchased bonds for $10, $25, or $40, while the community collection of several hundred dollars was comparable to more prosperous settlers and merchants, such as Francis Pettygrove, who took out a bond for $500.[13]

The French Prairie colonists' second form of support for the Anglo-American community was to provide militiamen for the prosecution of the Cayuse War. Following a public announcement, the settlers met at the home of Antoine Gregoire (French-Shushwap) on January 12, 1848, "for the purpose of taking into consideration the propriety of raising an additional company of volunteers, to march against the Cayuse Indians." François Xavier Matthieu, along with Americans Robert Newell, Willard Rees, and William Porteus (married to Antoine Gregoire's sister Sophie Gregoire), appear to have had a hand in managing the meeting, which included approximately 150 men from Champoeg, St. Paul, and St. Louis. Following an animated speech delivered in Chinook Jargon (and presumably French) by Thomas McKay, the mixed-race stepson of John McLoughlin, the assembly passed a resolution that read, "We Canadian Citizens of Champoeg county, feel it our duty to assist our adopted country in the prosecution of the existing war against the Cayuse Indians, for the horrible massacre, [committed] by them upon American citizens at Waiilatpu." Thirty men came forward to volunteer that day, and they unanimously chose McKay as their captain. Company D, also known as the "French Company," departed Oregon City on February 3, 1848, for Portland, and there joined about two hundred other volunteers headed to The Dalles to rendezvous with the advanced guard commanded by Colonel Cornelius Gilliam.[14]

The decision of the French Prairie settlers to provide financial backing and volunteers for the Cayuse War was based on a combination of factors, first among these being their own reaction to the killings at the Whitman mission and increasing tensions between settlers and Indians in the Willamette Valley in recent years.[15] The French Prairie settlers had cooperated with their American neighbors on local initiatives of mutual interest since the 1830s, and this approach had continued, with the French Prairie farmers contributing to the debate about the formation of a "public exporting company" and publicly supporting collective action in response to claim jumping.[16] In siding with their American neighbors and supporting a military response to the Cayuse attack on the Whitman mission, the French-Indian families may have intended to answer the allegations of an anti-American conspiracy articulated by Spalding and his supporters. Most importantly, they acted in their own self-interest, which coincided to some degree with the interests of the American settlers. However, the inhabitants of French Prairie approached the situation with a somewhat different attitude than that of the Americans, who brought a culture of anti-Indian intolerance to the military campaign against the Cayuse.[17]

A letter to the editor of the Salem-based *Oregon Spectator* from a literate observer, one "Veritas," provides some additional insight into the perspectives of the French Prairie families. Veritas, who penned the letter following the departure of McKay's French Company, commented on the accuracy of the newspaper's report of the February 12 meeting at Champoeg and the motives of the French Prairie volunteers. In the view of Veritas, the newspaper was too hasty in describing the volunteers as all Frenchmen, when in fact the party that departed for The Dalles "consisted of two Canadians, fifty or sixty half breeds—all British subjects—and two or three Americans citizens."[18] There is some truth to the numbers supplied by Veritas, but the enlistment rolls point to a somewhat more diverse group of volunteers. About fifty men made up the "French Company": approximately twenty settlers of French-Indian ancestry (40 percent), ten French Canadians (20 percent), fifteen Americans (30 percent), two Natives (4 percent), and three officers of Anglo-Indian ancestry (6 percent). Thus, a majority of the volunteers (60 percent) were French speakers, and twice as many younger mixed-race men offered to serve as compared to the older French Canadians.[19]

Veritas further argued that more of the French Canadians did not volunteer because they knew that winter was a poor time to wage war and that the provisional government's priorities should be to rescue the hostages, open negotiations with the Cayuse, and gather intelligence so as to be able to "act with propriety, decorum and energy, which the case required."[20] On one hand, the words of Veritas might be read as criticism at the lack of manliness on the part of the male farmers of French Prairie. They might be read alternatively as a general critique of the hurried nature of the larger war effort and as evidence of more moderate voices within the French-Indian community—voices that called for restraint rather than straightforward revenge in response to the killings at the Whitman mission. One French Canadian who publicly supported the provisional government actions yet also called for restraint and moderation was Archbishop F. N. Blanchet, sentiments which he expressed in a pastoral letter in the *Oregon Spectator* on March 9, 1848 (the letter was originally dated December 16, 1847).[21]

Although the sources on the French Company are quite limited in scope, they do provide some information on the volunteers' service in the Cayuse War. As a result of their biracial heritage and culture, knowledge of the regional fur trade and intercultural relations, and their familiarity with Native languages, including those of the Plateau region as well as Chinook Jargon, the French Prairie militiamen performed both military and diplomatic functions. During their march to Fort Wascopam (Fort Lee) at The Dalles, they helped transport a cannon across natural obstacles along the Columbia River Gorge. They were also actively involved in several of the engagements against the Cayuse, with Thomas McKay receiving particular praise for his leadership and performance on the battlefield. American observers also noted the French Company's contributions to negotiations and peace talks with the Cayuse and other regional Indian leaders, presumably as translators and cultural brokers.[22] The company included former French Canadian laborers who had worked in the Plateau and had in-laws there, such as Joseph Pin, as well as younger men whose mothers were natives of the region, including Xavier Plante (French-Cayuse), Charles Beauchemin (French–Walla Walla), and Olivier and Antoine Laferte (French–Pend d'Oreille).[23]

Robert Newell, a well-known American fur trader who had retired to French Prairie and served as a peace commissioner during the conflict, noted the differences in attitude and conduct between the French Prairie volunteers and some of the American troops: "This Army is composed of different kinds of men. Some have come to act legally[,] others to plunder and others for popularity and to [do] what we ought to do is easy to if we should do it together. Capt. McKay and Company deserve credit[,] in fact nearly all the officers appear to wish to do for the best."[24] The French Prairie volunteers may have met the initial expectations of military leaders and their own officers, but they were less interested in a long enlistment, especially given the need to attend to their farms in the Willamette Valley during the summer months. As a result, a number of the volunteers, including Tom McKay, returned to the valley in the spring of 1848. Reasons given for their return included illness, lack of supplies and clothing, and complaints that they had only signed up for three months (on the return trip, McKay led the escort that brought Colonel Gilliam's body back to Oregon City following his accidental death from a self-inflicted gunshot). The French Prairie volunteers who remained with the army in the Plateau joined new companies commanded by American officers, and these groups continued to pursue the Cayuse through 1848 and 1849.[25] The Cayuse War came to a close in 1850, when five Cayuse leaders, known as the Cayuse Five, agreed to surrender to U.S. officials in exchange for an end to the hostilities. Although the Cayuse argued that the men actually responsible for the killings at the Whitman mission were now dead, the Cayuse Five were summarily tried, convicted, and hanged by a territorial court in Oregon City. Archbishop F. N. Norbert Blanchet met with the Cayuse Five throughout their incarceration and trial and accompanied the men to the scaffold in the summer of 1850.[26]

❈   Gold was discovered at Sutter's Mill, California, in January 1848, and by the summer of 1848 settlers in western Oregon began to lose interest in the prosecution of the Cayuse War when word of the discovery reached the Willamette Valley. In the wake of reports from Sutter's Mill and the Sacramento Valley, several groups of Oregon settlers, including two from French Prairie, set about organizing prospecting forays to the California goldfields. The first group to leave French Prairie departed in the summer of 1848, and a second somewhat larger group left in May 1849, accompanied by Father Bartholomew Delorme, then pastor of the French Prairie parish of St. Louis. The French Prairie groups met with mixed success in California: a number of settlers were able to return to Oregon with gold dust, while the second group met with tragedy due to the infectious diseases circulating in the goldfields. F. N. Blanchet noted that about forty people in the second French Prairie brigade died of a "burning fever." The deceased included Pierre Bellique Sr., Hypolite Brouillet, Joseph Bourgeau, Joseph Crochère, Jean-Baptiste (Olivier) Dobin, Joseph Gagnon, Jean Baptiste Godin, and Marguerite Laverdure.[27]

The migration of Oregon settlers to the California goldfields had unanticipated consequences for Catholic institutions in the Willamette Valley. Facing reductions in enrollment, financial constraints, and a decline in the economic fortunes of Oregon City (Portland was then emerging as the more dominant city in Oregon), the Sisters of Notre Dame de Namur closed their schools in St. Paul and Oregon City. Aggressively recruited by José Sadoc Alemany, the bishop of California (later San Francisco), the sisters relocated permanently to the Bay Area in 1852. The closing of the girls' school, along with the shuttering of the Jesuit-run boys' school in St. Paul a few years earlier, curtailed both the educational and social service activities of the Church in the Willamette Valley for several years. Not surprisingly, these developments severely restrained the ability of the French Prairie families to overcome the illiteracy that had long characterized the community.[28]

On the whole, the California Gold Rush brought the Pacific Northwest into closer communication and economic integration with both California and the eastern United States. Trade increased substantially between Oregon and California, particularly with regard to grain, foodstuffs, timber, and other raw materials. While the trade with California initially served as a boost for Oregon's economy, an oversupply of products and greater competition from California firms, particularly in the goldfields of southern Oregon, later led to an economic depression in northern Oregon in the mid-1850s. This realignment of the Pacific Northwest economy coincided with the gradual withdrawal of the Hudson's Bay Company from the American territories south of the 49th parallel and the company's concentration on its fur trade operations in British Columbia and shipping activities in the Pacific region. The HBC also initiated financial negotiations with the U.S. federal government regarding its interests and properties in Oregon and Washington, which were concluded by 1860. As American immigrants continued to stream into California and the Pacific Northwest in the years before the Civil War, the Pacific Slope witnessed the emergence of a merchant class, a growth in land speculation, an increase in commercial agriculture, and the introduction of industrial operations in the timber and mining sectors.[29]

While news of the discovery of gold in California began to reach Oregon during the summer of 1848, the U.S Congress finally acted to extend formal political jurisdiction over the Pacific Northwest. Following the Whitman mission incident, Governor Abernethy and the Oregon Provisional Government dispatched the former fur trader Joseph Meek to Washington City in the spring of 1848 with a petition asking for the immediate formation of a territorial government. J. Quinn Thornton, who represented the interests of the Mission party (the former members of the Methodist mission settled in Oregon), also arrived in Washington with the group's suggestions for political appointments. Congress finally passed the Organic Act organizing the Oregon Territory by a slim margin, and President Polk signed the legislation in August 1848. Polk named Joseph Lane, a Mexican War veteran and Indiana Democrat, as Oregon's first territorial governor.

Upon Joseph Lane's arrival in Oregon City in March 1849, he set about organizing the territorial government, which included the executive, legislative, and judicial branches that were standard in other territorial acts of the antebellum period. The congressional legislation specified that voting rights were reserved for white male residents, twenty-one years of age, who were U.S. citizens or foreigners who had declared their intention to become citizens and had taken an oath to support the U.S. Constitution (the territorial legislature would have the power to alter these provisions for subsequent elections). The Organic Act further extended the Northwest Ordinance of 1787 over Oregon, thereby outlawing slavery and ostensibly recognizing Indian land rights (until Indian title could be extinguished). Since Congress had yet to negotiate with the Native peoples of the region, the land laws of the provisional government were ruled null and void.[30]

Although Congress appeared to protect indigenous land and resource rights in the Oregon Territorial Organic Act, the federal government's primary focus was to further the Anglo-American settlement and economic development of the Pacific Northwest. This aim was evident in the passage of the Oregon Donation Land Act in 1850, which provided for the transfer of so-called public lands to white settlers prior to congressional approval of any Indian treaties. The Donation Land Act granted 320 acres to single white male settlers, eighteen years of age, and 640 acres to married couples, each spouse owning 320 acres in his/ her own name. "American half-breed Indians" were eligible for land claims under the bill, but blacks, Hawaiians, and all other Indians were excluded. The race of the wife was not a factor in the granting of the claim; her "wifeship" or martial status was the only qualification required. The law recognized preemption privileges but not legal title to those who currently occupied claims in the Oregon Territory (Oregon, Washington, Idaho, and part of western Montana). In order to be awarded title to the land, claimants had to fulfill three other requirements: take up residency on or before December 1, 1850, reside on the land and cultivate it for four years, and make a declaration of intention to become a citizen on or before December 1, 1851.[31]

The legislation further stipulated that if a spouse should die before the patent was issued, the surviving spouse and children should equally share the deceased's property rights. Although the Oregon Donation Land Act did not grant women legal rights to sell or transfer their portion of a claim independent of their husbands, it did mark a small step in the slow evolution of married women's property rights in Oregon. The act also made provisions for settlers who arrived in the Pacific Northwest after 1850. Single male settlers could file a claim for up to

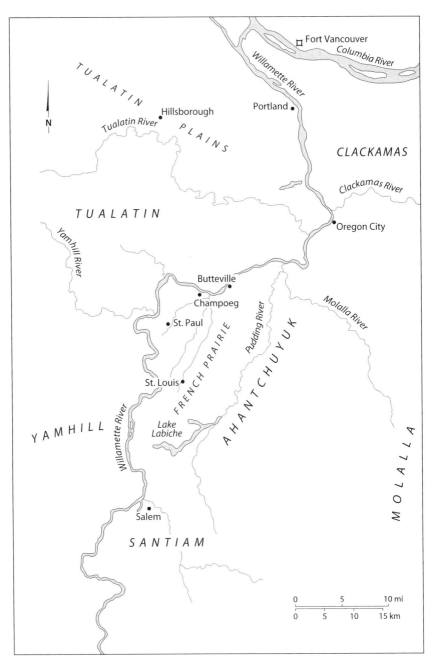

MAP 5. Lower Willamette Valley and French Prairie, 1850s. Map by Bill Nelson.

160 acres, and a couple could claim up to 320 acres, each in his/her own name. Later amendments to the original legislation advanced the final date when settlers could register claims to December 1, 1855, and extended the Preemption Law of 1841 to Oregon and Washington Territories that allowed settlement on both surveyed and unsurveyed land.[32] The legislation did coincide with additional American migration to the Pacific Northwest. During the period from 1849 to 1855, 34,050 emigrants arrived via the Oregon Trail, and between 1856 and 1860 some 7,500 more Americans completed the overland trek to the region. The U.S. Land Office ultimately granted patents to 7,437 residents in the state of Oregon, and these patents covered an estimated 2.5 million acres.[33]

The passage and implementation of the Oregon Donation Land Act served as a central mechanism of Anglo-American colonization in the Pacific Northwest, as it encouraged settlers to take control of Indian land and resources with the understanding that the region's Native people did not have equal (or even prior) claim to the land. This federal legislation, together with the discovery of precious metal deposits, had a ripple effect on the region during the 1850s, resulting in additional armed conflicts between settlers and Indians, a further consolidation of Anglo-American governance and economic control, and vocal calls from white settlers for the removal of indigenous peoples from their homelands. The major settler-Indian wars during this period—the Rogue River War and the Yakima War—stemmed directly from the actions of Anglo settlers to preempt indigenous land and resources and the failure of federal authorities to protect the interests and lives of Native people. Although the Indian groups of the Willamette Valley did not witness the same level of armed violence as the Indians of eastern Washington and southern Oregon, they did experience the comparable processes of cultural violence, interpersonal violence, dispossession, racial segregation, and removal during the 1850s.[34]

The methods that Anglo settlers employed to seize Indian territories in western Oregon—the "microtechniques of dispossession"—included preempting (squatting) on Indian land, driving Native people away from their villages, putting up fences to curtail the activities needed to maintain indigenous subsistence rounds, suppressing the Indians' annual burning of the land, continued hunting and despoliation of the flora and the fauna, and creating maps that erased the Indian presence from the landscape. During the early 1850s, the federal government sought to resolve the situation through the established treaty process of extinguishing Indian title and moving the Indians onto reservations. However, the initial agreements negotiated by the Willamette Valley Treaty Commission,

Superintendent Anson Dart, and his successor, Superintendent Joel Palmer, were not ratified because Oregon's territorial delegates to Congress, Samuel Thurston and Joseph Lane, effectively prevented any action by the Senate. Although some settlers in the Willamette Valley had been amenable to allowing the Kalapuyans and their neighbors to remain on small reserves in the valley so they could continue to be used as a labor force, Thurston and Lane had sought to block the treaties because they did not require the signatory groups to be removed east of the Cascade Mountains. Later treaties with the Kalapuyans and the Molalla were finally ratified by the U.S. Senate in March 1855 and March 1859.[35]

During the mid-1850s, a second round of treaties covering western Oregon were finally ratified by the U.S. Senate. At the same time, the Rogue River War, a genocidal campaign against the Native peoples of southern Oregon, wound down and federal officials sought removal of all the Indians of western Oregon onto reservations. The original Coast (Siletz) Reservation was established by executive order in 1855, and a temporary reservation, the "Grande Ronde Encampment," was hastily set up in the northern corner of the Coast Reservation. This later became the Grand Ronde Reservation by executive order in 1857. The Indian Office assigned the Willamette Valley peoples (the Kalapuyans, Molalla, and Upper Chinookans) and some of the groups from the Umpqua River watershed and the Rogue River area to Grand Ronde. The Willamette Valley Indians were forcibly removed to Grand Ronde over the fall and winter of 1855–1856. Following the Rogue River War, the plight of the surviving Rogue River and Umpqua groups was especially harrowing, as they were taken several hundred miles north by overland and sea routes in harsh, primitive conditions and placed on the Coast and Grand Ronde Reservations.[36]

At the same time that Anglo-Americans in Oregon proceeded with the appropriation of indigenous land and resources and the removal and segregation of Native peoples onto reservations to resolve the so-called Indian Problem in their midst, they also sought to exclude nonwhites from participation in the territory's political culture and limit their social and economic opportunities. During the era of the provisional government (1843–1849), French Canadian settlers had secured voting privileges for the adult sons of white men. Under Oregon's territorial system, however, voting rights were limited to white men, aged twenty-one years, which disenfranchised the French-Indian settlers in French Prairie who had reached their majority. In addition, although the French Canadians who remained in the Willamette Valley had accepted American rule and had publicly supported their Anglo-American neighbors in the Cayuse War, their motives and their loyalty remained suspect in the eyes of some Americans, especially those who still viewed the French Canadians and their mixed-race offspring as a possible fifth-column ready to abet anti-American conspiracies of the HBC and the Roman Catholic Church.

These views, which blended Pacific Northwest strains of Nativism with Anglo-Saxon racialism, were evident in debates about the provisions of the Oregon Donation Land Act. Prominent settler Jesse Applegate wrote Samuel Thurston, Oregon's first territorial delegate and author of the proposed legislation, and voiced his opinion that British subjects should only be allowed to claim, grant, and transfer land after they had taken an oath of allegiance to the United States. In 1849, Daniel Lownsdale, a Kentucky native then engaged in land speculation and development in Portland, wrote an extended letter to delegate Thurston on the subject of land rights for foreigners in the Pacific Northwest. In his letter, Lownsdale revisited Henry Spalding's view of Pacific Northwest history, detailing the apparently long-standing plot by Great Britain's proxy in the region, the HBC, to thwart the economic and political aspirations of Americans in the region. Lownsdale cited the efforts of John McLoughlin to claim large tracts of land in Oregon City and the apparent complicity of the HBC, its Indian and mixed-race minions, and Catholic missionaries in the Whitman mission incident as evidence of this long-standing plot against American interests, issues Lownsdale argued Congress ought to consider in drafting legislation on public lands in Oregon.[37]

During congressional deliberations over the Oregon land bill, Thurston, who had won his delegate seat on an anti-HBC, anti-Catholic campaign, expressed concerns about the troubling scenario of interracial mixing between blacks and Indians in the Pacific Northwest and the possibility of the HBC getting its hands on the land of its former servants and controlling their property. Thurston also questioned whether foreigners should automatically be allowed land grants under the proposed legislation, arguing that Canadians would need to qualify for land grants by agreeing to become naturalized citizens. As for the French Canadians' mixed-race offspring, Thurston took a paternalistic stance, reasoning that the French-Indians, all of whom "adhered to the whites," should be "protected"—presumably to ensure their commitment to Anglo-American settlement. Thurston argued further that contracts between aliens—that is, contracts between the HBC and its former employees—be declared null and void so as to reduce the economic influence of the London-based company. Thurston's vision for the Oregon Donation Land Act was essentially the one passed by Congress in 1850, with minor amendments in succeeding years.[38]

The French Canadians' response to concerns about their trustworthiness and their right to land grants can be gleaned from a few written sources of the period. In 1852, Edouard Dupuis, a Champoeg shopkeeper and one of the few literate French Canadians in the Willamette Valley, wrote a letter on behalf of his countrymen to Joseph Lane, who had replaced Thurston as Oregon's territorial delegate in Washington City. Dupuis asked for Lane's assistance in upholding the rights of the French Canadians and their family members under the Oregon Donation Land Act. He explained that "The majority of my fellow citizens are married to Indian women and the general opinion amongst the citizens of Oregon is that those Indian women will not hold land. Consequently the result is that a great many of our claims or parts of claims have been jump [*sic*] on those grounds[.] Next to the Half Breed, it is supposed that they cannot hold land, and you are well aware that some of them have splendid claims[,] well improved[,] and they are liable to be jumped. Also some of them are selling for little or nothing for they fear losing them altogether."[39] Dupuis further reminded Lane that he had served with other French Canadians and French-Indians in a regiment commanded by Thomas McKay for "upwards of six months" during the Cayuse War, and that the French Prairie settlers had been willing to "defend Oregon in time of danger." Dupuis asked Lane that if "Canadian Half Breeds" could not hold land under the Oregon Donation Land Act, special action be taken on their behalf, especially for the Cayuse War veterans.[40]

By emphasizing the French Prairie inhabitants' military service, Dupuis echoed Thurston's earlier rhetoric of the French Canadians earning the benefits of American citizenship and access to land grants by demonstrating their allegiance to the United States. Dupuis also noted the essential economic role of women in the settlement process and the disadvantaged status of bachelors who had served in the French regiment. The French Prairie shopkeeper wrote that "a person cannot hold land without being a permanent settler, and a Bachelor to be a permanent settler, you know yourself that is a matter of impossibility."[41] Although Dupuis may have misconstrued the acreage provisions in the Oregon Donation Land Act for single and married individuals, his allusion to the importance of women's role in the land grant process is noteworthy.

The provision in the federal legislation granting married women land claims in their own name was part of a larger national shift intended to protect the assets of middle-class families from creditors. Although married women did not gain property rights as individuals but rather through the mechanism of their marriage to men, married women's property acts at the state level did begin to limit

FIGURE 6. The American Village. SOURCE: Henry Warre, *Sketches in North America and the Oregon Territory* (1848). Courtesy of the Oregon Historical Society, OrHi 49029.

the reach of coverture. This evolution in married women's property laws apparently influenced Samuel Thurston and others in their work on the Oregon land bill. As demonstrated by the Dupuis letter, the French Prairie settlers understood this important role for married women in gaining land patents and were concerned about protecting the property rights of Indian women under the legislation. In *Vandolf* v. *Otis* (1854), a decision in response to a suit brought by the French Canadian Louis Vandal (the elder) agains a claim jumper, the Supreme Court of the Oregon Territory recognized the rights of Indian women to federal land claims based on their status as wives to white men, a decision that upheld the property rights of white men by relying on current notions of race and gender. The court also specified that the ruling did not apply to Indian men and their wives, who might be Indian or white.[42]

❋ Although the French Prairie families faced an increasingly racialized society under the Oregon territorial government, they continued to pursue both family and community interests during the 1850s. The available sources from the period provide some insights into the responses and experiences of the French-Indian community during the decade that preceded the Civil War and Oregon's achievement of statehood. The federal census of 1850, the first complete nominal census, reveals a general demographic stability in French Prairie at the start of the 1850s. According to the census rolls for Marion County (formerly Champoeg County), the total French-Indian population in French Prairie was about 557, which included 265 adults and 292 children under the age of twenty-one. Of 114 French-speaking households listed in the census rolls, 108 were headed by men and 6 by women. French Canadians continued to make up the majority of the male heads of households (80 of 108, or 80 percent), while their French-Indian sons made up a small minority (14 percent) and the Frenchmen and French Americans a tiny group (1.5 percent). Of the 108 male settlers, 73 percent (79) were married and 27 percent (29) were single.[43]

The census rolls point to the importance of endogamy within the French Prairie community and the male settlers' preference for *métis* women of French-Indian ancestry by the 1850s. Of the 79 wives of the settlers, the ethnic background of 77 could be identified: 58 percent (45) were French-Indian, 38 percent (29) Native, 2.5 percent Anglo-American (2), and 1 percent Anglo-Indian (1). The six female heads of household listed in the 1850 census included Angelique Marcellais, widow of François Gagnon; Marguerite Soulière, widow of David Dompiere; Marie Angelique Banak, widow of Louis Brousseau; Marguerite Yogalta, widow of Jean Baptiste Dubreuil; Sophie Grégoire, widow of William Porteous; and Catherine Delard, widow of Jean Baptiste Lucier dit Gardepied. Catholic Church records for St. Paul and St. Louis show that aside from Catherine Delard, all these women chose to marry local French-speaking farmers within a few years of their husbands' deaths. Angelique Marcellais wed Edouard Bellanger; Marguerite Soulière wed Joseph Rochbrune; Marie Angelique Banak wed Pierre Dépôt Jr.; Marguerite Yogalta married Charles Plante; and Sophie Grégoire married Frimin Lebrun.[44]

In addition to married couples, single men, and widows, the 1850 census records for Marion County reveal that 34 percent of the French-speaking households (39 of 114) included other adults in the households, both adult children (married and unmarried) and laborers. While the vast majority of the francophone settlers and their adult boarders were either farmers or farm laborers, a small number of the men had other identified professions: the Frenchman Pierre Bouelle was a clerk; the young Louisiana native Joseph Silvestre was a trader; Narcisse Vivette, boarding with Andre Longtain and Nancy Okanagan, was a tanner; and Marcel Gagnon, living with George Laroque, was a carpenter. It appears that some of the male laborers had either been unable to secure farms of their own or had lost or sold their claim. This was the case for Antoine Masta. The French Canadian had registered a land claim with the Oregon Provisional Government in the late 1840s, but by 1850 he and his wife Sophie Chinook and their two daughters, Victoire and Marie, were living with Joseph Despard and his wife Lisette Chinook and their four children. The French envoy Pierre Fournier de Saint Amant wrote of a strange encounter he had with Masta in the summer of 1851. In Saint Amant's telling, the aged French Canadian was a rustic individual given to drinking, violence against his wife, and periods of depression and self-doubt. Masta had apparently sold his land claim to an American settler before traveling to California to prospect for gold. According to Saint Amant, Masta explained that his wife had finally left him due to his mistreatment and that he was living alone in a cabin with a small hoard of gold because F. N. Blanchet, archbishop of Oregon City, would not allow him to marry a *métis* woman from French Prairie because he was still married to Sophie Chinook. For her part, Sophie had returned to her people near Astoria and apparently had a new beau as well.[45]

In contrast to outliers such as Antoine Masta, the available evidence from the 1850s suggests that most French Prairie settlers continued to prioritize the status and well-being of their families and the community at large and used the legal means at their disposal to advance these aims. Concerning issues of nationalism and culture, they were less committed to Great Britain than their American critics believed and less apt to share the views of their elite francophone critics who cherished middle-class notions of French cultural nationalism. Between 1849 and 1860, some 133 French Canadians, French-Indians, and Frenchmen in Marion County (87 percent from British North America and 13 percent from France) registered their declaration of intention to become citizens of the United States. The 133 foreign-born residents included elderly, long-time settlers from the 1820s and 1830s such as Jean Baptiste Desportes McKay, Joseph Gervais, Jean Baptiste Perrault, Amable Arquette, Joseph Delard, and Pierre Dépôt; middle-aged French Canadian fur trade laborers who retired to farms in French Prairie during the 1840s; and a smaller group of younger, literate emigrants from Lower Canada who were engaged in commercial activities, such as François-Xavier Matthieu, Medard Foisy, Edouard Dupuis, and Adolphe Jetté.[46]

In contrast to the Americans in Oregon who questioned the loyalties of the French Prairie inhabitants and their right to federal land grants, the French envoy Saint Amant expressed disappointment that the French Prairie settlers, both the French Canadians and their French-Indian offspring, demonstrated a less than vigorous interest in France, their ancestral homeland, and its national culture and that they spoke a "triple jargon of French, English, and Indian" rather than a more refined French. The French Prairie inhabitants enjoyed the visits of Frenchmen such as Saint Amant, but Saint Amant concluded that any sense of French nationalism had been extinguished among these descendants of the French diaspora. Aside from their concerns about the land survey process required for the implementation of the donation land bill, they appeared content to be left alone by the government. In Saint Amant's view, the French Canadians' primary motivation for making declarations of their intention to become citizens was to gain the legal patents to their farms. While Saint Amant's portrayal of the French Prairie settlers can be read as a nostalgic lament for France's lost empire in North America intended to be read by his countrymen in France, it is clear that a substantial number of French Canadians chose to remain in Oregon with their families under American rule rather than return to British North America after the international boundary settlement of 1846. American settler J. W. Grim, who arrived in Oregon in 1847, confirmed in an 1878 interview that as a group, the French Canadians wished to retain their land claims, and for this reason they declared their intention to become American citizens.[47]

Additional archival sources add further detail to the socioeconomic priorities of the French Prairie families during the 1850s. The Marion County records from 1847 to 1860 contain thirty-seven complete probate files for settlers with French surnames, all of whom are also listed in the local Catholic Church registers.[48] This group included thirty-six men and one woman, Catherine (née Russie) Chalifoux Comartin. The ethnicity of the deceased men indicates a continued prominence of French Canadians (and Frenchmen) as heads of household into the 1850s: 95 percent (34) were French Canadian or French and 5 percent (2) were of French-Indian ancestry. The vast majority of the men, 89 percent (32), were married while a small minority, 11 percent (4), were single. The ethnicity of the thirty-two widows illustrates the historic patterns of marriage practices in the community: 53 percent (17) were of French-Indian ancestry, 44 percent (14) were of Native ancestry, and one woman, Catherine Russie, was French Canadian. Russie had married Andre Chalifoux in Lower Canada in the mid-1830s and then traveled with him to his posting in the Columbia Department. Following Chalifoux's death in 1851, she married Hyacinthe Comartin in 1854, and upon her passing in 1860 her estate was in turn registered with the Marion County probate court (see table 11).[49]

Taken as a whole, the thirty-seven probate cases from Marion County suggest a number of patterns for social and economic realities in French Prairie during the transition to Anglo-Ameican rule in the 1850s. When the French Canadians and their Native and *métis* wives resettled the fertile lands of the Ahantchuyuk Kalapuyans in the 1830s and 1840s, they had limited financial resources to draw on, which necessitated a mixed economy based on subsistence agriculture, some commercial agriculture, stock raising, hunting and gathering, fur trapping, and communal labor. By the 1850s, the French-Indian families confronted a local settler economy that prioritized agriculture and livestock, as well as a larger industrial economy that relied on land speculation, capital accumulation, and more sophisticated systems of trade and banking, circumstances which led to higher levels of indebtedness among the French Prairie farmers. Compared with earlier decades, they were now demonstratively more dependent on kin, neighbors, friends, and local merchants for labor services, credit, loans, and cash or its equivalent. These conditions, evident in the probate files, led the French-Indian families to pursue a series of socioeconomic strategies in keeping with the times; and first among these was to clear the men's debts and make the best possible provisions for their widows and children.

The first step was to register the settlers' deaths with probate court and thereby protect their estates in the short term. This was particularly important in French Prairie because the majority of the thirty-seven deceased settlers (thirty-six men and one woman), 63 percent (twenty-three), died intestate, while a minority, 37 percent (fourteen), left wills (dictated and translated by the handful of literate French speakers). For the most part, French Canadians—white men—served as the executors and appraisers of the estates in question. The probate court would occasionally appoint Anglo-American settlers such as Robert Newell, John Findlay, and John David Crawford as coexecutors or appraisers, a practice that occurred more frequently in the late 1850s. It was not uncommon for the executors to be related to the deceased by blood or marriage. In some cases, a widow's new husband would serve as the executor of the estate, and on a few rare occasions widows assisted as coexecutrixes. Following the death of Joseph Gagnon in California in 1849, his brother Luc Gagnon became the executor of his estate and later bought the Joseph Gagnon land claim. Catherine Russie lost her first husband Andre Chalifoux in 1851, and she served as coexecutrix of his estate along with Laurent Quintal, Sylvain Bourgeau, and Louis Pichet. When David Gervais died in 1853 at the age of thirty, his widow Marie Anne Toupin was appointed

TABLE 11. Marion County probate records: Settlers with French surnames, 1847–1860

Deceased Name	Date	Spouse	Remarriage	Date
1. Hyacinthe Lavigeur	1847*	Marguerite Chaudière	[deceased 1848]	
2. Andre Picard	1847*	Marie Okanagan	Cuthbert Lambert	1846
3. Nazaire Dupré	1848	Catherine Lafantaisie	David Mongrain	1849
4. Charles Jeaudoin	1848	Marie Anne Servant	Louis Bergevin	1848
5. Pierre Bellique	1849	Genevieve St. Martin	Casimir Guardepie	1850
6. Hypolite Brouillet	1849	Angle Gingras	Cyrile Bertrand	1849
7. Joseph Bourgeau	1849	Angele Lafantaisie	Theodore Gervais	1850
8. Jean Baptiste Perrault	1849	Angele Chehalis	Sylvain Bourgeau	1857
9. Jean Baptiste (Olivier) Dobin	1849	Nancy of The Dalles	[deceased 1850]	
10. Joseph Gagnon	1849	Margeurite Desjarlais	Jean Claude dit Bellanger	1851
11. Joseph Plouff	1849	Therese Makaine	Baptiste Laroque	1850
12. Jean Baptiste Godin	1849	Julie (Louise) Shoshone	Charles Beauchemin	1849
13. Jean Baptiste Sylvestre	1851			
14. Andre Chalifoux	1851	Catherine Russie	Hyacinthe Comartin	1854
15. Stanislaus Liard	1852	Celeste Rochbrune	Honore Picard	1853
16. Joseph Rivet	1852	Marie Anne Despard	Xavier Gervais	1853
17. Etienne Lucier Sr.	1853	Marguerite Chinook	Edouard Daigneau	1856
18. Thomas Roy	1853	Marie Lafleur	[deceased 1853]	
19. David Gervais	1853	Marie Anne Toupin	François Robideau	1857
20. Flavius Loignon	1854			
21. Jacques Servant	1854	Josette Okanagan	Pierre Lacourse	1856
22. Eloi Ducheneau	1854			
23. Eli Giguère	1855	Victoire Cornoyer	Ambroise Gagnon	1855
24. Fabien Malouin	1855	Victoire Laderoute	Andre Cloutier	1855
25. Pascal Biscornet	1855	Louise Cowichan		
26. Charles Rondeau	1855	Elizabeth Indian	Jonathon Dupati	1856
27. Louis Aucent	1856	Mary Molala	Joseph Simoneau	1858
28. Jean Bapstiste Dalcourt	1856			
29. Jean Gingras	1856	Olive Forcier	François Brouillard	1860
30. Joseph Binet	1856	Marianne Felicité Indian	[deceased 1858]	
31. Octave Martel	1857	Mary Okanagan	Jean Genet	1859
32. Hercules Lebrun	1857	Louise Ouvre	Adolphe L'Oiseau (Lozeau)	1858
33. Laurent Sauvé	1858	Françoise Cayuse		
34. Felix Bergevin	1859	Olive Deguire	Narcisse Herpin	1859
35. Joseph Longtain	1859	Marie Ducharme	Luger Camiran	1861
36. Louis B. Vandal	1859	Marie Anne Delard	Medard Foisy	1860
37. Catherine (Russie) Comartin	1860			

NOTE: *Lavigeur and Picard died in 1846.
SOURCES: Marion County Probate Case Files, 1843–1898, OSA; Munnick, *CCRPNW-V; CCRPNW-SP; CCRPNW-SL.*

executrix of the estate along with her father Jean Toupin and her brother François Toupin. A few weeks after the death of Felix Bergevin in 1859, his common-law wife Olive Deguire formally married Narcisse Herpin, and Herpin then became primary executor of the Bergevin estate.[50]

Nearly all of the probate cases required an estate sale of some kind involving personal property, immovable property (real estate), or most often a combination of the two. The data from the Marion County probate records suggests that from the 1840s through the 1850s, the French-Indian families sought to keep the existing land base within the French Prairie community. A primary means for accomplishing this was to utilize the mechanisms of the probate court. The few literate French Canadians—such as Medard Foisy, Father Jean Baptiste Bolduc, Narcisse Cornoyer, and François Xavier Matthieu—often assisted with the court paperwork, including dictation and translation of wills, collection of written loans and indentures (mortgages), completion of inventory lists and estate sale statements, and writing of receipts and other statements needing to be witnessed. The estate sales organized by the various executors, including the public auction of land claims, afforded French Prairie families the opportunity to purchase useful items for their own farms, while also providing the funds needed to settle the debts of their neighbors and relations, which in many cases were owed to both French-speaking and English-speaking settlers and merchants in the Willamette Valley.

During the probate process, the court allowed the executors to provide maintenance for the deceased's widow and children, including paying school fees at local Catholic girls schools (the Sisters of Notre Dame de Namur and later the Sisters of Providence) and support payments for widows and children boarding with neighbors or family members. After the settlement of the debts, the widows and heirs would receive any remaining funds. Following the death of Hyacinthe Lavigeur in November 1846 and then his wife Marguerite Chaudière in April 1848, their daughter Josette Lavigeur boarded with the Sisters of Notre Dame de Namur in St. Paul while her older brothers Joseph and François boarded with local settlers, their maintenance fees paid by the sale of the Lavigeur estate. The probate court ordered final settlements to François Lavigeur in 1855 and to Joseph Lavigeur and Josette Lavigeur and her husband Joseph Bernier in 1859. Each of the three siblings received several hundred dollars in the final settlement, with François receiving about $100 less than his two siblings because he filed suit for payment prior to the final estate accounting in 1859.[51]

One exceptional case that demonstrates a general consensus among the French Prairie settlers to see probate cases settled appropriately was that of Eloi

Ducheneau, a young laborer from Lower Canada who may have made his way to Oregon via the Oregon Trail. After Ducheneau died intestate at the age of twenty-six in 1854 leaving no widow, children, or apparent heirs, the settlement of his estate became a concern for the community because it included $1,680 in monies owed to him by local settlers (via promissory notes) for labor services as well as a small amount of personal property. The literate executor of his estate, Medard Foisy (Cuthbert Lambert and Louis Aucent, the other two executors, were illiterate), may have sent word of Ducheneau's death to Lower Canada, because news did reach his widowed mother, Josette Dion, in the parish of St. Cesaire near Montreal. In 1858 she made a formal claim on Eloi's estate with the assistance of the Catholic clergy in Quebec and Father Jean Baptiste Brouillet in Vancouver. Ducheneau's mother presumably received the final settlement of the account, $1,112.50, sometime after 1858.[52]

Among the thirty-seven probate cases, thirty-one included land claims in the estate inventories, and of these thirty-one cases 70 percent (twenty-two) involved the loss of all or a portion of the men's half of the original land claim through a public auction or a prior mortgage; in nine of the cases involving immovable property, the widows retained the entire land claim. Of the twenty-two properties bought at auction or conveyed to mortgage holders, fifteen came into the possession of French Canadians and Frenchmen from the community and four into the possession of Anglo settlers, with three buyers unidentified. For example, in May 1848, French Canadian Nazaire Dupré died at the age of forty, leaving a wife, Catherine Lafantaisie, and two small children. The probate court appointed local settler David Mongrain and Catherine's brother, Charles Lafantaisie, executors of Nazaire's estate. After an appraisal by neighbors Patrick McKenzie, John McKay, and William McPherson, Mongrain and Lafantaisie held an estate sale and land auction. Local French Canadians, including Mongrain and Charles Lafantaisie, purchased much of the farm equipment, and Charles bought the land claim. Catherine later married David Mongrain in July 1849. In the final settlement of the Dupré estate in 1857, Catherine Lafantaisie and David Mongrain received $393.58 and Catherine's daughter Angelique Dupré received $44.50.[53]

The transfer of land claims from the estates of deceased French Canadian to Anglo ownership occurred in the period from 1856 to 1862, when local Americans acquired four of the last five properties to sell in full or in part. The last five farms sold during these years were the Jean Gingras claim, bought by Archibald McKinley in 1859; the Joseph Binet claim, bought by Charles Edward in 1858; the Hercules Lebrun claim, bought by Adolphe L'Oiseau (Lozeau), the widow

Lebrun's new husband, in 1859; the Laurent Sauvé claim, bought by William McAlster in 1860; and one-half of the Catherine (Russie) Comartin claim (originally belonging to Catherine and her first husband Andre Chalifoux), bought by James Coleman in 1862.[54]

For their part, the vast majority of the widows of the men whose estates went to probate utilized remarriage as a rational strategy to find a new male breadwinner to ensure a stable future for themselves and their children. Among the widows, 79 percent (26 of 32) remarried within about two years of their husbands' death, and, in keeping with existing patterns of endogamy, all married French Canadians, Frenchmen, and French-Indians from the local community. Among the six French Prairie widows associated with the Marion County probate records (1847–1860) who did not remarry, four died within a few years of their husbands' death: such was the fate of Marguerite Chaudière, widow of Hyacinthe Lavigeur; Nancy of The Dalles, widow of Jean Baptiste (Olivier) Dobin; Marie Lafleur, widow of Thomas Roy; and Marianne Felicité Indian, widow of Joseph Binet. Louise Cowichan, widow of Pascal Biscornet, never remarried after her husband's deaths in 1855. Although fifty acres of the Biscornet land claim were legally transferred to François Barget in 1856 in payment of a mortgage on that portion, Louise retained the rest of the farmland. She remained in the area with her children, Rose and Sophie Biscornet, who married two brothers, William and John McKay, local settlers of Scottish and Native ancestry. Louise died in St. Louis in 1883 at the age of about one hundred.[55]

The men making marriage alliances with widows in French Prairie would have been motivated by social and economic needs, if not romantic considerations. By combining households with a healthy woman of childbearing age, the new husbands might acquire additional financial resources, in addition to a new wife who could provide economic, domestic, and social reproductive labor essential for the local farm economy. For example, when Stanislaus (Tanis) Liard died in 1852 at the age of thirty-five, he left behind a teenage widow, Celeste Rochbrune, and an infant daughter, Marguerite. Fortunately for Celeste, she received assistance from her neighbors David Mongrain, Louis Bergevin, and Narcisse Cornoyer, who served as executors of the Liard estate. Cornoyer completed the paperwork for registering the Liard property under the Oregon Donation Land Act, organized an estate sale, and paid off Liard's debts to local settlers and merchants. Celeste married a young French Canadian, Honore Picard, in 1853, and they went on to have nine surviving children together before Celeste's death in childbirth at the age of forty-two in 1876. The Liard land claim was eventually patented by the U.S.

Land Office, and in 1870 it became the focus of a lawsuit between Celeste Liard
(and her husband Honore Picard) and Tanis and Celeste's daughter Marguerite
Liard (and her husband Adolphe Jetté).[56]

As the experience of Celeste Rochbrune suggests, the French Prairie settlers
sought to utilize both the probate court and the Oregon Donation Land Act
of 1850 to protect the land claims of families that experienced the death of the
male breadwinner, especially when a widow faced significant debts on her husband's estate. These strategies were in keeping with the intentions of middle-class
reformers who promoted married women's property laws as a means to retain
family assets in an expanding industrial economy that experienced occasional
periods of recession and depression. With the assistance of estate executors, kin,
and neighbors, all the French Prairie widows and children who retained their
family's entire land claim filed the necessary paperwork—including key affidavits
regarding residency, marriage, and citizenship intentions—to ensure they would
receive patents for their farms from the U.S. Land Office. The Land Office awarded
these nine patents to Genevieve St. Martin, widow of Pierre Bellique; Catherine
Russie, widow of Andre Chalifoux; Celeste Rochbrune, widow of Stanislaus
Liard; Marguerite Chinook, widow of Etienne Lucier; Elizabeth Indian, widow
of Charles Rondeau; the children of Jean Baptiste Dalcourt; Mary Okanagan,
widow of Octave Martel; Olive Deguire, widow of Felix Bergevin; and Marie
Anne Delard, widow of Louis B. Vandal. Eight other widows were able to obtain
patents on their own portion of the original land and any remaining acreage
from their husband's portion not sold or mortgaged through the probate process.
These included the estates of Eli Giguère, Fabien Malouin, Pascal Biscornet, Louis
Aucent, Jean Gingras, Hercule Lebrun, Laurent Sauvé, and Jacques Servant.[57]

Inventories, estate sale statements, and other accounting paperwork in the probate files confirm the economic challenges confronting the French-Indian settlers
from the late 1840s through the 1850s. They ran family farms focused on agriculture and animal husbandry. Given the production cycles of this economy, they
utilized credit accounts with local merchants such as François Xavier Matthieu
and Edouard Dupuis for foodstuffs (butter, coffee, tea, sugar, rice, salmon, oys-
ters, and fruit), alcohol (brandy, rum, and whiskey), and farming supplies and
equipment. They also became more implicated in the market revolution of the
mid-nineteenth century through their purchase of a wide variety of consumer
goods, such as thread and cloth (calico, cotton, denim), clothing (pants, socks,
women's hose), accessories (hats and scarves), boots, tobacco, pipes, playing
cards, matches, plates, candy, and castor oil. The French Prairie settlers depended

primarily on the sale of their livestock and farm harvests (wheat, oats, and barely) for income. However, the significant debts in the probate files indicate that they often did not have enough funds to meet their day-to-day needs and so relied on personal loans from their neighbors, credit accounts with the storeowners, and in some cases mortgages (also known as indentures) on portions of their land claims. For example, in November 1853, Jacques Servant signed a promissory note (with his mark) to Augustin Raymond, which was witnessed by Narcisse Cornoyer. In the note, Servant agreed to pay Raymond the sum of $1,400 at an interest rate of 6 percent per annum until the loan was paid. The promissory note further stipulated that if Servant died before the payment of the loan, a codicil to his will would take effect. In the codicil, Servant bequeathed a quarter-mile-wide section of his land claim to Augustin Raymond. Following Servant's death in June 1854, the probate court transferred the deed to this section of the Servant land claim to Raymond as per the codicil and the promissory note. The remaining land of the Jacques Servant and Josette Okanagan claim (484.29 acres) later received a patent from the U.S. Land Office.[58]

The Marion County probate files also provide a small window into domestic and marital relations in French Prairie from the late 1840s through the 1850s. The evidence from probate records—largely focused on legal issues and economic concerns for the sampling of French-Indian couples—suggests that on the whole, the marriages were fairly stable socioeconomic partnerships (if not romantic relationships). The fourteen wills in the files suggest affection between husbands and wives and a clear concern for the welfare of the surviving spouses and children. All of the wills appear to have been initially dictated in French to literate, bilingual members of the community, who then translated them into English (six of the fourteen cases include the original French versions). French Prairie forty-niner Pierre Bellique drafted a will with the assistance of Father Jean Baptiste Bolduc in January 1849 prior to his departure for the California goldfields. In his testament, Bellique instructed that his debts were to be paid, "solemn funeral services to be celebrated," and he outlined specific bequeaths to his wife, Genevieve "Jenny" St. Martin, and their six children. Genevieve was to receive one-third of all Bellique's movable and immovable property; his daughters Sophie, Genevieve, and Ester and his sons Jean Baptiste and Cyprien were to share $800 in equal parts; all of his children were to continue to possess the cows, oxen, and horses meant to be theirs; and finally, his eldest son, Pierre Bellique Jr., was to receive the remainder of Pierre Sr.'s movable and immovable property (Pierre Jr. was also designated Pierre Sr.'s universal legate). Following Pierre Bellique's death on his return journey from California to Oregon in late 1849, the family did receive assistance from the community and was able to complete the application process for the Bellique donation land claim. For her part, Genevieve St. Martin wed another French Canadian, Casimir Gardepie, in November 1850.[59]

In several of the probate cases, the individuals in question dictated a will prior to their death when they were demonstrably ill. Such was the case of Stanislaus "Tanis" Liard, the former voyageur from St. Jacques in Lower Canada. On December 29, 1851, he was "au lit malade" (sick in bed) when he dictated a testament in French, which was witnessed by his neighbor Hercule Lebrun and written by another French speaker, I. O. Chevrefils. It is clear from the text of the will that Tanis was a man facing the likelihood of his death. The purpose of the document was not only to "put his affairs in order" but also to "ensure a future for Celeste Laroque his wife." This concern for his young wife was likely motivated by affection as well as a sense of duty, for Tanis wished to ensure Celeste a "future for the good care that she has given him and continues to give him." Tanis bequeathed one-half of his movable property, immovable property, and animals to Celeste and the other half to his daughter Marguerite. He also instructed Celeste "to take his horse Blou, the cow, the bed, bedding, two suitcases, a table, the kitchenware, all the dishes, all the wheat in the barn and the pigs belonging to his wife for the support of herself and his child." As these items would be needed to set up a household, Tanis may have foreseen the possibility that Celeste and Marguerite would have to leave the farm. However, the dictation of his will set in motion a series of events that prevented the loss of the Liard land claim. Liard died in March 1852 and in April 1852, the executors of Tanis Liard's estate, David Mongrain and Louis Bergevin, renounced their position and called on prominent local settler Narcisse Cornoyer to act as sole executor, and he was duly appointed to the post.[60] Cornoyer filed the necessary papers to complete the donation land claim application, and for her part, Celeste Rochbune wed Honore Picard in February 1853.[61]

French Canadians and Frenchmen in Marion County pursued naturalization in order to secure the benefits of citizenship, including voting rights, standing in the judicial system, and access to federal land claims, all important tools to protect the interests of their families and the French Prairie community at large. At the same time, these men and their Indian and *métis* spouses faced constraints in their efforts to ensure the well-being of their biracial children and grandchildren within the increasingly racialized society of the 1850s. Suffrage in the Oregon Territory was limited to white men, yet there was some debate regarding the status and legal rights of mixed-raced individuals of European and Native ancestry in the years prior to Oregon statehood in 1859. In the political arena, regional debates about citizenship and racial minorities were closely bound up with the nation's larger sectional crisis over slavery, westward expansion, and the so-called Indian Problem, and Oregon's political culture reflected all of these national tensions.[62]

In 1855, the territorial legislature passed a law preventing mixed-race men from becoming citizens, thereby barring them from voting and preventing their participation in the court system and territorial politics. The legislators made their decision in the context of ongoing disputations about slavery and popular sovereignty in the Pacific Northwest, treaty negotiations with the Native groups of the Willamette Valley, the Rogue River War in southern Oregon, and the Yakima War in eastern Washington. The issue of civil rights for mixed-blood residents resurfaced in the Oregon legislative assembly shortly after the end of the Rogue River War and the removal of the Indians of western Oregon onto the Coast (Siletz) and Grand Ronde Reservations. In December 1856, J. W. Moffitt, a Democratic representative from Clatsop County, introduced a bill in the House to allow some mixed bloods ("half-breed Indians") to qualify for "citizenship in this Territory" (House Bill 28). In Moffitt's plan, the mixed-race individuals would need to meet several requirements: have a white father and Indian mother, be a permanent resident and landowner, both speak and write English, have "in all respects the education habits and associations of a white person," be a citizen of the United States or eligible for citizenship, and be a person of "good moral character." The granting of citizenship in the territory would be administered by the district courts.[63]

Moffitt's proposal was referred to committee and then returned to the House without a recommendation. At a full vote in January 1857, the heavily Democratic House voted down the bill 21 to 8. Only a portion of the legislators from Benton, Columbia, Marion, Multnomah, Washington, Wasco, and Clackamas Counties supported Moffitt's bill. Marion County's vote was split, with Jacob Conser voting in favor of the legislation and Lafayette Grover voting against it. Opposition to the granting of citizenship to mixed bloods was unanimous among legislators from southern Oregon, who represented Douglas, Umpqua, Coos, Curry, Jackson, and Josephine Counties—areas that had recently witnessed the brutal settler war against the Native peoples of the Rogue River watershed.[64]

Later that year, political leaders met for a month-long convention in Salem with the aim of producing a constitution to advance the cause of statehood for

Oregon. Delegates at the constitutional convention debated citizenship and voting rights for both native-born and foreign-born men, and while there was discussion as to the status of ethnic minorities, women, and immigrants, the delegates did not mention mixed bloods per se. Among the convention delegates, all
white men, there was little disagreement that full citizenship and voting rights
applied exclusively to white men such as themselves, because all other classes
(blacks, mulattoes, Indians, Chinese, Hawaiians, and women) were disquali-
fied by their perceived natural condition of handicap, be it race or gender. In
September, the delegates produced a draft constitution for Oregon that continued to limit suffrage to native-born white men and "white males of foreign birth"
who had resided in the United States for one year and declared their intention to
become citizens (Article II, Section 2). The draft constitution also stated that "no
Negro, Chinamen, or Mulatto shall have the right of suffrage" (Article II, Section
6). A special election on the draft constitution was held on November 9, 1857,
and included three additional questions: whether slavery would be allowed in
Oregon, whether free blacks would be allowed to reside in the future state, and
whether they would enjoy voting rights. A substantial majority voted to approve
the constitution, outlaw slavery, and forbid residency to free blacks. Despite the
support for slavery among some Oregon legislators, these results reflected the
free-soil aspirations of the white male voters and their aim to police the boundaries of race in a future state of Oregon.[65]

While action on Oregon's bid for statehood stalled in Congress due to the
larger sectional crisis over slavery, residents in Marion County responded to the
draft constitution by making a formal request for full citizenship for mixed-race
men. In January 1859, a group of American, French Canadian, and immigrant
settlers from French Prairie sent a petition to the territorial assembly on behalf of
the biracial men ("half-breed Indians") who were their sons, in-laws, neighbors,
customers, and business partners. Some 150 men signed the petition, including
Anglo and immigrant settlers such as John David Crawford, John Hoard, John
Hoefer, Robert Newell, and Willard Rees. Of the 150 signatories, more than 40
were French speakers. One finds the names of older French Canadian veterans of the fur trade, including François Bernier, Adolphe Chamberlain, Michel
Laframboise, Pierre Lacourse, George Laroque, Amable Petit, and Louis Vandal,
as well as younger French Canadian, French American, and Frenchmen who
married into the French Prairie community, including Narcisse Cornoyer,
Adolphe Jetté, François Xavier Matthieu, Honore Picard, and Joseph Simoneau.[66]
According to the petitioners, Oregon residents of one-half Indian ancestry were

subject to unjust treatment before the law because current statutes forbade them from testifying in cases involving white men. The territorial law thus operated "very unjustly on the party excluded" and "furnished to criminals and fraudulent debtors an opportunity for escaping from liabilities."[67]

The Marion County settlers also addressed the issue of suffrage. Within French Prairie there was a "large class" of people of one-half Indian ancestry who owned property, were intelligent, and were thereby competent to vote. Based on this logic, the petitioners requested a second change in Oregon's legal statutes so as to confer on these individuals the right to vote. The use of the term "large class" may have a double meaning: to indicate that a significant portion of the French Prairie community was of mixed ancestry; it may also be a literary device to accentuate a serious injustice. The petitioners felt it was necessary to emphasize that the mixed bloods were worthy candidates for full citizenship because they were intelligent, civilized, and responsible property owners. Echoing the earlier rhetoric of Representative Moffitt in 1856, the signatories of the 1859 petition sought to demonstrate that their mixed-race kin, neighbors, and customers had earned the right to vote by virtue of their successful integration into white society. To award them the franchise and the right to testify in court proceedings would not only "improve their condition, but would do away with the jealousies that now exist between said class and their fellow citizens."[68]

A few days after the territorial legislature received the petition from French Prairie, Representative J. H. Stevens, a Democrat from Marion County, introduced two bills, one (H.B. 93) that would "extend the right of suffrage to half-breeds," and a second (H.B. 94) that would "remove the incompetency of half-breeds in courts of justice." The committee charged with studying the two bills recommended that it "was inexpedient to legislate upon that subject at the present time." In response, Representative Stevens asked that the committee be required to produce a bill so as to put the matter to a vote of the people. This resolution was adopted. However, a few days later when a vote was called on this third bill, it failed by one vote, 11 to 10. Stevens's measure received support from colleagues in Marion, Yamhill, Linn, and Polk Counties and opposition from legislators in Clackamas, Washington, Benton, Douglas, Jackson, and Josephine Counties.[69] At the national level, Oregon's request for statehood finally moved forward in Congress after the House approved the act admitting Oregon to the Union on February 12, 1859 (the Senate had passed the bill in May 1858). President Buchanan signed the legislation on February 14, and in accordance with the voter-approved constitution, the new state of Oregon limited voting rights and full citizenship to white men.

✳ The political debate over citizenship and civil rights for mixed bloods that took place in Oregon during the 1850s mirrored events in other regions of the United States with bicultural communities born of the fur trade. During the earlier period of mercantile capitalism, mixed-race people filled intermediate roles in commerce, diplomacy, social relations, and cultural exchange. However, under an Anglo-American regime of U.S. territorial expansion and state formation, French-Indian families such as those in French Prairie found their social world contracting and their political and economic opportunities constricted. Anglo-Americans in Oregon, like their counterparts in the North, South, Midwest, Great Lakes, and Plains, fashioned a modern democratic society demarcated by race and gender. Anglo-Saxon racialism solidified the collective identity of white Americans, notably white men, and justified the banishment of nonwhites from the body politic. In the context of the sectional conflict over the expansion of slavery and the emergence of the free-soil movement, mixed-raced peoples threatened the boundaries of race, not only in the South with its large slave population but also in the West with its large Native population. Equally significant for the residents of French Prairie were their French culture and their Catholic religion, which left them vulnerable to charges of disloyalty in an era of Nativism and Know-Nothing agitation.[70]

In response to the efforts of Anglo-Americans in Oregon to limit the political, legal, and economic activities of the mixed-raced families, the French Prairie residents contested these limits and endeavored to make a place for themselves in an increasingly racialized society. As evidenced in their actions and appeals to authorities, the French-Indian families outwardly presented themselves as "civilized" contributors to a progressive American society. They continued to resettle the lands of the Ahantchuyuk Kalapuyans, transforming the landscape and the economy through their participation in the developing settler economy; they served in the settler militia during the Cayuse War; they declared their intention to become American citizens; and they made formal claim to their farms through the Donation Land Act of 1850. It is clear that the French Canadians and their French-Indian sons believed that they deserved the same rights as the Anglo-American newcomers. And in their quest for citizenship rights, they did receive support from their neighbors in French Prairie; however, in the end the specter of mixed-raced French-Indian men enjoying equal rights proved too ominous for Oregon legislators endeavoring to construct a white supremacist state. As Oregon joined the Union on the eve of the Civil War, the French Prairie settlers no longer held the same measure of influence they had enjoyed as an influential minority under the early provisional government of the mid-1840s.

Faced with the racial politics and social realities of the 1850s, the French-Indians in the Willamette Valley faced several choices in later decades, not unlike their biracial counterparts in other regions of the United States originally born of the fur trade. They could remain in French Prairie and slowly acculturate into the dominant Anglo-American culture; they could migrate to less settled areas of the Pacific Northwest where they might face less hostility because of their ethnicity, religion, and culture; or they could choose to rejoin the indigenous communities of their maternal ancestors, which were then undergoing processes of retribalization on Indian reservations throughout the region.

Epilogue

In 1870, a little more than a decade after Oregon achieved statehood and just a few years after Oregon legislators passed a complex miscegenation law banning inter-racial marriage, the descendants of the French-Indian settlers of the Willamette Valley continued to marry and have children, though not necessarily in French Prairie.[1] In January of that year, Father Jean Baptiste Brouillet baptized Delphine Lucier, the month-old daughter of Paul Lucier and Marguerite Pin of Frenchtown in Washington Territory. Marguerite was the younger sister of Nancy Pin, the pre-cocious youngster who had spent some time at the school of the Sisters of Notre Dame de Namur in St. Paul before her marriage to Gideon Gravelle. Paul Lucier and Marguerite Pin, along with Gideon Gravelle and Nancy Pin, had migrated to Walla Walla County earlier in the 1860s. In February 1870, Adrian Croquet, the Belgian missionary to the Grand Ronde Reservation, baptized newborn Josephine Petit, the daughter of Charles Petit and Sophie Gendron. Charles, the son of Amable Petit Sr. and Susanne Tawakon, had married Sophie Gendron in St. Paul in 1860, and the couple later moved to the Grand Ronde Reservation in Yamhill County, where they raised a large family. In June 1870, Honore Picard and Celeste Rochbrune welcomed another son, Joseph, to their growing family, and had him baptized in the church at St. Paul in French Prairie. Celeste's father, Joseph Rochbrune, a former voyageur with the HBC, served as godfather, and Celeste and Honore's eldest daughter Adele served as a sponsor. In September 1870, another Belgian priest, Alphonsus Glorieux, baptized little Rosalie Quintal, two years of age, the daughter of Louis Quintal and Cecile Norwest, who lived on Calapooia Creek in Douglas County, Oregon. In the early 1860s, Louis and Cecile had migrated from French Prairie south to Douglas County along with Louis's aged father Laurent Quintal, a former fur trapper with the Snake Country expeditions.[2]

As these baptisms suggest, the family trajectories of the French Prairie settlers after 1860 were both geographically and ethnically diverse. The major historical developments that marked the 1850s acted as both push and pull factors on the inhabitants of the French-Indian settlement, with some couples electing to leave the area while others chose to remain in French Prairie. More than two dozen family groups migrated to the Grand Ronde Indian Reservation, located near the foothills of the Coast Range. Other families left the Willamette Valley and joined their Native kin on recently created Indian reservations in eastern Oregon, Washington, Montana, and Idaho. Still others migrated to less settled areas throughout the Pacific Northwest, notably Frenchtown in eastern Washington and the French settlement near Roseburg, Oregon. These decisions were based on several factors, including economic opportunity, previous kin migrations, the racial atmosphere in the resettled areas of western Oregon, and cultural and family affiliations with retribalizing Indian communities. Although the French Prairie community did not witness the emergence of a distinctive Métis identity due to the short thirty-year time span of mercantile capitalism and the fur trade in the Pacific Northwest, the precipitous decline of the regional Native population in the 1830s, the massive influx of Anglo-Americans during the 1840s, and the time compression of Anglo-American colonization, it nevertheless left its imprint on the society and culture of the region.[3]

Whether they stayed in French Prairie through the nineteenth century, joined their maternal relations on Indian reservations throughout the region, or migrated to more remote areas, the French-Indian settlers continued to create new families and new communities. For example, by the latter decades of the nineteenth century, the French-Indian families at Grand Ronde, like their ethnically diverse neighbors on the reservation, began to marry outside their immediate cultural group as the Grand Ronde peoples progressively created a new indigenous community based on their shared history on the reservation. As part of this process of retribalization, the French-Indian families contributed to the persistence of Chinuk Wawa (Chinook Jargon), the language of the Confederated Tribes of Grand Ronde, and their contribution of French words and syntax has been noted in recent studies, including the community's Chinuk Wawa dictionary.[4] While the descendants of French Prairie families who migrated to Indian reservations strengthened cultural and ethnic ties with their indigenous kinfolk, those who remained in the mid-Willamette Valley progressively acculturated into the dominant Anglo-American society. As the fourth and fifth generations came of age in the late 1800s, they began to marry outside the community, generally choosing spouses from nearby Catholic immigrant families who were of Irish and German ancestry (though there were occasionally marriages to Protestants, which caused some scandal). By the early 1900s, English was the native language of French Prairie residents descended from French Canadians and their Indian wives; French and Chinook Jargon was then largely spoken only by the aging settlers born during the mid-1800s.[5]

The words penned by Pierre Fournier de Saint Amant in the 1850s—"at the hearth of the crossed races"—remain relevant today because the experiences of the French Prairie families provide a window into the multiracial history of the Pacific Northwest. The historical structures of Anglo settler colonialism, including the founding myths of the Oregon story, long obscured an alternative vision exemplified in the lived experiences of the biracial French-Indian families who challenged notions of white supremacy, racial separation, and social exclusion. Not only did they contribute to the development of new communities across the Pacific Northwest, they were also instrumental in bringing French Canadian religious orders to the region, such as the Sisters of Providence and the Sisters of the Holy Names, which today directly affect the lives of hundreds of thousands of residents through their work in education, social services, and health care.

The experience of the French Prairie community also elucidates the workings of settler colonialism, for the French-Indian families ultimately contributed to Anglo-American colonization in the Pacific Northwest through their agricultural and husbandry operations in the Willamette Valley and their transformation of the valley landscape. The biracial community, by resettling the fertile homeland of the Ahantchuyuk Kalapuyans, contributed to the progressive displacement of the indigenous population; indeed, the area was renamed French Prairie after the new residents, who became more numerous than the Ahantchuyuk. Although the French-Indian families provided financial support and manpower for the prosecution of the settler war against the Cayuse in the aftermath of the Whitman mission incident, the French Prairie inhabitants in turn faced displacement and exclusion in the 1850s as Anglo-Americans gained ascendancy over political, economic, and social institutions in the territory. While some French-Indian families gradually became white over several generations—not uncommon in the United States for people of mixed ancestry—other families migrated to Grand Ronde, the reserved lands of the Willamette Valley peoples. And so the tale of French Prairie has many endings, yet if this story is any indication, the chronicle of Oregon's past has many chapters yet to be written. It is a future history that the French-Indian families would certainly applaud.

APPENDIX 1 ✳ Pacific Fur Company Personnel in the Columbia Region, 1811–1814

Name	Capacity	Nationality (Ethnicity)	Transport
PARTNERS:			
John Clarke	Partner	Canadian	Beaver
Ramsey Crooks	Partner	American	overland
Wilson Price Hunt	Partner	American	overland
Alexander McKay	Partner	Canadian	Tonquin
Duncan MacDougall	Partner	Scottish	Tonquin
Donald McKenzie	Partner	Scottish	overland
Robert McClellan	Partner	American	overland
David Stuart	Partner	Scottish	Tonquin
Robert Stuart	Partner	Scottish	Tonquin
CLERKS:			
Benjamin Clapp	Clerk	American?	Beaver
Ross Cox	Clerk	Irish	Beaver
Russel Farnham	Clerk	American	Tonquin
Gabriel Franchere	Clerk	French Canadian	Tonquin
John Cook Halsey	Clerk	American	Beaver
Paul Denis Jeremie	Clerk & Labourer	French Canadian	Tonquin
James Lewis	Clerk	American	Tonquin
Charles A. Nicoll	Clerk	American?	Beaver
Thomas McKay	Clerk	Anglo-Indian	Tonquin
Donald McGillis	Clerk	Canadian	Tonquin
Donald McLennon	Clerk	Canadian?	Tonquin
William Wallace Matthews	Clerk	American	Tonquin
Ovid Montigny	Clerk	French Canadian	Tonquin
Francois B. Pillet [Payette]	Clerk	French Canadian	Tonquin
John Reid	Clerk	Irish	overland
Alexander Ross	Clerk	Scottish	Tonquin
Alfred Seton	Clerk	American	Beaver
William Wallace	Clerk	Canadian	Tonquin
ARTISANS/LABORERS/VOYAGEURS/HUNTERS:			
Job Aitken	Master of Shallop	Scottish	Tonquin
Joseph Aston	Sailor & Workman	British?	Beaver
Micajah Baker	Blacksmith/Free Hunter	American	Beaver
George Bell	Cooper	American	Tonquin
Antoine Belleau	Baker & Milieu	French Canadian	Tonquin

Name	Capacity	Nationality (Ethnicity)	Transport
Jean Baptiste Belleau	Milieu	French Canadian	Tonquin
Charles Boucher	Milieu	French Canadian	overland
Brazile Brousseau	Milieu	French Canadian	overland
Pierre Brugiere	Milieu	French Canadian	overland
Louis Brule	Gouvernail	French Canadian	Tonquin
William Cannon [Canning]	Millwright	American	overland
Guillaume Cardinal dit Le Roux	Voyageur	French Canadian	overland
Alexander Carson	Gunsmith	American	overland
George Cone	Milieu & Sawyer	French Canadian	overland
Joseph Cotte	Gouvernail	French Canadian	overland
Edward Cox	Laborer	Hawaiian?	Tonquin
Daniel	Laborer	American	Beaver
Francois Ducharquette	Voyageur	French Canadian & African	overland
Joseph Delauney	Milieu	French Canadian	overland
Pierre Delauney	Hunter	French & Native	overland
Jean Baptiste Dubreuil	Milieu	French Canadian	overland
Jean Baptiste Delorme	Milieu	French Canadian	overland
Louis Denille	Milieu	French Canadian	overland
Pierre Dorion [Jr.]	Interpreter/Hunter	French Canadian & Sioux	overland
Louis Dufresne	Milieu	French Canadian	overland
John Day	Hunter	American	overland
Prisque Felix	Gouvernail	French Canadian	overland
Moses Flanagan	Bookbinder	American	Beaver
Jean Baptiste Gardepied	Devant & Hunter	French & Creek	overland
Joseph Gervais	Milieu & Hunter	French Canadian	overland
Morise Guerin	Milieu	French Canadian	Beaver?
Harry	Blacksmith & Milieu	Hawaiian	Tonquin
Jacques Harteau	Free Hunter?	French Canadian?	
John Hobough	Free Hunter	American	overland
Francois William Hodgins	Blacksmith & Milieu	Canadian	overland
Charles Jacquette	Milieu	French Canadian	overland
Benjamin Jones	Hunter	American	overland
Johann Kaster	Laborer	Russian	Tonquin
William Karimou	Ship Carpenter	Hawaiian	Tonquin
James Keemoo	Laborer	Hawaiian	Tonquin
Francois Landrie	Milieu	French Canadian	overland
Joseph Landrie	Milieu	French Canadian	overland
Charles Lassier	Gouvernail	French Canadian?	Beaver?
Louis Laliberte	Milieu	French Canadian	overland
Jean Baptiste Labonté	Milieu	French Canadian	overland
Louis Labonté	Carpenter	French Canadian	overland
Andre Lachapelier	Milieu	French Canadian	overland
Jacques Lafantaisie	Milieu	French Canadian	Tonquin
Michel Laframboise	Milieu	French Canadian	Tonquin
Michel Lanson [Sanson]	Voyageur	French Canadian	overland
Ignace Roy dit Lapensee	Voyageur	French Canadian	Tonquin
Basil Roy dit Lapensee	Voyageur	French Canadian	Tonquin
Olivier Roy dit Lapensee	Voyageur	French Canadian	Tonquin
Joseph Lapierre	Milieu	French Canadian	Tonquin

Name	Capacity	Nationality (Ethnicity)	Transport
Louis Lavalle	Gouvernail	French Canadian	overland
Francois Leclerc	Voyageur	French Canadian	overland
Giles Leclerc	Laborer	French Canadian	Tonquin
Alexis Lecompte	Milieu	French Canadian	overland
John Little	Boat Builder	American	Beaver
Etienne Lucier	Hunter	French Canadian	overland
Alexis Macon	Milieu	French Canadian?	Beaver?
Francois Martial	Milieu & Sawyer	French Canadian	overland
Richard Milligan	Tailor	American	Beaver
George Naaco	Silversmith	Hawaiian	Tonquin
Joseph Nadeau	Voyageur	French Canadian	Tonquin
Jean Baptiste Ouvre	Milieu	French Canadian	overland
Peter Pahia	Laborer	Hawaiian	Tonquin
Dick Paow	Laborer	Hawaiian	Tonquin
John Patterson	Laborer	American	Beaver
Francois Payette	Milieu	French Canadian	Beaver?
Joseph [Archibald] Pelton*	mentally ill	French Canadian	overland
Antoine Pepin	Milieu	French Canadian	overland
Guillaume [William] Perreault	Apprentice Boy	French Canadian	Tonquin
Perry	Laborer	American	Beaver
Jean Baptiste Pillon	Milieu	French Canadian	overland
Antoine Plante	Milieu	French Canadian	overland
Louis Pion	Carpenter	French Canadian?	Beaver?
Paul Pooar	Laborer	Hawaiian	Tonquin
Jack Powrowrie	Laborer	Hawaiian	Tonquin
Bob Pookarakara	Laborer	Hawaiian	Tonquin
John Reveneau	Laborer	American	Beaver
Jacob Reznor	Free Hunter	American	overland
Francois Robert	Milieu	French Canadian	overland
Edward Robinson	Free Hunter	American	overland
Augustin Roussel	Blacksmith	French Canadian	Tonquin
Benjamin Roussel	Shoemaker	French Canadian	Tonquin
Olivier Roy	Milieu	French Canadian?	Beaver?
Henry Spicer	Laborer	American	Beaver
Ignace Shonowane	Free Hunter	Iroquois	overland
Joseph Saint Amant	Voyageur	French Canadian	overland
Louis St. Michel	Gouvernail	French Canadian	overland
Toby Too	Laborer	Hawaiian	Tonquin
John Travers	Laborer	American	Beaver
Francois Trepagnier	Milieu	French Canadian	overland
Jean Baptiste Turcotte	Gouvernail	French Canadian	overland
Thoms Tuana	Laborer	Hawaiian	Tonquin
Andre Valle	Voyageur	French Canadian	overland
Henry Willetts	Laborer	American	Beaver
William Wilson	Cooper	Canadian	Beaver?

Devant refers to the bowsman of the fur brigade canoe; *gouvernail* refers to the steersman; *milieu* refers to the middle paddler.

*Joseph Pelton was a mentally ill fur trader living with the Snake Indians (Paiute or Shoshone).

SOURCES: Franchère, *Journal*; Irving, *Astoria*; Jones, *Annals*; Porter, *Astor*; Porter, "Roll."
Rollins, *Discovery*; Ronda, *Astoria*; Seton, *Astorian*; HBCA, F.4/61, folios 6-7.
Watson, *Lives Lived West of the Divide,* 3 vols.

APPENDIX 2 ✳ The First Astorian to the Willamette Valley

Hubert H. Bancroft concluded that Pacific Fur Company (PFC) partner Robert Stuart led the first Astorian party to reconnoiter the Willamette Valley above the falls, a party that departed Astoria on December 5, 1811.[1] This conclusion is based on just one source: clerk Gabriel Franchère's *published* journal of the PFC enterprise. However, as W. Kaye Lamb notes in the introductory remarks to his authoritative edition, the manuscript used as the source for the published editions in French and English is not the original diary that Franchère kept in Astoria since that original was lost.[2] The recent publication of the Fort Astoria log and the journal of clerk Alfred Seton, both previously unpublished, provide compelling evidence that the first group of Euro-Americans to venture into the Willamette Valley above the falls was in fact Donald McKenzie's expedition, which left Astoria on March 31 and returned on May 11, 1812.[3] Additional sources documenting the Astorian enterprise lend credence to this conclusion; these include the narratives of partner Robert Stuart and the memoirs of clerk William Wallace Matthews.[4]

Gabriel Franchère's manuscript lists the Cowlitz River, not the Willamette River, as the destination for Robert Stuart's party that departed on December 5, 1811. It is the printed editions in French and English that list the Willamette as the objective. The passage from the Franchère manuscript reads as follows: "On the 5th of December [1811], having procured a guide, Mr. R. Stuart accompanied by Messrs' Pillet, McGillis and R. Bruguier (the latter as a hunter) and a few men left to go up to the Cowilitzk River [*sic*] to investigate whether a post in this area would be profitable." In the footnote to this passage, Lamb has written that Cowlitz River is rendered as the "Willamette River in the printed text, and it is evident that Willamette was meant."[5] Lamb's conclusion that Franchère meant to write "Willamette" may be correct, but Franchère's memory appears to have been faulty. Lamb's conclusion cannot be corroborated by any other source. There is no additional information on this party in Franchère's text, and Robert Stuart's own narrative, which recounts his overland return from Astoria to St. Louis in the summer of 1812, does not begin until June 29, 1812.

The Fort Astoria log, kept by partner Duncan McDougall, substantiates the original passage in the Franchère manuscript in which Franchère identifies the Cowlitz watershed as the destination for Robert Stuart's party. The notation for December 5, 1811, reads as follows: "About Noon Mr. Robert Stuart left the Fort, accompanied by Messrs. McGillis, Farnham & Brugier, the Carpenter [Michel Laframboise], Joseph Lapierre, George & Peter (Two Sandwich Islanders). Messrs. McGillis, Pillet & Bruguier, Lapierre & the two Sandwich Islanders were to proceed up the Cowlitsk [sic], with Mr. Stuart & the others to remain on board the Shallop [the Dolly]."[6]

The riverboat Dolly, probably manned by Russell Farnham and Michel Laframboise, returned on December 26 with "a cargo of Timber," likely from the Cowlitz River basin.[7] Robert Stuart and some men from the original party returned to Fort Astoria on January 26, 1812, "having left Mr. Bruguier, Joseph Lapiere & Peter Pahia (a Canaka) hunting Beaver."[8] Here it is important to note that the Cowlitz River Valley was familiar to the Astorians, as they had sent trapping and hunting parties there on at least two previous occasions: April 4, 1811, and June 16, 1811. In addition, the topography of the Cowlitz River Basin was amenable to the use of the Dolly because that river does not present a barrier such as the falls on the Willamette. Because the Cowlitz was known to the men and was much closer in proximity to Fort Astoria, it is not unreasonable that Robert Stuart's foray there lasted but one month and that he would leave a small party of three men to continue trapping in the area.

In Robert Stuart's overland narratives, he devoted a short section to the Willamette Valley for the day that his party was encamped at the mouth of the Willamette on their ascent of the Columbia in the summer of 1812.[9] A close reading of the passage would indicate that Stuart recorded what Donald McKenzie reported about the Willamette Valley. On July 3, 1812, Stuart wrote in his journal that above the falls, the Willamette River "soon after expands to about the same Width as below the Falls and continues so for a great distance till passing a number of tributary streams, it becomes perceptibly reduced in size, when Mr. Mackenzie was obliged to relinquish his enterprise, on account of some sickness among his men."[10] Here Stuart, whom Franchère supposedly identified as the first partner to explore the Willamette Valley, associated this very exploration to his colleague, Donald McKenzie. Alfred Seton, writing in August 1813 from the Willamette Valley, stated that "Mr. McKenzie was the first person of our party who explored & penetrated about 500 miles up it [the Willamette River]."[11] Alexander Ross, writing in the 1840s, also identified Donald McKenzie as the first Astorian to visit the valley, noting that Mackenzie's purpose was exploration, "seeing the Indians, and studying the topography of the country, than for the purpose of procuring beaver."[12]

In his narrative, Robert Stuart includes some remarks on the indigenous people along the Willamette River. He uses the term "Cathlapoo-yas" for the Kalapuyans.[13] However, his description of the Native geography about the Willamette Falls is faulty. He places the "Cath-lath-las," the Upper Chinookan Clackamas, among the upper Willamette valley population, when in fact they lived along the Clackamas River, which flows into the Willamette River a few miles below the falls. Since few travelers who visited Willamette Falls and the Willamette Valley made such obvious errors in their reports about the Native geography, Stuart's mistaken reporting places further doubt upon the hypothesis that he traveled to the Willamette Valley; more likely, he learned about it from Donald McKenzie.

Given the weight of evidence supporting Donald McKenzie's 1812 expedition as the first Euro-American foray into the Willamette Valley, one must address the question as to why historians have long held that Robert Stuart led the first party into the valley in the winter of 1811. I surmise that this perception first developed in the nineteenth century following the publication of Franchère's narrative in French (1820) and in English translation (1854). The editors of these volumes misread Franchère's manuscript, and the error was repeated in later editions, including W. Kaye Lamb's authoritative edition published in 1969. They may have interpreted Franchère's "Cowlisk" valley as the Willamette Valley because of the later attractiveness of the Willamette Valley for Euro-American colonization. Scholars have tended to repeat this error because the history of the Willamette Valley before the Oregon Trail migrations of the 1840s—and especially the early relations between the Kalapuyans and the fur traders—has not been a salient feature in Pacific Northwest historiography. As a result, there has been limited critical analysis of these early sources on the Willamette Valley.

In a similar vein, scholars have tended to overlook the factual errors and "historical fictions" contained in the published fur trade narratives for the Columbia region.[14] While the Fort Astoria logbook and the journals of Gabriel Franchère, Alfred Seton, Robert Stuart, and Alexander Henry the Younger appear to be more reliable sources, as they are originals (or copies of originals) recorded at the time, the narratives of clerks Ross Cox and Alexander Ross highlight the historical inaccuracies in later accounts. These inaccuracies are partially due to the dynamics of memory, because both men produced their narratives years after the events in question. Of equal importance is the nature of nineteenth-century travel literature itself. The purpose of travel narratives was to perform well in the burgeoning print market by providing readers with an engaging, dramatic account of some hitherto untold adventure. And if the writing of a particular adventurer lacked flair or contravened Victorian standards of propriety, editors would step in to reshape the narrative, making it acceptable to the reading public.[15]

Tricks of memory, personal idiosyncrasies, and the dictates of the marketplace all combined in the works of Ross Cox and Alexander Ross, resulting in narratives noteworthy for their factual errors, distortions, and misremembered, even imaginary incidents. H. Lloyd Keith observed that although Cox and Ross most likely did not intend to mislead readers or fabricate historical events, it is perhaps best to view the works of the two chroniclers as standing "somewhere between history and fiction."[16] Cox's *The Columbia River* (1831) and Ross's *Adventures of the First Settlers on the Oregon or Columbia River* (1849) and *Fur Hunters of the Far West* (1855) must therefore be rigorously compared with all other extant sources in the interests of historical accuracy.[17]

McKenzie himself left no record of his experiences in the Willamette Valley. In a lecture given at the Kingston [Ontario] Historical Society in 1919, L. J. Burpee quoted an unnamed source that Donald McKenzie "had a great aversion to writing." Cecil W. Mackenzie, grandson of Donald McKenzie and author of *Donald Mackenzie: King of the Northwest*, affirmed that Donald McKenzie left no personal writings. Cecil Mackenzie also quoted a story recorded by Ernest Cawcroft (and apparently current in the McKenzie family) that Donald McKenzie's second wife and widow, Adelgonde Humbert Droz, burned a manuscript containing McKenzie's memoirs because "that writing did not add to the amiability of a man of deed."[18]

APPENDIX 3 ✳ NWC Personnel in the Columbia Region, 1814–1820

	1814	1815	1816	1817	1818	1819	1820
Total including Owyee & Iroquois	157	168	156	223	237	254	239
Deduct Owyhee	14	17	17	64	61	56	38
Total Whites & Iroquois	143	151	139	159	176	198	201
Deduct those classed as Iroquois & Abenaks	11	33	38	45	49	65	66
Total Whites Including Proprietors &c &c	132	118	101	114	127	133	135

NOTES:

11 Iroquois deserted to Snakes

5 Sent to New Caledonia with 2 Whites & 2 Owyhee

2 ditto sent across with 5 Whites are not included in total of 1820

SOURCE: Memoranda Book of James Keith, 48.

APPENDIX 4 ❋ Individuals Admitted to the Methodist Mission, 1834–1838

Indian Name	English	When Adm.	Gender	Age	Tribe	When died or left
Sintwa	John Mark	Nov. 7, 1834	M	10	Kalapuyan	Left Oct. 27, 1835
Kyeatah	Lucy Hedding	Nov. 16, 1834	F	12	Kalapuyan	Died Oct. 5, 1836
Chilapoos	Charles Moorehead	Nov. 29, 1834	M	12	Kalapuyan	Absconded April 19, 1836
Kenoteesh		April 26, 1835	M	15	Silelah	Died Aug. 19, 1835
Kokallah		April 26, 1835	M	lad	Tillamook	Taken away June 17, 1835
Lassee	Ann Webster	Aug. 29, 1835	F	10	Kalapuyan	Died April 28, 1837
	Isabel Shangretta Denton	Oct. 18, 1835	F		Iroquois-Kalapuyan	Died Oct. 12, 1837*
	Joseph Shangretta	Oct. 18, 1835	M		Iroquois-Kalapuyan	
	Nicholas Shangretta	Oct. 18, 1835	M	8	Iroquois-Kalapuyan	Died Nov. 27, 1835
	Mary Sargent	Oct. 18, 1835	F		Yamhill	
Kartoosh	David Tucker	Oct. 18, 1835	M		Unknown	Absconded March 31, 1836
Marlooah	Amos Amsden	Oct. 18, 1835	M		Unknown	Absconded March 31, 1836
Sookta		Oct. 18, 1835	M		Unknown	Died Dec. 13, 1835
	Solomon Greene	Oct. 18, 1835	M	30	French-Shoshone	Died Dec. 14, 1835
	Sophie Carpentier	Sept. 8, 1835	F	3	Chinook	
	William Brooks	Nov. 9, 1835	M	youth	Chinook	
Klytes	Ozro Morrill	Nov. 9, 1835	M	youth	Willamette	
	Antoine Bingham	Nov. 12, 1835	M		Willamette	
Kohucha	Thomas Adams	March 1, 1836	M		Hawaiian-Indian	
	Charles Cohania	March 5, 1836	M		Chinook	
Tapal	Harriet Newell	June 7, 1836	F		Chinook	
Siahhen	Wilbur Fisk	July 16, 1836	M		Cayuse	
Wislahowitka	B.J. Hall	July 16, 1836	M		Cayuse	
Toa yahnu	Elijah Hedding	Aug. 13, 1836	M		Walla Walla	
Tomanasulta	Osman Baker	Aug. 13, 1836	M		Unknown	
Welaptulekt	John Lindsay	Sept. 6, 1836	M	adult	Cayuse	Left March 17, 1837
	James Charponka	Sept. 6, 1836	M	youth	Cayuse	Left March 17, 1837
Tshecooitsh	Clarissa Perkins	Sept. 6, 1836	F		Cayuse	
	Samuel Champa	Sept. 6, 1836	M	9	Cayuse	Died March 23, 1837
	Samson Wilder	Oct. 28, 1836	M	1	Shasta	Died March 15, 1837

Indian Name	English	When Adm.	Gender	Age	Tribe	When died or left
Cleekatuck	Jess Lee	Nov. 26, 1836	M		Walla Walla	
	Thomas Peka	Nov. 28, 1836	M		Hawaiian-Chinook	
	Marie Ann Bastien	Jan 4, 1837	F		French-Shasta	
Wattiat	Mary Hawkhurst	Jan. 17, 1837	F		Yamhill	Married Feb. 25, 1837
	Willam A. Slacum	Jan. 29, 1837	M		Willamette	
	Francoise Dupati McKay	March 13, 1837	F		French-Kalapuyan	
	Henry Pool	April 8, 1837	M		Yamhill	
	Sarah Stevens	April 8, 1837	F		Yamhill	
	Sally Soule	June 16, 1837	F		Yamhill	
	David Kilburn	July 17, 1837	M		Yamhill	
	Francis Hale	Sept. 6, 1837	M		Iroquois-Chinook	
	Angelique Carpentier	Oct. 22, 1837	F		French-Shoshone	
	Jared Perkins	Dec. 11, 1837	M		Yamhill	
	Emeline Davis	Jan. 2, 1838	F		Yamhill	
	Nathaniel Bangs	Jan. 17, 1838	M		Yamhill	
	Ann Webster	Feb. 3, 1838	F		Yamhill	
	Joshua Newhall	Feb. 20, 1838	M		Willamette Falls	
	Enoch Mudge	March 13, 1838	M		Tualatin	
	Oliver Howe	May 5, 1838	M		Walla Walla	
	Luther Town	June 20, 1838	M		Klikitat	
	Isaac Rich	June 20, 1838	M		Klikitat	
	Albert Brown	June 20, 1838	M		Klikitat	

*Isabel Shangretta married John Denton on March 7, 1835. See Carey "Mission Record Book," 263.

SOURCES: Carey, "Mission Record Book"; Munnick, *CCRPNW-SP*; Munnick, "Mission Roll Call."

APPENDIX 5 ❋ William Slacum's Census of Willamette Valley Settlers, 1837

Name	When Begun	Acres Enclosed	Acres Cultivated	Wheat Crop Bushels	Horses	Hogs	Houses	Misc.	Remarks
Jean Baptiste Desportes McKay	1831	69	35	556	33	22	3		Good
Andre Longtain	1835	45	24	400	3	33	2		Good
Charles Plante	1835	60	60	800	12	14	2		Good
Charles Rondeau	1836	24	24	200	9	10	1		Good
Louis Forcier	1835	34	34	540	9	10	1		Good
Joseph Gervais	1832	125	65	1,000	19	55	3	1 grist mill	Good
François Xavier Laderoute	1834	36	36	350	11	35	2		Good
Joseph Delard	1832	28	28	280	11	28	2		Good
Amable Arquette	1833	80	50	600	5	31	2		Good
Jean Baptiste Perrault	1832	80	60	500	4	20	3		Good
Etienne Lucier	1832	70	45	740	21	45	4	1 grist mill	Good
Pierre Bellique	1833	50	45	700	9	28	2		Good
Pierre Depot*	1833	40	35	500	8	39	2		Good
Ewing Young	1835	29	29	240	79 & 2 mules	30	2	1 distillery	Good
Lawrence Carmichael (1)									
William Johnson	1834	45	25	300	2	14	2		Good
James A. Neil & Thomas J. Hubbard (2)	1836	200	15	70	9	13	1	1 blacksmith's shop	
W. Canning, miller, millwright (3)									
Solomon H. Smith									
Winslow Anderson									
Charles Roe, carpenter									
Elisha Ezekiel, wheelwright									
John Hoard, carpenter									
Webley Hawkshurst, carpenter									
John Turner									
William Bailey									
Calvin Tibbets, stonemason									
John Rowling									
George Gay									

SLACUM'S NOTES: *The above thirteen are all Canadians, and have been in the employ of the HBC.
(1) Works on shares with Young
(2) Besides the crop of wheat, each of the above five have a large quantity of barely, oats, peas, and potatotes sufficient for their support.
(3) 300 lbs. sterling in the hands of the UBC.

ADDITIONAL NOTES: Charlot Iroquois Tsete, Joseph Despard, Michel Laferte dit Placide, Louis Labonté, Andre Picard, and William McKarty were not listed by Slacum.
The names of the settlers have been corrected for spelling.

SOURCE: "Slacum's Report on Oregon, 1836–37"

Notes

Introduction

1. French Prairie, the original territory of the Ahantchuyuk Kalapuyans, was named after the French-Indian families that settled there. Located in the mid-Willamette Valley, it is bounded by the Willamette River to the north and west, the Pudding River to the east, and what remains of Lake Labish (Lac labiche) to the south. The five major towns of French Prairie were Butteville, Champoeg, St. Paul, St. Louis, and Gervais. The original Champoeg town site, located on the river, was washed away in floods in 1861 and 1891 and is now a state park. John A. Hussey, *Champoeg: Place of Transition, A Disputed History* (Portland: Oregon Historical Society/Oregon State Highway Commission, 1967).

2. M. [Pierre Charles Fournier] de Saint Amant, *Voyages en Californie et dans l'Orégon* (Paris: Librairie L. Maison, 1854), 170. Saint Amant was one of the first to use a version of the term "French Prairie" in print, referring to the area as *les prairies françaises*.

3. Janet Lecompte, introduction to *French Fur Traders and Voyageurs in the American West*, ed. by LeRoy Hafen (Spokane, WA: Arthur H. Clark Co., 1995), 1–26; Carolyn Podruchny, *Making the Voyageur World: Travelers and Traders in the North American Fur Trade* (Lincoln: University of Nebraska Press, 2006), 1–10.

4. Meriwether Lewis and William Clark, *The Lewis and Clark Expedition*, ed. Nicholas Biddle and Paul Allen (Philadelphia: Lippincott, 1814); Fred Wilbur Powell, ed., *Hall J. Kelley on Oregon* (Princeton, NJ: Princeton University Press, 1932); Gustavus Hines, *Oregon: Its History, Conditions, and Prospects* (1851; reprint: New York: Arno Press, 1973); Frederick Jackson Turner, *Rereading Frederick Jackson Turner: "The Significance of the Frontier in American History" and Other Essays*, with commentary by John Mack Faragher (New York: Henry Holt, 1994); Richard White and Patricia Nelson Limerick, *The Frontier in American Culture*, edited by James R. Grossman (Berkeley: University of California Press, 1996).

5. James V. Walker, "Henry S. Tanner and Cartographic Expression of American Expansionism in the 1820s," *OHQ* 111:4 (Winter 2010): 416–441.

6. James P. Ronda, "Calculating Ouragon," *OHQ* 94: 2–3 (Summer–Fall 1993), 121.

7. Ronda, "Calculating Ouragon," 124–125. See also Amy S. Greenberg, *Manifest Destiny and American Territorial Expansion: A Brief History with Documents* (Boston: Bedford/St. Martin's 2012); Robert J. Miller, *Native America Discovered and Conquered: Thomas Jefferson, Lewis and Clark and Manifest Destiny* (Lincoln: University of Nebraska Press, 2008); Walter Nugent, *Habits of Empire: A History of American Exceptionalism* (New York: Alfred

A. Knopf, 2008); Steven E. Woodworth, *Manifest Destinies: America's Westward Expansion and the Road to Civil War* (New York: Alfred A. Knopf, 2010).

8. William G. Robbins, "Willamette Eden: The Ambiguous Legacy," in *Northwest Lands, Northwest Peoples: Readings in Environmental History*, ed. Dale D. Goble and Paul W. Hirt (Seattle: University of Washington Press, 1999), 95–110.

9. The Bancroft history largely written by Francis Fuller Victor solidified this interpretation: Hubert H. Bancroft, *History of Oregon*, 2 vols. (San Francisco: A. L. Bancroft & Co., 1886). See also Jean Barman, *French Canadians, Furs, and Indigenous Women in the Making of the Pacific Northwest* (Vancouver, BC: UBC Press, 2014), 318–336; Susan H. Armitage, "From the Inside Out: Rewriting Regional History," *Frontiers* 22:3 (2001): 32–47; David Peterson del Mar, *Oregon's Promise: An Interpretive History* (Corvallis: Oregon State University Press, 2003), 1–10; Kent D. Richards, "In Search of the Pacific Northwest: The Historiography of Oregon and Washington," *PHR* 50:4 (November 1981): 415–444; James R. Robertson, "The Social Evolution of Oregon," *OHQ* 3:1 (March 1902): 1–37.

10. Kent D. Richards noted that in the 1950s Norman Graebner was unable to "convince historians that merchant interests had much to do with bringing settlement to the Oregon Country." Richards, "Growth and Development of Government in the Far West," (Ph.D. diss., University of Wisconsin, 1966), 249. See also Norman Graebner, *Empire on the Pacific: A Study in American Continental Expansion* (New York: Ronald Press, 1955). William G. Robbins and Katrine Barber advocate for a much broader historiography of the "Greater Northwest" that transcends the U.S.–Canada border. Robbins and Barber, *Nature's Northwest: The North Pacific Slope in the Twentieth Century* (Tucson: University of Arizona Press, 2011). Local historians familiar with French Prairie presented a more moderate view of early Oregon history, notably J. Neilson Barry, who penned the short pamphlet, *The French Canadian Pioneers of the Willamette Valley* (Portland: Catholic Sentinel Press, 1933). With the development of Champoeg Park, John A. Hussey completed the commissioned work, *Champoeg: Place of Transition, A Disputed History* (1967) for the Oregon Historical Society and the Oregon State Highway Commission.

11. Perhaps the most strident articulation of the strong ethnic, religious, and nationalistic attitudes of many American settlers toward the French Canadians, Catholic missionaries, and the HBC was William H. Gray's *A History of Oregon, 1792–1849* (Portland: Harris & Holman, 1870). The most recent reiteration of the French Canadians' ostensible "loyalty" to the Hudson's Bay Company and Great Britain can be found in Dorothy Nafus Morrison, *Outpost: John McLoughlin and the Far Northwest* (Portland: Oregon Historical Society Press, 1999).

12. Colin M. Coates, "French Canadians' Ambivalence to the British Empire," in *Canada and the British Empire*, ed. Phillip Buckner (New York: Oxford University Press, 2008), 181–199.

13. Chad Reimer, "Borders of the Past: The Oregon Boundary Dispute and the Beginnings of Northwest Historiography," in *Parallel Destinies: Canadian-American Relations West of the Rockies*, ed. John M. Findlay and Ken S. Coates (Seattle and Montreal: University of Washington Press and McGill-Queen's University Press, 2002), 221–233. Sam W. Haynes explores American Anglophobia during this period in *Unfinished Revolution: The*

Early American Republic in a British World (Charlottesville: University of Virginia Press, 2010). John Phillip Reid's work on the Snake River Expeditions reconsiders the importance of the British-Canadian fur trade in the Pacific Northwest in the early 1800s. See Reid's *Contested Empire: Peter Skene Ogden and the Snake River Expeditions* (Norman: University of Oklahoma Press, 2002) and *Forging a Fur Trade Empire: Expeditions in the Snake River Country* (Norman: Arthur H. Clark Co., 2011).

14. Michel-Rolph Trouillot brilliantly outlines the process that results in the production of historical records and historical studies weighted in favor of those groups that wield the greatest power in *Silencing the Past: Power and the Production of History* (Boston: Beacon Press, 1995). See also Armitage, "From the Inside Out"; Susan Armitage, "Rethinking the Region: Gender, Race, and Class in Pacific Northwest History," in *Terra Northwest: Interpreting People and Place*, ed. David H. Stratton (Pullman: Washington State University Press, 2007), 199–216; Karen J. Blair, "The State of Research on Pacific Northwest Women," *Frontiers* 22:3 (2001): 48–56; Kimberly Jensen, "Revolutions in the Machinery: Oregon Women and Citizenship in Sesquicentennial Perspective," *OHQ* 110:3 (Fall 2009): 336–361.

15. The standard text on Pacific Northwest history into the 1980s, authored by Dorothy O. Johansen and Charles M. Gates, was the aptly titled *Empire of the Columbia: A History of the Pacific Northwest*, 2nd ed. (New York: Harper & Row Publishers, 1967). Two collections of essays signaled the beginning of diversification and complexity in Pacific Northwest History: Thomas Vaughan, ed., *The Western Shore: Oregon Country Essays Honoring the American Revolution* (Portland: Oregon Historical Society and American Revolution Bicentennial Commission of Oregon, 1976); and G. Thomas Edwards and Carlos A. Schwantes, eds. *Experiences in a Promised Land: Essays in Pacific Northwest History* (Seattle: University of Washington Press, 1986).

16. Andrew F. Fisher, *Shadow Tribe: The Making of Columbia River Identity* (Seattle: University of Washington Press, 2010); Alexandra Harmon, *Indians in the Making: Ethnic Relations and Indian Identities around Puget Sound* (Berkeley: University of California Press, 1998); Adele Perry, *On the Edge of Empire: Gender, Race, and the Making of British Columbia* (Toronto: University of Toronto Press, 2001); Cynthia Culver Prescott, *Gender and Generation on the Far Western Frontier* (Tucson: University of Arizona Press, 2007); Coll Thrush, *Native Seattle: Histories from the Crossing-Over Place* (Seattle: University of Washington Press, 2007); Gray H. Whaley, *Oregon and the Collapse of Illahee: U.S. Empire and the Transformation of an Indigenous World, 1792–1859* (Chapel Hill: University of North Carolina Press, 2010). Surveys of the expansive scholarship on European and American imperialism include the following: Michael Ada, "From Settler Colony to Global Hegemon: Integrating the Exceptionalist Narrative of the Ameican Experience into World History," *AHR* 116:5 (December 2011): 1692–1720; Paul A. Kramer, Review Essay, "Power and Connection: Imperial Histories of the United States in the World," *AHR* 116:5 (December 2011): 1348–1391; Patrick Wolfe, Review Essay, "History and Imperialism: A Century of Theory, from Marx to Postcolonialism," *AHR* 102:2 (April 1997): 388–420. Instructive sources on Anglo settler colonialism include James Belich, *Replenishing the Earth: The Settler Revolution and the Rise of the Anglo World, 1783–1939* (New York: Oxford University Press, 2009); Lisa Ford, *Settler Sovereignty: Jurisdiction and Indigenous People in America and Australia,*

1788–1836 (Cambridge, MA: Harvard University Press, 2010): Dolores Janiewski, "Gendering, Racializing and Classifying: Settler Colonization in the United States, 1590–1990," in *Unsettling Settler Societies: Articulations of Gender, Race, Ethnicity, and Class,* ed. Daiva Stasiulus and Nira Yuval-Davis (Thousand Oaks, CA: Sage Publications, 1995), 132–160; Daiva Stasiulus and Radha Jhappan, "The Fractious Politics of a Settler Society: Canada," in *Unsettling Settler Societies,* ed. Stasiulus and Yuval-Davis, 95–131; Patrick Wolfe, "Settler Colonialism and the Elimination of the Native," *Journal of Genocide Research* 8:5 (December 2006): 387–409.

17. Over the past several decades, David Brauner, Oregon State University, has headed this ongoing excavation and research program in collaboration with the Oregon State Office of Historic Preservation. See Melvin Aikens, Thomas J. Connolly, and Dennis L. Jenkins, Chapter 5: "The Willamette Valley," in their *Oregon Archaeology* (Corvallis: Oregon State University Press, 2011), 284–327. The fact that the Champoeg area is a state park has played a role in the preservation of sites for excavation.

18. Melinda Marie Jetté, "Betwixt and Between the Official Story: Tracing the History and Memory of a Family of French-Indian Ancestry in the Pacific Northwest," *OHQ* 111:2 (Summer 2010): 142–183.

19. Jean Barman, *French Canadians, Furs, and Indigenous Women*; John C. Jackson, *Children of the Fur Trade: Forgotten Métis of the Pacific Northwest* (1995. Reprint. Corvallis: Oregon State University Press, 1997).

20. Studies on family and community that have contributed to the larger historiography of nineteenth-century America include the following: John Demos, *A Little Commonwealth: Family and Community in Plymouth Colony* (New York: Oxford University Press, 1970); John Mack Faragher, *Sugar Creek: Life on the Illinois Prairie* (New Haven, CT: Yale University Press, 1986); Kenneth Lockridge, *New England Town, The First Hundred Years: Dedham, Massachusetts, 1636–1736,* expanded ed. (New York: W. W. Norton, 1985); Dean L. May, *Three Frontiers: Family, Land, and Society in the American West, 1850–1900* (New York: Cambridge University Press, 1994); Mary P. Ryan, *The Cradle of the Middle Class: The Family in Oneida, New York, 1790–1865* (New York: Cambridge University Press, 1981); Anthony F. C. Wallace, *Rockdale: The Growth of an American Village in the Early Industrial Revolution* (New York: W. W. Norton, 1972); Helena M. Wall, *Family and Community in Early America* (Cambridge, MA: Harvard University Press, 1990). For debates on the definition and meaning of "community" in American history/historiography, see Richard Beeman, "The New Social History and the Search for 'Community' in Colonial America," *American Quarterly* 29:4 (Fall 1977): 422–443; Thomas Bender, *Community and Social Change in America* (Baltimore: Johns Hopkins University Press, 1978); Robert V. Hine, *Community on the American Frontier* (Norman: University of Oklahoma Press, 1980).

21. Jay Gitlin, *Bourgeois Frontier: French Towns, French Traders, and American Expansion* (New Haven, CT: Yale University Press, 2010); David Alan Johnson, *Founding the Far West: California, Oregon, and Nevada, 1840–1890* (Berkeley: University of California Press, 1992); Susan Lee Johnson, *Roaring Camp: The Social World of the California Gold Rush* (New York: W. W. Norton, 2000); Peter J. Kastor, *The Nation's Crucible: The Louisiana Purchase and the Creation of America* (New Haven, CT: Yale University Press, 2004); Peter J.

Kastor, *William Clark's World: Describing America in an Age of Unknowns* (New Haven, CT: Yale University Press, 2011); Peter Kastor and François Weil, eds., *Empires of the Imagination: Transatlantic Histories of the Louisiana Purchase* (Charlottesville: University of Virginia Press, 2009); Andrés Reséndes, *Changing Native Identities at the Frontier: Texas and New Mexico, 1800–1850* (New York: Cambridge University Press, 2004); Mark Rifkin, *Manifesting America: The Imperial Construction of U.S. National Space* (New York: Oxford University Press, 2009); John R. Wunder and Joann M. Ross, *The Nebraska-Kansas Act of 1854* (Lincoln: University of Nebraska Press, 2008).

22. Anne F. Hyde, *Empires, Nations, and Families: A History of the North American West, 1800–1860* (Lincoln: University of Nebraska Press, 2011); María Raquél Casas, *Married to a Daughter of the Land: Spanish-Mexican Women and Interethnic Marriage in California, 1820–1880* (Reno: University of Nevada Press, 2007); Louise Pubols, *The Father of All: The de la Guerra Family, Power and Patriarchy in Mexican California* (Berkeley and San Marino: Huntington–USC Institute on the History of the West/University of California Press, 2009); Elizabeth Jameson and Susan Armitage, eds., *Writing the Range: Race, Class, and Culture in the Women's West* (Norman: University of Oklahoma Press, 1997); John Mack Faragher, "Americans, Mexican, Métis: A Community Approach to the Comparative Study of North American Frontiers," in *Under an Open Sky: Rethinking America's Western Past*, ed. William Cronon, George Miles, and Jay Gitlin (New York: W. W. Norton, 1992), 90–109.

23. Gray Whaley analyzes these processes on the regional level in *Oregon and the Collapse of Illahee.*

24. As Whaley has argued, the foundation for the construction of an Anglo-American world in the Pacific Northwest was the settlers' genocidal attitudes and actions toward Native people. See Whaley, *Oregon and the Collapse of Illahee*. Brendan Lindsay outlines the history of state-sponsored mass murder in nearby California during this same period in *Murder State: California's Native American Genocide, 1846–1873* (Durham, NC: Duke University Press, 2012).

25. Juliana Barr, *Peace Came in the Form of a Woman: Indians and Spaniards in the Texas Borderlands* (Chapel Hill: University of North Carolina Press, 2007); James F. Brooks, *Captives and Cousins: Slavery, Kinship, and Community in the Southwest Borderlands* (Chapel Hill: University of North Carolina Press, 2002); Kathleen DuVal, *The Native Ground: Indians and Colonists in the Heart of the Continent* (Philadelphia: University of Pennsylvania Press, 2006); Richard White, *The Middle Ground: Indians, Empires and Republics, in the Great Lakes Region, 1650–1815* (New York: Cambridge University Press, 1991). For an early landmark study on the Canadian context, see Arthur J. Ray, *Indians in the Fur Trade* (Toronto: University of Toronto Press, 1974; reprint, 1998).

26. Two recent longitudinal studies that trace this process for Native groups from the contact period to the present are Jeffrey P. Shepard's *We Are an Indian Nation: A History of the Hualapai People* (Tucson: University of Arizona Press, 2010) and Charles Wilkinson's *The People Are Dancing Again: The History of the Siletz Tribe of Western Oregon* (Seattle: University of Washington Press, 2010). See also John Mack Faragher, "'More Motley than Mackinaw': From Ethnic Mixing to Ethnic Cleansing on the Frontier of the Lower

Missouri, 1783–1833," in *Contact Points: American Frontiers from the Mohawk Valley to the Mississippi, 1750–1830*, ed. Andrew R. L. Cayton and Fredrika J. Teute (Chapel Hill: University of North Carolina Press, 1998), 304–326.

27. Nathan Douthit, *Uncertain Encounters: Indians and Whites at Peace and War in Southern Oregon, 1820s–1860s* (Corvallis: Oregon State University Press, 2002); E. A. Schwartz, *The Rogue River Indian War and Its Aftermath, 1850–1980* (Norman: University of Oklahoma Press, 1997); Whaley, *Oregon and the Collapse of Illahee*; Wilkinson, *The People Are Dancing Again*.

28. On the larger mixed-race history of the United States, see Gary B. Nash, "The History of Mestizo America," in *Sex, Love, Race: Crossing Boundaries in North American History*, ed. Martha Hodes (New York: New York University Press, 1999), 10–32.

29. In-depth analyses of Métis ethnogenesis include the following: Heather Devine, *The People Who Own Themselves: Aboriginal Ethnogenesis in a Canadian Family, 1660–1900* (Calgary: University of Calgary Press, 2004); Martha Harroun Foster, *We Know Who We Are: Métis Identity in a Montana Community* (Norman: University of Oklahoma Press, 2006); and Brenda Macdougall, *One of the Family: Metis Culture in Nineteenth-Century Northwest Saskatchewan* (Vancouver: UBC Press, 2010). See also Jacqueline Peterson and Jennifer S. H. Brown, eds., *The New Peoples: Being and Becoming Métis in North America* (Winnipeg: University of Manitoba Press, 1985); Gerhard J. Ens, *Homeland to Hinterland: The Changing Worlds of the Red River Métis in the Nineteenth Century* (Toronto: University of Toronto Press, 1996); Jonathan Anuik, Review Essay, "From Ethnogenesis to Nationhood: A Review of Three Recent Works in Métis Studies," *Native Studies Review* 17:2 (2008): 167–176; Jennifer S. H. Brown, "Cores and Boundaries: Métis Historiography Across a Generation," *Native Studies Review* 17:2 (2008): 1–18; Michel Hogue, "Between Race and Nation: The Creation of a Métis Borderlands on the Northern Plains," in *Bridging National Border in North America: Transnational and Comparative Histories*, ed. Benjamin H. Johnson and Andrew R. Graybill (Durham, NC: Duke University Press, 2010), 58–87; Nicole St. Onge, Carolyn Produchny, and Brenda Macdougall, eds., *Contours of a People: Metis Family, Mobility and History* (Norman: University of Oklahoma Press, 2012).

30. Susan Sleeper-Smith, *Indian Women and French Men: Rethinking Cultural Encounters in the Western Great Lakes* (Amherst: University of Massachusetts Press, 2001).

31. Tanis C. Thorne, *The Many Hands of My Relations: French and Indians on the Lower Missouri* (Columbia: University of Missouri Press, 1996), 12.

32. Jean Barman and Bruce W. Watson, "Fort Colvile's Fur Trade Families and the Dynamics of Race in the Pacific Northwest," *PNQ* 90:3 (Summer 1999): 140–153. See also Robert F. Berkhofer, *The White Man's Indian: Images of the American Indian from Columbus to the Present* (New York: Vintage, 1978); Robert E. Bieder, *Science Encounters the Indian, 1820–1880* (Norman: University of Oklahoma Press, 1986); Thomas F. Gossett, *Race: The History of an Idea in America* 1963. Reprint. New York: Schocken Books, 1965); Reginald Horsman, *Race and Manifest Destiny: The Origins of American Racial Anglo-Saxonism* (Cambridge, MA: Harvard University Press, 1981); Ronald T. Takaki, *Iron Cages: Race and Culture in Nineteenth-Century America* (Seattle: University of Washington Press, 1979).

33. Barman and Watson, "Fort Colvile's Fur Trade Families"; Andrew R. Graybill, "Helen P. Clarke in the 'Age of Tribes': Montana's Changing Racial Landscape, 1870–1920," *Montana: The Magazine of Western History* 61:1 (Spring 2011): 4–19; Melinda Marie Jetté, "Betwixt and Between the Official Story"; Sylvia Van Kirk, "Tracing the Fortunes of Five Founding Families of Victoria," *BC Studies* 115/116 (Winter 1997/1998): 148–179; Henry Zenk, "Chinook Jargon and Native Persistence in the Grand Ronde Indian Community, 1856–1907," Ph.D. diss., University of Oregon, 1984, 90–92, Recent studies on the development of white supremacy, racial classification, and biracial peoples in the United States include Lauren L. Basson, *White Enough to Be American: Race Mixing, Indigenous People, and the Boundaries of State and Nation* (Chapel Hill: University of North Carolina Press, 2008); Thomas N. Ingersoll, *To Intermix with Our White Brothers: Indian Mixed Bloods in the United States from the Earliest Times to the Indian Removals* (Albuquerque: University of New Mexico Press, 2005); Peggy Pascoe, *What Comes Naturally: Miscegenation Law and the Making of Race in America* (New York: Oxford University Press, 2009); Claudio Sant, *Black, White, and Indian: Race and the Unmaking of an American Family* (New York: Oxford University Press, 2005).

34. Foster, *We Know Who We Are*, 13–14; Peterson and Brown, *The New Peoples*, 1–8; Thorne, *Many Hands of My Relations*, 12.

35. Carlo Ginzburg, *The Cheese and the Worms: The Cosmos of a Sixteenth-Century Miller*, trans. John and Anne Tedeschi (1980. Reprint. New York: Penguin Books, 1982); Carlo Ginsburg, *Clues, Myths and the Historical Method*, trans. John and Anne Tedeschi (Baltimore: Johns Hopkins University Press, 1989); Carlo Ginzburg, "Microhistory: Two or Three Things that I Know about It," trans. John and Anne Tedeschi, *Critical Inquiry* 20:1 (Autumn 1993): 10–35.

36. Giovanni Levi has stressed that the "unifying principle of all microhistorical research is the belief that microscopic observation will reveal factors previously unobserved." See Levi, "On Microhistory," in *New Perspectives on Historical Writing*, ed. Peter Burke (University Park: Pennsylvania State University Press, 1991), 97. Richard D. Brown considers the challenges and applicability of microhistory in "Microhistory and the Post-Modern Challenge," *Journal of the Early Republic* 23:1 (Spring 2003): 1–20.

37. Tamara K. Hareven, "The History of the Family and the Complexity of Social Change," *AHR* 96:1 (February 1991): 95.

CHAPTER 1: Native–Fur Trader Relations in the Willamette Valley

1. Gabriel Franchère, *Journal of a Voyage on the North West Coast of North America during the Years 1811, 1812, 1813, and 1814*, ed. W. Kaye Lamb, trans. Wessie Tipping Lamb (Toronto: Champlain Society, 1969), 118; Fred S. Perrine, "Early Days on the Willamette," *OHQ* 25:4 (December 1924): 305–311; J. Neilson Barry, "Site of Wallace House, 1812–1814," *OHQ* 42:3 (September 1941): 206–207.

2. Robert F. Jones, ed., *Annals of Astoria: The Headquarters Log of the Pacific Fur Company on the Columbia River, 1811–1813* (New York: Fordham University Press, 1999), 137; J.

Neilson Barry, "Madame Dorion of the Astorians," *OHQ* 30:2 (September 1929): 272–277; Bruce McIntyre Watson, *Lives Lived West of the Divide: A Biographical Dictionary of Fur Traders Working West of the Rockies, 1793–1858*, vol. 1 (Kelowna, BC: Centre for Social, Spatial, and Economic Justice, 2010), 338–339; James P. Ronda, *Astoria and Empire* (Lincoln: University of Nebraska Press, 1990), 213.

3. Jones, *Annals of Astoria*, 151.

4. Ewart M. Baldwin, Elizabeth L. Orr, and William N. Orr, *Geology of Oregon*, 4th ed. (Dubuque, IA: Kendall/Hunt, 1992); Patricia A. Benner and James R. Sedell, "Upper Willamette River Landscape: A Historical Perspective," in *River Quality: Dynamics and Restoration*, ed. Antonius Laenen and David A. Dunnette (New York: CRC Publishers, 1997), 23–49; Samuel N. Dickens, "Western Oregon and Washington," in *The Pacific Northwest: An Overall Appreciation*, ed. Otis W. Freeman and Howard H. Martin, 2nd ed. (New York: John Wiley & Sons, 1954), 54–64; Jerry F. Franklin and C. T. Dryness, *Natural Vegetation of Oregon and Washington* (1973; reprint, Corvallis: Oregon State University Press, 1988); William G. Loy et al., *Atlas of Oregon*, 2nd ed. (Eugene: University of Oregon Press, 2001).

5. "Willamette" is derived from the name of an Upper Chinookan village *wálamt*, originally located on the west shore of the Willamette River, across from Oregon City. See Michael Silverstein, "Chinookans of the Lower Columbia," in *Handbook of North American Indians*, vol. 7, *Northwest Coast*, ed. Wayne Suttles (Washington, D.C.: Smithsonian Institution, 1990), 534.

6. Benner and Sedell, "Upper Willamette River Landscape," 24.

7. M. E. Peck, *A Manual of the Higher Plants of Oregon* (Portland: Binford & Mort, 1941), cited in James R. Habeck, "The Original Vegetation of the Mid-Willamette Valley, Oregon," *Northwest Science* 35:2 (May 1961), 66.

8. William A. Bowen, *Migration and Settlement on the Oregon Frontier* (Seattle: University of Washington Press, 1978), 6; George H. Taylor and Raymond R. Hatton, *The Oregon Weather Book* (Corvallis: Oregon State University Press, 1999), 8.

9. Habeck, "Original Vegetation," 65–77; Robert Boyd, "Strategies of Indian Burning in the Willamette Valley," in *Indians, Fire, and the Land in the Pacific Northwest*, ed. Robert Boyd (Corvallis: Oregon State University Press, 1999): 94–98; Franklin and Dryness, *Natural Vegetation*, 110–129; Carl L. Johannessen et al., "The Vegetation of the Willamette Valley," *Annals of the Association of American Geographers* 61:2 (June 1971): 286–303; Jerry Towle, "Changing Geography of Willamette Valley Woodlands," *OHQ* 83:1 (Spring 1983): 66–87.

10. Boyd, "Strategies," 95–97; B. Jennifer Guard, *Wetland Plants of Oregon and Washington* (Vancouver, BC: Lone Pine Publishing, 1995); Jim Pojar and Andy MacKinnon, eds., *Plants of the Pacific Northwest: Washington, Oregon, British Columbia, and Alaska* (Vancouver BC: Ministry of Forests & Lone Pine Publishing, 1994).

11. Boyd, "Strategies," 95–97; Stephen Dow Beckham, *The Indians of Western Oregon: This Land Was Theirs* (Coos Bay, OR: Arago Press, 1977), 33.

12. Due to the limited scope of the secondary literature on the Kalapuyans (based on a fragmentary primary source base), any study of the Willamette Valley's indigenous inhabitants in the early 1800s is speculative. Key anthropological studies include the following: Boyd, "Strategies"; Lloyd R. Collins, "The Cultural Position of the Kalapuya in the

Pacific Northwest" (M.A. thesis, University of Oregon, 1951); Yvonne Hajda, "Mary's River Kalapuyan: A Descriptive Phonology" (M.A. thesis, Portland State University, 1976); Melville Jacobs, ed., *Kalapuya Texts*, University of Washington Publications in Anthropology, vol. 11 (Seattle: University of Washington, 1945); Henry Zenk, "Contributions to Tualatin Ethnography: Subsistence and Ethnobiology" (M.A. thesis, Portland State University, 1976); Henry Zenk, "Tualatin Kalapuyan Villages: The Ethnographic Record," in *Contributions to the Archaeology of Oregon*, ed. Paul W. Baxter (Portland: Association of Oregon Archeologists, 1994), 146–165. See also C. Melvin Aikens, Thomas J. Connolly, and Dennis L. Jenkins, *Oregon Archaeology* (Corvallis: Oregon State University Press, 2011), 284–327.

13. Laurence C. Thompson and M. Dale Kinkade, "Languages," in *Handbook of the North American Indian*, vol. 7, *Northwest Coast*, 41; Henry B. Zenk, "Kalapuyans," in *Handbook of North American Indians*, vol. 7, *Northwest Coast*, 547–553.

14. Robert Boyd, table 16: "Lower Columbia Population History, Pre-1830s," in *The Coming of the Spirit Pestilence: Infectious Disease and Population Decline among Northwest Coast Indians, 1774–1874* (Seattle: University of Washington Press, 1999), 324–325.

15. Zenk, "Contributions to Tualatin Ethnography," 1–2.

16. Zenk, "Contributions to Tualatin Ethnography," 15.

17. Zenk, "Contributions to Tualatin Ethnography," 46.

18. Zenk, "Kalapuyans," 552. The only extant linguistic record in the Ahantchuyuk dialect of the Central Kalapuyan language is a short vocabulary list collected by Albert Gaschet in 1877. (Henry Zenk, personal communication, 2002).

19. Beckham, *Indians of Western Oregon*, 36. Henry Zenk noted, "There was a village somewhere near Champoeg State Park, on the north bank, or possibly both banks, of [the] Willamette River. While this village is mentioned in the Tualatin ethnography material (. . . giving *cámpuick* as the name of a 'town' in the French Prairie area where Indians gathered to dig the root *puicik*), it is not mentioned as having been Tualatin—I thus speculate that it was *hanciyuk* [Ahantchuyuk] unless . . . it represents some undocumented entity." Zenk, "Contributions to Tualatin Ethnography," 4. Zenk's 1976 speculation is based on the ethnographic field notes of Albert Gatschet, collected in 1877, and Hussey's analysis of historical documentation from the testimony of American settler William R. Rees. See John A. Hussey, *Champoeg: Place of Transition, A Disputed History* (Portland: Oregon Historical Society/Oregon State Highway Commission, 1967), 17 and n. 8, 341. Another hypothesis is that Gatschet's informant may have noted the name of the historical French-Indian town, Champoeg, rather than a contact-era Kalapuyan toponym. (Henry Zenk, personal communication, 2002).

20. Jacobs, *Kalapuya Texts*, 86.

21. Jacobs, *Kalapuya Texts*, 186–187. Henry Zenk indicates that there may likely have been a historical shift with American colonization and the push for treaty negotiations in the 1850s, which would have required identifiable chiefs to sign treaties with American officials. He notes, "The villages of this [Tualatin] and other Kalapuyan tribes were apparently politically basically autonomous. Treaty documents, and some ethnographic sources, further suggest that the tribes themselves were political entities, headed by tribal chiefs. However, it may also be that tribal chieftainship was a historical development, the result

of population considerations and government agents' demands to deal with authoritative representatives of tribes." Zenk, "Kalapuyans," 549. See also Collins, "Cultural Position of the Kalapuya," 48–49, where Collins discusses the historic chief Sande-am, who apparently held sway over several hamlets. Again, this may be the result of postcontact dynamics. Zenk, "Contributions to Tualatin Ethnography," 15–16.

22. Beckham, *Indians of Western Oregon*, 45.

23. Zenk, "Contributions to Tualatin Ethnography," 6.

24. Melville Jacobs, *Clackamas Chinook Texts*, vol. 2 (Bloomington: Indiana University Research Center in Anthropology, Folklore, and Linguistics/*International Journal of American Linguistics*, 1959), 517; Henry Zenk, personal communication, 2002. See also Leland Donald, *Aboriginal Slavery on the Northwest Coast of North America* (Berkeley: University of California Press, 1997).

25. Zenk, "Kalapuyans," 550.

26. Zenk, "Contributions to Tualatin Ethnography," 6.

27. Zenk, "Kalapuyans," 550.

28. Beckham, *Indians of Western Oregon*, 55; Jacobs, *Kalapuya Texts*, 45; Zenk, "Contributions to Tualatin Ethnography," 6; W. W. Oglesby, "The Calapooyas Indians," Mss. P-A 82, p. 6, H. H. Bancroft Library, Berkeley, California (hereafter BAN).

29. Jacobs, *Kalapuya Texts*, 43–45.

30. Jacobs, *Kalapuya Texts*, 191–192.

31. Peter G. Boag, *Environment and Experience: Settlement Culture in Nineteenth-Century Oregon* (Berkeley: University of California Press, 1992), 19; Robert Bunting, *The Pacific Raincoast: Environment and Culture in an American Eden, 1778–1900* (Lawrence: University Press of Kansas, 1997), 17–18.

32. Zenk, "Contributions to Tualatin Ethnography," 35; Zenk, "Kalapuyans," 547–553; Silverstein, "Chinookans of the Lower Columbia," 533–546; Joseph E. Taylor, *Making Salmon: An Environmental History of the Northwest Fisheries Crisis* (Seattle: University of Washington Press, 1999), 13–38.

33. Zenk, "Contributions to Tualatin Ethnography," 19–74; Zenk, "Kalapuyans," 547–548; Beckham, *Indians of Western Oregon*, 43–56; Robert Boyd, "Strategies," 94–128; Collins, "Cultural Position of the Kalapuya," 39–57; Harold Mackey, *The Kalapuyans: A Sourcebook on the Indians of the Willamette Valley*, 2nd ed. (Salem, OR: Mission Mill Museum Association in cooperation with the Confederated Tribes of Grand Ronde, 2004), 22–46.

34. Boyd, "Strategies," 121.

35. Jacobs, *Kalapuya Texts*, 34.

36. Philip Ashton Rollins, ed., *The Discovery of the Oregon Trail: Robert Stuart's Narratives of His Overland Trip Eastward from Astoria, 1812–13* (1935; reprint, Lincoln: University of Nebraska Press, 1995), 32–33.

37. For an overview of the importance of food production for the Native peoples of the Northwest Coast, see Dianne Newell, *Tangled Webs of History: Indians and the Law in Canada's Pacific Coast Fisheries* (Toronto: University of Toronto Press, 1993), 32–43.

38. Zenk, "Kalapuyans," 548. For the most detailed treatment of Kalapuyan ethnography, including society, culture, subsistence, diet, and food sources, see Zenk, "Contributions to Tualatin Ethnography."

39. Following agricultural settlement in the mid-nineteenth century, when American settlers forced a cessation of ancient burning practices, significant changes occurred in the Willamette Valley landscape. Those areas not used for agricultural production or grazing witnessed an increase in woodland and forest cover. The cessation of the regular burning led to a dominance of Douglas-fir trees, replacing the oak openings. Robert Boyd, "Strategies," 94–128; Johannessen et al., "Vegetation of the Willamette Valley," 286–301; Jerry C. Towle, "Woodland in the Willamette Valley: An Historical Geography" (Ph.D. diss., University of Oregon, 1974); Jerry C. Towle, "Changing Geography of Willamette Valley Woodlands, *OHQ* 83:1 (Spring 1983): 66–87; and Jerry C. Towle, "Settlement and Subsistence in the Willamette Valley: Some Additional Considerations," *Northwest Anthropological Research Notes* 13:1 (Spring 1979): 12–21.

40. Boyd, "Strategies," 128. See also Omer C. Stewart, *Forgotten Fires: Native Americans and the Transient Wilderness*, ed. Henry T. Lewis and M. Kat Anderson (Norman: University of Oklahoma Press, 2002); Carl O. Sauer, "Grassland Climax, Fire, and Man," *Journal of Range Management* 3:1 (January 1950): 16–21; Carl O. Sauer, "Man's Dominance by Use of Fire," *Geoscience and Man* 10 (1975): 1–13.

41. Boyd, "Strategies," 127.

42. Yvonne Hajda, "Regional Social Organization in the Greater Lower Columbia, 1792–1830" (Ph.D. diss. University of Washington, 1984), 1–3; Yvonne Hajda and Elizabeth Sobel, "Lower Columbia Trade and Exchange Systems," in *Chinookan Peoples of the Lower Columbia*, ed. Robert T. Boyd, Kenneth M. Ames, and Tony A. Johnson (Seattle: University of Washington Press, 2013), 106–114; Robert T. Boyd and Yvonne Hajda, "Seasonal Population Movement along the Lower Columbia River: The Social and Ecological Context," *American Ethnologist* 14:2 (May 1987): 308–326. Jerry R. Galm, "Prehistoric Trade and Exchange in the Interior Plateau of Northwestern North America," in *Prehistoric Exchange Systems in North America*, ed. Timothy G. Baugh and Jonathon E. Ericson (New York: Plenum Press, 1994), 275–305.

43. Studies on European and American activities on the Northwest Coast include Warren L. Cook, *Flood Tide of Empire: Spain and the Pacific Northwest, 1543–1819* (New Haven, CT: Yale University Press, 1973); James R. Gibson, *Otter Skins, Boston Ships, and China Goods: The Maritime Fur Trade of the Northwest Coast, 1785–1841* (Vancouver: UBC Press, 1992); Barry M. Gough, *The Northwest Coast: British Navigation, Trade and Discoveries to 1812* (Vancouver: UBC Press, 1992); Richard Mackie, *Trading Beyond the Mountains: The British Fur Trade on the Pacific, 1793–1843* (Vancouver: UBC Press, 1997).

44. Gibson, *Otter Skins*, 230–231; Mackie, *Trading Beyond the Mountains*, 284, 301; Robert H. Ruby and John A. Brown, *The Chinook Indians: Traders of the Lower Columbia River* (Norman: University of Oklahoma Press, 1976), 15–17; Fredric W. Howay, "A Yankee Trader on the Northwest Coast, 1791–1795," *Washington Historical Quarterly* 21:2 (April 1930), 84, cited in Ruby and Brown, *The Chinook Indians*, 17; Alexander Ross, *Adventure of the First Settlers on the Oregon or Columbia River*, with a new introduction by William G. Robbins (1904; reprint, Corvallis: Oregon State University Press, 2000), 104–105.

45. Hajda, "Regional Social Organization," 206; Verne F. Ray, *Lower Chinook Ethnographic Notes*, University of Washington Publications in Anthropology, vol. 7 (Seattle: University of Washington Press, 1938), 48–58, 99–101.

46. Hajda, "Regional Social Organization," 212–221; Silverstein, "Chinookans of the Lower Columbia," 533–543.

47. The classic fur trade studies on indigenous middlemen in the fur trade include Harold A. Innis, *The Fur Trade in Canada*, rev. ed. (Toronto: University of Toronto Press, 1956; reprint, 1999); Arthur J. Ray, *Indians in the Fur Trade* (Toronto: University of Toronto Press, 1974; reprint, 1998); Ruby and Brown, *The Chinook Indians*, 3–127; William Lang, "The Chinookan Exchange with Euro-Americans in the Lower Columbia River Valley," in *Chinookan Peoples of the Lower Columbia*, ed. Boyd, Ames, and Johnson, 250–271.

48. For the Lewis and Clark expedition's winter at Fort Clatsop, see Gary Moulton, ed., *The Definitive Journals of Lewis and Clark*, vol. 6: *Down the Columbia to Fort Clatsop*; and vol. 7: *From the Pacific to the Rockies* (Lincoln: University of Nebraska Press, 1990 and 1991); and James P. Ronda, *Lewis and Clark among the Indians*, with a new introduction (Lincoln: University of Nebraska Press, 1984; reprint, 2002). When the Chinook proper and their allies discovered that the Winship brothers were trying to establish a fur trading post upriver from their territory (at present-day Oak Point), the Natives quickly expressed their opposition. After several tense discussions and intimidating actions by the Chinook, the Winships decided to abandon the post, fearing that the twenty-five men in their company could not adequately defend themselves against an armed attack by the Chinook and their allies. See Ruby and Brown, *The Chinook Indians*, 119–124; William Dane Phelps, "Solid Men of Boston," in *Fur Traders from New England: The Boston Men in the North Pacific, 1787–1800*, ed. Briton C. Busch and Barry M. Gough (Spokane, WA: Arthur H. Company, 1997), 52–73.

49. For the most recent and comprehensive history of the PFC in the Pacific Northwest, see James P. Ronda, *Astoria and Empire* (Lincoln: University of Nebraska Press, 1990).

50. Jones, *Annals of Astoria*, 4–10; Ronda, *Astoria and Empire*, 197–201.

51. Jones, *Annals of Astoria*, 12–13.

52. Carolyn Podruchny, *Making the Voyageur World: Travelers and Traders in the North American Fur Trade* (Lincoln: University of Nebraska Press, 2006), 21–27; Scott Hamilton, "Dynamics of Social Complexity in Early Nineteenth-Century British Fur Trade Posts," *International Journal of Historical Archaeology* 4:3 (2000): 217–273.

53. Charles E. Simpson, "The Snake Country Freemen: British Free Trappers in Idaho" (M.A. thesis, University of Idaho, 1990).

54. Gray H. Whaley provides the most recent, in-depth analysis of intercultural relations in the lower Columbia during the early fur trade period in *Oregon and the Collapse of Illahee: U.S. Empire and the Transformation of an Indigenous World, 1792–1859* (Chapel Hill: University of North Carolina Press, 2010), 19–70. For the impact of the fur trade on the lower Columbia and larger Northwest Coast, see also Boyd, *The Coming of the Spirit Pestilence*; Daniel W. Clayton, *Islands of Truth: The Imperial Fashioning of Vancouver Island* (Vancouver: UBC Press, 2000); Donald Leland, *Aboriginal Slavery on the Northwest Coast of North America* (Berkeley: University of California Press, 1997); Thomas Vaughan and Bill Holm, *Soft Gold: The Fur Trade and Cultural Exchange on the Northwest Coast of America* (Portland: Oregon Historical Society Press, 1982); Douglas Cole and David Darling, "History of the Early Period," in *Handbook of North American Indians*, vol. 7:

Northwest Coast, 119–134; and Joyce Ann Wike, "The Effect of the Maritime Fur Trade on Northwest Coast Indian Society" (Ph.D. diss., Columbia University, 1951).

55. Ronda, *Lewis and Clark*, 208–210; Ronda, *Astoria and Empire*, 227–228; Whaley, *Collapse of Illahee*, 26–30; David Peterson del Mar, "Intermarriage and Agency: A Chinookan Case Study," *Ethnohistory* 42:1 (Winter 1995), 2–8; Matthias B. Bergman, "'We Should Lose Much by Their Absence': The Centrality of Chinookans and Kalapuyans to Life in Frontier Oregon," *OHQ* 109:1 (Spring 2008), 36–39. See also Helen Hyatt Norton, "Women and Resources of the Northwest Coast: Documentation from the 18th and 19th Centuries" (Ph.D. diss., University of Washington, 1985); Mary C. Wright, "The Circle, Broken: Gender, Family and Difference in the Pacific Northwest, 1811–1850" (Ph.D. diss., Rutgers University, 1996); and Leslie M. Scott, "Indian Women as Food Providers and Tribal Counselors," *OHQ* 29:3 (September 1928): 208–219.

56. Key studies on the central role of Native and Métis women in the North American fur trade include the following: Jennifer S. H. Brown, *Strangers in Blood: Fur Trade Families in Indian Country* (Vancouver: UBC Press, 1980); Heather Devine, *The People Who Own Themselves: Aboriginal Ethnogenesis in a Canadian Family, 1660–1900* (Calgary: University of Calgary Press, 2004); Lucy Eldersveld Murphy, *A Gathering of Rivers: Indians, Métis, and Mining in the Western Great Lakes, 1737–1832* (Lincoln: University of Nebraska Press, 2000); Susan Sleeper-Smith, *Indian Women and French Men: Rethinking Cultural Encounters in the Great Lakes* (Amherst: University of Massachusetts Press, 2001); Sylvia Van Kirk, *Many Tender Ties: Women in Fur-Trade Society, 1670–1870* (Norman: University of Oklahoma Press, 1980).

57. Susan Kardas, "'The People Bought This Land and the Clatsop Became Rich': A View of Nineteenth-Century Fur Trade Relations on the Lower Columbia Between Chinookan Speakers, Whites, and Kanakas" (Ph.D. diss., Bryn Mawr College, 1971), 224–225; Brett Rushforth, "Trading Language: Chinook Jargon, Race, and Nation at Fort Vancouver, 1824–1853," in *Aboriginal Peoples and the Fur Trade: Proceedings of the Eighth North American Fur Trade Conference, Akwesasne*, ed. Louise Johnston (Cornwall, ON/Roosevelton, NY: Akwesasne Notes, 2001), 194–199; Henry Zenk with Tony A. Johnson, "A Northwest Language of Contact, Diplomacy, and Identity: Chinuk Wawa/Chinook Jargon," *OHQ* 111:4 (Winter 2010): 444–461; and Henry Zenk, "Chinook Jargon and Native Cultural Persistence in the Grand Ronde Indian Community, 1856–1907" (Ph.D. diss., University of Oregon, 1984).

58. Jones, *Annals of Astoria*, 79; Franchère, *Journal of a Voyage*, 112.

59. Rollins, *Discovery of the Oregon Trail*, 32.

60. Rollins, *Discovery of the Oregon Trail*, 33.

61. Franchère, *Journal of a Voyage*, 116; Jones, *Annals of Astoria*, 89; "An account of events at Fort Astoria during more than one year (1811–1812)," in Rollins, *Discovery of the Oregon Trail*, 280.

62. Jones, *Annals of Astoria*, 155.

63. Jones, *Annals of Astoria*, 155.

64. Jones, *Annals of Astoria*, 155.

65. Jones, *Annals of Astoria*, 156.

66. Jones, *Annals of Astoria*, 158.

67. Franchère, *Journal of a Voyage*, 118.

68. Jones, *Annals of Astoria*, 160.

69. Jones, *Annals of Astoria*, 160.

70. Jones, *Annals of Astoria*, 161.

71. Jones, *Annals of Astoria*, 162.

72. Jones, *Annals of Astoria*, 165.

73. Elizabeth A. Sobel concluded that the archeological record supports stability in the Native-Native exchange system between the Columbia River Chinookans and Willamette Valley peoples during the contact period of the early 1800s. See Sobel, "An Archaeological Test of the 'Exchange Expansion Model' of Contact Era Change on the Northwest Coast," *Journal of Anthropological Archaeology* 31 (2012): 1–21.

74. The Astorians likely traded for Kalapuyan vegetable resources to alleviate problems with scurvy. Gabriel Franchère noted that on February 15, 1813, he sent "a canoe load" of sturgeon to Fort Astoria, "which was very acceptable as the men had stopped working some time before for lack of sufficient food." Franchère added that he "made a big camp near Oak Point and Mr. McDougall sent [him] all the men suffering from scurvy to recover their health." Franchère, *Journal of a Voyage*, 118.

75. Susan Marsden and Robert Galois have demonstrated a similar situation between the Tsimshian and other inland groups during the 1820s when the Hudson's Bay Company sought to expand is operations in northern British Columbia; see Susan Marsden and Robert Galois, "The Tsimshian, the Hudson's Bay Company, and the Geopolitics of the Northwest Coast Fur Trade, 1787–1840," *Canadian Geographer* 39:2 (1995): 169–183.

76. For a rendering of Upper Chinookan villages and ethnic affiliations of this part of the Columbia River, see David H. French and Katherine S. French, "Wasco, Wishram, and Cascades," in *Handbook of North American Indians*, vol. 12: *Plateau*, ed. Deward E. Walker (Washington, D.C.: Smithsonian Institution, 1998), 362–363.

77. Ronda, *Lewis and Clark*, 163–213.

78. John Phillip Reid, "Restraint of Vengeance: Retaliation-in-Kind and the Use of Indian Law in the Old Oregon Country," *OHQ* 95:1 (Spring 1994): 48–92. See also John Phillip Reid, *Patterns of Vengeance: Crosscultural Homicide in the North American Fur Trade* (Pasadena, CA: Ninth Judicial Circuit Historical Society, 1999).

79. Ronda, *Astoria and Empire*, 222; J. F. Santee, "Comcomly and the Chinooks," *OHQ* 33:3 (September 1932), 271.

80. Jones, *Annals of Astoria*, 165.

81. Jones, 186. Franchère places their return to Astoria at the end of May. Franchère, *Journal of a Voyage*, 119. The PFC Inventory for McKay's Fort [Willamette River Post] lists the return as June 1, 1813; see Kenneth Wiggins Porter, *John Jacob Astor, Business Man*, vol. 1 (Cambridge, MA: Harvard University Press, 1931), 531.

82. Jones, *Annals of Astoria*, 186; Porter, *John Jacob Astor*, 531. Alexander Carson and Pierre Delaunay had joined the overland PFC expedition in the Upper Missouri Country around May 11, 1811. They left the company in September 1811 and thereafter contracted as free trappers. See Kenneth Wiggins Porter, "Roll of Overland Astorians, 1819–1812," *OHQ* 43:2 (June 1933): 101–112.

83. Elizabeth Vibert, *Narratives of Cultural Encounters in the Columbia Plateau, 1807–1846* (Norman: University of Oklahoma Press, 1997), 119–126.

84. Jones, *Annals of Astoria*, 186.

85. Ross, *Adventures of the First Settlers*, 230.

86. Ross misidentifies the Cathlakamaps headman Casino as a Kalapuyan leader; see Ross, *Adventures*, 230.

87. Ross, *Adventures of the First Settlers*, 230.

88. Frits Pannekoek, "Alexander Ross," *in DBC* vol. 8: *1851–1860*, ed. Francess G. Halpenny and Jean Hamelin (Toronto: University of Toronto Press, 1985), 849–852; John Phillip Reid, *Forging a Fur Trade Empire: Expeditions in the Snake River Country, 1809–1824* (Norman, OK: Arthur H. Clark Co., 2011), 101–118, 169–196; Sylvia Van Kirk, "'What If Mama Is an Indian?': The Cultural Ambivalence of the Alexander Ross Family," in *The New Peoples: Being and Becoming Métis in North America*, ed. Jacqueline Brown and Jennifer S. H. Brown (Winnipeg: University of Manitoba Press, 1985), 207–217.

89. Jones, *Annals of Astoria*, 186, fn. 71.

90. Allan Richardson, "The Control of Productive Resources on the Northwest Coast of North America," in *Resource Managers: North American and Australian Hunter-Gatherers*, ed. Nancy M. Williams and Eugene S. Hunn (Boulder, CO: Westview Press/American Association for the Advancement of Science, 1982), 93–112.

91. Richard A. Gould, "To Have and Have Not: The Ecology of Sharing among Hunter-Gatherers," in *Resource Managers*, ed. Williams and Hunn, 69–92.

92. Jones, *Annals of Astoria*, 186.

93. Ronda, *Astoria and Empire*, 23; see also "Notes and Documents: The Appeal of the North West Company to the British Government to Forestall John Jacob Astor's Columbian Enterprise," *Canadian Historical Review* 17 (September 1936): 301–306.

94. Jones, *Annals of Astoria*, 222; Ronda, *Astoria and Empire*, 277–301; T. C. Elliot, "Sale of Astoria, 1813," *OHQ* 33:1 (March 1932): 45–50.

95. Jones, *Annals of Astoria*, 222.

96. Alexander Henry, *The Journal of Alexander Henry the Younger, 1799–1814*, vol. 2, ed. Barry M. Gough (Toronto: Champlain Society, 1992), 611.

97. For the meaning and origin of the toponym "Champoeg," see Henry Zenk, "Notes on Native Place-names of the Willamette Valley Region," *OHQ* 109:1 (Spring 2008), 14–15.

98. Alfred Seton, *Astorian Adventure: The Journal of Alfred Seton, 1811–1813*, ed. Robert F. Jones (New York: Fordham University Press, 1993), 134.

99. Seton, *Astorian Adventure*, 135.

100. Henry, *Journal of Alexander Henry*, 628–629.

101. Henry, *Journal of Alexander Henry*, 629.

102. Robert J. Miller, *Native America Discovered and Conquered: Thomas Jefferson, Lewis and Clark, and Manifest Destiny* (Lincoln: University of Nebraska Press, 2008), 1–24.

103. William G. Robbins, introduction to Alexander Ross, *Adventures of the First Settlers*, xiii.

104. There is no indication of marriage alliances between the fur traders and Kalapuyans during the 1810s in the existing documentary record.

105. Whaley, *Collapse of Illahee*, 41; Jones, *Annals of Astoria*, 203; Peterson del Mar, "Intermarriage and Agency," 2–7. Susan Kardas analyzed population data and marriage patterns at the fur trade laborers' ethnically mixed "Kanaka Village" at Fort Vancouver for a slightly later period (1820s–1830s), and she found very few Native women from the Willamette Valley in residence at the village. Kardas concluded that population distribution "confirms the dominating influence of the lower Chinook and agrees with reports that Indians immediately around Fort Vancouver and in the Willamette Valley were not responsive to the fur trade." Kardas, "'The People Bought This Land,'" 212.

106. Henry, *Journal of Alexander Henry*, 658.

107. Barry Gough, introduction to Henry, *Journal of Alexander Henry*, vol. 1, lxvi–lxvii.

108. Henry, *Journal of Alexander Henry*, 658. Robert Boyd has suggested that conjunctivitis and trachoma may have been indigenous eye ailments on the Northwest Coast. See Boyd, *The Coming of the Spirit Pestilence*, 287.

109. Henry, *Journal of Alexander Henry*, 659.

110. Henry, *Journal of Alexander Henry*, 663.

111. Elizabeth Vibert, "Real Men Hunt Buffalo: Masculinity, Race, and Class in British Fur Traders' Narratives," *Gender and History* 8:1 (April 1996): 4–21.

112. Henry, *Journal of Alexander Henry*, 658.

113. Henry, *Journal of Alexander Henry*, 664.

114. Henry, *Journal of Alexander Henry*, 662.

115. Henry, *Journal of Alexander Henry*, 661.

116. Henry, *Journal of Alexander Henry*, 662.

117. This was the position of the Native people of southern Oregon, whom the fur traders called "rogues" for their unwillingness to establish close ties with the Euro-Americans. See Nathan Douthit, *Uncertain Encounters: Indians and Whites at Peace and War in Southern Oregon, 1820s–1860s* (Corvallis: Oregon State University Press, 2002), 11–35; Stephen Dow Beckham, *Requiem for a People: The Rogue Indians and the Frontiersmen* (Coos Bay, OR: Arago Press, 1971), 23–35.

118. Henry, *Journal of Alexander Henry*, 662–663.

119. Henry, *Journal of Alexander Henry*, 704.

120. Memoranda Book of James Keith (1811–1821), James Keith Papers, A-676, A-2 , National Archives of Canada, Ottawa; Alexander Ross, *Fur Hunters of the Far West*, ed. Kenneth A. Spaulding (Norman: University of Oklahoma Press, 1956).

121. Ross, *Fur Hunters*, 56–81; Pannekoek, "Alexander Ross," 849–852.

122. Ross, *Fur Hunters*, 74.

123. Ross, *Fur Hunters*, 76.

124. Ross, *Fur Hunters*, 77.

125. Reid, *Forging a Fur Trade Empire*, 169–196.

126. T. C. Elliot, ed., "Letter of Donald Mackenzie to Wilson Price Hunt" [April 20, 1821], *OHQ* 43:1 (March 1942), 12.

CHAPTER 2: Agrarian Colonization and the Intermittent Fever

1. The parents of Jean Baptiste Desportes McKay dit Dupati (ca. 1793–1853) were identified as "Jean Baptiste Depati and an infidel woman of Temiscaming" (thus Algonquin). See Harriet Munnick, ed. *Catholic Church Records of Pacific Northwest-Saint Paul*, vol. 1, compiled by Harriet Munnick and Mikell Delores Warner (Portland, OR: Binford & Mort, 1979), 86, hereafter Munnick, *CCRPNW-SP*. Agathe Kalapuya [Dupati] was baptized at the temporary Catholic mission in the Willamette Valley on January 21, 1839, at the age of thirteen. See Harriet Munnick, "Annotations," in *CCRPNW-SP*, A-29, and Harriet Munnick, ed. *CCRPNW-Vancouver*, vol. 1 (St. Paul, OR: French Prairie Press, 1972), 26, hereafter Munnick, *CCRPNW-V*. As for the identity of the Agathe's Kalapuyan mother, there is one clue suggesting that her given French name was Marguerite. On August 8, 1847, Jean Baptiste Dupati (I), age seventeen, was baptized in the French Prairie parish of Saint Louis. His mother is listed as "Marguerite, Indian." He would have been born in 1830, the period when Jean Baptiste Desportes McKay and his Kalapuyan wife were together. See Harriet Munnick, ed. *CCRPNW-Saint Louis*, vol. 1 (Portland, OR: Binford & Mort, 1982), 3, hereafter *CCRPNW-SL*. There is much variation in the secondary surname for this family (Dupati, Dupatti, Depati, Depaté). I have used one of the more prominent names indicated by the research of Harriet Munnick.

2. Munnick, *CCRPNW-V*, vol. 1, 25. Marie Lisette Dupati was sixteen when she was baptized and married Irishman John Hoard in January 1839. Her mother, Catherine Chehalis, was then deceased.

3. Two excellent studies on long-term processes of ethnogenesis of Métis peoples in North America are Martha Harroun Foster's *We Know Who We Are: Métis Identity in a Montana Community* and Brenda Macdougall's *One of the Family; Metis Culture in Nineteenth-Century Northwestern Saskatchewan*.

4. The standard sources for the HBC and its West Coast operations include John S. Galbraith, *The Hudson's Bay Company as an Imperial Factor* (Berkeley: University of California Press, 1957); Richard Mackie, *Trading Beyond the Mountains: The British Fur Trade on the Pacific, 1793–1843* (Vancouver: UBC Press, 1997); E. E. Rich, *Hudson's Bay Company, 1670–1870*, vol. 3 (New York: Macmillan Company, 1961).

5. Mackie, *Trading Beyond the Mountains*, 35.

6. Frederick Merk, *The Oregon Question: Essays in Anglo-American Diplomacy and Politics* (Cambridge, MA: Harvard University Press, 1967), 30–45.

7. Mackie, *Trading Beyond the Mountains*, 38–39.

8. Mackie, *Trading Beyond the Mountains*, 44–45.

9. Dorothy O. Johansen, "Introduction," in *Peter Skene Ogden's Snake Country Journal, 1826–27*, ed. K. G. Davies, assisted by A. M. Johnson (London: Hudson's Bay Records Society, 1961), xv; Lorne Hammond, "Marketing Wildlife: The Hudson's Bay Company and the Pacific Northwest, 1821–1849," *Forest and Conservation Policy* 37 (January 1993): 16–17; Jennifer Ott, "'Ruining' the Rivers in the Snake Country: The Hudson's Bay Company Fur Desert Policy," *OHQ* 104:2 (Summer 2003): 166–195.

10. Gloria Griffin Cline, *Peter Skene Ogden and the Hudson's Bay Company* (Norman:

University of Oklahoma Press, 1974); Alice Bay Maloney, ed., *Fur Brigade to the Bonaventura: John Work's California Expedition, 1832–1833 for the Hudson's Bay Company* (San Francisco: California Historical Society, 1945); Doyce B. Nunis, ed., *The Hudson's Bay Company's First Fur Brigade to the Sacramento Valley: Alexander McLeod's 1829 Hunt* (Fair Oaks, CA: Sacramento Book Collectors Club, 1968); John Phillip Reid, *Forging a Fur Empire: Expeditions in the Snake River Country, 1809–1824* (Norman, OK: Arthur H. Clarke Co., 2011); John Phillip Reid, *Contested Empire: Peter Skene Ogden and the Snake River Expeditions* (Norman: University of Oklahoma Press, 2002); John Work, *The Snake Expedition of 1830–1831: John Work's Field Journal*, ed. Francis D. Haines (Norman: University of Oklahoma Press, 1971).

11. Ott, "'Ruining' the Rivers," 166–191; Steven Fountain, "Stealing Shoes in the Fur Desert: Hudson's Bay Company Policy in the Columbia Department, 1824–1840," in *Aboriginal People and the Fur Trade: Proceedings of the Eighth North American Fur Trade Conference, Akwesasne*, ed. Louise Johnston (Cornwall, ON, and Roosevelton, NY: Akwesasne Notes Publishing, 2001), 187–193; Colin G. Calloway, "Snake Frontiers: The Eastern Shoshone in the Eighteenth Century," *Annals of Wyoming* 63 (Summer 1991): 82–92.

12. Johansen, "Introduction," xix.

13. W. Kaye Lamb, introduction to *The Letters of John McLoughlin: 1st Series, 1825–38*, ed. E. E. Rich (London: Hudson's Bay Record Society, 1941), lx–cxiii.; Mackie, *Trading Beyond the Mountains*, 44–122.

14. Charles E. Simpson, "The Snake Country Freemen: British Fur Trappers in Idaho" (M.A. thesis, University of Idaho, 1990), 203.

15. Philip Goldring, *Papers on the Labour System of the Hudson's Bay Company, 1821–1900*, vol. 1 (Ottawa: Canada Parks Service, 1979), 64.

16. Ott, "'Ruining' the Rivers," 173–178.

17. Horace S. Lyman, ed., "Reminiscences of Louis Labonte," *OHQ* 1:2 (June 1900), 175.

18. Willard Rees, "Annual Address [1879]," *TOPA* 7 (1880), 23–25; T. C. Elliott, ed., "The Peter Skene Ogden Journals," *OHQ* 10:4 (December 1909), 364; Alexander R. McLeod, "Journal of a Trapping Expedition along the Coast South of the Columbia River," in Davies, *Snake Country Journals, 1826–1827*, 143–150.

19. McLeod, "Journal of a Trapping Expedition," 147–146; John A. Hussey, *Champoeg: Place of Transition, A Disputed History* (Portland: Oregon Historical Society/Oregon State Highway Commission, 1967), 47–48.

20. For regional Native and fur trader views on violence between the two groups during this period, see R. Scott Byram, "Colonial Power and Indigenous Justice: Fur Trader Violence and Its Aftermath in Yaquina Narrative," *OHQ* 109:3 (Fall 2008): 358–387; Jonathan Dean, "The Hudson's Bay Company and Its Use of Force, 1828–1829," *OHQ* 98:3 (Fall 1997): 262–295; Francis Ermatinger, *Fur Trade Letters of Francis Ermatinger, 1818–1853*, ed. Lois Halliday McDonald (Glendale, CA: Arthur H. Clark Co., 1980), 96–117; and Gray Whaley, *Oregon and the Collapse of Illahee: U.S. Empire and the Transformation of an Indigenous World, 1792–1859* (Chapel Hill: University of North Carolina Press, 2010), 83–91.

21. David Douglas, *The Oregon Journals of David Douglas*, ed. David Lavender, vol. 1, (Ashland: Oregon Book Society, 1972), 68.

22. David Douglas, *Journal Kept by David Douglas during His Travels in North America, 1823–1827.* (1914. Reprint. New York: Antiquarian Press, 1959), 237.

23. On the tendency of Northwest Coast Natives to supplement (rather than reorder) their existing economic activities with the exchange of furs, foodstuff, and labor in the fur trade economy, see, for example, Robert Bunting, *The Pacific Raincoast: Environment and Culture in an American Eden, 1778–1900* (Lawrence: University Press of Kansas, 1997), 22–35; and Lissa K. Wadewitz, *The Nature of Borders: Salmon, Boundaries, and Bandits on the Salish Sea* (Seattle: University of Washington Press, 2012), 30–51.

24. Mackie, *Trading Beyond the Mountains*, chapter 12: "The Native Foundation of Trade and Labour," 282–310. See also Mathias D. Bergman, "'We should lose much by their absence': The Centrality of Chinookans and Kalapuyans to Life in Frontier Oregon," *OHQ* 109:1 (Spring 2008): 40–42.

25. Douglas, *Journal Kept by David Douglas*, 226.

26. For the conception of fur traders as guests of the indigenous peoples of the Pacific Northwest, see Duane Thomson and Marianne Ignace, "'They Made Themselves Our Guests': Power Relationships in the Interior Plateau Region of the Cordillera in the Fur Trade Era," *BC Studies* 146 (Summer 2005): 3–35.

27. The major works in Canada and the United States on the history of intermarriage between Euro-American fur traders and Native women include the following: Jennifer S. H. Brown, *Strangers in Blood: Fur Trade Families in Indian County* (Vancouver: University of British Columbia Press, 1980); Jennifer S. H. Brown, "Partial Truths: A Closer Look at Fur Trade Marriage," in *From Rupert's Land to Canada*, ed. Theodore Binnema, Gerhard J. Ens, and R. C. Macleod (Edmonton: University of Alberta Press, 2001), 59–80; Jacqueline Peterson and Jennifer S. H. Brown, eds., *The New Peoples: Being and Becoming Métis in North America* (Winnipeg: University of Manitoba Press, 1985); Susan Sleeper-Smith, *Indian Women and French Men: Rethinking Cultural Encounters in the Western Great Lakes* (Amherst: University of Massachusetts Press, 2001); Tanis C. Thorne, *The Many Hands of My Relations: French and Indians on the Lower Missouri* (Columbia: University of Missouri Press, 1996); and Sylvia Van Kirk, *Many Tender Ties: Women in Fur Trade Society, 1670–1870* (Norman: University of Oklahoma Press, 1980). For the importance of social and kin relations between indigenous people and fur traders in the Pacific Northwest, see Susan Armitage, "Making Connections: Gender, Race, and Place in Oregon Country," in *One Step Over the Line: Toward a History of Women in the North American Wests*, ed. Elizabeth Jameson and Sheila McManus (Edmonton: University of Alberta Press, 2008), 55–79; and Alexandra Harmon, *Indians in the Making: Ethnic Relations and Indian Identities around Puget Sound* (Berkeley: University of California Press, 1998), 13–42.

28. David Peterson del Mar, "Intermarriage and Agency: A Chinookan Case Study," *Ethnohistory* 42:1 (Winter 1995): 1–30; Gray Whaley, "'Complete Liberty'?: Gender, Sexuality, Race, and Social Change on the Lower Columbia River, 1805–1838," *Ethnohistory* 54:4 (Fall 2007): 669–695. Ron Bourgeault has argued for an alternative view, one that emphasizes the sexual and economic exploitation of Indian women in the fur trade. His arguments, informed by Marxist theory, minimize the agency of Native women. See Ron Bourgeault,

"Race, Class, and Gender: Colonial Domination of Indian Women," in *Race, Class, Gender: Bonds and Barriers*, ed. Jess Vorst et al., revised ed. (Toronto: Society for Socialist Studies/ Garamond Press, 1991), 88–117.

29. There is one other documented long-term relationship between a Kalapuyan woman and a fur trader during this period. In the late 1810s, Louis Shangretta, an Iroquois who worked as voyageur and later free trapper with the Northwest Company, began a relationship with a Chelamela Kalapuyan woman from the Long Tom River area. The couple had at least three living children together. Sometime between 1827 and 1835, the Kalapuyan woman died, and in 1835 Louis Shangretta passed away. The HBC and local settlers arranged for the American Methodist missionaries recently arrived in the Willamette Valley to care for the couple's children. Within a few years, son Nicholas and daughter Isabel also died. However, one of the couple's sons, Joseph Shangretta, did survive. He later married a Chinook woman and became a leader on the Grand Ronde Reservation, where the Shangretta descendants are enrolled today. For background on the Shangretta family, see June Olson, "My Long Ago Che-lam-e-la Grandmother," in *The Kalapuyans: A Sourcebook on the Indians of the Willamette Valley*, by Harold Mackey, 2nd ed, (Salem, OR: Mission Mill Museum Association, in cooperation with the Confederated Tribes of Grand Ronde 2004), 198–200; and Harriet D. Munnik, "Mission Roll Call," *Marion County History* 11 (1972–1976): 23–26.

30. Helen Codere, "Kwakiutl Traditional Culture," in *Handbook of North Ameican Indians*, vol. 7: *Northwest Coast*, ed. Wayne Suttles (Washington, D.C.: Smithsonian Institution, 1990), 360, 363; Robert Boyd, personal communication, 2009.

31. Leland Donald, *Aboriginal Slavery on the Northwest Coast of North America* (Berkeley: University of California Press, 1997), 140–142; Yvonne P. Hajda, "Slavery in the Greater Lower Columbia Region," *Ethnohistory* 52:3 (Summer 2005): 563–588.

32. Peterson del Mar, "Intermarriage and Agency," 1–12.

33. Mary C. Wright, "The Circle Broken: Gender, Family, and Difference in the Pacific Northwest, 1811–1850" (Ph.D. diss., Rutgers, State University of New Jersey, 1996), 50–101; Jean Barman, *French Canadians, Furs, and Indigenous Women in the Making of the Pacific Northwest* (Vancouver: UBC Press, 2014), 107–142.

34. Elliott, "Ogden Journals," 364; Rees, "Annual Address," 23.

35. John McLoughlin, "Copy of a Document Found among the Private Papers of John McLoughlin," *TOPA* 8 (1880): 48–49.

36. Lyman, "Reminiscences of Louis Labonte," 173.

37. Ermatinger, *Fur Trade Letters*, 203.

38. For a wide-ranging analysis of the motivations of French Canadian men who chose to remain in the Pacific Northwest rather than return to Lower Canada, see Barman, *French Canadians, Furs, and Indigenous Women*, 76–103. See also W. L. Morton, "The Significance of Site in the Settlement of the American and Canadian Wests," *Agricultural History* 25 (1951), 97. For the later Anglo-American settlement of the Willamette Valley, see Peter G. Boag, *Environment and Experience: Settlement Culture in Nineteenth-Century Oregon* (Berkeley: University of California Press, 1992); and Bunting, *The Pacific Raincoast*.

39. David Brauner, "The French-Canadian Archaeological Project, Willamette Valley, Oregon: Site Inventory and Settlement Pattern Analysis," report submitted to the Oregon State Preservation Office (Corvallis: Oregon State University Department of Anthropology, 1989), cited in Jun R. Kinoshita, "Little Houses on the Prairie: A Predictive Model of French-Canadian Settlement in Oregon's Willamette Valley" (M.A. thesis, Oregon State University, 2004), 58.

40. Philip Goldring, *Papers on the Labour System of the Hudson's Bay Company, 1821–1900*, vol. 1 (Ottawa: Canada Parks Service, 1979), 64; Allan Greer, *Peasant, Lord, and Merchant: Rural Society in Three Quebec Parishes, 1740–1840* (Toronto: University of Toronto Press, 1985), 177–193; Carolyn Podruchny, *Making the Voyageur World: Travelers and Traders in the North American Fur Trade* (Lincoln: University of Nebraska Press, 2006), 18–51.

41. Colin M. Coates, *The Metamorphoses of Landscape and Community in Early Quebec* (Montreal: McGill-Queen's Press, 2000), 32–54; Louise Dechêne, *Habitants and Merchants in Seventeenth-Century Montreal* (Montreal: McGill-Queen's University Press, 1992), 127–196; Allan Greer, *The People of New France* (Toronto: University of Toronto Press, 1997), 27–42.

42. Carl J. Ekberg, *French Roots in the Illinois Country: The Mississippi Frontier in Colonial Times* (Chicago: University of Illinois Press, 1998), 5–30, 104–110; Gerhard J. Ens, *Homeland to Hinterland: The Changing Worlds of the Red River Metis in the Nineteenth Century* (Toronto: University of Toronto Press, 1996), 114–117; Richard Colebrook Harris, *The Seigneurial System in Early Canada: A Geographical Study* (Madison/Quebec City: University of Wisconsin Press/Les Press de l'Université Laval, 1966), 117–138; Harlow Ziner Head, "The Oregon Donation Land Claims and Their Patterns" (Ph.D. diss., University of Oregon, 1971), 138–160.

43. Brauner, "French-Canadian Archaeological Project," 25; cited in Kinoshita, "Little Houses on the Prairie," 27.

44. Harris, *The Seigneurial System*, 63–87; Jeanne Pomerleau, *Corvées et quêtes: Un parcours au Canada français* (Montreal: Éditions Hurtubise, 2002), 27–32. See also François Noël, *The Christie Seigneuries: Estate Management and Settlement in the Upper Richelieu Valley, 1760–1854* (Montreal: McGill-Queen's University Press, 1992). Historians of French Canada have argued for an economic crisis in Lower Canada during the early 1800s that placed strains on the existing patterns of peasant agriculture, though there is ongoing disagreement as to the causes and extent of the crisis. For the "classic" interpretation of the agricultural crisis, see Fernand Ouellet, *Economic and Social History of Quebec, 1760–1850* (Toronto: Gage Publishing/Institute of Canadian Studies, Carleton University, 1980), 332–394; and Fernand Ouellet, *Lower Canada, 1791–1840: Social Changes and Nationalism* (Toronto: McClelland & Stewart, 1980), 117–135. For a critical review of the historiography and the existing evidence, including a reconsideration of the biases of elite observers and the adaptive strategies of the French Canadian *habitants*, see Serge Courville, "La crise agricole du Bas-Canada: Éléments d'une réflexion géographique," *Cahier du géographie du Québec* 24:62 (September 1980): 193–224 and 24:63 (December 1980): 385–428; R. M. McInnis, "A Reconsideration of the State of Agriculture in Lower Canada," *Canadian Papers in Rural History* 2 (1982): 9–49. Gilles Paquet and Jean-Pierre Wallot demonstrate the need for

a rethinking of Ouellet's thesis and conclude that Lower Canada likely did not experience an agricultural crisis before 1830: Paquet and Wallot, *Un Québec modern, 1760–1840: Essai d'histoire économique and sociale* (Montreal: Éditions Hurtubise, 2007), 297–303, 349–412.

45. Greer, *Peasant, Lord, and Merchant*, 20–47, 177–193.

46. Hussey, *Champoeg*, 56–58.

47. In studying land settlement patterns and village life, researchers on French Canada noted a marked individualism among French Canadian *habitants* dating from the settlement of New France during the 1600s. There is disagreement as to the origins of this individualism: whether the dispersed settlement patterns caused an individualist streak among the settlers or whether the French colonists created dispersed settlements as a result of an individualistic culture they brought with them from France. However, the result was a culture that allowed the *habitants* more control over their choices and resources, thereby limiting the power of both village and governmental structures. See Carl Ekberg's discussion in *French Roots in the Illinois Country*, 9–14.

48. Alexander McLeod to John McLoughlin, September 18, 1828, in Nunis, *Hudson's Bay Company's First Fur Brigade*, 12.

49. Nunis, 12.

50. Simpson, *Fur Trade*, 124.

51. Nathan Douthit, *Uncertain Encounters: Indians and Whites at Peace and War in Southern Oregon, 1820s–1860s* (Corvallis: Oregon State University Press, 2002), 10.

52. The *habitants* of Lower Canada had long pursued adaptive economic strategies that mixed agriculture (subsistence and market) with wage labor in the fur trade and other activities. See Greer, *Peasant, Lord, and Merchant*, 177–193.

53. The importance of family and especially the long-term welfare of one's children and the transmission of inheritable property were particularly pronounced among the rural *habitants* of Lower Canada through the 1800s. See Paquet and Wallot, *Un Québec modern*, 442–449; Greer, *Peasant, Lord, and Merchant*, 20–47; Gérard Bouchard, *Quelques arpents d'Amérique: Population, économie, famille au Saguenay, 1838–1971* (Montreal: Boréal, 1996), 157–276; Coates, *Metamorphoses of Landscape*, 55–76. For the importance of family relations and place in the Pacific Northwest for both Native people and bicultural fur trade families during the early 1800s, see Armitage, "Making Connections," 55–63.

54. See chapters 1, 3, and 5 in Podruchny, *Making the Voyageur World*, 1–17, 52–85, 134–164.

55. McLoughlin, "Copy of a Document," 49–50.

56. McLoughlin, "Copy of a Document," 49–50.

57. McLoughlin, "Copy of a Document," 49–50.

58. Nathaniel Wyeth, *The Correspondence and Journals of Captain Nathaniel J. Wyeth*, ed. Frederick G. Young. (1899. Reprint. Arno Press, 1973), 92; William A. Slacum, "Slacum's Report on Oregon, 1836–37," *OHQ* 13:2 (June 1912), 197–198.

59. Lyman, "Reminiscences of Louis Labonte," 173–175; Hussey, *Champoeg*, 43–61.

60. Louis Labonté initially settled across the river in the territory of the Yamhill Kalapuyans.

61. This number is a conservative estimate based on Robert Boyd's pre-1830s population tables. In 1805 the Central Kalapuyans numbered about six thousand. In dividing this 1805 figure between the ten known Central subdivisions, one returns a total of

about six hundred per Central Kalapuyan group. Boyd, *The Coming of the Spirit Pestilence*, 325.

62. Mathias D. Bergmann, "Cross-Cultural Interactions, Interdependencies, and Insecurities on the Lower Columbia River Valley, 1810–1855" (M.A. thesis, Washington State University, 2000); Morag Maclachlan, ed., *The Fort Langley Journals* (Vancouver: University of British Columbia Press, 1998); Brett Rushforth, "'The Great Spirit Was Grieved': Religion and Environment among the Cowlitz Indians," *PNQ* 93:4 (Fall 2002), 190–191; Theodore Stern, *Chiefs and Chief Traders: Indian Relations at Fort Nez Percés, 1818–1855* (Corvallis: Oregon State University Press, 1993).

63. Lyman, "Reminiscences of Louis Labonte," 175.

64. Lyman, "Reminiscences of Louis Labonte," 172.

65. Lyman, "Reminiscences of Louis Labonte," 175–176.

66. John McLoughlin, *The Letters of John McLoughlin from Fort Vancouver, 1st Series*, edited by R. R. Rich (London: Hudson's Bay Company Record Society, 1941), 172–173.

67. McLoughlin, *Letters, 1st Series*, 172–173.

68. Lyman, "Reminiscences of Louis Labonte," 171.

69. McLoughlin, *Letters, 1st Series*, 171–173.

70. McLoughlin, *Letters, 1st Series*, 173.

71. McLoughlin, "Copy of a Document," 48.

72. McLoughlin, "Copy of a Document," 51–52; Horace S. Lyman, ed., "Reminiscences of F. X. Matthieu," *OHQ* 1:1 (March 1900), 89.

73. John McLoughlin cited in S. A. Clarke, *Pioneer Days of Oregon History*, vol. 1 (Portland, OR: J. K. Gill Co., 1905), 220–221.

74. Lyman, "Reminiscences of F. X. Matthieu," 89.

75. McLoughlin cited in Clarke, *Pioneer Days*, vol. 1, 220.

76. Goldring, *Papers on the Labour System*, vol. 3, 34; William R. Swagerty and Dick A. Wilson, "Faithful Service under Different Flags: A Socioeconomic Profile of the Columbia District, Hudson's Bay Company and the Upper Missouri Outfit, American Fur Company, 1825–1835, in *The Fur Trade Revisited: Selected Papers of the Sixth North American Fur Trade Conference, Mackinac Island, Michigan, 1991*, ed. Jennifer S. H. Brown, W. J. Eccles, and Donald P. Heldman (East Lansing: Michigan State University Press, 1994): 243–267.

77. Lyman, "Reminiscences of Louis Labonte," 172–173.

78. Lyman, "Reminscences of Louis Labonte," 173.

79. Slacum, "Report on Oregon," 175–224; Maloney, *Fur Brigade to the Bonaventura*, 82–83; Hussey, *Champoeg*, 47–66; J. Neilson Barry, *The French Canadian Pioneers of the Willamette* Valley (Portland, OR: Catholic Sentinel, 1933); J. Neilson Barry, "Astorians Who Settled in Oregon," *WHQ* 24 (1933): 221–231, 282–301; Harriet D. Munnick, "The Prairie That Slacum Saw," *MCH* 9 (1965–1968): 25–32; Oswald West, "Oregon's First White Settlers in French Prairie," *OHQ* 43:3 (September 1942): 198–209; John Ball, *Born to Wander: Autobiography of John Ball*, comp. Kate Ball Powers, Flora Ball Hopkins, and Lucy Ball, with a new introduction by Gary Burbridge (1925; reprint, Grand Rapids, MI: Grand Rapids Historical Society, 1994); *Genealogical Material in Oregon Provisional Land Claims: Abstracted from Applications*, vol. 1-8: *1845–1849* (Portland: Genealogical Forum of Portland, Oregon, 1982), 11, 41.

80. Lyman, "Reminiscences of Louis Labonte," 172.

81. Lyman, "Reminiscences Louis Labonte," 173–177; Barry, "Astorians Who Settled in Oregon," 283.

82. John Hussey did include Jean Baptiste Desportes McKay as one of the original colonists of French Prairie in his 1967 history of Champoeg. See Hussey, *Champoeg*, 54–55.

83. Ball, *Born to Wander*, 61–63; John Ball, "Letters of John Ball, 1832–1833," ed. M. M. Quaife, *MCH* 4:5 (March 1919): 450–468.

84. Johannessen et al., "The Vegetation of the Willamette Valley," *Annals of the Association of American Geographers* 61:2 (June 1971), 286; James L. Ratcliff, "What Happened to the Kalapuya?: A Study of the Depletion of Their Economic Base," *Indian Historian* 6:3 (Summer 1973), 30–31.

85. Harvey McKay's oral interviews with the elderly descendants of the French Prairie settlers in the late 1970s suggest that Chinook Jargon was a native tongue of the second and third generations born to French-Indian families in the mid-1800s. Harvey McKay, *St. Paul, Oregon, 1830–1890* (Portland, OR: Binford & Mort, 1980), 133.

86. John Ball, "Across the Continent Seventy Years Ago," *OHQ* 3:2 (June 1902), 103.

87. For the system of slavery in the Pacific Northwest, see Elsie Francis Dennis, "Slavery in the Pacific Northwest," Part 2, *OHQ* 31:2 (1930), 192–195; Hajda, "Slavery in the Greater Lower Columbia Region"; and Leland Donald, *Aboriginal Slavery*.

88. Ball, "Across the Continent," 103–105.

89. Frederick L. Dunn, "Malaria," in *The Cambridge World History of Human Disease*, ed. Kenneth F. Kipple (Cambridge: Cambridge University Press, 1993), 860; Randall M. Packard, *The Making of a Tropical Disease: A Short History of Malaria* (Baltimore: Johns Hopkins University Press, 2007), 36–66.

90. Boyd, *The Coming of the Spirit Pestilence*, 84.

91. Boyd, *The Coming of the Spirit Pestilence*, 84; S. F. Cook, "The Epidemic of 1830–1833 in California and Oregon," *University of California Publications in American Archaeology and Ethnology* 43:3 (May 1955): 303–326; Herbert C. Taylor and Lester L. Hoaglin, "The 'Intermittent Fever' Epidemic of the 1830s on the Lower Columbia River," *Ethnohistory* 9:1 (Winter 1962): 160–178. See also Gray Whaley's overview of the Columbia region, *Oregon and the Collapse of Illahee*, 91–94.

92. Boyd, *The Coming of the Spirit Pestilence*, 100.

93. John Kirk Townsend, *Narrative of a Journey Across the Rocky Mountains to the Columbia River*, with an introduction by George A. Jobanek (1839. Reprint. Corvallis: Oregon State University Press, 1999), 128.

94. Boyd, *The Coming of the Spirit Pestilence*, 10; Cook, "The Epidemic of 1830–1833," 307–308; Dunn, "Malaria," 855–856; Jacques M. May, "The Ecology of Malaria," in *Studies in Disease Ecology*, ed. Jacques M. May (New York: Hafner Publishing, 1961): 161–171.

95. Peter Skene Ogden, *Traits of American Indian Life* (1933. Reprint. Fairfield, WA: Ye Galleon Press, 1998), 100.

96. McLoughlin, *Letters, 1st Series*, 88.

97. Ogden, *Traits of American Indian Life*, 100.

98. Ogden, *Traits*, 100.

99. Boyd, *The Coming of the Spirit Pestilence*, 107; William Fraser Tolmie, *Journal of William Fraser Tolmie*, ed. Howard R. Mitchell and Janet R. Mitchell (Vancouver, BC: Mitchell Press, 1963), 171, 175; Donald Culross Peattie, *A Natural History of Western Trees* (New York: Bonanza Books, 1953), 653–655.

100. McLoughlin, *Letters, 1st Series*, 88.

101. Boyd, *The Coming of the Spirit Pestilence*, 86–92; Cook, "The Epidemic of 1830–1833," 305; Taylor and Hoaglin, "The 'Intermittent Fever' Epidemic," 160.

102. Boyd, *The Coming of the Spirit Pestilence*, 18–20.

103. Carl Landerholm, ed. and trans., *Notices and Voyages of the Famed Quebec Mission to the Pacific Northwest* (Portland: Oregon Historical Society, 1956), 18.

104. Boyd, *The Coming of the Spirit Pestilence*, 108.

105. Boyd, *The Coming of the Spirit Pestilence*, 109.

106. Alfred Crosby, "Virgin Soil Epidemics as a Factor in the Aboriginal Depopulation in America," *William and Mary Quarterly* 3rd Series, 33:2 (April 1976), 296.

107. Crosby, "Virgin Soil Epidemics," 297; Robert J. Wolfe, "Alaska's Great Sickness, 1900: An Epidemic of Measles and Influenza in a Virgin Soil Population," *Proceedings of the American Philosophical Society* 126: 2 (1982): 91–121; Daniel T. Reff, *Disease, Depopulation, and Culture Change in Northwestern New Spain, 1518–1764* (Salt Lake City: University of Utah Press, 1991).

108. Crosby, "Virgin Soil Epidemics," 294.

109. Landerholm, *Notices and Voyages of the Famed Quebec Mission*, 18.

110. Boyd, *The Coming of the Spirit Pestilence*, 86–87.

111. Boyd, *The Coming of the Spirit Pestilence*, 109–112; George B. Roberts, "Recollections," BAN, P-A 83, 38; Francis Fuller Victor, "Flotsam and Jetsam of the Pacific: the *Owyhee*, the *Sultana*, and the *May Dacre*," *OHQ* 2:1 (March 1901): 39.

112. Boyd, *The Coming of the Spirit Pestilence*, 85.

113. Boyd, *The Coming of the Spirit Pestilence*, 109.

114. Henry F. Dobyns, "Native American Trade Centers as Contagious Disease Foci," in *Disease and Demography in the Americas*, ed. John W. Verano and Douglas H. Ubelaker (Washington, D.C.: Smithsonian Institution Press, 1992): 215–222; Arthur J. Ray, "Diffusion of Disease in the Western Interior of Canada, 1830–1850," *Geographic Review* 66:2 (1976): 139–157.

115. Boyd, *The Coming of the Spirit Pestilence*, 92; Taylor and Hoaglin, "The 'Intermittent Fever' Epidemic," 169.

116. Boyd, *The Coming of the Spirit Pestilence*, 95.

117. Boyd, *The Coming of the Spirit Pestilence*, 99.

118. Slacum, "Report on Oregon," 201.

119. Ball, *Born to Wander*, 61–63.

120. Maloney, *Fur Brigade to the Bonaventura*, 81–83.

121. Ball, "Across the Continent," 104; Ball, *Born to Wander*, 62.

122. Melville Jacobs, ed., *Clackamas Chinook Texts*, vol. 2 (Bloomington: Indiana University Research Center in Anthropology, Folklore and Linguistics/*International Journal of American Linguistics*, 1959), 538, 546–547. See also Siobhan Senier, *Voice of American Indian*

Assimilation and Resistance: Helen Hunt Jackson, Sarah Winnemucca, and Victoria Howard (Norman: University of Oklahoma Press, 2001).

123. Victoria Howard was raised largely by her Clackamas grandmother, from whom she learned the Clackamas language as well as the historical and mythical stories she related to Melville Jacobs. For her first marriage, Victoria married into a prominent Clackamas family, the Wachenos. As a result she gained additional knowledge of Clackamas history and culture from her mother-in-law. Her second husband was Eustace Howard of Santiam Kalapuyan ancestry. Henry Zenk, personal communication, 2002.

124. Jacobs, *Clackamas Chinook Texts*, 546.

125. Ball, *Born to Wander*, 97.

126. Ball, *Born to Wander*, 99.

127. Jacobs, *Clackamas Chinook Texts*, 546–547.

128. Boyd, *The Coming of the Spirit Pestilence*, 278.

129. Boyd, *The Coming of the Spirit Pestilence*, 97.

130. Boyd, *The Coming of the Spirit Pestilence*, 97; Melville Jacobs, ed., *Kalapuya Texts*, University of Washington Texts in Anthropology, vol. 11 (Seattle: University of Washington, 1945), 89–90.

131. Boyd, *The Coming of the Spirit Pestilence*, 244, 325, 327.

132. John Minto, "The Number and Condition of the Native Race in Oregon When First Seen by White Men," *Oregon Historical Quarterly* 1:3 (September 1900), 298; Leslie M. Scott, "Indian Disease as Aids to the Pacific Northwest Settlement," *OHQ* 29 (1928), 144.

133. For several decades, there has been disagreement among scholars regarding the historical demography of Native North America since the 1500s. Points of contention include methodology, the analysis and reliability of European sources, an early tendency to estimate low population numbers in the precontact period (1400s), and ethics of attributing the majority of indigenous population losses to inadvertently introduced epidemic diseases from Europe (and elsewhere) rather than to the actions and decisions of the European invaders. Two important works on the controversies are Henry F. Dobyns, with an essay by William R. Swagerty, *Their Numbers Become Thinned: Native American Population Dynamics in Eastern North America* (Knoxville: University of Tennessee Press, 1983); and Ann F. Ramenofsky, *Vectors of Death: The Archaeology of European Contact* (Albuquerque: University of New Mexico Press, 1987).

134. Boyd, *The Coming of the Spirit Pestilence*, 244.

135. Boyd, *The Coming of the Spirit Pestilence*, 258–261; Robert Boyd, "Population Decline from Two Epidemics on the Northwest Coast," in *Disease and Demography in the Americas*, ed. John W. Verano and Douglas H. Ubelaker (Washington, D.C.: Smithsonian Institution Press, 1992), 251.

136. Boyd, *The Coming of the Spirit Pestilence*, 245.

137. Landerholm, *Notices and Voyages of the Famed Quebec Mission*, 84.

138. Joseph Taylor, *Making Salmon: An Environmental History of the Northwest Coast Fisheries Crisis* (Seattle: University of Washington Press, 1999), 42–43.

139. Boyd, "Strategies of Indian Burning," 99–100; Taylor, *Making Salmon, 42*.

140. Boyd, *The Coming of the Spirit Pestilence*, 84–116; Whaley, *Oregon and the Collapse*

of Illahee, 71–98; and William G. Robbins, *Landscapes of Promise: The Oregon Story, 1800–1940* (Seattle: University of Washington Press, 1997), 50–80.

CHAPTER 3: Methodist Missionaries and Community Relations

1. Joseph Provencher to Joseph Signay, Archbishop of Quebec City, June 9, 1835, British Columbia Records, 26 CN, Archives of the Archdiocese of Quebec (AAQ), Quebec City; Francis Norbert Blanchet, The Catholic Missionaries of Oregon, P-A 5, BAN, 3; Francis Norbert Blanchet, *Historical Sketches of the Catholic Church in Oregon*, ed. Edward J. Kowrach (1878. Reprint. Fairfield, WA: Ye Galleon Press, 1998), 38.

2. Provencher to Signay, June 9, 1835. These passages, translated from the French by the author, are Provencher's paraphrasing of the French Canadians' letter. According to officials at La Société historique de St. Boniface in Winnipeg, Manitoba, which holds the early Red River Catholic records, neither the originals nor copies of the 1834 and 1835 letters have survived. The Archives of Archdiocese of Quebec likewise does not have copies of these two initial letters.

3. Jason Lee, "The Diary of Rev. Jason Lee," *OHQ* 17:3 (September 1916), 261; Cyrus Shepard, *Diary of Cyrus Shepard*, ed. Gerry Gilman (Vancouver: Clark County Genealogical Society, 1986), 65; Robert J. Loewenberg, *Equality on the Oregon Frontier: Jason Lee and the Methodist Mission, 1834–43* (Seattle: University of Washington Press, 1976), 80–82.

4. Gray H. Whaley, "'Trophies for God': Native Morality, Racial Ideology, and the Methodist Mission of Lower Oregon, 1834–1844," *OHQ* 107: 1 (Spring 2006): 6–35.

5. For representative views of early Oregon historiography and its emphasis on Anglo-Americans, see the Hubert H. Bancroft volumes largely written by Francis Fuller Victor, *History of Oregon*, 2 vols. (San Francisco: The History Company, 1886), and James R. Robertson, "The Social Evolution of Oregon," *OHQ* 3:1 (March 1902): 1–37. For recent assessments of Pacific Northwest historiography, see Keith D. Richards, "In Search of the Pacific Northwest: The Historiography of Oregon and Washington," *PHR* 50:4 (November 1981): 415–444; James P. Ronda, "Calculating Ouragon," *OHQ* 94:2–3 (Summer-Fall 1993):121–140; Susan H. Armitage, "From the Inside Out: Rewriting Regional History," *Frontiers* 22:3 (2001): 32–47; David Peterson del Mar, *Oregon's Promise: An Interpretive History* (Corvallis: Oregon State University Press, 2003), 1–10.

6. Larry Cebula, *Plateau Indians and the Quest for Spiritual Power, 1700–1850* (Lincoln: University of Nebraska Press, 2003), 86–89; Francis Haines, *The Nez Percés: Tribesmen of the Columbia Plateau* (Norman: University of Oklahoma Press, 1955), 57–70; Christopher L. Miller, *Prophetic Worlds: Indians and Whites on the Columbia Plateau*, with a new foreword by Chris Friday (1985. Reprint. Seattle: University of Washington Press, 2003), 59–62; Alvin M. Josephy, *The Nez Perce Indians and the Opening of the Northwest* (1965. Reprint. New York: Mariner Books, 1997), 92–96.

7. Cebula, *Plateau Indians*, 68–83; Miller, *Prophetic Worlds*, 37–57.

8. Loewenberg, *Equality on the Oregon Frontier*, 78; Ray Allen Billington and Martin Ridge, *Westward Expansion: A History of the American Frontier*, 5th ed. (New York:

Macmillan Publishing, 1982), 458–459; Ray A. Billington, "Oregon Epic: A Letter that Jarred America," *The Pacific Historian* (Summer 1968): 30–37; Albert Furtwangler, *Bringing Indians to the Book* (Seattle: University of Washington Press, 2005), 24, 191–200.

9. For an insightful discussion of how the Methodists interpreted the Nez Perce–Flathead delegation's visit to St. Louis in 1831 and the cultural misunderstandings that accompanied it, see Furtwangler, *Bringing Indians to the Book*, 13–56.

10. Susan Neylan, *The Heavens Are Changing: Nineteenth-Century Protestant Missions and Tsimshian Christianity* (Montreal: McGill-Queen's University Press, 2003), 66.

11. Dee E. Andrews, *The Methodists and Revolutionary America, 1760–1800* (Princeton, NJ: Princeton University Press, 2000), 55–72.

12. Sydney A. Alhstrom, *A Religious History of the American People* (New Haven: Yale University Press, 1972), 360–384; Nathan O. Hatch, *The Democratization of American Christianity* (New Haven, CT: Yale University Press, 1989), 3–16; Mark A. Noll, *A History of Christianity in the United States and Canada* (Grand Rapids, MI: William B. Eerdmans, 1992), 115–118.

13. Noll, *A History of Christianity*, 166–169. Whitney E. Cross, *The Burned-Over District: The Social and Intellectual History of Enthusiastic Religion in Western New York, 1800–1850* (Ithaca, NY: Cornell University Press, 1950).

14. Francis L. Moates, "The Rise of Methodism in the Middle West," *MVHR* 15:1 (June 1928): 69–88; William Warren Sweet, *Religion on the American Frontier*, vol. 4, *The Methodists* (Chicago: University of Chicago Press, 1946), 42–68.

15. Robert F. Berkhofer, *Salvation and the Savage: An Analysis of Protestant Missions and American Indian Responses* (New York: Atheneum, 1976); C. L. Higman, *Noble, Wretched, and Redeemable: Protestant Missionaries to the Indians of Canada and the United States, 1820–1900* (Albuquerque: University of New Mexico Press, 2000); Keith Widder, *Battle for the Soul: Métis Children Encounter Evangelical Protestants at Mackinaw Mission, 1823–1837* (East Lansing: Michigan State University Press, 1999).

16. Loewenberg, *Equality on the Oregon Frontier*, 78–79.

17. Robert Moulton Gatke, ed., "A Document of Missionary History, 1833–43," *OHQ* 36:1 (March 1935), 72–74.

18. Charles Henry Carey, ed., "The Mission Record Book of the Methodist Episcopal Church, Willamette Station, Oregon Territory, Commenced 1834," *Oregon Hitorical Quarterly* 23:3 (September 1922), 232.

19. For narratives of the Wyeth's second expedition and the Methodist missionaries, see Jason Lee, "Diary of the Rev. Jason Lee," 116–146, 240–261; Shepard, *Diary of Cyrus Shepard*, 4–84; John Kirk Townsend, *Narrative of a Journey Across the Rocky Mountains to the Columbia River,* with an introduction by George A. Jobanek (1839. Reprint. Corvallis: Oregon State University Press, 1999); Nathaniel J. Wyeth, *The Correspondence and Journals of Captain Nathaniel J. Wyeth, 1831–6*, ed. Frederick G. Young (1899. Reprint. New York: Arno Press, 1973), 131–143; Nathaniel J. Wyeth, *The Journals of Captain Nathaniel J. Wyeth's Expeditions to the Oregon Country, 1831–1836*, ed. Don Johnson (Fairfield, WA: Ye Galleon Press, 1984), 71–82.

20. Jason Lee, "Diary of the Rev. Jason Lee," 139–143.

21. Jason Lee, "Diary of the Rev. Jason Lee," 240–260; Shepard, *Diary of Cyrus Shepard*, 44–45.

22. Carey, "Mission Record Book," 234.

23. John McLoughlin, "Copy of a Document Found Among the Papers of John McLoughlin," *TOPA*, vol. 8 (Salem: E. M. Waite, 1881), 50. John McLoughlin had mentioned the importance of "civilizing" the Indians of the Willamette Valley in a letter from 1836: John McLoughlin to Edward Ermatinger, February 1, 1836, in "Documentary: Letters of Dr. John McLoughlin," ed. T. C. Elliot, *OHQ* 23:4 (December 1922), 368.

24. Jason Lee, "Diary of the Rev. Jason Lee," 264.

25. Jason Lee, "Diary of the Rev. Jason Lee," 264. The brackets are included in the published version of the Lee diary; they indicate a break or illegible passage in the manuscript.

26. Daniel Lee and Joseph H. Frost, *Ten Years in Oregon* 1844. (1844. Reprint. Fairfield, WA: Ye Galleon Press, 1968), 90.

27. Gray Whaley has argued that this approach to intercultural relations reflects the larger shift in Indian policy and Indian-white relations during the Jacksonian period. See Whaley, *Oregon and the Collapse of Illahee*, 8–9, 30.

28. Jason Lee, "Diary of the Rev. Jason Lee," 265.

29. Robert James Decker, "Jason Lee, Missionary to Oregon: A Re-Evaluation" (Ph.D. diss., Indiana University, 1961), 51–52.

30. Lee and Frost, *Ten Years in Oregon*, 127–128.

31. Higham, *Noble, Wretched, and Redeemable*, 16; Decker, "Jason Lee," 52–53; Loewenberg, *Equality on the Oregon Frontier*, 78–105. For an overview of the ambivalent attitudes of the Lees and other Protestant missionaries in the Pacific Northwest during the 1830s and 1840s, including their eventual disillusionment with missionizing the Indians, see Furtwangler, *Bringing Indians to the Book*, 57–114.

32. Whaley, *Oregon and the Collapse of Illahee*, 8–9; Brian W. Dippie, *The Vanishing American: White Attitudes and U.S. Indian Policy* (Lawrence: University Press of Kansas, 1982), 10–31; David S. Jones, *Rationalizing Epidemics: Meanings and Uses of American Indian Mortality since 1600* (Cambridge, MA: Harvard University Press, 2004), 137–144. See also Stephen Dow Beckham, "The Myth of the Vanishing Kalapuyans," in *What Price Eden? The Willamette Valley in Transition, 1812–1855* (Salem, OR: Mission Mill Museum, 1988).

33. Jason Lee, "Diary of the Rev. Jason Lee," 264–265; Carey, "Mission Record Book," 234; Shepard, *Diary of Shepard Cyrus*, 67–68.

34. Loewenberg, *Equality on the Oregon Frontier*, 63; Judith A. Sanders, Mary K. Weber, and David R. Brauner, *Willamette Mission Archeological Assessment*, Anthropology Northwest, No. 1 (Corvallis: Oregon State University Anthropology Department, 1983), 15; J. Neilson Barry, "Site of the Historic Granary of the Methodist Mission," *OHQ* 43:3 (September 1942): 286–289.

35. Whaley, *Oregon and the Collapse of Illahee*, 144–115.

36. Kenneth L. Homes, *Ewing Young: Master Trapper* (Portland: Binford & Mort, 1967), 93–97.

37. Daniel Lee and Joseph Frost, *Ten Years in Oregon*, 128–129; Shepard, *Diary of Cyrus Shepard*, 71–73; Holmes, *Ewing Young*, 103–105.

38. Jason Lee, "Diary of the Rev. Jason Lee," 401.

39. Carey, "Mission Record Book," 235.

40. Jason Lee to Wilbur Fisk, cited in Cornelius J. Brosnan, *Jason Lee: Prophet of the New Oregon* (New York: Macmillian, 1932), 73. There is an age discrepancy for Sintwa between the "Mission Record Book" and Lee's letter to Brosnan. However, the timing and details of the two sources indicate that the Kalapuyan youth described in both sources was in fact the same individual.

41. Carey, "Mission Record Book," 265–266.

42. While many of the children from the Lower Columbia River–Willamette region (where the population losses from the intermittent fever were the most severe) were probably orphans; parents from the middle Columbia and the Plateau region placed a number of children at the mission because they wanted them to receive a Euro-American education. This was the case for Kenooteesh, a Silelah (Celilo?) lad, and Kokallah, a Tillamook youth, both of whom HBC translator Michel Laframboise brought to the mission "for the purpose of having them educated" on April 26, 1835. However, Kokallah left with his father on June 17, 1835. At one point, the missionaries received two Chinook youths who requested admittance to the mission on the advice of John McLoughlin. In July 1836, Welaptulekt, identified as Cayuse, visited the mission, bringing his two sons, Wislahowitka and Siahhen. Welaptulekt had traveled with the missionaries on the portion of their overland journey from Fort Hall to Fort Walla Walla (Fort Nez Perces) in fall 1834. He too brought his sons to the mission to "have them remain with the [missionaries] to be educated." Carey, "Mission Record Book," 244.

43. Carey, "Mission Record Book," 237–245; Robert Boyd, *The Coming of the Spirit Pestilence: Introduced Infectious Disease and Population Decline among Northwest Coast Indians, 1774–1874* (Seattle: University of Washington Press, 1999), 136–138.

44. Jason Lee to Wilbur Fisk, March 15, 1836, cited in Brosnan, *Jason Lee*, 79.

45. Jason Lee to Wilbur Fisk, March, 15, 1836.

46. Jason Lee to Wilbur Fisk, February 6, 1835, cited in Brosnan, *Jason Lee*, 73–74. See also Samuel Parker, *Journal of an Exploring Tour Beyond the Rocky Mountains*, 3rd ed. (1843; reprint, Moscow: University of Idaho Press, 1990), 176.

47. Lee to Fisk, March 15, 1836, cited in Brosnan, *Jason Lee*, 79.

48. Decker, "Jason Lee," 75; Juliet T. Pollard, "The Making of the Metis in the Pacific Northwest, Fur Trade Children: Race, Class, and Gender" (Ph.D. diss., University of British Columbia, 1990), 332.

49. Jason Lee wrote that the French Canadian settlers were "all very friendly and seem much pleased that we have come among them." See "Jason Lee to the Corresponding Secretary of the Missionary Society of the Methodist E. Church" [Lee's Original Diary, July 2, 1834–Feb. 6, 1835], in *The Oregon Crusade: Across Land and Sea to Oregon*, ed. Archer Butler Hulbert and Dorothy Printup, Overland to the Pacific series, vol. 5 (Denver: Steward Commission of Colorado College/Denver Public Library, 1935), 182.

50. George B. Roberts, "Recollections," P-A 83, BAN, 40; George B. Roberts to Mrs. F. F. Victory, January 20, 1879, "Letters to Mrs. F. F. Victory," *OHQ* 63:2-3 (June–September 1962), 200.

51. Carey, "Mission Record Book," 242–243.

52. Harriet D. Munnick, "Annotations," in *CCRPNW-SP*, A-14, and A-28 and St. Paul, vol. 1, 98; Carey, "Mission Record Book," 265–266; Shepard, *Diary of Cyrus Shepard*, 47, 82; Bruce McIntyre Watson, *Lives Lived West of the Divide: A Biographical Dictionary of Fur Traders Working West of the Rockies, 1793–1858*, vol. 1 (Kelowna: Centre for Social, Spatial, and Economic Justice, University of British Columbia-Kelowna, 2010), 252.

53. Harriett D. Munnick, "Mission Roll Call," *MCH* 11 (1972–1976): 23–26; June Olson, "My Long Ago Che-lam-e-la Grandmother," in *The Kalapuyans: A Sourcebook on the Indians of the Willamette Valley*, by Harold Mackey, 2nd ed. (Salem, OR: Mission Mill Museum Association with the cooperation of the Confederated Tribes of Grand Ronde, 2004), 198–200.

54. Munnick, "Mission Roll Call," 23; Munnick, *CCRPNW-SP*, vol 2, 7; Waston, *Lives Lived West of the Divide*, vol. 1, 178; Donald, *Aboriginal Slavery*, 140–141.

55. Carey, "Mission Record Book," 239–242.

56. Key sources on the Methodist' cultural views and their educational efforts include Read Bain, "Educational Plans and Efforts by Methodists in Oregon to 1860," *OHQ* 21:1 (March 1920): 63–94; Albert Furtwangler, *Bringing Indians to the Book*; Robert Moulton Gatke, "The First Indian School of the Pacific Northwest," *OHQ* 23:1 (March 1922): 70–83; Loewenberg, *Equality on the Oregon Frontier*; Z. A. Mudge, *The Missionary Teacher: A Memoir of Cyrus Shepard*; Harriet Munnick, "The Earliest Three R's in Oregon, 1830–1840," *MCH* 5 (June 1959): 52–56; Pollard, "The Making of the Metis."

57. Mudge, *The Missionary Teacher*, 155–156.

58. Mudge, *The Missionary Teacher*, 197–198.

59. Carey, "Mission Record Book," 235; Lee and Frost, *Ten Years in Oregon*, 132; Samuel A. Clarke, *Pioneer Days in Old Oregon*, vol. 1 (Portland: J. K. Gill), 340.

60. Furtwangler, *Bringing Indians to the Book*, 79–82; Whaley, *Oregon and the Collapse of Illahee*, 112–116.

61. Susan Armitage, "Making Connections: Gender, Race, and Place in Oregon Country," in *One Step Over the Line: Toward a History of Women in the North American Wests*, ed. Elizabeth Jameson and Sheila McManus (Edmonton and Athabasca: University of Alberta Press/University of Athabasca Press, 2008), 55–63.

62. Carey, "Mission Record Book," 264.

63. Tanis Thorne, *The Many Hands of My Relations: French and Indians on the Lower Missouri* (Columbia: University of Missouri Press, 1996), 64–97; Carolyn Podruchny, *Making the Voyageur World: Travelers and Traders in the North American Fur Trade* (Lincoln: University of Nebraska Press, 2006), 80–85.

64. Jenny Franchot, *Roads to Rome: The Antebellum Protestant Encounter with Catholicism* (Berkeley: University of California Press, 1994); Nancy Lusignan Schultz, *Fire and Rose: The Burning of the Charlestown Convent, 1834* (New York: The Free Press, 2000).

65. Furtwangler, *Bringing Indians to the Book*, 90–91.

66. Brosnan, *Jason Lee*, 87–90.

67. See Hubert Howe Bancroft, *History of Oregon*, vol. 1, *1834–1848* (San Francisco: The History Company, 1886), chapters 4 and 6; Gustavus Hines, *Oregon: Its History, Conditions, and Prospectus* (1851; reprint, New York: Arno Press, 1973), chapter 1.

68. Anne F. Hyde, *Empires, Nations, and Families: A History of the North American West, 1800–1860* (Lincoln: University of Nebraska Press, 2011); Bethel Saler and Carolyn Produchny, "Glass Curtains and Storied Landscapes: The Fur Trade, National Boundaries, and Historians," in *Bridging National Borders in North America: Transnational and Comparative Histories*, ed. Benjamin H. Johnson and Andrew R. Graybill (Durham, NC: Duke University Press, 2010), 273–302.

69. Courtney Walker, "Sketch of Ewing Young," *TOPA* (1880): 57–58.

70. John McLoughlin, *The Letters of John McLoughlin from Fort Vancouver, 1st Series*, ed. E. E. Rich (London: Hudson's Bay Record Society, 1941), 208.

71. A. J. Allen, comp., *Ten Years in Oregon: Travels and Adventures of Doctor E. White and Lady West of the Rocky Mountains* (Ithaca, NY: Mack, Andrus, & Co., 1848), 78.

72. Carey, "Mission Record Book," 242.

73. Allen, *Ten Years in Oregon*, 78.

74. Carey, "Mission Record Book," 248; Lee and Frost, *Ten Years in Oregon*, 141.

75. William A. Slacum, "Slacum's Report on Oregon," *OHQ* 13:2 (June 1912), 212–213. Among the English speakers in the Willamette Valley, William Bailey, William Johnson, William McKarty, and John Rowling did not sign. Among the French speakers, Joseph Despard, Michel Laferte dit Placide, and Andre Longtain did not affix their mark.

76. Carey, "Mission Record Book," 248–250; Slacum, "Slacum's Report," 211–213.

77. Carey, "Mission Record Book," 248–250; Slacum, "Slacum's Report," 211–213; Lee and Frost, *Ten Years Ago*, 141.

78. Slacum, "Slacum's Report," 195–196.

79. Slacum, "Slacum's Report," 213.

80. Slacum, "Slacum's Report," 208–209.

81. Slacum, "Slacum's Report," 196, 208–209; Receipts, Willamette Cattle Company Records, Mss. 500, OHS.

82. Clarke, *Pioneer Days in Old Oregon*, vol. 1., 306–309; H.O. Lang, *History of the Willamette Valley* (Portland: Geo. H. Himes, 1885), 230.

83. F. G. Young, ed., "Ewing Young and His Estate," *OHQ* 21: 3 (September 1920), 208–209.

84. For detailed accounts of the cattle drive from Spanish California to the Willamette Valley, see Holmes, *Ewing Young*, 122–134; Philip Leget Edwards, *The Diary of Philip Leget Edwards* (San Francisco: Grabhorn Press, 1932).

85. James R. Gibson, *Farming the Frontier: The Agricultural Opening of the Oregon Country, 1786–1846* (Seattle: University of Washington Press, 1985), 143–144.

86. Bancroft, *History of Oregon*, vol. 1, 102. The Bancroft–Victor Fuller interpretation stressed the crucial role of William Slacum.

87. Loewenberg, *Equality on the Oregon Frontier*, 170.

88. Lee and Frost, *Ten Years in Oregon*, 140–141.

89. Gerhad J. Ens, *Homeland to Hinterland: The Changing Worlds of the Red River Metis in the Nineteenth Century* (Toronto: University of Toronto Press, 1996), 72–92; Martha Harroun Foster, *We Know Who We Are: Métis Identity in a Montana Community* (Norman: University of Oklahoma Press, 2006), 51–89; Brenda Macdougall, *One of the Family: Metis Culture in Nineteenth-Century Northwestern Saskatchewan* (Vancouver: UBC Press,

2010), 183–239. For a recent assessment of the French Prairie settlers' focus on economic self-sufficiency, see Jean Barman, *French Canadians, Furs, and Indigenous Women in the Making of the Pacific Northwest* (Vancouver: UBC Press, 2014), 167–192.

90. Slacum, "Slacum's Report," 196–198.

91. Slacum, "Slacum's Report," 195.

92. Townsend, *Narrative of a Journey*, 77.

93. Podruchny, *Making the Voyageur World*, 80.

94. Thorne, *The Many Hands of My Relations*, 188–205; Edith I. Burley, *Servants of the Honourable Company: Work, Discipline, and Conflict in the Hudson's Bay Company, 1770–1879* (Toronto: Oxford University Press, 1997), 131–139.

95. Allen, *Ten Years in Oregon*, 78.

96. The "moral restraint" phrase is a quote from William Slacum, "Slacum's Report," 195.

97. Provencher to Signay, June 9, 1835, AAQ; Willamette Settlers [Joseph Gervais et al.] to the Bishop of Juliopolis, March 22, 1836, OHS, Mss 83. The letter from the French Canadian settlers was transcribed and printed in *Les Cloches de Saint-Boniface* 31:6 (June 1932): 143–144.

98. Willamette Settlers [Joseph Gervais et al.] to the Bishop of Juliopolis, March 22, 1836.

99. Louis Labonté I., did not sign the petition because he was then foreman of the Thomas McKay farm near Scappoose. See H. S. Lyman, "Reminiscences of Louis Labonte," *OHQ* 1:2 (June 1900): 168–188.

100. Munnick, "Annotations," *CCRPNW-SP*; J. Neilson Barry, "Astorians Who Became Permanent Settlers," *WaHQ* 34 (1933): 221–301; Watson, *Lives Lived West of the Divide*, 3 vols.

101. The French Canadians' familiarity with seeking the assistance of literate or semi-literate individuals to write letters on their behalf is evident in the undelivered letters of French Canadian voyageurs employed by the HBC and the undelivered letters from their families in Lower Canada. See Judith Hudson Beattie and Helen M. Buss, ed., *Undelivered Letters to Hudson's Bay Company Men on the Northwest Coast of America, 1830–1857* (Vancouver: UBC Press, 2003), 285–311. See also Allan Greer, "The Pattern of Literacy in Quebec, 1745–1899," *Histoire sociale—Social History* 9:22 (November 1978): 292–335.

102. Stephen Woolworth identifies HBC chief factor John McLoughlin as the instigator of the French Canadians' early petitions to Bishop Provencher. Woolworth apparently restates the views of Herbert Beaver, an Anglican minister who came into conflict with McLoughlin while stationed at Fort Vancouver, but he provides no additional evidence and neglects to mention the actual missives from the Willamette settlers to Provencher or the correspondence among Catholic Church leaders in Canada. See Stephen Woolworth, "The School is under My Direction: The Politics of Education at Fort Vancouver, 1836–1838," *OHQ* 104:2 (Summer 2003): 232–233; Herbert Beaver, *Reports and Letters of Herbert Beaver*, ed. Thomas E. Jessett (Portland, OR: Champoeg Press, 1959); Herbert Beaver, "Experiences of a Chaplain of Fort Vancouver, 1836–1838, ed. R. C. Clark, *OHQ* 39:1 (March 1939): 22–38.

103. Francis N. Blanchet to George Simpson, November 15, 1841, Francis N. Blanchet Collection, Archdiocese of Portland in Oregon Archives (APOA).

264 NOTES TO CHAPTER 3

104. John A. Hussey, *Champoeg: Place of Transition, A Disputed History* (Portland: Oregon Historical Society/Oregon State Highway Department, 1967), 86. John Hoard's surname was also spelled "Hord" and occasionally "Howard."

105. Allan Greer, *The Patriot and the People: The Rebellion of 1837 in Rural Lower Canada* (Toronto: University of Toronto Press, 1993), 60–63; Peter N. Moogk, *La Nouvelle France: The Making of French Canada—A Cultural History* (East Lansing: Michigan State University Press, 2000), 212–213.

106. Willamette Settlers [Pierre Bellique et al.] to the Bishop of Juliopolis, March 8, 1837, OHS, Mss 83. This letter was also transcribed and printed in *Les Cloches de Saint-Boniface* 31:7 (July 1932): 165–66.

107. Although the transcribed name "Atoam Lafourty" appears to correspond to "Antoine Laferte," it most likely refers to Michel Laferte dit Placide rather than his eight-year-old son Antoine, who is the only "Antoine Laferte" in the Catholic Church records of the period. See Munnick, *CCRPNW-SP*, vol. 1,118, and "Annotations," 52.

108. Parker, *Journal of an Exploring Tour*, 174.

109. Parker, *Journal of an Exploring Tour*, 176.

110. These estimates are the result of cross-referencing the two letters to Bishop Provencher in Red River, Slacum's census, and Munnick, *CCRPNW-V* and *CCRPNW-SP*. By adding 2.5 children per family, this comes to a population of about 85 people for the French Prairie settlement: 18 men, 19 women, and some 45+ children. The 18 families were headed by: (1) Amable Arquette and Marguerite Chinook, (2) Pierre Bellique and Genevieve St. Martin; (3) Joseph Delard and Lisette Shushwap, (4) Pierre Dépôt and Marguerite Clackamas, (5) Joseph Despard and Lisette Chinook, (6) Jean Baptiste Desportes McKay and his two wives: Eugenie (Jane) Wanakske and Marguerite Kalapuya, (7) Louis Forcier and Catherine Canaman, (8) Joseph Gervais and Yiamust Clatsop, (9) Louis Labonté I and Kilkatoh Clatsop, (10) François Xavier Laderoute and Julie Gervais, (11) Michel Laferte dit Placide and Josephte Nez Perce, (12) Andre Longtain and Nancy Okanagan, (13) Etienne Lucier and Josette Nouette, (14) Andre Picard and Marie Okanagan, (15) Jean Baptiste Perrault and Angèle Chehalis, (16) Andre Picard and Marie Okanagan, (17) Charles Plante and Agathe Cayuse, and (18) Charles Rondeau and Agathe Dupati McKay. Charlot Iroquois Tsete was listed in the first letter to Bishop Provencher, and his marriage to Marie Thomas (Iroquois–Upper Chinookan) was recorded in Munnick, *CCRPNW-V*. See table 7 and Munnick, *CCRPNW-V* and *CCRPNW-SP*. James R. Gibson estimated that there were 17–18 families in French Prairie in 1836, which he calculated returned 83–95 people, including 59 children. See Gibson, *Farming the Frontier*, 131.

111. Watson, *Lives Lived West of the Divide*, vol. 2, 491.

112. Gibson, *Farming the Frontier*, 142–143.

113. Gibson, *Farming the Frontier*, 143; William A. Bowen, *The Willamette Valley: Migration and Settlement on the Oregon Frontier* (Seattle: University of Washington Press, 1978), 91–93.

114. In comparison, five of the eighteen English-speaking male settlers had enclosed an average of 55 acres and were farming an average of 14 acres, with their average annual wheat production at 122 bushels. The most successful of the anglophone settlers—Ewing

Young, Lawrence Carmichael, William Johnson, James Neil, and Thomas Jefferson Hubbard—also invested in the cattle company enterprise (see appendix 5 and table 6 in this volume).

CHAPTER 4: Catholic Missionaries and Community Tensions

1. *Sen. Doc.*154, 25th Cong., 3rd Sess., January 28, 1839, reprinted in Cornelius J. Brosnan, *Jason Lee: Prophet of the New Oregon* (New York: Macmillan: 1932), 220–223; Cornelius Brosnan, "The Oregon Memorial of 1838," *OHQ* 34:1 (March 1933): 68–77; Cornelius Brosnan, "The Signers of the Oregon Memorial of 1838," *WHQ* 24:3 (July 1933): 174–189; Robert J. Loewenberg, "Saving Oregon Again: A Western Perennial?" *OHQ* 76:4 (December 1977), 341–342; and C. J. Pike. "Petitions of Oregon Settlers, 1838–48," *OHQ* 34:3 (September 1933): 216–235.

2. American scholars have made limited use of the Blanchet collection because the majority of the documents were written in French. A noteworthy exception is Letitia Mary Lyons, *Francis Norbert Blanchet and the Founding of the Oregon Missions* (Washington, D.C.: Catholic University of America Press, 1940). However, in keeping with earlier trends in religious history, Lyons focuses on the institutional history of the Oregon Catholic Mission and the role of the male clergy, as opposed to the experiences and perspectives of the laity. Robert J. Loewenberg largely relies on the English translations of the Blanchet materials included in Letitia Lyons's study, though he does cite the Francis N. Blanchet Collection in his bibliography for *Equality on the Frontier: Jason Lee and the Method Mission, 1834–1843* (Seattle: University of Washington Press, 1976). Wilfred P. Schoenberg's useful institutional history, *A History of the Catholic Church in the Pacific Northwest, 1743–1983*, relies on published primary sources rather than archival material. See also Roberta Stringham Brown and Patricia O'Connell Killen, eds., *Selected Letters of A. M. A. Blanchet, Bishop of Walla Walla and Nesqually (1847–1879)*, trans. Roberta Stringham Brown (Seattle: University of Washington Press, 2013).

3. Joseph Provencher to Willamette Settlers, June 8, 1835, cited in Francis Norbert Blanchet, *Historical Sketches of the Catholic Church in Oregon*, ed. Edward J. Kowrach (Fairfield, WA: Ye Galleon Press, 1983), 44; Joseph Provencher to Joseph Signay, June 9, 1835, British Columbia Records, 36 CN, AAQ.

4. Provencher to Signay, June 9, 1835; Provencher to Signay, November 24, 1835, Red River Records, 330 CN, AAQ.

5. Blanchet, *Historical Sketches*, 42; Francis N. Blanchet, "The Catholic Missionaries to Oregon," Mss. P-A 5, BAN, 3.

6. Governor and Committee to John McLoughlin, January 25, 1837, A.6/24, folios 64d-65, HBCA, cited by E. E. Rich in John McLoughlin, *The Letters of John McLoughlin from Fort Vancouver*, vol. 1 (London: Hudson's Bay Company Record Society, 1941), 202; E. E. Rich, *The Hudson's Bay Company, 1670–1870*, vol. 3 (New York: Macmillan, 1961), 682.

7. McLoughlin to the Governor and Committee, October 31, 1837, in McLoughlin, *The Letters*, vol. 1, 202–203.

8. Richard G. Montgomery, *The White-Headed Eagle: John McLoughlin, Builder of an Empire* (1931; reprint, Freeport, NH: Books for Libraries Press, 1971), 2–13; Suzanne Prince, "Marie-Louise McLoughlin," *DBC*, vol. 7 (Toronto/Quebec City: University of Toronto Press/Les Presses de l'Université Laval, 1988), 620–621.

9. E. E. Rich, *Hudson's Bay Company, 1670–1870*, vol. 3: *1821–1870* (New York: Macmillan, 1961), 682.

10. George Simpson to Joseph Signay, February 17, 1838, cited in Blanchet, *Historical Sketches*, 45.

11. Rich, *Hudson's Bay Company*, 682–687.

12. Blanchet, *Historical Sketches*, 46; Patricia Brandt and Lillian A. Pereyra, *Adapting in Eden: Oregon Catholic Minority, 1838–1986* (Pullman: Washington State University Press, 2002), 3–4; Lucien Lemieux, *L'Établissement de la première province ecclésiatique au Canada, 1783–1844* (Montreal: Éditions Fides, 1968), 415–417; Schoenberg, *A History of the Catholic Church*, 26–31.

13. Brandt and Pereyra, *Adapting in Eden*, 4; Schoenberg, *A History of the Catholic Church*, 32.

14. For Blanchet's contemporary account of the long overland trek from Montreal to Fort Vancouver, see his letter to Archbishop Signay, dated March 17, 1839, cited in Blanchet, *Historical Sketches*, 52–62. See also Blanchet's first official mission report, dated January 1839, in Carl Landerholm, trans., *Notices and Voyages of the Famed Quebec Mission to the Pacific Northwest* (Portland: Oregon Historical Society, 1956), 1–9.

15. Harriet Munnick wrote a short biographical sketch of Augustin Rochon, one of the French Canadian voyageurs to accompany Blanchet and Demers to Fort Vancouver. See Harriet Munnick, "An Odor of Sanctity," *MCH* 8 (1962–1964): 12–15.

16. Harriet Munnick, ed., *CCRPNW-V*, vol. 1 (St. Paul, OR: French Prairie Press, 1972), 1–17; Joseph Signay to Francis N. Blanchet, October 22, 1838, Francis N. Blanchet Collection, APOA; Sylvia Van Kirk, *Many Tender Ties: Women in Fur Trade Society, 1670–1870* (Norman: University of Oklahoma Press, 1980), 157.

17. Blanchet, *Historical Sketches*, 63; Francis N. Blanchet, First Willamette Mission Report, 1839, Francis N. Blanchet Collection, APOA. Blanchet recalled that a much larger contingent from the Willamette settlement had earlier traveled to Fort Vancouver to await the arrival of the missionaries. However, most had to return home after the missionaries were delayed following a drowning tragedy in the Columbia near The Dalles—the English name for the dangerous rapids known to French Canadians as *les Dalles de Mort*, "the flagstones of death." See Blanchet, *Historical Sketches*, 63.

18. Blanchet, *Historical Sketches*, 71.

19. Blanchet, *Historical Sketches*, 71.

20. Blanchet, *Historical Sketches*, 73; Munnick, ed., *CCRPNW-V*, vol. 1, 17–19. The most detailed study of the Kanaka Village is Susan Kardas's "'The People Bought This Land and the Clatsop Became Rich': A View of Nineteenth-Century Trade Relations on the Lower Columbia between Chinookan Speakers, Whites, and Kanakas" (Ph.D. diss., Bryn Mawr College, 1971).

21. Blanchet, *Historical Sketches*, 77–78; Landerholm, *Notices and Voyages*, 10–11; Munnick, ed., *CCRPNW-V*, vol. 1, 19–33.

22. Landerholm, *Notices and Voyages*, 11, 13; Francis N. Blanchet, First Willamette Mission Report, 1839, Francis N. Blanchet Collection, APOA.

23. Harriet Munnick, introduction to *CCRPNW-SP* (Portland, OR: Binford & Mort, 1979), xviii; Blanchet, *Historical Sketches*, 79.

24. Blanchet, First Willamette Report; Landerholm, *Notices and Voyages*, 11.

25. For two useful studies on the religious culture and institutionalized rituals of the Roman Catholic Church in Lower Canada, see Ollivier Hubert, *Sur la terre comme au ciel: La gestion des rites par l'Église Catholique du Québec, fin XVIIe— mi-XIXe siècle* (Sainte-Foy, QC: Les Presses de l'Université Laval, 2000), and René Hardy, *Contrôle social et mutation de la culture religieuse au Québec, 1830–1930* (Montreal: Boréal, 1999).

26. Landerholm, *Notices and Voyages*, 11.

27. Landerholm, *Notices and Voyages*, 12.

28. Blanchet, First Willamette Report, 5–6; Landerholm, *Notices and Voyages*, 11–13. Evidence that Jacquet, like all of the other first-generation French-speaking settlers, could not write his name can be found in Munnick, ed., *CCRPNW-V* and *CCRPNW-SP*: see, for example, *CCRPNW-V*, vol. 1, 27, 79, 115. Harriet Munnick initially mistakenly identified two individuals with the surname Jacquet, "Pierre" and "Stanislas," without cross-referencing the register entries with the Blanchet writings. In the annotations section, Munnick later clarifies that there was one individual named Pierre Stanislas Jacquet in French Prairie, *CCRPNW-SP*, A-46.

29. Gray H. Whaley, *Oregon and the Collapse of Illahee: U.S. Empire and the Transformation of an Indigenous World* (Chapel Hill, NC: University of North Carolina Press, 2010), 27–30, 43–50; Leland Donald, *Aboriginal Slavery on the Northwest Coast of North America* (Berkeley: University of California Press, 1997), 309–312; Yvonne P. Hajda, "Slavery in the Greater Lower Columbia Region," *Ethnohistory* 52:3 (Summer 2005): 582. Ron G. Bourgeault has argued that the sexual exploitation of Indian women was central to the fur trade in North America rather than a marginal historical development. While Bourgeault downplays female agency, it would also be inaccurate to overlook the role of French Canadian laborers in the sexual exploitation of Indian women within the class, gender, and racial structures of the fur trade. See Rob G. Bourgeault, "The Indian, the Métis, and the Fur Trade: Class, Sexism, and Racism in the Transition from 'Communism' to Capitalism," *Studies in Political Economy* 12 (1983): 45–80; Ron Bourgeault, "Race, Class, and Gender: Colonial Domination of Indian Women," in *Race, Class, Gender: Bonds and Barriers*, ed. Jess Vorst et al., rev. ed. (Winnipeg/Toronto: Society for Socialist Studies/Garamond Press, 1991), 88–117.

30. William Slacum noted that at Kanaka Village outside Fort Vancouver, "nearly every man has a wife, or lives with an Indian or half-breed woman, and . . . each family has from two to five slaves." William Slacum, " Slacum's Report on Oregon, 1836–38," *OHQ* 13: 2 (June 1912), 186; Elsie Frances Dennis, "Indian Slavery in the Pacific Northwest," Part 2, *OHQ* 31: 2 (1930), 193–195; Mathias D. Bergmann, "'We lose much by their absence': The Centrality of Chinookans and Kalapuyans to Life in Frontier Oregon," *OHQ* 109:1 (Spring 2008), 44–45.

31. Blanchet, First Willamette Mission Report, 1–5, 11–12; Landerholm, *Notices and Voyages*, 11–13.

32. Munnick, ed., *CCRPNW-V*, vol. 1, 29–37 and *CCRPNW-SP*, vol. 1, 1–23.

33. Willard Rees, "Annual Address [1879]," TOPA 7 (1880), 24.

34. Blanchet, First Willamette Report, 1; Landerholm, *Notices and Voyages*, 13.

35. Joseph Provencher to Francis N. Blanchet, June 22, 1839, Blanchet Collection, APOA.

36. Provencher to Blanchet, June 22, 1839.

37. Francis N. Blanchet to Joseph Signay, March 3, 1840, Francis N. Blanchet Collection, APOA; Blanchet, "Catholic Missionaries," 4.

38. Blanchet, "Catholic Missionaries," 4; Blanchet, *Historical Sketches*, 91; Landerholm, *Notices and Voyages*, 25.

39. Jeanne Pomerleau, *Corvées et quêtes: Un parcours au Canada français* (Montreal: Éditions Hurtubise HMH, 2002).

40. Blanchet to Signay, March 3, 1840.

41. Blanchet to Signay, March 3, 1840.

42. Allan Greer, *The Patriots and the People: The Rebellion of 1837 in Rural Lower Canada* (Toronto: University of Toronto Press, 1993), 121–152, 356–359; Ollivier Hubert, "Ritual Performance and Parish Sociability: French-Canadian Catholic Families at Mass from the Seventeenth to the Nineteenth Century," in *Households of Faith: Family, Gender, and Community in Canada, 1760–1969*, ed. Nancy Christie (Montreal: McGill-Queen's University Press, 2002), 37–39; Christine Hudon and Ollivier Hubert, " The Emergence of a Statistical Approach to Social Issues in Administrative Practices of the Catholic Church in the Province of Quebec," in *The Churches and Social Order in Nineteenth- and Twentieth-Century Canada*, ed. Michael Gauvreau and Ollivier Hubert (Montreal: McGill-Queen's University Press, 2006), 57; Yvan Lamonde, *Histoire sociale des idées au Québec, 1760–1896* (Montreal: Fides, 2000), 359–381; Lucien Lemieux, *Histoire du catholicisme québécoise: Les XVIIIᵉ et XIXᵉ siècles*, vol. 1, *Les années difficiles (1760–1839)*, ed. Nive Voisine (Montreal: Boréal 1989), 369–401; Susan Mann, *The Dream of a Nation: A Social and Intellectual History of Quebec* (Montreal: McGill-Queen's University Press, 1982), 48–83.

43. Francis N. Blanchet to Modeste Demers, September 1, 1840, Francis N. Blanchet Collection, APOA.

44. Blanchet to Signay, March 3, 1840.

45. Blanchet, Third Willamette Mission Report, March 19, 1840, Francis N. Blanchet Collection, APOA.

46. Blanchet, Third Willamette Mission Report, March 19, 1840.

47. Blanchet, *Historical Sketches*, 72.

48. Hubert, "Ritual Performance and Parish Sociability," 53–59; Hubert, *Sur la terre comme au ciel*, 280–284.

49. For an example of the inability of early French Catholic missionaries to adapt to cross-cultural marriages between Frenchmen and Indian women in the Great Lakes region, see Susan Sleeper-Smith, *Indian Women and French Men: Rethinking Cultural Encounters in the Western Great Lakes* (Amherst: University of Massachusetts Press, 2001), 16–17.

50. Hardy, *Contrôle social*, 67–153; Hubert, "Ritual Performance and Parish Sociability," 37–39; Ollivier Hubert, "Ritualité ultramontaine et pouvoir pastoral clérical dans le Québec de la seconde moitié du XIXᵉ siècle," in *La régulation sociale entre l'acteur et l'institution: Pour une problématique historique de l'interaction/Agency and Institutions in Social*

Regulation: Toward an Historical Understanding of Their Interaction (Sainte Foy, QC: Les Presses de l'Université du Québec, 2005), 438–447; Lemieux, *Histoire du catholicisme québécois*, 345–359; Ralph Gibson, *A Social History of French Catholicism, 1789–1914* (New York: Routledge, 989), 15–29.

51. Schoenberg, *A History of the Catholic Church in the Pacific Northwest*, 42.

52. This estimate includes the 27 couples married during the two missions, some 51 children, Jean Baptiste Desportes McKay, his two wives, their 3 younger children, and Michel Laferte dit Placide, Josephte Nez Perce and their 5 children. The estimate of 120 people does not include an unknownd number of Indian slaves in the French-Indian households of French Prairie.

53. Munnick, ed., *CCRPNW-V*, vol. 1, 25–34.

54. Kardas, "The People Bought This Land," 206–212.

55. The centrality of matrifocal residence and its connection to social networks in early colonial settlements has been noted in the Pacific Northwest and elsewhere in North America. See Susan Sleeper-Smith, *Indian Women and French Men*; Susan Armitage, "Marking Connections: Gender, Race, and Place in Oregon Country," in *One Step Over the Line: Toward a History of Women in the North American Wests*, ed. Elizabeth Jameson and Sheila McManus (Edmonton/Athabasca: University of Alberta Press/Athabasca University Press, 2008), 55–65; Brenda Macdougall, *One of the Family: Metis Culture in Nineteenth-Century Saskatchewan* (Vancouver: UBC Press, 2010), 51–126.

56. In the late 1800s, L. H. Poujade, the son of French emigrant Jean Pierre Poujade (1790–1875), remarked to journalist Samuel Clarke that Nicholas Montour had told Poujade, "after the arrival of Father Blanchet they [the French Canadian and French-Indian men] were allowed to have but one wife." S. A. Clarke, *Pioneer Days of Oregon History*, vol. 2 (Portland: J. K. Gill Co., 1905), 592.

57. Blanchet, Second Willamette Report, 1839.

58. Munnick, ed., *CCRPNW-V*, vol. 1, 25–32; Munnick, ed., *CCRPNW-SP*, vo1. 1, 86.

59. Joseph Signay to Francis N. Blanchet, April 10, 1840, Blanchet Collection, APOA. Drawing on ancient history, Signay argued that in early Christianity, marriages between Christians and non-Christians were valid. It was not until the fifth century that the marriages were declared invalid by the Roman emperors and not until the twelfth century that such marriages were officially repudiated by the Catholic Church. Signay therefore concluded that a Christian man married to a non-Christian woman (*une infidèle*) who was in good standing in the Church was not living in sin. Signay further concluded that a missionary passing quickly in a region could leave these married couples as they were if the priest believed that they would not profit from their situation. The missionary could theoretically validate existing common-law marriages in these circumstances.

60. Francis Norbert Blanchet, *A Comprehensive, Explanatory, Correct Pronouncing Dictionary and Jargon Vocabulary; to which is added numerous conversations enabling any person to speak Chinook Jargon* (Portland, Oregon Territory: S. J. McCormick, 1853).

61. Philip M. Hanley, *History of the Catholic Ladder*, ed. Edward J. Kowrach (Fairfield, WA: Ye Galleon Press, 1993); Kris A. White and Janice St. Laurent, "Mysterious Journey: The Catholic Ladder of 1840," *OHQ* 97:1 (Spring 1997): 70–90; Francis Paul Prucha, "Two

Roads to Conversion: Protestant and Catholic Missionaries in the Pacific Northwest, *PNQ* 79:3 (October 1981): 130–137; Nellie Pipes, "The Protestant Ladder," *OHQ* 37 (1936): 237–240.

62. Francis N. Blanchet, Third Willamette Report, 1840.

63. Blanchet to Signay, March 3, 1840.

64. Blanchet to Signay, March 3, 1840. For an overview of the roles of Native women in the larger regional fur trade and the attitudes of Euro-American male observers toward these women, see Jean Barman, *French Canadians, Furs, and Indigenous Women in the Making of the Pacific Northwest* (Vancouver, BC: UBC Press, 2014), 107–166.

65. See Hubert, "Ritual Performance and Parish Sociability," 37–65; Gibson, *A Social History of French Catholicism*; John R. Ditchl, *Frontiers of Faith: Bringing Catholicism to the West in the Early Republic* (Lexington: University Press of Kentucky, 2008); and Michael Pasquier, *Fathers on the Frontier: French Missionaries and the Roman Catholic Priesthood in the United States, 1789–1870* (New York: Oxford University Press, 2010).

66. Blanchet, Third Willamette Report, 1840.

67. See, for example, Jacqueline Peterson with Laura Peers, *Sacred Encounters: Father DeSmet and the Indians of the Rocky Mountain West* (Norman: University of Oklahoma Press, 1993).

68. Blanchet, Second Willamette Report; Munnick, ed., *CCRPNW-V*, vol. 1, 42.

69. Blanchet to Demers, September 1, 1840. Although there were two Poirer brothers (Toussaint and Basile) in the Lower Columbia region, the Poirer to whom Blanchet refers in his letter to Demers is very likely Toussaint because Blanchet married Toussaint Poirer and Catherine Clatsop at the first Willamette Mission in January 1839 as they were then living in French Prairie (Blanchet referred to Toussaint Poirer as a "farmer of this place" in the marriage notation). Basile Poirer remained employed as a baker at Fort Vancouver until his death in 1844. Munnick, ed., *CCRPNW-V*, 27, and *CCRPNW-SP*, "Annotations," A-81–82; Bruce McIntyre Watson, *Lives Lived West of the Divide: A Biographical Dictionary of Fur Traders Working West of the Rockies, 1793–1858*, vol. 2 (Kelowna: Centre for Social, Spatial, and Economic Justice, University of British Columbia, 2010), 786–787.

70. Blanchet to Demers, September 1, 1840.

71. Susan Neylan, *The Heavens Are Changing: Nineteenth-Century Protestant Missions and Tshimsian Christianity* (Montreal: McGill-Queen's University Press, 2003), 105–127; Emma Milliken found some comparable examples in the experiences of the Native wives of English-speaking laborers at the HBC's Fort Nisqually in her article "Choosing between Corsets and Freedom: Native, Mixed-Blood, and White Wives of Laborers at Fort Nisqually, 1833–1860," *PNQ* 96:2 (Spring 2005): 95–101.

72. Mary C. Wright, "The Circle Broken: Gender, Family, and Difference in the Pacific Northwest, 1811–1850" (Ph.D. diss., University of Washington, 1996), 246.

73. See Ray Allen Billington, *The Protestant Crusade, 1800–1860: A Study of the Origins of American Nativism* (1938; reprint, Chicago: Quadrangle Books, 1964); Jenny Franchot, *Roads to Rome: The Antebellum Protestant Encounter with Catholicism* (Berkeley: University of California Press, 1994); Nancy Lusignan Schultz, *Fire and Roses: The Burning of the Charlestown Convent, 1834* (New York: Free Press, 2000).

74. Landerholm, *Notices and Voyages*, 53–54; Malcolm Clark, "The Bigot Disclosed: 90 Years of Nativism," *OHQ* 75:2 (1974), 111–112.

75. Alan Greer, *The Patriot and the People: The Rebellion of 1837 in Rural Lower Canada* (Toronto: University of Toronto Press, 1993), 233–235; Gibson, *A Social History*, 60–61; Mann, *The Dream of a Nation*, 48–53; Mark Noll, *A History of Christianity in the United States and Canada* (Grand Rapids, MI: William B. Eerdmans, 1992), 250–255; Fernand Ouellet, *Lower Canada, 1791–1840: Social Change and Nationalism*, trans. Patricia Claxton (Toronto: McClelland and Stewart, 1980), 165–170.

76. William L. Barney, *The Passage of the Republic: An Interdisciplinary History of Nineteenth-Century America* (Lexington, MA: D.C. Heath and Co., 1987), 9–49, 87–115, 121–152; Walter A. McDougall, *Throes of Democracy: The American Civil War Era, 1829–1877* (New York: Harper Perennial, 2008), 1–228; Charles Seller, *The Market Revolution: Jacksonian America, 1815–1846* (New York: Oxford University Press, 1991), 1–33.

77. Billington, *The Protestant Crusade*; Sam W. Haynes, *Unfinished Revolution: The Early American Republic in a British World* (Charlottesville: University of Virginia Press, 2010), 3–23, 106–132, 177–250.

78. LeRoy R. Hafen and Ann Hafen, eds., *To the Rockies and Oregon, 1839–1842* (Glendale, CA: Arthur H. Clark Co., 1955), 19–24.

79. Hafen and Hafen, eds., *To the Rockies and Oregon*, 19–24; Cornelius Brosnan, *Jason Lee: Prophet of the New Oregon* 100–102; S. J. Clarke, *Pioneer History of Oregon*, vol. 2 (Portland: J. K. Gill Co., 1905), 442–447; Steven E. Woodworth, *Manifest Destinies: America's Westward Expansion and the Road to the Civil War* (New York: Alfred Knopf, 2010), 59–63. In the sources on Jason Lee's return to the United States in 1839, the Indian pupil Thomas Adams is variously identified as Chinook (Lower Chinookan), Kalalapuyan, and "Willamette" (Upper Chinookan). The "Mission Record Book" lists him as "Willamette." See appendix 4 in this volume. William Brooks (Chinook) died in May 1839 while on a lecture tour along the Erie Canal with Jason Lee and Thomas Adams. See Brosnan, *Jason Lee*, 139–140.

80. Amy S. Greenberg, *Manifest Destiny and American Territorial Expansion: A Brief History with Documents* (Boston: Bedford/St. Martin's, 2012), 14–17; Will Bagley, *So Rugged and Mountainous: Blazing Trails to Oregon and California, 1812–1848* (Norman: University of Nebraska Press, 2010), 67; Woodworth, *Manifest Destinies*, 60.

81. Thomas J. Farnham, *Travels in the Great Western Prairies*, vol. 2, ed. Reuben Gold Thwaites (1843; reprint, Cleveland: Arthur H. Clark Co., 1906), 23.

82. Reuben Thwaites noted that "An act of parliament was passed (about 1837) at the instigation of Dr. McLoughlin, extending the jurisdiction and civil laws of Canada over the British subjects of Oregon territory. Under this law James Douglas was commissioned justice of the peace for criminal matters and for civil suits under £200 in value. Imprisonment was possible either in the forts of Hudson's Bay Company or the jails of Canada." Farnham, *Travels in the Great Western Prairies*, 23, n. 16.

83. Farnham, *Travels in the Great Western Prairies*, 23.

84. Farnham, *Travels in the Great Western Prairies*, 25.

85. Farnham, *Travels in the Great Western Prairies*, 23; H. H. Bancroft, *History of Oregon*. vol. 1 (San Francisco: A. L. Bancroft & Co., 1886), 230–236; Pike, "Petitions of Oregon Settlers," 222–223; Francis N. Blanchet to John McLoughlin, February 12, 1840, copy enclosed in Francis N. Blanchet to A. M. A. Blanchet, February, 8, 1841, Francis N. Blanchet

Collection, APOA. The petition, signed "David Leslie and others," is registered as *Sen. Doc* 514, 26 Cong., 1st sess., June 4, 1840. A hand-written copy can be found in Fort Vancouver Correspondence-Outward, B.223/b/25, HBCA, Provincial Archives of Manitoba.

86. Farnham, *Travels in the Great Western Prairies*, 23.

87. For Captain Belcher's visit to the Pacific Northwest and the expedition's focus on Russian America, see Bancroft, *History of Oregon*, vol. 1, 232–233.

88. Loewenberg, *Equality on the Oregon Frontier*, 146–147. Malcolm Clark described the Farnham petition as "an exercise in cooperative mendacity," and "unadulterated humbuggery." See Malcolm Clark, *Eden Seekers: The Settlement of Oregon, 1818–1862* (Boston: Houghton Mifflin, 1981), 123.

89. Copy of Farnham Memorial, Fort Vancouver Correspondence-Outward, B.223/b/25, HBCA.

90. Katharine B. Judson, introduction to "John McLoughlin's Last Letter to the Hudson's Bay Company as Chief Factor, in Charge at Fort Vancouver, 1845," *AHR* 21:1 (October 1915), 109.

91. Francis N. Blanchet to McLoughlin, February 12, 1840.

92. Joseph Delard et al. to John McLoughlin, March 18, 1840, Fort Vancouver Correspondence-Outward, B.223/b/25, HBCA. The eighteen settlers who affixed their mark or signed the petition were Joseph Delard, François Xavier Laderoute, Joseph Gervais, David Gervais, Toussaint Poirier, William Johnson, Andre Longtain, Joseph Despard Sr., Joseph Despard Jr., Etienne Lucier, Louis Lucier, Pierre Bellique, Jean Baptiste Perrault, Amabale Arquette, Antoine Rivet, Jean Baptiste Aubichon, Thomas McKay, and Charles Rondeau.

93. Susan (Downing) Shepard to Ann Lloyd, September 15, 1839, Mss. 1219, OHS.

94. A letter written by mission member Lewis H. Judson seconded this view of Blanchet and the French Canadians. Judson wrote: "While Bro. Lee was gone to the United States there came two of the gentlemen clergy; liege subjects of His Holiness the Pope, and took up their abode in this territory and they immediately suceeded in making those Frenchmen who had attended our people's meetings verily believe that they would be sent to Hell unless they renounced all connect and fellowship with us Hereticks and consequently they forsook us and genuine religion together for mummeries of a fallen church who may justly be called 'the Mother of Harlots.'" Copy of letter from Lewis H. Judson to Amos Star Cooke, August 12, 1842, Amos Star Cooke Letters, Mss. 1223, OHS.

95. Francis N. Blancher to Modeste Demers, January 13, 1840, APOA; Z. A. Mudge, *The Missionary Teacher: A Memoir of Cyrus Shepard* (New York: Carlton & Porter, 1848), 207–211; Gustavus Hines, *Oregon: Its History, Condition and Prospects* (1851; reprint, New York: Arno Press, 1973), 35.

96. Mudge, *The Missionary Teacher*, 208–209.

97. Billington, *The Protestant Crusade*, 99–108.

98. Landerholm, *Notices and Voyages*, 53–54; Clark, "The Bigot Disclosed," 111–112; F. N. Blanchet to A. M. A. Blanchet, February 8, 1841, Francis N. Blanchet Collection, APOA.

99. F. N. Blanchet to A. M. A. Blanchet, February 8, 1841. There is no mention of this controversy in the Reverend Zachariah Mudge's hagiographic biography of Cyrus Shepard, *The Missionary Teacher*.

100. James Douglas to Francis N. Blanchet, January 14, 1840, and Blanchet to Douglas, February 10, 1840, enclosed in F. N. Blanchet to A. M.A. Blanchet, February 8, 1841.

101. Douglas to Blanchet, January 14, 1840.

102. Blanchet to Douglas, February 10, 1840.

103. Blanchet to Douglas, February 10, 1840.

104. Blanchet to Douglas, February 10, 1840.

105. Billington, *The Protestant Crusade*, 1–135; Noll, 205–211, 219–244, 256–262.

106. Blanchet to Douglas, February 10, 1840.

107. Blanchet to Douglas, February 10, 1840.

108. Allan Greer, *The People of New France* (Toronto: University of Toronto Press, 1997), 71–75; Hubert, "Ritual Performance and Parish Sociability," 54–59; Jan Noel, *Women in New France* (Ottawa: Canadian Historical Association, 1998), 2–8.

109. Blanchet did not identify the couple. However, at the time Elijah White wrote to Blanchet, "If it shall appear that Saddy root has done me injustice"; Dr. White to Francis N. Blanchet, n.d. [circa March 1840], copy enclosed in F. N. Blanchet to A. M. A. Blanchet, February 8, 1841. In Elijah White's "Census of Settlers in the Oregon Country, 1842," he enumerated François Xavier Laderoute and his family as "Laddyroot, X." See Letters Received by the Office of Indian Affairs, 1824-81, Oregon Superintendency, 1842-1880, Bureau of Indian Affairs, National Archives of the United States, Washington D.C, Record Group 75 (microfilm roll 607).

110. Francis N. Blanchet to Elijah White, February 1, 1840, copy enclosed in F. N. Blanchet to A. M. A. Blanchet, February 8, 1841.

111. Douglas to Blanchet, February 26, 1840, copy enclosed in F. N. Blanchet to A.M.A. Blanchet, February 8, 1841.

112. Allen, *Ten Years in Oregon*. Daniel Waldo, an American settler who arrived in the Willamette Valley in 1843, held a rather negative view of the sexual conduct of the male Methodist missionaries. In an 1878 interview, he stated, "The missionaries were all Yankees and close fisted fellows. They had one Indian converted; she said they converted her, all of them. She was a young person. [Hamilton] Campbell said she pulled his breeches down and his wife came in. I guess he tried to screw her. He put her in prison for it. That was the upshot of it. She said she was good enough for any white men because all the missionaries had screwed her." Daniel Waldo, Critiques, Mss. P-A 74. BAN,

113. F. N. Blanchet to A. M. A. Blanchet, February 8, 1841; R. J. Loewenberg, "Elijah White vs. Jason Lee: A Tale of Hard Times," *Journal of the West* 11:4 (October 1972), 654–655.

114. F. N. Blanchet to A.M.A. Blanchet, February 8, 1841.

115. Elijah White to Francis N. Blanchet, n.d. [circa March 1840].

116. F. N. Blanchet to A. M. A. Blanchet, February 8, 1841.

117. Brosnan, *Jason Lee*, 155–189. Brosnan identified fifty-one people, but he did not include Adelia Judson, who married the carpenter James Olley just before the *Lausanne* sailed. The *Lausanne* party included Adelia Judson's brother Lewis H. Judson and his wife and children. See Loewenberg, *Equality on the Oregon Frontier*, 129–132. For the activities and expansion of the Methodist mission after 1840, see also Elisabeth Brigham Walton, "'Mill Place' on the Willamette: A New Mission House for the Methodists in Oregon, 1841–1844" (Ph.D. diss., University of Delaware, 1965); Robert Boyd, *People of the Dalles: The Indians of Wascopam Mission* (Lincoln: University of Nebraska Press, 1996).

118. Copy of a letter from Mrs. Olley, Willamette, Ore., to Mrs. Amos S. Cooke, Honolulu, Oahu, S.I., November 31, 1840, Amos Starr Cooke Letters, Mss. 1223, OHS.

119. Mrs. Olley to Mrs. Amos S. Cooke.

120. Mrs. Olley to Mrs. Amos S. Cooke.

121. Allen, *Ten Years in Oregon*, 85.

122. Allen, *Ten Years in Oregon*, 86.

123. F. N. Blanchet to A. M. A. Blanchet, February 8, 1841.

124. Lyons, *Francis Norbert Blanchet*, 82–84.

125. Loewenberg, "Elijah White vs. Jason Lee," 636–662.

126. F. N. Blanchet to A. M. A. Blanchet, February 8, 1841.

127. Jason Lee to the Missionary Board of the Methodist Episcopal Church, September 15, 1840, University of Puget Sound Archives, cited in Loewenberg, "Elijah White vs. Jason Lee," 657–658.

128. Loewenberg, "Elijah White vs. Jason Lee," 652–653.

129. F. N. Blanchet to A. M. A. Blanchet, February 8, 1841.

130. Elijah White to Francis N. Blanchet, September 9, 1840, copy enclosed in F. N. Blanchet to A. M. A. Blanchet, February 8, 1841.

131. The term "Oregon" entered the American lexicon in the late eighteenth century with the publication of Jonathan Carver's *Travels through the Interior Parts of North America*. This volume contained the first printed citation of "Oregon" as referring to the Great River of the West. Robert Rogers, who had hired Carver to explore the Far West in the 1760s, believed that the River Oregon could be reached by following the Missouri River to it source. Although the overland travels of the Lewis and Clark expedition and John Jacob Astor's PFC cast doubt on Roger's earlier notions about the course of the River Oregon, the publications resulting from these expeditions disseminated popular notions about the region that came to be known as the Oregon Country. See Jonathan Carver, *Travels through the Interior Parts of North America in the Years 1766, 1767, and 1768* (1778. Reprint. Minneapolis: Ross and Haines, 1956); Jonathan Carver, *The Journals of Jonathan Carver and Related Documents, 1766–1770* (St. Paul: Minnesota Historical Society, 1976); Scott Byram and David G. Lewis, "Ourigan: Wealth of the Northwest Coast," *OHQ* 102:2 (Summer 2001): 127–157.

132. John Mack Faragher, *Sugar Creek: Life on the Illinois Prairie* (New Haven: Yale University Press, 1986); Reginald Horsman, *The Frontier in the Formative Years, 1783–1815* (New York: Holt, Rinehart, and Winston, 1970); Malcolm Rohrbough, *The Trans-Appalachian Frontier* (New York: Oxford University Press, 1978).

133. Elliott West, "American Frontier," in *The Oxford History of the American West*, ed. Clyde A. Milner, Carol A. O'Connor, and Martha A. Sandweiss (New York: Oxford University Press, 1994), 115–150; Richard White, *"It's Your Misfortune and None of My Own": A New History of the American West* (Norman: University of Oklahoma Press, 1991), 61–84; Ralph Morris, "The Notion of a Great American Desert East of the Rockies," *MVHR* 13:2 (September 1926): 190–200.

134. Clifford M. Drury, *"The Oregonian and Indian's Advocate," PNQ* 56:4 (October 1965): 159–167; Whaley, *Oregon and the Collapse of Illahee*, 148–155.

135. For studies of American imperialism, territorial expansion, and the Oregon Trail migrations, see Will Bagley, *So Rugged and Mountainous*; Amy S. Greenberg, *Manifest Destiny*;

Sam W. Haynes and Christopher Morris, eds., *Manifest Destiny and Empire: American Ante-bellum Expansionism* (College Station: Texas A & M University Press, 1997); Reginald Hors-man, *Race and Manifest Destiny: The Origins of American Racial Anglo-Saxonism* (Cam-bridge, MA: Harvard University Press, 1981); Robert J. Miller, *Native America, Discovered and Conquered: Thomas Jefferson, Lewis and Clark, and Manifest Destiny* (Lincoln: University of Nebraska Press, 2008); Walter Nugent, *Habits of Empire: A History of American Expansion* (New York: Alfred Knopf, 2008); John D. Unruh, *The Plains Across: The Overland Emigrants and the Trans-Mississippi West, 1840–60* (Urbana: University of Illinois Press, 1979); Gray Whaley, *Oregon and the Collapse of Illahee*; Steven E. Woodworth, *Manifest Destinies*.

136. Whaley, *Oregon and the Collapse of Illahee*, 157.

CHAPTER 5: American Settlers and Political Initiatives

1. Eugène Duflot de Mofras, *Duflot de Mofras' Travels on the Pacific Coast*, vol. 2, trans. and ed. Marguerite Eyer Wilbur (Santa Ana, CA: The Fine Arts Press, 1937), 111–112. See also the original French version, [Eugène] Duflot de Mofras, *Exploration du territoire de l'Orégon, des Californies et de la Mer Vermeille exécutée pendant les années 1840, 1841 et 1842*. vol. 2 (Paris: Arthus Bertand, 1844), 213–214. Aside from two phrases, this citation fol-lows the Wilbur translation: *ce qui vient de France* I have translated as "who have emigrated from France" rather than as "those who have just come from France"; *un Métis Iroquois* I have translated as "an Iroquois Métis" rather than as "an Iroquois half-breed."

2. Marguerite Wilbur, introduction to *Duflot de Mofras' Travels*, vol. 1, xi–xii and xix–xx.

3. Wilbur, introduction, xxx–xxxii. For a classic treatment of the literary license taken by European travel writers, see Percy G. Adams's *Travelers and Travel Liars, 1660–1800*, 2nd ed. (New York: Dover Publications, 1980).

4. "Piastre" is a common term in Canadian French that refers to local currencies in North America and remains in use today. For a source on its use in Oregon, see Francis N. Blanchet, Willamette Mission Report, 1839, Blanchet Collection, APOA.

5. John D. Unruh Jr., *The Plains Across: The Overland Emigrants and the Trans-Missis-sippi West, 1840–60* (Urbana: University of Illinois Press, 1979), 119.

6. Richard Somerset Mackie, *Trading Beyond the Mountains: The British Fur Trade on the Pacific, 1793–1843* (Vancouver: UBC Press, 1997), 238; John McLoughlin, *The Letters of John McLoughlin from Fort Vancouver, 2nd Series, 1839–44*, ed. E. E. Rich (Toronto: The Champlain Society, 1943), 77–79; Jesse S. Douglas, "Origins of the Population of Oregon in 1850," *PNQ* 41:2 (April 1950): 95–114. Paul Bourke and Donald DeBats, *Washington County: Politics and Community in Antebellum America* (Baltimore: Johns Hopkins University Press, 1995), 47–51; William J. Betts, "From Red River to the Columbia," *Beaver Outfit* 301:1 (Spring 1971): 50–56.

7. F. X. Matthieu, Refugee, Trapper, and Settler, Mss. P-A 49, BAN; Horace S. Lyman, ed., "Reminiscences of F. X. Matthieu," *OHQ* 1:1 (March 1900), 79. H.H. Bancroft, *His-tory of Oregon*, vol. 2 (San Francisco: The History Company, 1886), 259. In his 1878 inter-view for the Bancroft history, Matthieu noted the names of three of the six other French

Canadians: Peter [Pierre] Gautier, Paul Ojet, and Chamberlain. "Chamberlain" was likely Adolphe Chamberlain, who worked as a tinsmith for the HBC at Fort Vancouver until 1841, returned East, and then journeyed back to Oregon in 1842. See Bruce McIntyre Watson, *Lives Lived West of the Divide*, vol. 1 (Kelowna: Centre for Social, Spatial and Economic Justice, University of British Columbia, 2010), 258.

8. Unruh, *The Plains Across*, 119.

9. Charles Wilkes, *Narrative of the United States Exploring Expedition for the Years 1838, 1839, 1841, 1842*, vol. 4 (Philadelphia: Lea & Blanchard, 1845), 354; Charles Wilkes, "Document: Report on the Territory of Oregon," *OHQ* 12:3 (September 1911), 291.

10. Robert Boyd estimated that following the losses due to the intermittent fever, the total Kalapuyan population (including the Yoncalla) ranged between 1,200 and 1,500 during the 1830s. Robert Boyd, *The Coming of the Spirit Pestilence: Introduced Infectious Diseases and Population Decline among Northwest Coast Indians* (Seattle: University of Washington Press, 1999), 326–327.

11. Wilkes, "Report on the Oregon Territory," 292. Robert Boyd has noted that the estimate of 600 for the Kalapuyan population for the 1840s is also reflective of Protestant and Catholic missionary accounts of the period. See Boyd, *The Coming of the Spirit Pestilence*, 326–327.

12. The number of sixty French-Indian families for the early 1840s is based on the 1842 census of Elijah White and George Simpson's estimate from 1842: George Simpson, *An Overland Journey Round the World During the Years 1841 and 1843* (Philadelphia: Lee and Blanchard, 1947), 144. In 1844, Catholic missionary Modeste Demers also gave an estimate of 600 people for the French-Indian settlement in French Prairie: See Carl Landerholm, ed. and trans., *Notices and Voyages of the Famed Quebec Mission to the Pacific Northwest* (Portland: Oregon Historical Society, 1956), 207. Demers estimated another 100 French-Indian individuals at Fort Vancouver and 100 at Cowlitz. This number corresponds to Lieutenant Howison's estimate of 700–800 mixed-bloods for the whole of the Oregon Country in 1846: Neil M. Howison, "Report of Lieutenant Neil M. Howison on Oregon, 1846," *OHQ* 14:1 (March 1913), 24.

13. Unruh, *The Plains Across*, 119.

14. Joseph Schafer, ed., "Documents Relative to Warre and Vavasour's Military Reconnaissance in Oregon, 1845–1846," *OHQ* 10:1 (March 1909), 50.

15. Wilkes, *Narrative of the United States Exploring Expedition*, 358.

16. John Dunn, *The Oregon Territory and the British North American Fur Trade* (Philadelphia: G. B. Zieber & Co., 1845), 126–138; Watson, *Lives Lived West of the Divide*, vol. 1, 350.

17. See Edward Watts, *In This Remote Country: French Colonial Culture in the Anglo-American Imagination, 1780–1860* (Chapel Hill: University of North Carolina Press, 2006).

18. Francis Parkman, *The Oregon Trail*, ed. Bernard Rosenthal (1849; reprint, New York: Oxford University Press, 1996); Francis Parkman, *France and England in North America*, 2 vols. (1865–1892; reprint, New York: Library of America, 1983); Reginald Horsman, *Race and Manifest Destiny: The Origins of American Racial Anglo-Saxonism* (Cambridge: Harvard University Press, 1981).

19. James P. Ronda, "Calculating Ouragon," *OHQ* 94: 2–3 (Summer-Fall 1993): 121–140; William G. Robbins, "Willamette Eden: The Ambiguous Legacy," in *Northwest Lands,*

Northwest Peoples: Readings in Environmental History, ed. Dale D. Goble and Paul W. Hirt (Seattle: University of Washington Press, 1999), 95–110; Gray H. Whaley, *Oregon and the Collapse of Illahee: U.S Empire and the Transformation of an Indigenous World, 1792–1859* (Chapel Hill: University of North Carolina Press, 2010), 125–190.

20. Robert Bunting, "The Environment and Settler Society in Western Oregon," *PHR* 64:3 (August 1995): 413–443; Robert Bunting, *The Pacific Raincoast: Environment and Culture in an American Eden, 1778–1900* (Lawrence: University Press of Kansas, 1997); Peter Boag, *Environment and Experience: Settlement Culture in Nineteenth-Century Oregon* (Berkeley: University of California Press, 1992); Richard White, *Land Use, Environment, and Social Change: The Shaping of Island County, Washington* (Seattle: University of Washington Press, 1980); Richard White, "The Altered Landscape: Social Change and the Land in the Pacific Northwest," in *Regionalism and the Pacific Northwest*, ed. William G. Robbins, Robert J. Frank, and Richard E. Ross (Corvallis: Oregon State University Press, 1983), 109–127.

21. For an overview of the HBC's Pacific trade system, see Mackie, *Trading Beyond the Mountains*, 309–322.

22. Duflot de Mofras, *Duflot de Mofras' Travels*, vol. 2, 105; Medorem Crawford, Missionaries and Their Works, Mss. P-A 19, 9–10, BAN.

23. James R. Gibson, *Farming the Frontier: The Agricultural Opening of the Oregon Country, 1786–1846* (Seattle: University of Washington Press, 1985), 142.

24. Gibson, *Farming the Frontier*, 94, 143; Mackie, *Trading Beyond the Mountains*, 182.

25. William Bowen, *The Willamette Valley: Migration and Settlement on the Oregon Frontier* (Seattle: University of Washington Press, 1978), 89–90. For Elijah White's "Census of Settlers in the Oregon Country, 1842," see Letters Received by the Office of Indian Affairs, 1824-81, Oregon Superintendency, 1842-1880, Bureau of Indian Affairs, National Archives of the United States, Washington D.C, Record Group 75 (microfilm roll 607).

26. Gerhard Ens, *Homeland to Hinterland: The Changing Worlds of the Red River Métis* (Toronto: University of Toronto Press, 1996), 72–92; Susan Sleeper-Smith, *Indian Women and French Men: Rethinking Cultural Encounter in the Western Great Lakes* (Amherst: University of Massachusetts Press, 2001), 73–115.

27. Duflot de Mofras, *Duflot de Mofras' Travels*, vol. 2, 111. Bowen, *The Willamette Valley*, 91–93. Bowen notes that although the number of farmers with a substantial cultivation of fruits was small, about eight, the two most prominent orchardists in the Willamette Valley were French Canadians Etienne Lucier and Achilles Peault. See Bowen, *The Willamette Valley*, 93.

28. Wilkes, "Report on the Territory of Oregon," 285.

29. Wilkes, "Report on the Territory of Oregon," 285–287.

30. James Henry Gilbert, *Trade and Currency in Early Oregon: A Study in the Commercial and Monetary History of the Pacific Northwest* (New York: Columbia University Press, 1907), 32–42. For a detailed overview of the various communal labor practices and rituals in French Canada, involving seigeneuries, communities, public events, religious practices, and seasonal harvests, see Jeanne Pomerleau, *Corvées et quêtes: Un parcours au Canada français* (Montreal: Les Éditions Hurtubise HMH Limitée, 2002).

31. Jesse A. Applegate, *A Day with Cow Column in 1843* (1934; reprint, Fairfield, WA: Ye Galleon Press, 1990), 149–150.

278 NOTES TO CHAPTER 5

32. Margaret Jewett Bailey, *The Grains or Passages in the Life of Ruth Rover, with Occasional Pictures of Oregon, Natural and Moral*, ed. Evelyn Leasher and Robert J. Frank (Corvallis: Oregon State University Press, 1986), 195, 220.

33. Bailey, *The Grains*, 193.

34. Cynthia Culver Prescott outlines the socioeconomic and cultural roles of Anglo-American settler women in the Willamette Valley from 1845 to 1900 using the more detailed sources on the Americans in *Gender and Generation on the Far Western Frontier* (Tucson: University of Arizona Press, 2007). See also Joan Jenson, *Loosening the Bonds: Mid-Atlantic Farm Women, 1759–1850* (New Haven: Yale University Press, 1986).

35. Harriet Munnick, "The Mission Mills at St. Paul, *MCH* 11 (1972–1976), 27–28.

36. Duflot de Mofras, *Duflot de Mofras' Travels*, vol. 2, 111; F.N. Blanchet to Philip Foster, September 14, 1843, and February 14, 1844, Philip Foster Papers, Willamette Cattle Company Records, Series C: General Files, Mss.996, OHS; List of Men Imployed (*sic*) for the Cattle Company, and Willamette Cattle Company in Account with Philip Foster, Philip Foster Papers, Willamette Cattle Company Records, Series C: General Files, Mss.99, OHS.

37. For an overview of communal labor practices in French Canada (*la corvée*), see Pomerleau, *Corvées et quêtes*. See also Colin M. Coates, *The Metamorphoses of Landscape and Community in Early Quebec* (Montreal: McGill-Queen's University Press, 2000); *Louise* Dechêne, *Habitants and Merchants in Seventeenth-Century Montreal* (Montreal: McGill-Queen's University Press, 1991); Allan Greer, *Peasant, Lord, and Merchant: Rural Society in Three Quebec Parishes, 1740–1840* (Toronto: University of Toronto Press, 1985).

38. James L. Ratcliff. "What Happened to the Kalapuya? A Study of the Depletion of Their Economic Base," *Indian Historian* 6:3 (Summer 1973): 27–33; William G. Robbins, *Landscapes of Promise: The Oregon Story, 1800–1940* (Seattle: University of Washington Press, 1997), 71–78; Bunting, *The Pacific Raincoast*, 72–88; White, *Land Use, Environment, and Social Change*, 35–53.

39. Bowen, *The Willamette Valley*, 79–88; Gibson, *Farming the Frontier*, 143–142.

40. Ratcliff, "What Happened to the Kalapuya?" 31; Applegate, *A Day with the Cow Column*, 150.

41. Ratcliff, "What Happened to the Kalapuya?" 32; Boag, *Environment and Experience*, 41–73; Robert Boyd, *The Coming of the Spirit Pestilence*, 116–171, 231–278, 326–327; Bunting, *The Pacific Raincoast*, 55–56; Melville Jacobs, "Preface," *Kalapuya Texts*, University of Washington Publications in Anthropology (Seattle: University of Washington, 1945), 8.

42. Jacobs, *Kalapuya Texts*, 67; Boag, *Environment and Experience*, 22; Jarold Ramsey, ed., *Coyote Was Going There: Indian Literature of the Oregon Country* (Seattle: University of Washington Press, 1977), 104.

43. Wilkes, "Report on the Territory of Oregon," 290. Applegate, *A Day with the Cow Column*, 158–160, 188; T.N. Ramsdell, Indians of Oregon, OHS, Mss. 853; Mathias D. Bergmann, "'We should lose much by their absence': The Centrality of Kalapuyans to Life in Frontier Oregon," *OHQ* 109:1 (Spring 2008), 48–52

44. Lyman, "Reminiscences of F. X. Matthieu," 101.

45. Willard Rees, "Annual Address" [1879], *TOPA* 7 (1880), 24; T.N. Ramsdell, Indians of Oregon.

46. John Minto, Early Days, P-A 50, 29–30, BAN.

47. Lyman, "Reminiscences of F. X. Matthieu," 90.

48. Duflot de Mofras, *Duflot de Mofras' Travels*, vol. 2, 109.

49. Rees, "Annual Address," 19.

50. Evelyn Leasher and Robert J. Frank, introduction to Bailey, *The Grains*, 1–20; Janice C. Duncan, "'Ruth Rover'—Vindictive Falsehood or Historical Truth?" *Journal of the West* 12:2 (April 1973): 240–253; Herbert B. Nelson, "Ruth Rover's Cup of Sorrow," *PNQ* 50:3 (July 1959): 91–98; David C. Thomas, "Against the Grains: Margaret Jewett Bailey's Social and Spiritual Independence, Oregon, 1837–1854," *Methodist History* 35:1 (October 1996): 28–42.

51. Bailey, *The Grains*, 194.

52. Bailey, *The Grains*, 223.

53. Bailey, *The Grains*, 221.

54. The Catholic Church Records for St. Paul identify Angelique Carpentier's husband as "Anderson, a métis Kanaka" and later as "Peter Anderson." Harriet Munnick, ed., *CCRP-NW-SP*, vol. 1, 136, and vol. 2, 51 (Portland, OR: Binford & Mort), 1979. The U.S. census of 1850 identified Angelique Carpentier's husband as Peter Anderson, a carpenter from the Sandwich Islands (Hawaii). See Elsie Y. Browning, trans., "Marion County," *1850 Federal Census, Oregon Territory* (Lebanon, OR: End Trail Researchers, 1970), 144.

55. Bailey, *The Grains*, 222. Bailey identified the missionary woman whom Angelique Carpentier was forced to serve as "Mrs. S____," a not-so-subtle reference to Mrs. Cyrus Shepard. See O. W. Frost, "Margaret J. Bailey, Oregon Pioneer Author," *MCH* 5 (June 1959), 65.

56. Munnick, ed., *CCRPNW-SP*, vol. 1, 98, 136, and vol. 2, 14, 51, Annotations, A-14.

57. Bailey, *The Grains*, 232. Bailey identifies the woman as "Madame Lucien, a Chenook Indian woman"; Etienne Lucier's first wife Josette Nouette died in January 1840, and he married Marie Marguerite Chinook in August 1840. Munnick, ed., *CCRPNW-SP.* vol. 1, 4, 16.

58. Bailey, *The Grains*, 220.

59. Bailey, *The Grains*, 238.

60. Martha Anna (Morrison) Minto, Female Pioneering in Oregon, Mss. P-A 51, 1–9, BAN. For analysis of the life of Celiast (Clatsop) Smith, see David Peterson del Mar, "Intermarriage and Agency: A Chinookan Case Study," *Ethnohistory* 42:1 (Winter 1995): 1–30.

61. Elizabeth (Miller) Wilson, Oregon Sketches, Mss. P-A 55, 19–20, BAN.

62. Susan Armitage, "Making Connections: Gender, Race, and Place in Oregon Country," in *One Step Over the Line: Toward a History of Women in the North American Wests*, ed. Elizabeth Jameson and Sheila McManus (Edmonton: University of Alberta Press/Athabasca University Press, 2008), 55–79; Jean Barman, *French Canadians, Furs, and Indigenous Women in the Making of the Pacific Northwest* (Vancouver: UBC Press, 2014), 107–166; Jean Barman and Bruce M. Watson, "Fort Colvile's Fur Trade Families and the Dynamics of Race in the Pacific Northwest," *PNQ* 90:3 (Summer (1999): 140–153; Juliet T. Pollard, "The Making of the Metis in the Pacific Northwest, Fur Trade Children: Race, Class, and Gender" (Ph.D diss., University of British Columbia), 1990. See also Nancy F. Cott, *The Bonds of Womanhood: "Women Sphere" in New England, 1780–1835*, 2nd ed. (New Haven: Yale University Press, 1997); Barbara Welter, "The Cult of True Womanhood, 1820–1860," *American Quarterly* 18:2 (Summer 1966): 151–174.

63. See Jennifer S. H. Brown, *Strangers in Blood: Fur Trade Company Families in Indian Country* (Vancouver: UBC Press, 1980); Albert L. Hurtado, *Intimate Frontiers: Sex, Gender, and Culture in Old California* (Albuquerque: University of New Mexico Press, 1999); Susan Lee Johnson, *Roaring Camp: The Social World of the California Gold Rush* (New York: W. W. Norton, 2000); Adele Perry, *On the Edge of Empire: Gender, Race, and the Making of British Columbia, 1849–1871* (Toronto: University of Toronto Press, 2001); Cynthia Culver Prescott, *Gender and Generation on the Far Western Frontier* (Tucson: University of Arizona Press, 2007); Laura E. Wentworth-Ney, *Women in the American West* (Santa Barbara, CA: ABC-CLIO, 2008); Sylvia Van Kirk, *Many Tender Ties: Women in Fur Trade Society, 1670–1870* (Norman: University of Oklahoma Press, 1980).

64. Bailey, *The Grains*, 194.

65. Bailey, *The Grains*, 198.

66. Bailey, *The Grains*, 198 and 195. See Harriet Munnick's annotation on François Quesnel Sr. where she notes the connection between Bailey's "Indian woman, wife of a neighbor, buried to day" and the burial of Marie Chehalis, Quesnel's wife: Munnick, ed., *CCRPNW-SP*, Annotations, A-83.

67. Bailey, *The Grains*, 198.

68. Crawford, Missionaries, 11.

69. Francis N. Blanchet to Modeste Demers, February 9, 1842, Francis N. Blanchet Collection, APOA.

70. Blanchet to Demers, February 9, 1842.

71. Francis N. Blanchet to Joseph Signay, n. d. [fall?] 1842, Francis N. Blanchet Collection, APOA.

72. Duflot de Mofras, *Duflot de Mofras' Travels*, vol. 2, 113–114.

73. Ollivier Hubert, "Ritual Performance and Parish Sociability: French-Canadian Catholic Families at Mass from the Seventeenth to the Nineteenth Century," in *Households of Faith: Family, Gender, and Community in Canada, 1760–1969*, ed. Nancy Christie (Montreal: McGill-Queen's University Press, 2002), 44.

74. Landerholm, *Notices and Voyages*, 77; Francis N. Blanchet to George Simpson, November 15, 1841; Francis N. Blanchet to Joseph Provencher, March 22, 1842, Francis N. Blanchet Collection, APOA.

75. Bailey, *The Grains*, 139.

76. Bailey, *The Grains*, 139; Munnick, ed., *CCRPNW-SP*, vol. 1, 98, 136., vol. 2, 51.

77. Pierre-Jean DeSmet, *Oregon Mission and Travels over the Rocky Mountains, 1845–46* (1847; rpt; Fairfield, WA: Ye Galleon Press, 1978), 79; Duflot de Mofras, *Duflot de Mofras' Travels*, vol. 2, 113.

78. Landerholm, *Notices and Voyages*, 75; Francis Norbert Blanchet. *Historical Sketches of the Catholic Church in Oregon*, ed. Edward Kowrach (Fairfield, WA: Ye Galleon Press, 1983), 110–111; Jean Baptiste Zacharie Bolduc, *Mission of the Columbia*, ed. Edward J. Kowrach (Fairfield, WA: Ye Galleon Press, 1979).

79. At this period in the history of Catholic religious orders, the term "nun" referred to members of cloistered orders. However, following the approach used by current researchers in the field, I utilize the terms "nun" and "sister" interchangeably to refer to female

members of Catholic religious orders, both those enclosed and those engaged in mission-ary and apostolic work beyond the cloister. See Sarah A. Curtis, *Civilizing Habits: Women Missionaries and the Revival of French Empire* (New York: Oxford University Press, 2010), 274; Anne Butler, *Across God's Frontiers: Catholic Sisters in the American West, 1850–1920* (Chapel Hill: University of North Carolina Press, 2012), 9.

80. Wildred P. Schoenberg, *A History of the Catholic Church in the Pacific Northwest, 1743–1983* (Washington, D.C.: Pastoral Press, 1987), 81, 88.

81. Sister Mary Dominica McNamee, *Willamette Interlude* (Palo Alto, CA: Pacific Books, 1959), 1–62; List of first and second groups of Sisters of Notre Dame de Namur to Oregon, 1843–1847, California Province Archives, Sisters of Notre Dame de Namur, Notre Dame de Namur University, Belmont, California.

82. *Notice sur le territoire et sur la mission de l'Orégon suivie de quelques lettres des soeurs de Notre-Dame établies à Saint Paul du Wallamette* (Brussels: Bureau de publications de la Bibliotèque d'éducation, 1847), 116–119.

83. *Notice sur le territoire*, 121.

84. *Notice sur le territoire*, 122–125.

85. Shawna Lea Gandy, Tables A–K, "Fur Trade Daughters of the Oregon Country: Stu-dents of the Sisters of Notre Dame de Namur, 1850" (M.A. thesis, Portland State University, 2004), 211–220. The mother of Marie Press was "a Stikine woman." "Stikine" refers to one of the Tlingit groups of present-day southern Alaska. See Frederick De Laguna, "Tlingit," in *Handbook of North American Indians*, vol. 7, *Northwest Coast*, ed. Wayne Suttles (Washing-ton, D.C.: Smithsonian Institution, 1990), 204.

86. Curtis, *Civilizing Habits,* 1–46, 53–64; Ralph Gibson, *A Social History of French Catholicism 1789–1914* (New York: Routledge, 1989).

87. *Notice sur le territoire*, 133–134; Gandy, "Fur Trade Daughters," 114–136; Pollard, "The Making of the Metis," 319–336; Mary C. Wright, "The Circle Broken: Gender, Family, and Dif-ference in the Pacific Northwest, 1811–1850" (Ph.D diss., Rutgers University, 1996), 149–201.

88. *Notice sur le territoire*, 134–135.

89. Curtis, *Civilizing Habits*, 1–46, 53–64; Wright, "The Circle Broken," 202–293; Butler, *Across God's Frontiers*, 36–42, 233–246; Lesley Erickson, "Repositioning the Missionary: Sara Riel, the Grey Nuns, and Aboriginal Women in Catholic Missions in the Northwest," in *Recollecting: Lives of Aboriginal Women in the Canadian Northwest and Borderlands*, ed. Sarah Carter and Patricia A. McCormack (Edmonton: Athabasca University Press, 2011), 115–134.

90. *Notice sur le territoire*, 133, 136, 149, 169; McNamee, Willamette Interlude, 159–175. See also Joseph G. Mannard, "Maternity . . . of the Spirit: Nuns and Domesticity in Antebellum America," in *History of Women in the United States: Historical Articles on Women's Lives and Activities*, vol. 13, *Religion*, ed. Nancy F. Cott (Munich: K. G. Saur, 1993), 74–92.

91. *Notice sur le territoire*, 133.

92. H. S. Lyman, "Reminiscences of Hugh Cosgrove," *OHQ* 1 (March–December 1900), 267–268.

93. John Minto, Early Days of Oregon, Mss. P-A 50, BAN.

94. Charles Wilkes, *Narrative of the United States Exploring Expedition*, vol. 4, 370.

95. *Notice sur le territoire*, 134, 155, 162; McNamee, *Willamette Interlude*, 159–175.

96. *Notice sur le territoire*, 169.

97. Munnick, ed., *CCRPNW-SP*, vol. 1, 149, Annotations, A-79; Watson, *Lives Lived West of the Divide*, vol. 2, 417–418; *Genealogical Material in Oregon Provisional Land Claims: Abstracted from Applications*, vols. 1–8, *1845–1849* (Portland, OR: Genealogical Forum of Oregon, 1982), 10.

98. Munnick, ed., *CCRPNW-V*, vol 1, 41; Annotations, A-70; Watson, *Lives Lived West of the Divide*, vol. 2, 779–780.

99. David D. Duniway and Neil R. Riggs, eds., "The Oregon Archives, 1841–1843," *OHQ* 60:2 (June 1959), 261.

100. Munnick, ed., *CCRPNW-SP*, Annotations, A-79; Watson, *Lives Lived West of the Divide*, vol. 3, 417–418.

101. For a discussion of the pressures on the daughters of French-Indian families to seek to marry more acculturated mixed-race men or white men by the 1850s, see Gandy, "Fur Trade Daughters."

102. John A. Hussey, *Champoeg: Place of Transition, A Disputed History* (Portland: Oregon Historical Society/Oregon State Highway Commission, 1967); Robert J. Loewenberg, "Creating a Provisional Government in Oregon: A Revision," *PNQ* 86:1 (January 1977): 13–24; Kent David Richards, "Growth and Development of Government in the Far West" (Ph.D. diss., University of Wisconsin, 1966); Kent D. Richards, "The Methodists and the Formation of the Oregon Provisional Government," *PNQ* 61:2 (April 1970): 87–93.

103. John H. Frost, "Journal of John H. Frost," ed. Nellie B. Pipes, *OHQ* 35:1 (March 1934), 64–66; Francis N. Blanchet to Modeste Demers, February 11, 1841, Francis N. Blanchet Collection, APOA.

104. Blanchet to Demers, February 11, 1841. Blanchet does not identify Perrault in this initial letter to Demers but in a subsequent report to Archbishop Signay of Quebec City. See Francis N. Blanchet, 1841 Mission Report (June 10–October 12, 1841), Francis N. Blanchet Collection, APOA. Here Blanchet spells Perrault's surname as "Perreau." This "Perreau" undoubtedly refers to Jean Baptiste Perrault because there is no other French Canadian of a remotely similar surname listed as living in the Willamette Valley in either the Catholic Church Records or in Elijah White's census of a year later.

105. Francis N. Blanchet to Jason Lee, January 6, 1841, copy enclosed in Blanchet to Demers, February 11, 1841.

106. Jason Lee to Francis N. Blanchet, January 7, 1841, copy enclosed in Blanchet to Demers, February 11, 1841.

107. Hubert, "Ritual Performance," 37–76.

108. Allan Greer, *The Patriots and the People: The Rebellion of 1837 in Rural Lower Canada* (Toronto: University of Toronto Press, 1993), 91–100.

109. Jason Lee to Francis N. Blanchet, January 7, 1841, copy enclosed in Blanchet to Demers, February 11, 1841.

110. Blanchet baptized Reine Perrault, age twenty, during the Christmas vigil, December 24, 1840. See Munnick, ed., *CCRPNW-SP*, vol. 1, 20.

111. Hubert, "Ritual Performance," 37–76; Ollivier Hubert, *Sur la terre come au ciel: La gestion des rites par l'Église catholique du Québec (fin XVIIe – mi-XIXe siècle)* (Sainte Foy,

QC: Les Presses de l'Université Laval, 2000), 263–285.

112. Blanchet to Demers, February 11, 1841.

113. Blanchet to Demers, February 11, 1841.

114. Josiah L. Parrish, Anecdotes of Intercourse with the Indians, P-A 4,97–98, BAN. Duniway and Riggs, eds. "The Oregon Archives," 216–217. For the 1842 statistics on the Ewing Young Estate, see Elijah White, "Census of Settlers in the Oregon Country, 1842." Letters Received by the Office of Indian Affairs, 1824-81, Oregon Superintendency, 1842-1880, Bureau of Indian Affairs, National Archives of the United States, Washington D.C, Record Group 75 (microfilm roll 607).

115. Duniway and Riggs, "The Oregon Archives," 216–217; Gustavus Hines, *Oregon: Its History, Condition, and Prospects* (1851; reprint, New York: Arno Press, 1973), 418–419.

116. Blanchet to Demers, February 11, 1841 [February 23, 1841]. Blanchet started writing this long missive on February 11, 1841, but did not complete it until February 23, dispatching it sometime later. Therefore, in this letter dated February 11, 1841, Blanchet documents the historic events that took place on February 17 and 18, 1841.

117. Loewenberg, "Creating a Provisional Government," 13–24; Kent D. Richards, "The Methodists," 87–93; Russell B. Thomas, "Truth and Fiction of the Champoeg Meeting," *OHQ* 30:3 (September 1929): 218–237. Loewenberg identifies this interpretive tradition with Francis Fuller Victor, the ghostwriter of H. H. Bancroft's two-volume *History of Oregon* (1886). Victor relied on William H. Gray's flawed, bombastic denunciation of what he perceived as Roman Catholic and HBC conspiracies to snatch Oregon from the United States. See William H. Gray, *A History of Oregon, 1792–1849* (Portland, OR: Harris & Holman, 1870). For an example of the Catholic clergy's supposed influence on the French Canadian settlers, see Bancroft, *History of Oregon*, vol. 1, 235; Leslie Scott, "Oregon's Provisional Government, 1843–49," *OHQ* 30:3 (September 1929): 207–217.

118. Loewenberg, "Creating a Provisional Government," 14–15.

119. Blanchet to Demers, February 11, 1841; Duniway and Riggs, "The Oregon Archives," 216–218; Richards, "Growth and Development," 40–41.

120. Blanchet to Demers, February 11, 1841.

121. Parrish, Anecdotes of Intercourse with the Indians, 76.

122. Blanchet to Demers, February 11, 1841.

123. Duniway and Riggs, "The Oregon Archives," 217–218.

124. Duniway and Riggs, "The Oregon Archives," 218–219; Francis N. Blanchet, 1841 Willamette Mission Report, Blanchet Collection, APOA.

125. Wilkes, *Narrative of the United States Exploring Expedition*, vol. 4, 352–353; Blanchet, 1841 Willamette Mission Report; Hines, *A History of Oregon*, 420–421.

126. According to Wilkes, the fact that additional officers and expenditures were not needed in the colony was an important factor in the waning of the organizing efforts. He quoted a settler by the name of Johnson (likely William Johnson), a former HBC fur trapper, who told Wilkes "that they yet lived in the bush, and let all do right, there was no necessity for laws, lawyers, or magistrates." Wilkes, *Narrative of the United States Exploring Expedition*, vol. 4, 349.

127. Hines, *A History of Oregon*, 421; Bancroft, *History of Oregon*, vol. 1, 296–297.

128. Hussey, *A History of Oregon: Place of Transition*, 144–145.

129. Robbins, *Landscapes of Promise*, 89.

130. Duniway and Riggs, "The Oregon Archives," 226.

131. Duniway and Riggs, "The Oregon Archives," 227.

132. Duniway and Riggs, "The Oregon Archives," 236.

133. Robert Newell, *Oregon Herald*, December 9, 1866. See also Thomas, "Truth and Fiction of the Champoeg Meeting," 219–237; Loewenberg, "Creating a Provisional Government," 13–24; Frederick V. Holman, "A Brief History of the Oregon Provisional Government and What Caused its Formation," *OHQ* 13:2 (June 1912): 89–139.

134. Duniway and Riggs, "The Oregon Archives," 221–272. See also Lyman, "Reminiscences of F. X. Matthieu," 90–99; Parrish, Anecdotes of Intercourse with the Indians, 99–100; and Leslie M. Scott, "First Taxes in Oregon, 1844," *OHQ* 31:1 (March 1930): 1–10.

135. Newell, *Oregon Herald*, December 9, 1866. In 1912, Frederick Holman published a list of the names of those who voted for and against the establishment of a provisional government on May 2, 1843. His list included 52 who voted for organization (42 Americans, 1 Irishman, 2 Scotsman, 5 with unspecified nationality, and 2 Canadians, F. X. Matthieu and Etienne Lucier) and 50 who voted against organization (50 French Canadians). Given Robert Newell's evidence, the lack of direct written evidence from the meeting, and the various conflicting sources, Holman's list is best seen as an approximate rather than the definitive tally of the day's vote. See Holman, "A Brief History," 114–116.

136. John McLoughlin, "Document: A Narrative of John McLoughlin," *OHQ* 1:2 (June 1900), 198–199.

137. The most recent reiteration of this interpretation can be seen in Dorothy Nafus Morrison, *Outpost: John McLoughlin and the Far Northwest* (Portland: Oregon Historical Society Press, 1999).

138. Abner Sylvester Baker III, "The Oregon Pioneer Tradition in the Nineteenth Century: A Study of Recollection and Self-Definition" (Ph.D. diss., University of Oregon, 1969).

139. For William H. Gray's anti-British, anti-HBC, and anti-Catholic views and his conspiracy theories relating to the organization of the provisional government, see his *History of Oregon,* 279–281.

140. Lyman, "Reminiscences of F. X Matthieu," 94. This is how Matthieu remembered his reasons for voting for the formation of a government. Josiah Parrish remembered that one man, "Gervais Laderoute," voted with the majority. Joseph Gervais and François Xavier Laderoute were two different people. Parrish, Anecdotes of Intercourse with the Indians, 76–77.

141. P. J. Frien, trans., "Address [by the Canadian Settlers of the Willamette Valley to the American Settlers on Proposed Political Organization]," *OHQ* 13:4 (December 1912): 338–343; J. Neilson Barry, "The Champoeg Meeting of March 4, 1844," *OHQ* 38:4 (December 1837): 425–432.

142. Duniway and Riggs, "The Oregon Archives," 273–280; Hussey, *Champoeg: Place of Transition,* 165–167; Matthew P. Deady, comp., *The Organic and Other Laws of Oregon, 1845-1864* (Portland: Henry L. Pittock, 1866), 58–65, 80–83.

143. Lyman, "Reminiscences of F. X. Matthieu," 95.

144. *Oregon Supreme Court Record: An Original Printing of Cases and Other Matter Contained in a Manuscript Labeled Book I, 1844-1848* (Portland, OR: Stevens-Ness Law

Publishing Co., 1938), 8–9; Harriet D. Munnick, "Medard Godard Foisy, Pioneer Printer," *MCH* 10 (1969–1971), 5; La Fayette Grover, ed., *The Oregon Archives* (Salem: Asahel Bush, 1852), 71–72, 155, 221.

145. Scott, "First Taxes in Oregon, 1844," 1–10; Leslie M. Scott, ed., "First Taxpayers in Oregon, 1844," *OHQ* 31:1 (March 1930): 11–24; *Genealogical Material in Oregon Provisional Land Claims: Abstracted from Applications,* Vols. 1–8, *1845–1849* (Portland: Genealogical Forum of Portland, Oregon, Inc. 1982). This list of 91 of French-speaking claimants is an approximate number because some 10–15 individuals with apparently French surnames were not included in the list as their identity could not be cross-referenced with the *Catholic Church Records of the Pacific Northwest.* In addition, some settlers did not register their land claims as evidenced by the 13 prominent French Canadians whose farms were apparently unregistered, but whose land was described in the claims of neighboring settlers.

146. Katharine B. Judson, ed., "Documents: Dr. John McLaughlin's Last Letter to the Hudson's Bay Company as Chief Factor, 1845," *AHR* 21:1 (October 1915): 104–135.

147. Duniway and Riggs, "The Oregon Archives," 258; Eric Foner, *Free Soil, Free Labor, Free Men: The Ideology of the Republican Party Before the Civil War* (New York: Oxford University Press, 1995).

148. Horsman, *Race and Manifest Destiny*; Alexander Keyssar, *The Right to Vote: The Contested History of Democracy in the United States*, revised ed. (New York: Basic Books, 2000).

149. Quintard Taylor, "Slaves and Free Men: Blacks in the Oregon Country, 1840–1860," *OHQ* 83:2 (Summer 1982), 153–170; Thomas A. McClintock, "James Saules, Peter Burnett, and the Oregon Black Exclusion Law of June 1844," *PNQ* 86:3 (Summer 1995): 121–130.

150. Taylor, "Slaves and Free Men," 157.

CHAPTER 6: Under an Anglo-American Regime

1. J. B. A. Brouillet, *Protestantism in Oregon. Account of the Murder of Dr. Whitman and the Ungrateful Calumnies of H.H. Spalding, Protestant Missionary* (New York: M. T. Cozans, 1853); George Belknap, "Authentic Account of the Murder of Dr. Whitman: The History of a Pamphlet," *The Papers of the Bibliographical Society of America* 55 (1961), 319–325; Malcolm Clark, "The Bigot Disclosed: 90 Years of Nativism," *OHQ* 75:2 (June 1974), 115–119; Sister Marian Josephine Thomas, "Abbé Jean-Baptiste Abraham Brouillet, First Vicar General of the Diocese of Seattle" (M.A. thesis, Seattle University, 1950). In using the term "Whitman Mission incident" rather than "Whitman Massacre," I have followed the perspective of the Cayuse in whose territory Marcus Whitman established his mission. For an explanation of the historical context of the incident and the *tewatat* "medicine doctor" tradition of the Cayuse that holds healers responsible for the health of their patients whereby a healer's life may be forfeit if a patient is not cured, see Antone Minthorn (Cayuse), "Wars, Treaties, and the Beginning of Reservation Life," in *As days go by / wiyáxayxt / wiyáa awn—Our History, Our Land, and Our People: The Cayuse, Umatilla, and Walla Walla*, ed. Jennifer Karson (Pendleton, OR: Tamástslikt Cultural Institute, 2006), 64.

2. David G. Lewis, "Four Deaths: The Near Destruction of Western Oregon Tribes

and Native Lifeways, Removal to the Reservation, and Erasure from History," *OHQ* 115:3 (Fall 2104): 414–437; Gray H. Whaley, "A Reflection on Genocide in Southwest Oregon in Honor of George Bundy Wasson, Jr.," *OHQ* 115:3 (Fall 2104):438–440. Recent studies on the Pacific Northwest and the Pacific Slope during this period include the following: Brendan C. Lindsey, *Murder State: California's Native American Genocide, 1846–1873* (Lincoln: University of Nebraska Press, 2012); E. A. Schwartz, *The Rogue River Indian War and Its Aftermath, 1850–1980* (Norman: University of Oklahoma Press, 1997); Gray Whaley, *Oregon and the Collapse of Illahee: U.S. Empire and the Transformation of an Indigenous World, 1792–1859* (Chapel Hill: University of North Carolina Press, 2010); Charles Wilkinson, *The People Are Dancing Again: The History of the Siletz Tribe of Western Oregon* (Seattle: University of Washington Press, 2010). For an overview of the early Anglo-American tradition that marginalized Native peoples within historiography of the Pacific Northwest, see Chad Reimer, "Border of the Past: The Oregon Boundary Dispute and the Beginnings of Northwest Historiography," in *Parallel Destinies: Canadian-American Relations West of the Rockies*, ed. John M. Findlay and Ken S. Coates (Seattle: University of Washington Press, 2002), 221–245.

3. Patricia Brandt and Lillian A. Pereyra, *Adapting in Eden: Oregon's Catholic Minority, 1838–1986* (Pullman: Washington State University Press, 2002), 13–16; Wilfred P. Schoenberg, *A History of the Catholic Church in the Pacific Northwest, 1743–1983* (Washington, D.C.: Pastoral Press, 1987), 89–95.

4. Brandt and Pereyra, *Adapting in Eden*, 13–17; Schoenberg, *A History of the Catholic Church* 99–106.

5. Robert James Decker, "Jason Lee, Missionary to Oregon: A Re-evaluation" (Ph.D. diss., Indiana University, 1961), 235–275; Robert J. Loewenberg, *Equality on the Oregon Frontier: Jason Lee and the Methodist Mission, 1834–1843* (Seattle: University of Washington Press, 1976), 229–240.

6. Hubert Howe Bancroft, *History of Oregon*, vol. 1 (San Francisco: The History Company, 1886), 104–138; Clifford Merrill Drury, ed., *The Mountains We Have Crossed: Diaries and Letters of the Oregon Mission, 1838* (1966; reprint, Lincoln: University of Nebraska Press, 1999); Dorothy O. Johansen, *Empire of the Columbia*, 2nd ed. (New York: Harper & Row, 1957), 165–172.

7. Minthorn, "Wars, Treaties, and the Beginning of Reservation Life," 62–63; Larry Cebula, *Plateau Indians and the Quest for Spiritual Power, 1700–1850* (Lincoln: University of Nebraska Press, 2003), 99–127; Christopher L. Miller, *Prophetic Worlds: Indians and Whites on the Columbia Plateau* (1985; reprint, Seattle: University of Washington Press, 2003), 89–102; David Peterson del Mar, *Oregon's Promise: An Interpretive History* (Corvallis: Oregon State University Press), 56–57.

8. Cebula, *Plateau Indians*, 103–116; Miller, *Prophetic Worlds*, 124–127; Minthorn, "Wars, Treaties, and the Beginning of Reservation Life," 62–64; Peterson, *Oregon's Promise*, 57–58; Julie Roy Jeffery, *Converting the West: A Biography of Narcissa Whitman* (Norman: University of Oklahoma Press, 1991), 205–221.

9. Francis Norbert Blanchet, *Historical Sketches of the Catholic Church in Oregon*, ed. Edward J. Kowrach (Fairfield, WA: Ye Galleon Press, 1983), 132–135; Francis Fuller Victor, *The Early Indian Wars of Oregon* (Salem, OR: Frank C. Baker, State Printer, 1894), 110–113.

10. Blanchet, *Historical Sketches*, 134–135; Fuller, *The Early Indian Wars*, 113–124.

11. Belknap, "Authentic Account," 321–322; Clark, "The Bigot Disclosed," 115–117; William I. Marshall, *Acquisition of Oregon and the Long Suppressed Evidence about Marcus Whitman*, vol. 1 (Seattle: Lowman & Hanford Co., 1911), 199–269.

12. Blanchet, *Historical Sketches*, 136; Fuller, *The Early Indian Wars*, 159–161, 221; Priscilla Knuth, "Nativism in Oregon," *Frances Greenburg Armitage Prize Winning Essays, Reed College Bulletin* 24:2 (January 1946): 8–11.

13. Cayuse War Bonds, 1847–1850. Ref. 2/21/07/04, OSA.

14. *Oregon Spectator*, January 20, 1848; *Oregon Spectator*, February 10, 1848; J. W. Grim, J. W. Grim's Narrative, Mss. P-A. 38, 8–9, BAN.

15. See, for example, the short notice on "Indian Difficulty" in the *Oregon Spectator*, July 4, 1846, and "Indian Disturbances" in the *Oregon Spectator*, May 27, 1847.

16. *Oregon Spectator*, March 4, 1847; *Oregon Spectator*, March 18, 1847; *Oregon Spectator*, May 27, 1847.

17. See, for example, Richard Drinnon, *Facing West: The Metaphysics of Indian-Hating and Empire-Building* (Norman: University of Oklahoma Press, 1980).

18. *Oregon Spectator*, February 10, 1848.

19. Robert Newell, letter to editor, *Oregon Spectator*, April 6, 1848; Fuller, *The Early Indian Wars*, 503–519. The French Prairie volunteers initially served in Company D. Those who remained through the summer and fall of 1848 moved to other companies after Thomas McKay, who was ill, returned to the Willamette Valley in March 1848 with other volunteers who had also become sick.

20. *Oregon Spectator*, February 10, 1848.

21. *Oregon Spectator*, March 9, 1848.

22. Fuller, *The Early Indian Wars*, 169–210; David Lavender, "Thomas McKay," in *The Mountain Men and the Fur Trade of the Far West*, ed. LeRoy R. Hafen, vol. 6 (Glendale, CA: Arthur H. Clark Co., 1969), 275–276.

23. Robert Newell, letter to editor, *Oregon Spectator*, April 6, 1848; Fuller, *The Early Indian Wars*, 503–519.

24. Robert Newell, *Robert Newell's Memoranda*, ed. Dorothy O. Johansen (Portland, OR: Champoeg Press, 1959), 111–113.

25. Lavender, "Thomas McKay," 276; Fuller, *The Early Indian Wars*, 503–519.

26. Schoenberg, *A History of the Catholic Church*, 128–129; Minthorn, "Wars, Treaties, and the Beginning of Reservation Life," 64–65; Ronald B. Lansing, *Juggernaut: The Whitman Massacre Trial, 1850* (n.p.: Ninth Judicial Circuit Historical Society, 1993).

27. Blanchet, *Historical Sketches*, 139–140; Harriet Munnick, ed., *CCRPNW-SL*, vol. 1 (Portland, OR: Binford & Mort, 1982), 21; Harvey McKay, *St. Paul, Oregon, 1830–1890* (Portland: Binford & Mort, 1980), 26–30.

28. Mary Dominica McNamee, *Willamette Interlude* (Palo Alto, CA: Pacific Books, 1959), 216–267; Schoenberg, *A History of the Catholic Church*, 124–134; Anne N. Butler, *Across God's Frontiers: Catholic Sisters in the American West, 1850–1920* (Chapel Hill: University of North Carolina Press, 2012), 154–156; Shawna Lee Gander, "Fur Trade Daughters of the Oregon Country: Students of the Sisters of Notre Dame de Namur, 1850" (M.A. thesis, Portland State University, 2004), 177.

29. Earl Pomeroy, *The Pacific Slope* (New York: Alfred A. Knopf, 1968), 37–54, 83–119; James Henry Gilbert, *Trade and Currency in Early Oregon: A Study of the Commercial and Monetary History of the Pacific Northwest* (1907; reprint, New York: AMS Press, 1967), 73–94; Elaine Tanner, "A Study of the Underlying Causes of the Depression of 1854," in *Frances Greenburg Armitage Prize Winning Essays, Reed College Bulletin* 25:3 (April 1947): 35–65.

30. Johansen, *Empire of the Columbia*, 225–230; Autobiography of J. Henry Brown, Mss. 1002, 21–22, OHS,

31. Matthew P. Deady, comp., *The Organic and Other General Laws of Oregon, 1845–1864* (Portland, OR: Henry Pittock, State Printer, 1866), 84–90.

32. Deady, *The Organic and Other General Laws*, 84–97; Richard H. Chused, "The Oregon Donation Act of 1850 and Nineteenth Century Federal Married Women's Property Law," *Law and History Review* 2:1 (Spring 1984): 44–78.

33. John D. Unruh, *The Plains Across: The Overland Emigrants and the Trans-Mississippi West, 1840–60* (Urbana: University of Illinois Press, 1993), 120; Johansen, *Empire of the Columbia*, 230–234; Dorothy O. Johansen, "The Role of Land Laws in the Settlement of Oregon," in *Genealogical Material in Oregon Donation Land Claims*, vol.1 (Portland: Genealogical Forum of Portland, 1992), n.p.

34. David G. Lewis, "Four Deaths," 420–428; William G. Robbins, "The Indian Question in Western Oregon: The Making of a Colonial People," in *Experiences in a Promised Land: Essays in Pacific Northwest History*, ed. G. Thomas Edwards and Carlos A. Schwantes (Seattle: University of Washington Press, 1986), 51–67; Gray H. Whaley, *Oregon and the Collapse of Illahee*, 191–226.

35. Stephen Dow Beckham, "History of Western Oregon Since 1846," in *Handbook of North American Indians*, vol. 7, *Northwest Coast*, ed. Wayne Suttles (Washington D.C.: Smithsonian Institution, 1990), 180–183; C. F. Coan, "The First Stage of Federal Indian Policy in the Pacific Northwest, 1849–1852," *OHQ* 22: 1 (March 1921): 46–89; C. F. Coan, "The Adoption of the Reservation Policy in the Pacific Northwest," *OHQ* 23:1 (March 1923): 1–38; Cole Harris, "How Did Colonialism Dispossess? Comments from the Edge of an Empire," *Annals of the Association of American Geographers* 94:1 (2004): 165–182; Douglas Dale Martin, "Indian-White Relations on the Pacific Slope, 1850–1890" (Ph.D. diss., University of Washington, 1969), 54–68; Paige Raibmon, "Unmaking Native Space: A Genealogy of Indian Policy, Settler Practice, and the Microtechniques of Dispossession," in *The Power of Promises: Rethinking Indian Treaties in the Pacific Northwest*, ed. Alexandra Harmon (Seattle: University of Washington Press, 2008), 56–85.

36. Beckham, "History of Western Oregon," 180–183; Brent Merrill and Yvonne Hajda, "The Confederated Tribes of the Grand Ronde Community of Oregon," in *The First Oregonians*, 2nd ed., ed. Laura Berg (Portland: Oregon Council for the Humanities, 2007), 121–125; Ronald Spores, "Too Small a Place: The Removal of the Willamette Valley Indians, 1850–1856," *American Indian Quarterly* 17:2 (Spring 1993): 171–191.

37. Jesse Applegate to Samuel Thurston, n.d. [circa 1849], Thurston Family Papers, Mss. 379, OHS; Clarence Bagley, ed., "Letter by Daniel H. Lownsdale to Samuel R. Thurston, First Territorial Delegate from Oregon To Congress," *OHQ* 14:3 (September 1913): 213–249.

38. Samuel Thurston, "Letter of the Delegate from Oregon to the Members of the House of Representatives on Behalf of His Constituents, Touching on the Oregon Land Bill," Thurston Family Papers; Samuel Thurston to Samuel Parker and Wesley Shannon, August 31, 1850, Thurston Family Papers; James M. Berquist, "The Oregon Donation Act and National Land Policy," *OHQ* 58; 1 (March 1957): 17–35; Knuth, "Nativism in Oregon," 16–21.

39. Edward Dupuis to Joseph Lane, February 3, 1852, Joseph Lane Papers, Mss. 1146, OHS.

40. Edward Dupuis to Joseph Lane, February 3, 1852.

41. Jean Barman, *French Canadians, Furs, and Indigenous Women* (Vancouver, BC: UBC Press, 2014), Edward Dupuis to Joseph Lane, February 3, 1852.

42. Chused, "The Oregon Donation Act of 1850," 44–78; Richard Chused, "Married Women's Property Law, 1800–1850," *Georgetown Law Review* 71 (1982–1983): 1359–1425; Richard Chused, "Late Nineteenth-Century Married Women's Property Law: Reception of the Early Married Women's Property Acts by Courts and Legislatures," *American Journal of Legal History* 29:1 (1985): 3–35; Peggy Pascoe, *What Comes Naturally: Miscegenation Law and the Making of Race in America* (New York: Oxford University Press, 2009), 95–97; Kimberly Jensen, "Revolutions in the Machinery: Oregon Women and Citizenship in Sesquicentennial Perspective," *OHQ* 110:3 (Fall 2009): 337–341; Kristen Tegtmeier Oertel, *Bleeding Borders: Race, Gender, and Violence in Pre-Civil War Kansas* (Baton Rouge: Louisiana State University Press, 2009), 118–119.

43. Elsie Y. Browning, trans., *1850 Federal Census, Oregon Territory* (Lebanon, OR: End of the Trail Researchers, 1970), 132–192.

44. Browning, *1850 Federal Census, Oregon Territory*, 132–190; See Munnick, ed., *CCRPNW-SP* and *CCRPNW-SL*.

45. Browning, *1850 Federal Census, Oregon Territory*, 132–190; M. [Pierre Charles Fournier] de Saint Amant, *Voyages en Californie and dans l'Orégon* (Paris: Librairie L. Maison, 1854), 194–201.

46. Declarations of Intention, 1849–1860, Marion County Naturalization Records, OSA.

47. Saint Amant, *Voyages en Californie*, 196–211; Grim, Grim's Narrative, 7–8.

48. Marion County Probate Case Files (hereafter MCPCF), 1843–1898, OSA; Munnick, ed., *CCRPNW-V, CCRPNW-SP, CCRPNW-SL*. Two cases were excluded from the sample because the only paperwork in the surviving file was the executor's bond: Baptiste Dorion (1849) and Antoine Bonenfant (1850).

49. For Andre Chalifoux and Catherine Russie, see Munnick, ed., *CCRPNW-SP*, Annotations, A-15 and A-86.

50. Joseph Gagnon, case no. 11 (1849); Andre Chalifoux, case no. 54 (1851); David Gervais, case no. 83 (1853); Felix Bergevin, case no. 189 (1859); MCPCF, OSA.

51. Hyacinthe Lavigeur, case no. 15, MCPCF, OSA.

52. Eloi Ducheneau, case no. 104 (1854), MCPCF, OSA.

53. Nazaire Dupré, case no. 7 (1849), MCPCF, OSA.

54. MCPCF, OSA. The case file numbers are as follows: Jean Gingras, no. 145 (1856); Joseph Binet, no. 166 (1856); Hercules Lebrun, no. 172 (1857); Laurent Sauvé, no. 168 (1858); and Catherine Comartin, no. 196 (1860).

55. For Louise Cowichan Biscornet, see Munnick, ed., *CCRPNW-SL*, vol. II, 110; for Françoise Cayuse (also identified as Walla Walla), see Munnick, ed., *CCRPNW-SP*, Annotations, A-41, A-88, A-90.

56. Stanislaus Liard, case no. 55 (1852), MCPCF, OSA; Melinda Marie Jetté, "Betwixt and Between the Official Story: Tracing the History and Memory of a Family of French-Indian Ancestry in the Pacific Northwest," *OHQ* 111:2 (Summer 2010): 142–183. Marguerite Liard Jetté was the author's great-great grandmother.

57. MCPCF, 1847–1860, OSA; *Genealogical Material in Oregon Land Claims*, vols. 1, 2, 4, 5 (Portland: Genealogical Forum of Oregon, 1957–1994); *Index: Oregon Donation Land Claims*, 2nd ed. (Portland: Genealogical Forum of Oregon, 1992).

58. Jacques Servant, MCPCF, case file no. 102 (1854); Heirs of Jacques Servant, donation land claim certificate number 1740, *Index: Oregon Donation Land Claims*, 137.

59. Pierre Bellique, MCPCF, case file no. 2. (1850), OSA. For the Bellique family, see Munnick, *CCRPNW-SP*, Annotations, A-6 and A-7.

60. Stanislaus Liard, MCPCF, case file no. 55 (1852), OSA. For the Liard family, see Munnick, ed., *CCRPNW-SP*, Annotations, A-59, and Jetté, "Betwixt and Between the Official Story," 146–150.

61. Stanislaus Liard case file, MCPCF.

62. Eugene H. Berwanger, *The Frontier Against Slavery: Western Anti-Negro Prejudice and the Slavery Extension Controversy* (Urbana: University of Illinois Press, 1967), 78–96; Melinda Marie Jetté and Tim Zacharias, "The State of Oregon," in *The Uniting States: The Story of Statehood for the Fifty United States*, ed. Benjamin F. Shearer, vol. 3 (Westport, CT: Greenwood Press, 2005), 1003–1013; Robert W. Johannsen, *Frontier Politics on the Eve of the Civil War* (Seattle: University of Washington Press, 1955), 15–50.

63. Bill to Allow Half-Breeds to Become Citizens, 1856, H.B. 28, Oregon Territorial Legislative Assembly Records, OSA.

64. Bill to Allow Half-Breeds to Become Citizens, 1856, H.B. 28; *Journal of the House of Representatives of the Territory of Oregon: During the Eighth Regular Session, 1856–7* (Salem, OR: Asahel Bush, Territorial Printer, 1857), 45–49, 54–56, 74; Territorial Government Legislators and Staff Guide, Eighth Regular Session (1856), Oregon Legislators and Staff Guide, Oregon Legislature Records, OSA.

65. Charles Henry Carey, *The Oregon Constitution and Proceedings of the Debates of the Constitutional Convention of 1857* (Portland: Oregon Historical Society Press, 1984); David Alan Johnson, *Founding the Far West: California, Oregon, and Nevada, 1840–1890* (Berkeley: University of California Press, 1992), 178–181; Eric Foner, *The Story of American Freedom* (New York: W. W. Norton, 1998), 69–94; Alexander Keyssar, *The Right to Vote: The Contested History of Democracy in the United States*, rev. ed. (New York: Basic Books, 2000), 43–56; Helen Leonard Seagraves, "Oregon's 1857 Convention," *Frances Greenburg Armitage Prize Essays, Reed College Bulletin* 30: 4 (June 1952): 15–21; Berwanger, *The Frontier Against Slavery*, 78–96; Johannsen, *Frontier Politics*, 15–50.

66. The French American Narcisse Cornoyer married Sophie Bellique, daughter of Pierre Bellique and Genevieve St. Martin; Adolphe Jetté lost his first wife, Julie Rogue, in 1865 and later married Marguerite Liard, daughter of Celeste Rochbrune and Tanis Liard; François Xavier Mattieu married Rose Aucent, daughter of Louis Aucent and a Native

woman (possibly Catherine Cayuse); Honore Picard married Celeste Rochbrune, daughter of Joseph Rochbrune and Lisette Walla, and widow of Tanis Liard; Joseph Simoneau married Mary (Molalla) Aucent, widow of Louis Aucent. See Munnick, ed., *CCRPNW-SP* and *CCRPNW-SL*.

67. Petition to Allow Half-Breed Indian Voting, 1859, Legislative Petitions, Oregon Territorial Records, OSA.

68. Petition to Allow Half-Breed Indian Voting, 1859.

69. *Journal of the House of Representatives of the Territory of Oregon*, 304–310; Territorial Government Legislators and Staff Guide, Regular Session, First Pre-Admission (1858), Oregon Legislators and Staff Guide, Oregon Legislature Records, OSA.

70. Berwanger, *Frontier Against Slavery*, 78–96; Johansen, *Frontier Politics*, 15–50; Oertel, *Bleeding Borders*, 110–115; Lauren L. Basson, *White Enough to Be American: Race Mixing, Indigenous People, and the Boundaries of State and Nation* (Chapel Hill: University of North Carolina Press, 2008), 7–16; Thomas N. Ingersoll, *To Intermix with Our White Brothers: Indian Mixed Bloods in the United States from the Earliest Times to the Indian Removals* (Albuquerque: University of New Mexico Press, 2005), 171–172; Jeremy Mumford, "Métis and the Vote in 19th-Century America," *Journal of the West* 39:3 (Summer 2000): 38–45; James Z. Schwartz, *Conflict on the Michigan Frontier: Yankee Borderland Cultures, 1815–1840* (Dekalb: Northern Illinois University Press, 2009), 12–29, 89–94.

Epilogue

1. Peggy Pascoe, "'A Mistake to Simmer the Question Down to Black and White': The History of Oregon's Miscegenation Law," in *Seeing Color: Indigenous Peoples and Racialized Minorities in Oregon*, ed. Jun Xing et al. (Lanham, MD: University Press of America, 2007), 27–43. See also Peggy Pascoe, *What Comes Naturally: Miscegenation Law and the Making of Race in America* (New York: Oxford University Press, 2009).

2. The histories of these families can be traced through Harriet Munnick, ed., *Catholic Church Records of the Pacific Northwest*, 7 vols. (Portland, OR: Binford & Mort, 1972–1989). See the volumes on Vancouver, St. Paul, St. Louis, Roseburg, Grand Ronde, and St. Ann among the Cayuse, Walla Walla, and Frenchtown. See also Bruce Watson, *Lives Lived West of the Divide: A Biographical Dictionary of Fur Traders Working West of the Rockies, 1793–1858*, 3 vols. (Kelowna: Centre for Social, Spatial, and Economic Justice, University of British Columbia, 2010). For an overview of the tragic death of Angelique Carpentier in 1859, see Melinda Marie Jetté, "Dislodging Oregon's History from its Mythical Mooring: Reflections on Death and the Settling and Unsettling of Oregon," *OHQ* 115:3 (Fall 2014): 444–445.

3. For comparative family histories on the regional and continental scale, see Jean Barman, *French Canadians, Furs, and Indigenous Women in the Making of the Pacific Northwest* (Vancouver: UBC Press, 2014); and Anne F. Hyde's *Empires, Nations, and Families: A History of the North American West, 1800–1860* (Lincoln: University of Nebraska Press, 2011).

4. Tracy Neal Leavelle, "'We Will Make It Our Own Place': Agricultural Adaptation at the Grand Ronde Reservation, 1856–1887," *American Indian Quarterly* 22:4 (Fall 1998):

433–456; June L. Olson, *Living in the Great Circle: The Grande Ronde Indian Reservation, 1855–1905* (Clackamas, OR: A. Menard Publications, 2011); Henry Zenk, "Chinook Jargon and Native Cultural Persistence in the Grand Ronde Indian Community, 1856–1907: A Special Case of Creolization" (Ph.D. diss., University of Oregon, 1984), 80–141; *Chinuk Wawa / kakwa nsayka ulman-tilixam laska mnk-kemeks nsayka / As Our Elders Teach Us to Speak It*, The Chinuk Wawa Dictionary Project (Grand Ronde, OR: Confederate Tribes of the Grand Ronde, 2012).

   5. Melinda Marie Jetté, "Betwixt and Between the Official Story: Tracing the History and Memory of a Family of French-Indian Ancestry in the Pacific Northwest," *OHQ* 111:2 (Summer 2010): 142–183.

APPENDIX 2: The First Astorian to the Willamette Valley

   1. H. H. Bancroft, *History of the Northwest Coast*, vol. 2 (San Francisco: A. L. Bancroft & Co., 1884), 177.

   2. See W. Kaye Lamb's footnote in Gabriel Franchère, *Journal of a Voyage on the North West Coast of North America during the Years 1811, 1812, 1813, and 1814*, ed. W. Kaye Lamb, trans. Wessie Tipping Lamb (Toronto: The Champlain Society, 1969), 96, fn 1; See also Fred S. Perrine, "Early Days on the Willamette," *OHQ* 25:4 (December 1924), 301–302, which follows the published edition of Franchère's narrative.

   3. Alfred Seton, *Astorian Adventure: The Journal of Alfred Seton, 1811–1813*, ed. Robert F. Jones (New York: Fordham University Press, 1993); and Robert F. Jones, ed., *Annals of Astoria: The Headquarters Log of the Pacific Fur Company on the Columbia River, 1811–1813* (New York: Fordham University Press, 1999). Robert Carlton Clark makes no mention of the Stuart or McKenzie parties in *History of the Willamette Valley*, vol. 1 (Chicago: S. J. Clarke Co., 1929), 135–136.

   4. Philip Ashton Rollins, ed., *The Discovery of the Oregon Trail: Robert Stuart's Narratives of His Overland Trip Eastward from Astoria 1812–13* (1935; reprint, Lincoln: University of Nebraska Presss, 1995); Jesse S. Douglas, ed., "Matthews' Adventures on the Columbia: A Pacific Fur Company Document," *OHQ* 40:2 (June 1939): 105–148. John Langdon Sullivan, a civil engineer with the U.S. government's Board of Engineers for Internal Improvements, recorded William Wallace Matthew's memoirs in 1824. Matthew's memoirs, as recorded by Sullivan, are contained in the Papers of the Board of Engineers for Internal Improvements for 1824–1826 at the National Archives in Washington, D.C. Sullivan used Matthews's memoirs to prepare an undelivered report addressed to Secretary of War John C. Calhoun, dated December 24, 1824.

   5. Franchère, *Journal of a Voyage*, 96.

   6. Jones, *Annals of Astoria*, 62.

   7. Jones, *Annals of Astoria*, 65.

   8. Jones, *Annals of Astoria*, 69.

   9. Robert Stuart's narratives were the journal of his overland return to Montreal, which begins on June 29, 1812, and his travel memoranda, written sometime after his return to the East. Philip Ashton Rollins discusses the differences between the two narratives in his

foreword to Stuart, cvii–cxii. Rollins included the additional passages from the later travel memoranda in *The Discovery of the Oregon Trail*. Kenneth A. Spaulding edited a separate edition of the travel memoranda: *On the Oregon Trail: Robert Stuart's Journey of Discovery* (Norman: University of Oklahoma Press, 1953).

10. Rollins, ed., *The Discovery of the Oregon Trail*, 32.

11. Seton, *Astorian Adventure*, 121.

12. Alexander Ross, *Adventures of the First Settlers on the Oregon or Columbia River, 1810–1813*, with a new introduction by William G. Robbins (1904; reprint, Corvallis: Oregon State University Press, 2000), 229.

13. Rollins, ed., *The Discovery of the Oregon Trail*, 33.

14. H. Lloyd Keith, "Adventure Narrative as History: Alexander Ross and *The Fur Hunters of the Far West*," Paper presented before the Pacific Northwest History Conference, April 25–26, 2004; H. Lloyd Keith, "The Historical Fictions of Ross Cox," unpublished manuscript, November 1986.

15. I. S. Maclaren, "Paul Kane and the Authorship of *A Wandering Artist*," in *From Rupert's Land to Canada*, ed. Theodore Binnema, Gerhard J. Ens, and R.C. Macleod (Edmonton: University of Alberta Press, 2001), 225–243. See also Percy G. Adams's classic study of European travel literature, *Travelers and Travel Liars, 1660–1800*, 2nd ed. (New York: Dover Publications, 1980).

16. Keith, "Adventure Narrative as History," 12; Keith, "The Historical Fictions of Ross Cox," 18–19.

17. Ross Cox, *The Columbia River*, ed. Edgar I. Stewart and Jane R. Stewart (Norman: University of Oklahoma Press, 1957); Alexander Ross, *Adventures of the First Settlers*; Alexander Ross, *The Fur Hunters of the Far West*, ed. Kenneth A. Spaulding (Norman: University of Oklahoma Press, 1956).

18. L. J. Burpee, "A Forgotten Adventure of the Fur Trade," *Queen's Quarterly* 26:4 (April–June 1919): 365; Cecil W. Mackenzie, *Donald Mackenzie: King of the Northwest* (Los Angeles: Ivan Beach, 1937); Ernest Cawcroft, "Donald Mackenzie: King of the Northwest," *Canadian Magazine* 50 (Nov. 1917–April 1918): 347.

Bibliography

Primary Sources

ARCHIVAL MANUSCRIPTS

Archdiocese of Portland in Oregon Archives, Portland, Oregon. Francis N. Blanchet Collection.

Archives of the Archdiocese of Quebec. Joseph Provencher Letters.

H. H. Bancroft Library, Berkeley, California:

Blanchet, Francis N. Catholic Missionaries of Oregon. P-A 5.

Crawford, Medorem. Missionaries and Their Works. P-A 19.

Ebberts, George W. A Trapper's Life in the Rocky Mountains of Oregon from 1828 to 1839. P-A 28.

Grim, J. W. J. W. Grim's Narrative. P-A 38.

Holman, Joseph. The Peoria Party. P-A 41.

Matthieu, F. X. Refugee, Trapper, Settler. P-A 49.

Minto, John. Early Days of Oregon. P-A 50.

Minto, Martha Anna (Morrison). Female Pioneering in Oregon. P-A 51.

Oglesby, W. W. The Calapooyas Indians. P-A 82.

Parrish, Josiah L. Anecdotes of Intercourse with the Indians. P-A 59.

Roberts, George B. Recollections. P-A 83.

Waldo, Daniel. Critiques. P-A 74.

White, Elijah. Government and Emigration to Oregon. P-A 76.

Wilson, Elizabeth (Miller). Oregon Sketches. P-A 55.

Hudson's Bay Company Archives, Winnipeg, Manitoba.

B.76. Fort George (Columbia) Records.

B.223. Fort Vancouver Records.

F.3 to F.5. Northwest Company Records.

National Archives of Canada, Ottawa, Ontario. Memoranda Book of James Keith, 1811–1821. James Keith Papers. A-676, A-2.

National Archives of the United States, Washington, D.C. Bureau of Indian Affairs. Letters Received by the Office of Indian Affairs, 1824–81. Oregon Superintendency, 1842–1880. Record Group 75. [microfilm roll 607]

Oregon Historical Society Research Library, Portland:
  Autobiography of J. Henry Brown. Mss. 1002.
  John Ball Papers. Mss. 195.
  Amos Cooke Papers. Mss. 1223.
  Philip Foster Papers. Mss. 996.
  Joseph Lane Papers. Mss. 1146.
  Daniel Lee Papers. Mss. 1211.
  Jason Lee Papers. Mss. 1212.
  Robert Newell Papers. Mss. 1197.
  T. N. Ramsdell. Indians of Oregon. Mss. 853.
  Cyrus Shepard Correspondence. Mss. 1219.
  Thurston Family Papers. Mss. 379.
  Willamette Cattle Records. Mss. 500.
  Willamette Settlers' Letters to the Bishop of Juliopolis. Mss. 83.
Oregon State Archives, Salem:
  Bill to Allow Half-Breeds to Become Citizens, 1856. H.B. 28. Oregon Territorial Legislative Assembly Records.
  Cayuse War Bonds.
  Marion County Naturalization Records.
  Marion County Probate Case Files.
  Oregon Legislators and Staff Guide. Oregon Legislative Records. http:/arceweb.sos
  .state.or.us.
Sisters of Notre Dame de Namur, California Province Archives, Notre Dame de Namur University, Belmont, California. List of First and Second Groups of Sisters of Notre Dame de Namur to Oregon, 1843–1847.

PUBLISHED PRIMARY SOURCES: NEWSPAPERS

Oregon Herald
Oregon Spectator
Oregon Statesman

PUBLISHED PRIMARY SOURCES: BOOKS

Allen, A. J., comp. *Ten Years in Oregon: Travels and Adventures of Doctor E. White and Lady West of the Rocky Mountains.* Ithaca, NY: Mack, Andrus, & Co., 1848.
Applegate, Jesse A. *A Day with the Cow Column in 1843.* 1934. Reprint. Fairfield, WA: Ye Galleon Press, 1990.
Bailey, Margaret Jewett. *The Grains or Passages in the Life of Ruth Rover.* Edited by Evelyn Leasher and Robert J. Frank. Corvallis: Oregon State University Press, 1986.
Ball, John. *Autobiography.* Compiled by Kate Ball Powers and Flora Ball Hopkins. Glendale, CA: Arthur H. Clark Co., 1925.
———. *Born to Wander: Autobiography of John Ball, 1794–1884.* Compiled by Kate Ball

Powers and Flora Ball Hopkins. Annotated with a new introduction by Gary Burbridge. Grand Rapids, MI: Grand Rapids Historical Commission, 1994.

Beattie, Judith Hudson, and Helen M. Buss, eds. *Undelivered Letters to Hudson's Bay Company Men on the Northwest Coast of North America, 1830–1857*. Vancouver: UBC Press, 2003.

Beaver, Herbert. *Reports and Letters of Herbert Beaver*. Edited by Thomas E. Jessett. Portland: Champoeg Press, 1959.

Blanchet, Francis Norbert. *Historical Sketches of the Catholic Church in Oregon*. Edited by Edward Kowrach. Fairfield, WA: Ye Galleon Press, 1983.

Bolduc, Jean Baptiste Zacharie. *Mission of the Columbia*. Edited and translated by Edward J. Kowrach. Fairfield, WA: Ye Galleon Press, 1979.

Brouillet, J. B. A. *Protestantism in Oregon: Account of the Murder of Dr. Whitman and the Ungrateful Calumnies of H. H. Spalding, Protestant Missionary*. New York: M. T. Cozens, 1853.

Browning, Elsie Y., trans. *1850 Federal Census, Oregon Territory*. Lebanon, OR: End of the Trail Researchers, 1970.

Carey, Charles Henry. *The Oregon Constitution and Proceedings of the Debates of the Constitutional Convention of 1857*. Portland: Oregon Historical Society Press, 1984.

Carver, Jonathan. *The Journals of Jonathan Carver and Related Documents, 1766–1770*. St. Paul: Minnesota Historical Society, 1976.

———. *Travels through the Interior Parts of North America in the Years 1766, 1767, and 1768*. 1778. Reprint. Minneapolis: Ross and Haines, 1956.

Cox, Ross. *The Columbia River*. Edited by Edgar I. Stewart and Jane R. Stewart. Norman: University of Oklahoma Press, 1957.

Davies, K. G., and A. M. Johnson, eds. *Peter Skene Ogden's Snake Country Journal, 1826–27*. With an introduction by Dorothy O. Johansen. London: Hudson's Bay Record Society, 1961.

Deady, Matthew P., comp. *The Organic and Other Laws of Oregon, 1845–1864*. Portland: Henry L. Pittock, 1866.

De Smet, Pierre-Jean. *Oregon Mission and Travels over the Rocky Mountains, 1845–46*. 1847. Reprint: Fairfield, WA: Ye Galleon Press, 1978.

Douglas, David. *Journal Kept by David Douglas during his Travels in North America, 1823–1827*. 1914. Reprint. New York: Antiquarian Press, 1959.

———. *The Oregon Journals of David Douglas*. 2 vols. Edited by David Lavender. Ashland: Oregon Book Society, 1972.

Drury, Merrill, ed. *The Mountains We Have Crossed: Diaries and Letters of the Oregon Mission, 1838*. 1966. Reprint. Lincoln: University of Nebraska Press, 1999.

DuFlot de Mofras, Eugène. *Duflot de Mofras' Travels on the Pacific Coast*. 2 vols. Translated and edited by Marguerite Eyer Wilbur. Santa Ana, CA: Fine Arts Press, 1937.

———. *Exploration du Territoire de l'Orégon, des Californies, et de la Mer Vermeille*. Paris: Arthus Bertrand, 1844.

Dunn, John. *The Oregon Territory and the British North American Fur Trade*. Philadelphia: G. B: Zieber and Co., 1845.

Edwards, Philip L. *The Diary of Philip Leget Edwards.* San Francisco: Grabhorn Press, 1932.

——. *Sketch of the Oregon Territory.* 1842. Reprint. Fairfield, WA: Ye Galleon Press, 1971.

Ermatinger, Francis. *The Fur Trade Letters of Francis Ermantinger, 1818–1853.* Edited by Lois McDonald. Glendale, CA: Arthur H. Clark, 1980.

Farnham, Thomas J. *Travels in the Great Western Prairies.* Edited by Reuben Gold Thwaites. 2 vols. Cleveland, OH: Arthur H. Clark, 1906.

Franchère, Gabriel. *Journal of a Voyage on the North West Coast of North America during the Years 1811, 1812, 1813.* Edited by W. Kaye Lamb. Translated by Wessie Tipping Lamb. Toronto: Champlain Society, 1969.

Genealogical Material in Oregon Provisional Land Claims: Abstracted from Applications, vols. 1–8, *1845–1849.* Portland: Genealogical Forum of Portland, Oregon, 1982.

Gray, William H. *A History of Oregon, 1792–1849.* Portland: Harris & Holman, 1870.

Greenhow, Robert. *The History of Oregon and California.* 2nd ed. Boston: Charles C. Little & James Brown, 1845.

Grover, La Fayette, ed. *The Oregon Archives.* Salem: Asahel Bush, 1852.

Hafen, LeRoy R., and Ann W. Hafen, eds. *To the Rockies and Oregon, 1839–42.* Glendale, CA: Arthur H. Clark, 1955.

Harmon, Daniel Williams. *Sixteen Years in the Indian Country: The Journal of Daniel Williams Harmon, 1800–1816.* Edited by W. Kaye Lamb. Toronto: Macmillan, 1957.

Henry, Alexander. *Journal of Alexander Henry the Younger, 1799–1814.* 2 vols. Edited by Barry Gough. Toronto: Champlain Society, 1988 and 1992.

Hines, Gustavus. *Oregon: Its History, Condition, and Prospects.* 1851. Reprint. New York: Arno Press, 1973.

Howay, Frederic H., ed. *Voyages of the "Columbia" to the Northwest Coast, 1787–1790 and 1790–1793.* 1941. Reprint. Portland: Oregon Historical Society, 1990.

Hulbert, Archer B., and Dorothy P. Hulbert, eds. Overland to the Pacific series, vol. 5: *The Oregon Crusade: Across Land and Sea to Oregon.* Denver: Denver Public Library, 1935.

Irving, Washington. *Astoria: Or, Anecdotes of an Enterprise beyond the Rocky Mountains.* Edited by Edgeley W. Todd. Norman: University of Oklahoma Press, 1964.

Jacobs, Melville, ed. *Clackamas Chinook Texts.* 2 vols. Bloomington: Indiana University Research Center in Anthropology, Folklore, and Linguistics/*International Journal of American Linguistics,* 1958–1959.

——. *Kalapuya Texts.* University of Washington Texts in Anthropology, vol. 11. Seattle: University of Washington, 1945.

Jones, Robert F., ed. *Annals of Astoria: The Headquarters Log of the Pacific Fur Company on the Columbia River, 1811–1813.* New York: Fordham University Press, 1999.

Journal of the House of Representatives of the Territory of Oregon: During the Eighth Regular Session, 1856–57. Salem: Asahel Bush, Territorial Printer, 1857.

Journal of the House of Representatives of the Territory of Oregon: During the Tenth Regular Session, 1858–59. Salem: Asahel Bush, Territorial Printer, 1859.

Landerholm Carl, ed. and trans. *Notices and Voyages of the Famed Quebec Mission to the Pacific Northwest.* Portland: Oregon Historical Society, 1956.

Lansing, Ronald B. *Juggernaut: The Whitman Massacre Trial, 1850.* Pasadena, CA: Ninth Judicial Circuit Historical Society, 1993.

Lee, Daniel, and Joseph Frost. *Ten Years in Oregon.* 1844. Reprint. Fairfield, WA: Ye Galleon Press, 1968.

Lewis, Meriwether, and William Clark. *The Lewis and Clark Expedition.* Edited by Nicholas Biddle and Paul Allen. Philadelphia: Lippincott, 1814.

Maclachlan, Morag, ed. *The Fort Langley Journals.* Vancouver, BC: UBC Press, 1998.

McLoughlin, John. *Letters of Dr. John McLoughlin Written at Fort Vancouver, 1829–1832.* Edited by Burt Brown Barker. Portland: Binfords & Mort/Oregon Historical Society, 1948.

———. *The Letters of John McLoughlin from Fort Vancouver.* 3 vols. Edited by E. E. Rich. London: Hudson's Bay Record Society, 1941–1944.

Merk, Frederick, ed. *Fur Trade and Empire: George Simpson's Journal.* Rev. ed. Cambridge, MA: Harvard University Press, 1968.

Moulton, Gary E., ed. *The Journals of Lewis and Clark.* Vols. 5, 6, and 7. Lincoln: University of Nebraska Press, 1988–1991.

Mudge, Z. A. *The Missionary Teacher: A Memoir of Cyrus Shepard.* New York: Carlton and Porter, 1848.

Munnick, Harriet, ed. *Catholic Church Records of the Pacific Northwest.* 7 vols. Portland: Binford & Mort, 1972–1989.

Newell, Robert. *Robert Newell's Memoranda.* Edited by Dorothy Johansen. Portland, OR: Champoeg Press, 1959.

Notice sur la territorire et sur la mission de l'Orégon suivie de quelques lettres des soeurs de Notre-Dame établies à Saint Paul du Wallamette. Brussels: Bureau de publications de la Bibliotèque d'éducation, 1847.

Nunis, Doyce B., ed. *The Hudson's Bay Company's First Fur Brigade to the Sacramento Valley: Alexander McLeod's 1829 Hunt.* Fair Oak, CA: Sacramento Book Collectors Club, 1968.

Ogden, Peter Skene. *Traits of American Indian Life.* 1933. Reprint. Fairfield, WA: Ye Galleon Press, 1998.

Oregon Supreme Court Record: An Original Printing of Cases and Other Matter Contained in a Manuscript Label Book I, 1844–1848. Portland, OR: Stevens-Nevens Law Publishing Co., 1938.

Parker, Samuel. *Journal of an Exploring Tour beyond the Rocky Mountains.* 1842. Reprint. 3rd ed. With a new introduction by Larry R. Jones. Moscow: University of Idaho Press, 1990.

Parkman, Francis. *The Oregon Trail.* 1849. Reprint, edited with an introduction by Bernard Rosenthal. New York: Oxford University Press, 1996.

Powell, Fred Wilbur, ed. *Hall J. Kelley on Oregon.* Princeton, NJ: Princeton University Press, 1932.

Ramsey, Jarold, ed. *Coyote Was Going There: Indian Literature of the Oregon Country.* Seattle: University of Washington Press, 1977.

Ray, Verne. *Lower Chinook Ethnographic Notes.* University of Washington Publications in Anthropology, vol. 7, no. 2. Seattle: University of Washington, 1938.

Rollins, Philip Ashton, ed. *The Discovery of the Oregon Trail: Robert Stuart's Narratives of His Overland Trip Eastward from Astoria, 1812–13*. 1935. Reprint. Lincoln: University of Nebraska Press, 1995.

Ross, Alexander. *Adventures of the First Settlers on the Oregon or Columbia River, 1810–1813*. 1904. Reprint, with a new introduction by William G. Robbins. Corvallis: Oregon State University Press, 2000.

———. *The Fur Hunters of the Far West*. Edited by Kenneth A. Spaulding. Norman: University of Oklahoma Press, 1956.

Saint-Amant, M. [Pierre Charles Fournier] de. *Voyages en Californie et dans l'Orégon*. Paris: Librairie L. Maison, 1854.

Seton, Alfred. *Astorian Adventure: The Journal of Alfred Seton, 1811–1813*. Edited by Robert F. Jones. New York: Fordham University Press, 1993.

Shepard, Cyrus. *Diary of Cyrus Shepard, March 4, 1834–Dec. 20, 1835*. Edited by Gerry Gileman. Vancouver, WA: Clark County Genealogical Society, 1986.

Simpson, George. *An Overland Journey Round the World During the Years 1841 and 1842*. Philadelphia: Lea and Blanchard, 1847.

Sweet, William Warren. *Religion on the American Frontier, 1793–1840*. Vol. 4: *The Methodists: A Collection of Source Materials*. Chicago: University of Chicago Press, 1946.

Thompson, David. *David Thompson's Narrative, 1784–1812*. Edited by Richard Glover. Toronto: Champlain Society, 1962.

Tolmie, William Fraser. *The Journals of William Fraser Tolmie, Physician and Fur Trader*. Vancouver, BC: Mitchell Press, 1963.

Townsend, John Kirk. *Narrative of a Journey across the Rocky Mountains to the Columbia River*. Reprinted with an introduction and annotations by George A. Jobnek. 1839. Reprint. Corvallis: Oregon State University Press, 1999.

Wallace, W. Stewart, ed. *Documents Relating to the North West Company*. Toronto: Champlain Society, 1934.

Wilkes, Charles. *The Diary of Charles Wilkes in the Pacific Northwest*. Edited by Edmond S. Meany. Seattle: University of Washington Press, 1926.

———. *Narrative of the United States Exploring Expedition during the Years 1838, 1839, 1840, 1841, 1842*. Vols. 1, 4, and 5. Philadelphia: Lea and Blanchard, 1845.

Work, John. *Fur Brigade to the Bonaventura: John Work's California Expedition, 1832–1833*. Edited by Alice Maloney. San Francisco: California Historical Society, 1945.

———. *The Snake Expedition of 1830–1831: John Work's Field Journal*. Edited by Francis D. Haines. Norman: University of Oklahoma Press, 1971.

Wyeth, Nathaniel. *The Correspondence and Journals of Nathaniel J. Wyeth*. Edited by F. G. Young. 1899. Reprint. New York: Arno Press, 1973.

———. *The Journals of Captain Nathaniel J. Wyeth's Expedition to the Oregon Country, 1831–1836*. Edited by Don Johnson. Fairfield, WA: Ye Galleon Press, 1984.

Vancouver, George. *Voyage of George Vancouver, 1791–1795*. Edited by W. Kaye Lamb. Vol. 2. London: Hakluyt Society, 1984.

PUBLISHED PRIMARY SOURCES: ARTICLES

Bagley, Clarence, ed. "Letter by Daniel H. Lownsdale to Samuel R. Thurston, First Territorial Delegate from Oregon To Congress." *Oregon Historical Quarterly* 14:3 (September 1913): 213–249.

Ball, John. "Across the Continent Seventy Years Ago." *Oregon Historical Quarterly* 3:1 (March 1902): 82–106.

———. "Letters of John Ball, 1832–33." Edited by Milo M. Quaife. *Mississippi Valley Historical Review* 5: 4 (March 1919): 450–468.

Barry, J. Neilson, ed. "Documents: Primary Sources in Early Government [in Oregon]. *Washington Historical Quarterly* 15:2 (April 1934): 139–147.

Beaver, Herbert. "Experiences of a Chaplain at Fort Vancouver, 1836–1838." Edited by R. C. Clark. *Oregon Historical Quarterly* 39:1 (March 1938): 22–38.

Bridgewater, Dorothy Wildes, ed. "John Jacob Aster [*sic*] Relative to His Settlement on the Columbia River." *Yale University Library Gazette* 24:2 (October 1949): 47–69.

Brosnan, Cornelius, ed. "The Oregon Memorial of 1838." *Oregon Historical Quarterly* 39:1 (March 1933): 68–77.

Carey, Charles Henry, ed. "The Mission Record Book of the Methodist Episcopal Church, Willamette Station, Oregon Territory, Commenced 1834," *Oregon Historical Quarterly* 23:3 (September 1922): 230–266.

Dart, Anson. "Annual Report of the Oregon Superintendency of Indian Affairs, 1851." *Sen. Ex. Doc.* 1, 32nd Cong., 1 Sess.

Douglas, James. "The James Douglas Report on the 'Beaver Affair.'" Edited by W. Kaye Lamb. *Oregon Historical Quarterly* 47:1 (March 1946): 16–28.

Douglas, Jesse, ed. "Matthews' Adventures on the Columbia: A Pacific Fur Company Document." *Oregon Historical Quarterly* 40:2 (June 1939): 105–148.

Duniway, David C., and Neil R. Riggs, eds. "The Oregon Archives." *Oregon Historical Quarterly* 60:2 (July 1959): 210–290.

Elliot, T. C., ed. "Letter of Donald Mackenzie to Wilson Price Hunt" [April 20, 1821]. *Oregon Historical Quarterly* 43:1 (March 1942): 10–13.

———. "Peter Skene Ogden Journals: Snake Expedition, 1825–1826." *Oregon Historical Quarterly* 10:4 (December 1909): 331–365.

———. "Sale of Astoria, 1813." *Oregon Historical Quarterly* 33:1 (March 1932): 45–50.

Frien, P. J., trans. "Address" [of the Canadian Settlers of the Willamette Valley]. *Oregon Historical Quarterly* 13:4 (December 1912): 338–343.

Frost, John H. "The Journal of John H. Frost." Edited by Nellie B. Pipes. *Oregon Historical Quarterly* 35:1–4 (1934): 50–73, 137–167, 235–262, 348–375.

Gatke, Robert Moulton, ed. "A Document of Missionary History, 1833–1834" [Part 1]. *Oregon Historical Quarterly* 36:1 (March 1935): 71–93.

———. "A Document of Missionary History, 1833–1834" [Part 2]. *Oregon Historical Quarterly* 36:2 (June 1935): 163–181.

Howison, Neil M. "Report of Lieutenant Neil M. Howison on Oregon, 1846." *Oregon Historical Quarterly* 14:1 (March 1913): 1–60.

Judson, Katharine B., ed. "John McLoughlin's Last Letter to the Hudson's Bay Company as Chief Factor in Charge of Fort Vancouver, 1845." *American Historical Review* 21:1 (October 1915): 104–134.

Lee, Jason. "Diary of Rev. Jason Lee." *Oregon Historical Quarterly* 17:2–4 (1917): 116–146, 240–266, 397–429.

Lyman, H. S., ed. "Reminiscences of F. X. Matthieu." *Oregon Historical Quarterly* 1:1 (March 1900): 73–104.

———. "Reminiscences of Hugh Cosgrove." *Oregon Historical Quarterly* 1 (March–December 1990): 267–268.

———. "Reminiscences of Louis Labonte." *Oregon Historical Quarterly* 1:2 (June 1900): 169–188.

McLoughlin, John. "Copy of a Document Found among the Private Papers of the late Dr. John McLoughlin." *Transactions of the Oregon Pioneers Association* 8 (1880): 46–55.

———. "Document: A Narrative of John McLoughlin." *Oregon Historical Quarterly* 1:2 (June 1900): 198–199.

———. "Documentary: Letters of Dr. John McLoughlin." Edited by T. C. Elliot. *Oregon Historical Quarterly* 23:4 (December 1922): 365–371.

———. "Letter, March 1, 1832." *Washington Historical Quarterly* 2:1 (1908): 40–41.

Miller, John F. "Grand Ronde Indian Agent's Annual Report." In *Annual Report of the Commissioner of Indian Affairs for the Year 1859.* Washington: Government Printing Office, 1859, 429–432.

"Notes and Documents: The Appeal of the North West Company to the British Government to Forestall John Jacob Astor's Columbia Enterprise." *Canadian Historical Review* 17 (September 1936): 301–306.

Phelps, William Dane. "Solid Men of Boston." In *Fur Traders from New England: The Boston Men in the North Pacific, 1787–1800.* Edited by Briton C. Busch and Barry M. Gough. Spokane, WA: Arthur H. Clark Company, 1997, 52–73.

Rees, Willard. "Annual Address, [1879]." *Transactions of the Oregon Pioneer Association* 7 (1880), 18–31.

Roberts, George. "Letters to Mrs. F. F. Victor." *Oregon Historical Quarterly* 63:2–3 (June–September 1962): 175–241.

Schafer, Joseph, ed. "Documents Relative to the Warre and Vavasour's Military Reconnaissance in Oregon, 1845–1846." *Oregon Historical Quarterly* 10:1 (1909): 1–99.

Scott, Leslie, ed. "First Taxpayers in Oregon, 1844." *Oregon Historical Quarterly* 31:1 (March 1930): 11–24.

Simpson, George. "Letters of Sir George Simpson." Edited by Joseph Schafer. *American Historical Review* 14:1 (October 1908): 70–94.

Slacum, William A. "Slacum's Report on Oregon, 1836–37." *Oregon Historical Quarterly* 13:2 (June 1912), 197–198.

Walker, Courtney. "Sketch of Ewing Young." *Transactions of the Oregon Pioneer Association* 8 (1880): 56–58.

Wilkes, Charles. "Report on the Territory of Oregon." *Oregon Historical Quarterly* 12:3 (September 1911): 269–299.

Work, John. "John Work's Journey from Fort Vancouver to Umpqua River and Return in 1834." Edited by Leslie M. Scott. *Oregon Historical Quarterly* 24:3 (September 1923): 238–268.

———. "Journal of John Work, November and December, 1824." Edited by T. C. Elliott. *Washington Historical Quarterly* 3 (October 1908–October 1912): 198–228.

Young, Frederick G., ed. "Ewing Young and His Estate." *Oregon Historical Quarterly* 21:3 (September 1920): 171–315.

Secondary Sources

PUBLISHED SECONDARY SOURCES: BOOKS

Ackerknecht, Erwin W. *Malaria in the Upper Mississippi Valley, 1760–1900.* Supplement to the *Bulletin of the History of Medicine,* vol. 4. Edited by Henry E. Sigerist. Baltimore: Johns Hopkins University Press, 1945.

Adams, Percy G. *Travelers and Travel Liars, 1660–1800.* 2nd ed. New York: Dover Publications, 1980.

Ahlstrom, Sydney. *A Religious History of the American People.* New Haven, CT: Yale University Press, 1972.

Aikens, C. Melvin, Thomas J. Connolly, and Dennis L. Jenkins. *Oregon Archaeology.* Corvallis: Oregon State University Press, 2011.

Andrews, Dee E. *The Methodists in Revolutionary America, 1760–1800: The Shaping of Evangelical Culture.* Princeton, NJ: Princeton University Press, 2000.

Bagley, Will. *So Rugged and Mountainous: Blazing Trails to Oregon and California, 1812–1848.* Norman: University of Oklahoma Press, 2010.

Baldwin, Ewart M., Elizabeth L. Orr, and William N. Orr. *Geology of Oregon.* 4th ed. Dubuque, IA: Kendall/Hunt, 1992.

Bancroft, H. H. *History of the Northwest Coast.* 2 vols. San Francisco: A. L. Bancroft & Co., 1884.

———. *History of Oregon.* 2 vols. San Francisco: A. L. Bancroft & Co., 1886.

Barman, Jean. *French Canadians, Furs, and Indigenous Women in the Making of the Pacific Northwest.* Vancouver, BC: UBC Press, 2014.

———. *The West Beyond the West: A History of British Columbia.* Rev. ed. Toronto: University of Toronto Press, 1996.

Barney, William L. *The Passage of the Republic: An Interdisciplinary History of Nineteenth-Century America.* Lexington, MA: D. C. Heath and Co., 1987.

Barry, J. Neilson. *The French Canadian Pioneers of the Willamette Valley.* Portland, OR: Catholic Sentinel Press, 1933.

Basson, Lauren L. *White Enough to Be American: Race Mixing, Indigenous People, and the Boundaries of State and Nation.* Chapel Hill: University of North Carolina Press, 2008.

Beckham, Stephen Dow. *The Indians of Western Oregon: This Land Was Theirs.* Coos Bay, OR: Arago Press, 1977.

————. *Requiem for a People: The Rogue Indians and the Frontiersmen.* Coos Bay, OR: Arago Press, 1971.

Berkhofer, Robert J. *Salvation and the Savage: An Analysis of Protestant Missions and American Indian Responses, 1787–1862.* Lexington: University Press of Kentucky, 1965.

Berwanger, Eugene H. *The Frontier against Slavery: Western Anti-Negro Prejudice and the Slavery Extension Controversy.* Urbana: University of Illinois Press, 1967.

Billington, Ray Allen. *The Protestant Crusade, 1880–1860: A Study of the Origins of American Nativism.* 1938. Reprint. Chicago: Quadrangle Books, 1964.

Billington, Ray Allen, and Martin Ridge. *Westward Expansion: A History of the American Frontier.* New York: Macmillan, 1982.

Boag, Peter G. *Environment and Experience: Settlement Culture in Nineteenth-Century Oregon.* Berkeley: University of California Press, 1992.

Bouchard, Gérard. *Quelques arpents d'Amérique: Population, économie, famille au Saguenay, 1838–1971.* Montreal: Boréal, 1996.

Bourke, Paul, and Donald DeBats. *Washington County: Politics and Community in Antebellum America.* Baltimore: Johns Hopkins University Press, 1995.

Bowen, William. *Migration and Settlement on the Oregon Frontier.* Seattle: University of Washington Press, 1978.

Boyd, Robert. *The Coming of the Spirit Pestilence: Introduced Infectious Disease and Population Decline among Northwest Coast Indians, 1774–1874.* Seattle: University of Washington Press, 1999.

Brandt, Patricia, and Lillian A. Pereyra. *Adapting in Eden: Oregon's Catholic Minority, 1838–1986.* Pullman: Washington State University Press, 2002.

Brosnan, Cornelius. *Jason Lee: Prophet of the New Oregon.* New York: Macmillan, 1932.

Brown, Jennifer S. H. *Strangers in Blood: Fur Trade Company Families in Indian Country.* Vancouver: University of British Columbia Press, 1980.

Bunting, Robert. *The Pacific Raincoast: Environment and Culture in an American Eden, 1778–1900.* Lawrence: University Press of Kansas, 1997.

Burely, Edith I. *Servants of the Honourable Company: Work, Discipline, and Conflict in the Hudson's Bay Company, 1770–1870.* Toronto: Oxford University Press, 1997.

Butler, Anne. *Across God's Frontiers: Catholic Sisters in the American West, 1850–1920.* Chapel Hill: University of North Carolina Press, 2012.

Cebula, Larry. *Plateau Indians and the Quest for Spiritual Power, 1700–1850.* Lincoln: University of Nebraska Press, 2003.

Clark, Malcolm. *Eden Seekers: The Settlement of Oregon, 1818–1862.* Boston: Houghton Mifflin, 1981.

Clarke, S. A. *Pioneer Days of Oregon History.* 2 vols. Portland, OR: J. K. Gill Co., 1905.

Cline, Gloria Griffen. *Peter Skene Ogden and the HBC.* Norman: University of Oklahoma Press, 1974.

Coates, Colin M. *The Metamorphoses of Landscape and Community in Early Quebec.* Montreal: McGill-Queen's University Press, 2000.

Confederated Tribes of the Grand Ronde. *Chinuk Wawa / kakwa nsayka ulman-tilixam laska mnk-kemeks nsayka / As Our Elders Teach Us to Speak It.* The Chinuk Wawa

Dictionary Project. Grand Ronde, OR: Confederate Tribes of the Grand Ronde, 2012.

Cott, Nancy. *The Bonds of Womanhood: "Women's Sphere" in New England, 1780–1835.* 2nd ed. New Haven, CT: Yale University Press, 1997.

Crosby, Alfred W. *The Columbian Exchange: Biological Consequences of 1492.* Westport, CT: Westview Press, 1972.

Cross, Whitney E. *The Burned-Over District: The Social and Intellectual History of Enthusiastic Religion in Western New York, 1800–1850.* Ithaca, NY: Cornell University Press, 1950.

Curtis, Sarah A. *Civilizing Habits: Women Missionaries and the Revival of French Empire.* New York: Oxford University Press, 2010.

Dechêne, Louise. *Habitants and Merchants in Seventeenth-Century Montreal.* Montreal: McGill-Queen's University Press, 1992.

Dichtl, John R. *Frontiers of Faith: Bringing Catholicism to the West in the Early Republic.* Lexington: University Press of Kentucky, 2008.

Dippie, Brian. *The Vanishing American: White Attitudes and U.S. Indian Policy.* Lawrence: University Press of Kansas, 1982.

Dobyns, Henry F. *Their Numbers Become Thinned: Native American Population Dynamics in Eastern North America.* Knoxville: University of Tennessee Press, 1983.

Donald, Leland. *Aboriginal Slavery on the Northwest Coast of North America.* Berkeley: University of California Press, 1997.

Douthit, Nathan. *Uncertain Encounters: Indians and Whites at Peace and War in Southern Oregon, 1820s–1860s.* Corvallis: Oregon State University Press, 2002.

Ekberg, Carl J. *French Roots in the Illinois Country: The Mississippi Frontier in Colonial Times.* Urbana: University of Illinois Press, 1998.

Ens, Gerhard J. *Homeland to Hinterland: The Changing Worlds of the Red River Metis in the Nineteenth Century.* Toronto: University of Toronto Press, 1996.

Faragher, John Mack. *Sugar Creek: Life on the Illinois Prairie.* New Haven, CT: Yale University Press, 1986.

Foner, Eric. *The Story of American Freedom.* New York: W. W. Norton, 1998.

Foster, Martha Harroun. *We Know Who We Are: Métis Identity in a Montana Community.* Norman: University of Oklahoma Press, 2006.

Franchot, Jenny. *Roads to Rome: The Antebellum Protestant Encounter with Catholicism.* Berkeley: University of California Press, 1994.

Franklin, Jerry F., and C. T. Dryness. *Natural Vegetation of Oregon and Washington.* 1973. Reprint. Corvallis: Oregon State University Press, 1988.

Furtwangler, Albert. *Bringing Indians to the Book.* Seattle: University of Washington Press, 2005.

Galbraith, John S. *The HBC as an Imperial Factor, 1821–1869.* Berkeley: University of California Press, 1957.

Gibbs, George. *Tribes of Western Washington and Northwest Oregon.* Vol 2. Contributions in North American Ethnology. Washington, D.C.: Government Printing Office, 1877.

Gibson, James. *Farming the Frontier: The Agricultural Opening of the Oregon Country, 1786–1846*. Seattle: University of Washington Press, 1985.

———. *The Lifeline of the Oregon Country: The Fraser-Columbia Brigade System, 1811–1847*. Vancouver: UBC Press, 1997.

———. *Otter Skins, Boston Ships, and China Goods: The Maritime Fur Trade on the Northwest Coast, 1785–1841*. Montreal: McGill-Queen's Press, 1992.

Gibson, Ralph. *A Social History of French Catholicism, 1789–1914*. New York: Routledge, 1989.

Gilbert, J. H. *Trade and Currency in Early Oregon: A Study in the Commercial and Monetary History of the Pacific Northwest*. 1907. Reprint. New York: AMS Press, 1967.

Goldring, Philip. *Papers on the Labour System of the Hudson's Bay Company, 1821–1900*. 3 vols. Ottawa: Canada Parks Service, 1979.

Greenberg, Amy S. *Manifest Destiny and American Territorial Expansion: A Brief History with Documents*. Boston: Bedford/St. Martin's Press, 2012.

Greer, Allan. *The Patriots and the People: The Rebellion of 1837 in Rural Lower Quebec*. Toronto: University of Toronto Press, 1993.

———. *Peasant, Lord, and Merchant: Rural Society in Three Quebec Parishes, 1740–1840*. Toronto: University of Toronto Press, 1985.

———. *The People of New France*. Toronto: University of Toronto Press, 1997.

Guard, B. Jennifer. *Wetland Plants of Oregon and Washington*. Vancouver, BC: Lone Pine Publishing, 1995.

Haeger, John Denis. *John Jacob Astor: Business and Finance in the Early Republic*. Detroit: Wayne State University Press, 1991.

Hafen, Le Roy R., ed. *French Fur Traders and Voyageurs in the American West*. With an introduction by Janet Lecompte. Spokane, WA: Arthur H. Clarke Company, 1995.

Haines, Francis. *The Nez Percés: Tribesmen of the Columbia Plateau*. Norman: University of Oklahoma Press, 1955.

Hanley, Philip M. *History of the Catholic Ladder*. Edited by Edward J. Kowrach. Fairfield, WA: Ye Galleon Press, 1993.

Hardy, Rene. *Contrôle social et mutation de la culture religieuse au Québec, 1830–1930*. Montreal: Boréal, 1999.

Harmon, Alexandra. *Indians in the Making: Ethnic Relations and Indian Identities around Puget Sound*. Berkeley: University of California Press, 1998.

Harris, Cole. *The Resettlement of British Columbia: Essays on Colonialism and Geographic Change*. Vancouver: UBC Press, 1997.

Harris, Richard Colebrook. *The Seigneurial System in Early Canada: A Geographical Study*. Madison/Quebec City: University of Wisconsin Press/Les Presses de l'Université Laval, 1966.

Hatch, Nathan O. *The Democratization of American Christianity*. New Haven, CT: Yale University Press, 1989.

Haynes, Sam W. *Unfinished Revolution: The Early American Republic in a British World*. Charlottesville: University of Virginia Press, 2010.

Hietala, Thomas. *Manifest Destiny: Anxious Aggrandizement in Late Jacksonian America*. Ithaca, NY: Cornell University Press, 1985.

Higham, C. L. *Noble, Wretched, & Redeemable: Protestant Missionaries to the Indians of Canada and The United States, 1820–1900*. Albuquerque: University of New Mexico Press, 2000.

Holmes, Kenneth L. *Ewing Young: Master Trapper*. Portland, OR: Binfords & Mort, 1967.

Horsman, Reginald. *The Frontier in the Formative Years, 1783–1815*. New York: Holt, Rinehart & Winston, 1970.

Hubert, Ollivier. *Sur la terre comme au ciel: La gestion des rites par l'Église Catholique au Québec, fin XVIIᵉ–mi XIXᵉ siècle*. Sainte Foy, QC: Les Presses de l'Université Laval, 2000.

Hunn Eugene S., with James Selam and Family. *Nch'I-Wána, "The Big River": Mid-Columbia River Indians and Their Land*. Seattle: University of Washington Press, 1990.

Hunn, Eugene S., and Nancy M. Williams. *Resource Managers: North American and Australian Hunter-Gathers*. Boulder, CO: Westview Press, 1982.

Hussey, John A. *Champoeg: Place of Transition, A Disputed History*. Portland: Oregon Historical Society/Oregon State Highway Commission, 1967.

Hyde, Anne. *Empires, Nations, and Families: A History of the North American Wests, 1800–1860*. Lincoln: University of Nebraska Press, 2011.

Ingersoll, Thomas N. *To Intermix with Our White Brothers: Indian Mixed Bloods in the United States from the Earliest Times to the Indian Removals*. Albuquerque: University of New Mexico Press, 2005.

Innis, Harold. *The Fur Trade in Canada*. Rev. ed. Toronto: University of Toronto Press, 1956; reprint: 1998.

Jackson, John C. *Children of the Fur Trade: Forgotten Métis of the Pacific Northwest*. 1995. Reprint. Corvallis: Oregon State University Press, 2007.

Jacob, Roland. *Votre nom est son histoire: Les noms de famille au Québec*. Montreal: Les Éditions de l'Homme, 2006.

Jeffrey, Julie Roy. *Converting the West: A Biography of Narcissa Whitman*. Norman: University of Oklahoma Press, 1991.

Johannsen, Robert W. *Frontier Politics on the Eve of the Civil War*. Seattle: University of Washington Press, 1955.

Johansen, Dorothy O., and Charles M. Gates. *Empire of the Columbia*. 2nd ed. New York: Harper & Row, 1967.

Johnson, David Alan, *Founding the Far West: California, Oregon, and Nevada, 1840–1890*. Berkeley: University of California Press, 1992.

Jones, David S. *Rationalizing Epidemics: Meanings and Use of American Indian Morality since 1600*. Cambridge, MA: Harvard University Press, 2004.

Josephy, Alvin M. *The Nez Perce Indians and the Opening of the Northwest*. 1965. Reprint. New York: Mariner Books, 1997.

Karson, Jennifer, ed. *As days go by / wiyáxayxt / wiyáa awn: Our History, Our Land, and Our People—The Cayuse, Umatilla, and Walla Walla*. Pendleton, OR: Tamástslikt Cultural Institute, 2006.

Keyssar, Alexander. *The Right to Vote: The Contested History of Democracy in the United States*, Rev. ed. New York: Basic Books, 2000.

Lamonde, Yvan. *Historial sociale des idées au Québec, 1760–1896*. Montreal: Fides, 2000.

Lang, H. O. *History of the Willamette Valley*. Portland, OR: Geo. H. Himes, 1885.

Lemieux, Lucien. *L'Établissment de la première province ecclésiatique au Canada, 1783–1844*. Montreal: Éditions Fides, 1968.

———. *Histoire du catholicisme québécois: Les XVIIIe et XIXe siècles*. Vol. 1: *Les années difficiles (1760–1839)*. Edited by Nive Voisine. Montreal: Éditions du Boreal, 1989.

Limerick, Patricia Nelson. *The Legacy of Conquest: The Unbroken Past of the American West*. New York: W. W. Norton, 1987.

Limerick, Patricia Nelson, Clyde A. Milner, and Charles E. Rankin, eds. *Trails: Toward a New Western History*. Lawrence: Kansas University Press, 1999.

Loewenberg, Robert J. *Equality on the Oregon Frontier: Jason Lee and the Methodist Mission, 1834–43*. Seattle: University of Washington Press, 1976.

Loy, William G., Stuart Allan, Aileen R. Buckley, and James E. Meacham. *Atlas of Oregon*. 2nd ed. Eugene: University of Oregon Press, 2001.

Lyons, Letitia Mary. *Francis Norbert Blanchet and the Founding of the Oregon Missions (1838–1848)*. Washington, D.C.: Catholic University of America Press, 1940.

Macdougall, Brenda. *One of the Family: Metis Culture in Nineteenth-Century Northwestern Saskatchewan*. Vancouver: UBC Press, 2010.

Mackenzie, Cecil W. *Donald Mackenzie: King of the Northwest*. Los Angeles: Ivan Beach, Jr., 1937.

Mackey, Harold. *The Kalapuyans: A Sourcebook on the Indians of the Willamette Valley*. 2nd ed. Salem: Mission Mill Museum Association with the cooperation of the Confederated Tribes of Grand Ronde, 2004.

Mackie, Richard Somerset. *Trading Beyond the Mountains: The British Fur Trade on the Pacific Slope, 1793–1843*. Vancouver: UBC Press, 1997.

Mann, Susan. *The Dream of a Nation: A Social and Intellectual History of Quebec*. Montreal: McGill-Queen's University Press, 1982.

Marshall, William I. *Acquisition of Oregon and the Long Suppressed Evidence about Marcus Whitman*. Vol. 1. Seattle: Lowman & Hanford Co., 1911.

McArthur, Lewis A. *Oregon Geographic Names*. 5th ed. Revised and enlarged by Lewis L. McArthur. Portland: Oregon Historical Society Press, 1982.

McDougall, Walter A. *Throes of Democracy: The American Civil War Era, 1829–1846*. New York: Harper Perennial, 2008.

McKamee, Sister Mary Dominica. *Willamette Interlude*. Palo Alto, CA: Pacific Books, 1959.

McKay, Harvey. *St. Paul, Oregon, 1830–1890*. Portland: Binford & Mort, 1980.

Meinig, D. W. *The Great Columbia Plain: A Historical Geography, 1805–1910*. 2nd ed. Seattle: University of Washington Press, 1995.

Miller, Christopher. *Prophetic Worlds: Indians and Whites on the Columbia Plateau*. 1985; reprint: Seattle: University of Washington Press, 2003.

Miller, Robert J. *Native America Discovered and Conquered: Thomas Jefferson, Lewis and Clark, and Manifest Destiny*. Lincoln: University of Nebraska Press, 2008.

Minor, Rick, Stephen Dow Beckham, Phyllis E. Lancefield-Stevens, and Kathryn Anne Toepel. *Cultural Resources Overview of BLM Lands in Northwestern Oregon:*

Archeology, Ethnography, and History. Edited by C. Melvin Aikens. Eugene: University of Oregon Department of Anthropology, 1980.

Montgomery, Richard G. *The White-Headed Eagle: John McLoughlin, Builder of an Empire*. 1931; reprint: Freeport, NH: Books for Librairies Press, 1971.

Moogk, Peter N. *La Nouvelle France: The Making of French Canada—A Cultural History*. East Lansing: Michigan State University Press, 2000.

Morice, A. G. *History of the Catholic Church in Western Canada: From Lake Superior to the Pacific (1695–1895)*. Vol 1. Toronto: Musson Book Company, 1910.

Morrison, Dorothy Nafus. *Outpost: John McLoughlin and the Far Northwest*. Portland: Oregon Historical Society Press, 1999.

Morrison, Kenneth M. *The Solidarity of Kin: Ethnohistory, Religious Studies and the Algonkian-French Religious Encounter*. Albany: State University of New York Press, 2003.

Newell, Dianne. *Tangled Webs of History: Indians and the Law in Canada's Pacific Coast Fisheries*. Toronto: University of Toronto Press, 1993.

Neylan, Susan. *The Heavens Are Changing: Nineteenth-Century Protestant Missions and Tsimshian Christianity*. Montreal: McGill-Queen's University Press, 2003.

Noel, Jan. *Women in New France*. Ottawa: Canadian Historical Association, 1998.

Noll, Mark A. *A History of Christianity in the United States and Canada*. Grand Rapids, MI: William B. Eerdmans Publishing, 1992.

Nute, Grace Lee. *The Voyageur*. 1931. Reprint. St. Paul: Minnesota Historical Society Press, 1955.

Oertel, Kristen Tegtmeier. *Bleeding Borders: Race, Gender, and Violence in Pre-Civil War Kansas*. Baton Rouge: Louisiana State University Press, 2009.

Olson, June L. *Living in the Great Circle: The Grande Ronde Indian Reservation, 1855–1905*. Clackamas, OR: A. Menard Publications, 2011.

Osborn-Ryan, Sharon. *Cumulative Baptism Index to the Catholic Church Records of the Pacific Northwest*. Portland: Oregon Heritage Press, 1999.

———. *Cumulative Death Index to the Catholic Church Records of the Pacific Northwest*. Portland: Oregon Heritage Press, 1998.

———. *Cumulative Marriage Index to the Catholic Church Records of the Pacific Northwest*. Portland: Oregon Heritage Press, 1998.

Ouellet, Fernand. *Lower Canada, 1791–1840: Social Change and Nationalism*. Translated by Patricia Claxton. Toronto: McClelland and Stewart, 1980.

Packard, Randall M. *The Making of a Tropical Disease: A Short History of Malaria*. Baltimore: Johns Hopkins University Press, 2007.

Parkman, Francis. *France and England in North America*. 2 vols. 1865–1892. Reprint. New York: Library of America, 1983.

Pascoe, Peggy. *What Comes Naturally: Miscegenation Law and the Making of Race in America*. New York: Oxford University Press, 2009.

Pasquier, Michael. *Fathers on the Frontier: French Missionaries and the Roman Catholic Priesthood in the United States, 1789–1870*. New York: Oxford University Press, 2010.

Peattie, Donald Culross. *A Natural History of Western Trees*. New York: Bonanza Books, 1953.

Peterson, Jacqueline, and Jennifer S. H. Brown, eds. *The New Peoples: Being and Becoming Métis in North America*. Winnipeg: University of Manitoba Press, 1985.

Peterson del Mar, David. *Oregon's Promise: An Interpretive History*. Corvallis: Oregon State University Press, 2003.

Pojar, Jim, and Andy MacKinnon, eds. *Plants of the Pacific Northwest: Washington, Oregon, British Columbia, and Alaska*. Vancouver: B.C. Ministry of Forests & Lone Pine Publishing, 1994.

Pomerlau, Jeanne. *Corvées and quêtes: Un parcours au Canada français*. Montreal: Éditions Hurtubise, 2002.

Pomeroy, Earl. *The Pacific Slope*. New York: Alfred A. Knopf, 1968.

Porter, Kenneth Wiggins. *John Jacob Astor, Business Man*. Vol. 1. Cambridge, MA: Harvard University Press, 1931.

Prescott, Cynthia Culver. *Gender and Generation on the Far Western Frontier*. Tucson: University of Arizona Press, 2007.

Prodruchny, Carolyn. *Making the Voyageur World: Travelers and Traders in the North American Fur Trade*. Lincoln: University of Nebraska Press, 2006.

Ramenofsky, Ann. *Vectors of Death: The Archeology of European Contact*. Albuquerque: University of New Mexico Press, 1987.

Ray, Arthur. *Indians in the Fur Trade*. Toronto: University of Toronto Press, 1974; reprint: 1998.

Ray, Verne F. *Lower Chinook Ethnographic Notes*. University of Washington Publications in Anthropology. Vol. 7. Seattle: University of Washington, 1938.

Reff, Daniel T. *Disease, Depopulation, and Culture Change in Northwestern New Spain, 1518–1764*. Salt Lake City: University of Utah Press, 1991.

Reid, John Phillip. *Contested Empire: Peter Skene Ogden and the Snake River Expeditions*. Norman: University of Oklahoma Press, 2002.

———. *Forging a Fur Trade Empire: Expeditions in the Snake Country, 1809–1834*. Norman, OK: Arthur H. Clark Co., 2011.

Rich, E. E. *Hudson's Bay Company, 1670–1870*. 3 vols. New York: Macmillan, 1961.

Robbins, William G. *Landscapes of Promise: The Oregon Story, 1800–1940*. Seattle: University of Washington Press, 1997.

Rohrbough, Malcolm. *The Trans-Appalachian Frontier*. New York: Oxford University Press, 1978.

Ronda, James. *Astoria and Empire*. Lincoln: University of Nebraska Press, 1990.

———. *Lewis and Clark among the Indians*. 1984. Reprint, with a new introduction. Lincoln: University of Nebraska Press, 2002.

Ruby, Robert H., and John A. Brown. *The Chinook Indians: Traders of the Lower Columbia*. Norman: University of Oklahoma Press, 1976.

Sanders, Judith A., Mary K. Weber, and David R. Brauner. *Willamette Mission Archeological Project: Phase III Assessment*. Monograph Prepared for the Oregon State Historic Preservation Office. Corvallis: Department of Anthropology, Oregon State University, 1983.

Schwantes, Carlos Arnaldo. *The Pacific Northwest: An Interpretative History*. Rev. ed. Lincoln: University of Nebraska Press, 1996.

Schoenberg, Wilfred P. *A History of the Catholic Church in the Pacific Northwest, 1743–1983.* Washington, D.C.: Pastoral Press, 1987.

Schultz, Nancy Lusignan. *Fire & Roses: The Burning of the Charlestown Convent, 1834.* New York: Free Press, 2000.

Schwartz, James Z. *Conflict on the Michigan Frontier: Yankee Borderland Cultures, 1815–1840.* Dekalb: Northern Illinois University Press, 2009.

Sleeper-Smith, Susan. *Indian Women and French Men: Rethinking Cultural Encounters in the Western Great Lakes.* Amherst: University of Massachusetts Press, 2001.

Stern, Theodore. *Chiefs & Chief Traders: Indian Relations at Fort Nez Percés, 1818–1855.* Corvallis: Oregon State University Press, 1993.

Sweet, William Warren. *Religion on the American Frontier.* Vol. 4: *The Methodists.* Chicago: University of Chicago Press, 1946.

Sylvain, Philippe, and Nive Voisine. *Histoire du catholicisme québécois: Les XVIIIe et XIXe siècles.* Vol. 2: *Réveil et consolidation (1840–1898).* Montréal: Éditions du Boréal, 1991.

Taylor, George, and Raymond R. Hatton. *The Oregon Weather Book.* Corvallis: Oregon State University Press, 1999.

Taylor, Joseph. *Making Salmon: An Environmental History of the Northwest Coast Fisheries Crisis.* Seattle: University of Washington Press, 1999.

Thomas, Edward Harper. *Chinook: A History and Dictionary.* Portland, OR: Binfords & Mort, 1935.

Thorne, Tanis C. *The Many Hands of My Relations: French and Indians on the Lower Missouri.* Columbia: University of Missouri Press, 1996.

Turner, Frederick Jackson, *Rereading Frederick Jackson Turner: "The Significance of the Frontier in American History" and Other Essays.* With commentary by John Mack Faragher. New York: Henry Holt, 1994.

Unruh, John D. *The Plains Across: The Overland Emigrants and the Trans-Mississippi West, 1840–60.* Chicago: University of Illinois Press, 1979.

Van Kirk, Sylvia. *Many Tender Ties: Women in Fur Trade Society, 1670–1870.* Norman: University of Oklahoma Press, 1980.

Vibert, Elizabeth. *Traders Tales: Narratives of Cultural Encounters in the Columbia Plateau, 1807–1846.* Norman: University of Oklahoma Press, 1997.

Victor, Francis Fuller. *The Early Indian Wars of Oregon.* Salem, OR: Frank C. Baker, State Printer, 1894.

Wadewitz, Lissa A. *The Nature of Borders: Salmon, Boundaries, and Bandits on the Salish Sea.* Seattle: University of Washington Press, 2012.

Watson, Bruce McIntyre. *Lives Lived West of the Divide: A Biographical Dictionary of Fur Traders Working West of the Rockies, 1793–1858.* 3 vols. Kelowna: Centre for Social, Spatial, and Economic Justice, University of British Columbia, 2010.

Watts, Edward. *In This Remote Country: French Colonial Culture in the Anglo-American Imagination, 1780–1860.* Chapel Hill: University of North Carolina Press, 2006.

Whaley, Gray H. *Oregon and the Collapse of Illahee: U.S. Empire and the Transformation of an Indigenous World, 1792–1859.* Chapel Hill: University of North Carolina Press, 2010.

White, Richard. *"It's Your Misfortune and None of My Own"*: A New History of the American West. Norman: Oklahoma University Press, 1991.

———. *Land Use, Environment, and Social Change: The Shaping of Island County, Washington*. 2nd ed. Seattle: University of Washington Press, 1992.

———. *The Middle Ground: Indians, Empire, and Republics in the Great Lakes Region, 1650–1815*. New York: Cambridge University Press, 1991.

White, Richard, and Patricia Nelson Limerick. *The Frontier in American Culture*. Edited by James R. Grossman. Berkeley: University of California Press, 1994.

Widder, Keith. *Battle for the Soul: Métis Children Encounter Evangelical Protestants at Mackinaw Mission, 1823–1837*. East Lansing: Michigan State University Press, 1999.

Woodworth, Steven E. *Manifest Destinies: America's Westward Expansion and the Road to the Civil War*. New York: Alfred Knopf, 2010.

PUBLISHED SECONDARY SOURCES: ARTICLES

Armitage, Susan. "From the Inside Out: Rewriting Regional History." *Frontiers* 22:3 (2001): 32–47.

———. "Making Connections: Gender, Race, and Place in Oregon Country." In *One Step over the Line: Toward a History of Women in the North American Wests*. Edited by Elizabeth Jameson and Sheila McManus. Edmonton, AB: Athabasca University Press, 2008, 55–79.

Bain, Read. "Educational Plans and Efforts by Methodists in Oregon to 1860." *Oregon Historical Quarterly* 21:1 (March 1920): 63–94.

Barman, Jean, and Bruce M. Watson. "Fort Colvile Fur Trade Families and the Dynamics of Race in the Pacific Northwest." *Pacific Northwest Quarterly* 32:4 (Summer 1999): 140–155.

Barry, J. Neilson. "Astorians Who Became Permanent Settlers." *Washington Historical Quarterly* 24 (1933): 221–231, 282–301.

———. "The Champoeg Meeting of March 4, 1844." *Oregon Historical Quarterly* 38:3 (December 1937): 425–432.

———. "Early Oregon Country Forts." *Oregon Historical Quarterly* 44:2 (June 1945): 109–110.

———. "Madame Dorion of the Astorians." *Oregon Historical Quarterly* 30:2 (September 1929): 272–277.

———. "Site of the Historic Granary of the Methodist Mission." *Oregon Historical Quarterly* 43:3 (Summer 1942): 286–289.

———. "Site of Wallace House, 1812–1814." *Oregon Historical Quarterly* 42:3 (September 1941): 206–207.

Beckham, Stephen Dow. "History of Western Oregon Since 1846." In *Handbook of North American Indians*. Vol. 7: *Northwest Coast*. Edited by Wayne Suttles. Washington, D.C.: Smithsonian Institution, 1990, 180–188.

———. "The Myth of the Vanishing Kalapuyans." In *What Price Eden? The Willamette Valley in Transition*. Salem, OR: Mission Mill Museum, 1988, 53–64.

Belknap, George. "Authentic Account of the Murder of Dr. Whitman: The History of a Pamphlet." *Papers of the Bibliographic Society of America* 55 (1961): 319–325.

Benner, Patricia A., and Sedell R. James. "Upper Willamette River Landscape: A Historic Perspective." In *River Quality: Dynamics and Restoration*. Edited by Antonius Laenen and David Dunnette. New York: CRC Press, 1997, 23–49.

Bergmann, Mathias D. "'We should lose much by their absence': The Centrality of Chinookans and Kalapuyans to Frontier Life in Oregon." *Oregon Historical Quarterly* 109:1 (Spring 2008): 34–59.

Berquist, James M. "The Oregon Donation Act and National Land Policy." *Oregon Historical Quarterly* 58:1 (March 1957): 17–35.

Betts, William J. "From Red River to the Columbia." *Beaver Outfit* 301:4 (Spring 1971): 50–56.

Billington, Ray A. "Oregon Epic: A Letter That Jarred America." *Pacific Historian* (Summer 1968): 30–37.

Bourgeault, Ron. "The Indian, the Métis, and the Fur Trade: Class, Sexism, and Racism in the Transition from 'Communism' to Capitalism." *Studies in Political Economy* 12 (1983): 45–80.

———. "Race, Class, and Gender: Colonial Domination of Indian Women." In *Race, Class, Gender: Bonds and Barriers*. Edited by Jess Vorst et al. Rev. ed. Toronto: Society for Socialist Studies/Garamond Press, 1991, 88–117.

Boyd, Robert. "Population Decline from Two Epidemics on the Northwest Coast." In *Disease and Demography in the Americas*. Edited by John W. Verano and Douglas H. Ubelaker. Washington, D.C.: Smithsonian Institution Press, 1992, 249–255.

———. "Strategies of Indian Burning in the Willamette Valley." In *Indians, Fire, and the Land in the Pacific Northwest*. Edited by Robert Boyd. Corvallis: Oregon State University Press, 1999, 94–138.

Brosnan, Cornelius J. "The Signers of the Oregon Memorial of 1838." *Washington Historical Quarterly* 24:3 (July 1933): 174–189.

Brown, Jennifer S. H. "Partial Truths: A Close Look at Fur Trade Marriage." In *From Rupert's Land to Canada*. Edited by Theodore Binnema, Gerhard J. Ens, and R. C. Macleod. Edmonton: University of Alberta Press, 2001, 59–80.

Bunting, Robert. "The Environmental and Settler Society in Western Oregon." *Pacific Historical Review* 64:3 (August 1995): 413–443.

Burpee, L. J. "A Forgotten Adventure of the Fur Trade." *Queen's Quarterly* 26:4 (April–June 1919): 363–380.

Byram, R. Scott. "Colonial Power and Indigenous Justice: Fur Trader Violence and Its Aftermath in Yaquina Narrative." *Oregon Historical Quarterly* 109:3 (Fall 2008): 358–387.

Byram, R. Scott, and David G. Lewis. "Ourigan: Wealth of the Northwest Coast." *Oregon Historical Quarterly* 102:2 (Summer 2001): 127–157.

Calloway, Colin. "Snake Frontiers: The Eastern Shoshone in the Eighteenth Century." *Annals of Wyoming* 63 (Summer 1991): 82–92.

Cawcroft, Ernest. "Donald Mackenzie: King of the Northwest." *Canadian Magazine* 50:2 (Nov. 1917–April 1918): 342–349.

Chused, Richard H. "Late Nineteenth-Century Married Women's Property Law: Reception of the Early Married Women's Property Acts by Courts and Legislatures." *American Journal of Legal History* 29:1 (1985): 3–35.

———. "Married Women's Property Law, 1800–1850." *Georgetown Law Review* 71 (1982–1983): 1359–1425.

———. "The Oregon Donation Act of 1850 and Nineteenth Century Federal Married Women's Property Law." *Law and History Review* 2:1 (Spring 1984): 44–78.

Clark, Malcolm. "The Bigot Disclosed: 90 Years of Nativism." *Oregon Historical Quarterly* 75:2 (1974): 109–190.

Coates, Colin M. "French Canadians' Ambivalence to the British Empire." In *Canada and the British Empire*. Edited by Phillip Buckner. New York: Oxford University Press, 2008, 181–199.

Coates, Ken S. "Border Crossings: Patterns and Processes along the Canada–United States Boundary West of the Rockies." In *Parallel Destinies: Canadian-American Relations West of the Rockies*. Edited by John M. Findlay and Ken S. Coates. Seattle and Montreal: University of Washington Press and McGill-Queen's University Press, 2002, 3–27.

Codere, Helen. "Kwakiutl Traditional Culture." In *Handbook of North American Indians*. Vol. 7: *Northwest Coast*. Edited by Wayne Suttles. Washington, D.C.: Smithsonian Institution, 1990, 359–377.

Cook, Sherburne F. "The Epidemic of 1830–1833 in California and Oregon." *University of California Publications in American Archaeology and Ethnology* 43:3 (May 1955): 303–326.

Cook, Sherburne F., and Cesare Marino. "Roman Catholic Missions in California and the Southwest." In *Handbook of North American Indians*. Vol. 4: *History of Indian-White Relations*. Edited by Wilcomb E. Washburn. Washington, D.C.: Smithsonian Institution, 1988, 472–480.

Crampton, C. Gregory, and Gloria G. Cline. "The San Buenaventura, Mythical River of the West." *Pacific Historical Review* 25 (1956): 163–171.

Crosby, Alfred. "Virgin Soil Epidemics as a Factor in the Aboriginal Depopulation in America." *William and Mary Quarterly* 3rd Series 33:2 (April 1976): 289–299.

Dean, Jonathan. "The Hudson's Bay Company and Its Use of Force, 1828–1829." *Oregon Historical Quarterly* 98:3 (Fall 1997): 262–295.

Dennis, Elise Francis. "Slavery in the Pacific Northwest." Part 2. *Oregon Historical Quarterly* 31:2 (1930): 181–195.

Dickason, Olive Patricia. "From 'One Nation' in the Northeast to 'New Nation' in the Northwest: A Look at the Emergence of the Métis." In *The New Peoples: Being and Becoming Métis in North America*. Edited by Jacqueline Peterson and Jennifer S. H. Brown. Winnipeg: University of Manitoba Press, 1985, 19–36.

Dickens, Samuel N. "Western Oregon and Washington." In *The Pacific Northwest: An Overall Appreciation*. 2nd ed. Edited by Otis W. Freeman and Howard H. Martin. New York: John Wiley & Sons, 54–64.

Dobyns, Henry. "Native American Trade Centers as Contagious Disease Foci." In *Disease and Demography in the Americas*. Edited by John Verano and Douglas Ukelbaker. Washington, D.C.: Smithsonian Institution, 1992, 215–222.

Douglas, Jesse S. "Origins of the Population of Oregon in 1850." *Pacific Northwest Quarterly* 41:2 (April 1950): 95–114.

Drumm, Stella M. "More about Astorians." *Oregon Historical Quarterly* 24:4 (December 1923): 335–360.

Drury, Clifford M. "The Oregonian and Indian's Advocate." *Pacific Northwest Quarterly* 56:4 (October 1965): 159–167.

Duncan, Janice. "'Ruth Rover'—Vindictive Falsehood or Historical Truth?" *Journal of the West* 13:2 (April 1973): 24–253.

Dunn, Frederick L. "Malaria." In *The Cambridge World History of Human Disease*. Edited by Kenneth F. Kipple. New York: Cambridge University Press, 1993, 855–862.

Elliot, T. C. "Peter Skene Ogden, Fur Trader." *Oregon Historical Quarterly* 11:3 (September 1910):229–279.

Erickson, Lesley. "Repositioning the Missionary: Sara Riel, the Grey Nuns, and Aboriginal Women in the Catholic Missions of the Northwest." In *Recollecting: Lives of Aboriginal Women in the Canadian Northwest and Borderlands*. Edited by Sarah Carter and Patricia A. McCormack. Edmonton, AB: Athabasca University Press, 2011, 115–134.

Faragher, John Mack. "'More Motley than Mackinaw': From Ethnic Mixing to Ethnic Cleansing on the Frontier of the Lower Missouri, 1783–1833." In *Contact Points: American Frontiers from the Mohawk Valley to the Mississippi, 1750–1830*. Edited by Andrew R. L. Cayton and Frederika J. Teute. Chapel Hill: University of North Carolina Press, 1998, 304–326.

Fountain, Steven. "Stealing Shoes in the Fur Desert: Hudson's Bay Company Policy in the Columbia Department, 1824–1840." In *Aboriginal Peoples and the Fur Trade: Proceedings of the Eighth Annual North American Fur Trade Conference, Akwesasne*. Edited by Louise Johnston. Cornwall, ON/Rooseveltown, NH: Akwesasne Notes, 2001, 187–193.

French, David H., and Katherine S. French. "Wasco, Wishram, and Cascades." In *Handbook of North American Indians*. Vol. 12: *Plateau*. Edited by Deward E. Walker Jr. Washington, D.C.: Smithsonian Institution, 1998, 360–377.

Frost, O. W. "Margaret J. Bailey, Oregon Pioneer Author." *Marion County History* 5 (June 1959): 64–70.

Galm, Jerry R. "Prehistoric Trade and Exchange in the Interior Plateau of Northwestern North America." In *Prehistoric Trade Systems in North America*. Edited by Timothy G. Baugh and Jonathon E. Ericson. New York: Plenum Press, 1994, 275–305.

Gatke, Robert Moulton. "The First Indian School of the Pacific Northwest." *Oregon Historical Quarterly* 23:1 (March 1922): 70–83.

Ginzburg, Carlo. "Microhistory: Two or Three Things That I Know about It." Translated by John and Anne Tedeschi. *Critical Inquiry* 20:1 (Autumn 1993): 10–35.

Gould, Richard A. "To Have and Have Not: The Ecology of Sharing among Hunter-Gatherers." In *Resource Managers: North American and Australian Hunter-Gatherers*. Edited by Nancy M. Williams and Eugene S. Hunn. Boulder, CO: Westview Press/American Association for the Advancement of Science, 1982, 69–92.

Grabowski, Jan, and Nicole St-Onge. "Montreal Iroquois *Engagés* in the Western Fur Trade." In *From Rupert's Land to Canada*. Edited by Theodore Binnema, Gerhard J. Ens, and R. C. Macleod. Calgary, AB: University of Calgary Press, 2001, 23–58.

Graybill, Andrew R. "Helen P. Clarke in the 'Age of Tribes': Montana's Changing Racial Landscape, 1870–1920." *Montana: The Magazine of Western History* 61:1 (Spring 2011): 4–19.

Greer, Allan. "The Pattern of Literacy in Quebec, 1745–1899." *Histoire sociale/Social History* 11:22 (November 1978): 293–335.

Habeck, James. "The Original Vegetation of the Mid-Willamette Valley, Oregon." *Northwest Science* 35:2 (May 1961): 65–77.

Hayda, Yvonne P. "Slavery in the Greater Lower Columbia Region." *Ethnohistory* 52:3 (Summer 2005): 563–588.

Hajda, Yvonne, and Elizabeth Sobel. "Lower Columbia Trade and Exchange Systems." In *Chinookan Peoples of the Lower Columbia*. Edited by Robert T. Boyd, Kenneth M. Annes, and Tony Johnson. Seattle: University of Washington Press, 106–124.

Hamilton, Scott. "Dynamics of Social Complexity in Early Nineteenth-Century British Fur Trade Posts." *International Journal of Historical Archaeology* 4:2 (2000): 217–273.

Hammond, Lorne. "Marketing Wildlife: The Hudson's Bay Company and the Pacific Northwest, 1821–1849." *Forest and Conservation Policy* 37 (January 1993): 14–25.

Hareven, Tamara. "The History of the Family and the Complexity of Social Change." *American Historical Review* 96:1 (February 1991): 95–124.

———. "The Search for Generational Memory." In *Oral History: An Interdisciplinary Anthology*. Edited by David K. Dunaway and Willa K. Buam. Nashville, TN: American Association for State and Local History, 1984.

Harris, Cole. "How Did Colonialism Dispossess? Comments from the Edge of an Empire." *Annals of the Association of American Geographers* 94:1 (2004): 165–182.

Holman, Federick V. "A Brief History of the Oregon Provisional Government and What Caused Its Formation." *Oregon Historical Quarterly* 13:2 (June 1912): 89–139.

Hubert, Ollivier. "Ritual Performance and Parish Sociability: French-Canadian Catholic Families at Mass from the Seventeenth to the Nineteenth Century." In *Households of Faith: Family, Gender, and Community in Canada, 1760–1969*. Edited by Nancy Christie. Montreal: McGill-Queen's University Press, 2002, 37–76.

———. "Ritualité ultramontaine et pouvoir pastorale clérical dans le Québec de la seconde moitié du XIXe." In *La régulation sociale entre l'acteur et l'institution: Pour une problematique historique de l'interaction/Agency and Institutions in Social Regulation: Toward a Historical Understanding of Their Interaction.*" Sainte Foy, QC: Les Presses de l'Université Laval, 2005, 438–447.

Hudon, Christine, and Ollivier Hubert. "The Emergence of a Statistical Approach to Social Issue in Administrative Practices of the Catholic Church in the Province of Quebec." In *The Churches and Social Order in Nineteenth- and Twentieth-Century Canada*. Edited by Michael Gauvreau and Ollivier Hubert. Montreal: McGill-Queen's University Press, 2006, 1–65.

Innes, Frank C. "Disease Ecologies of North America." In *The Cambridge World History of Human Disease*. Edited by Kenneth F. Kiple. New York: Cambridge University Press, 1993, 519–535.

Jensen, Kimberly. "Revolutions in the Machinery: Oregon Women and Citizenship in Sesquicentennial Perspective." *Oregon Historical Quarterly* 110:3 (Fall 2009): 336–361.

Jetté, Melinda Marie. "Betwixt and Between the Official Story: Tracing the History and Memory of a Family of French-Indian Ancestry in the Pacific Northwest." *Oregon Historical Quarterly* 111:2 (Summer 2010): 142–183.

———. "Dislodging Oregon's History from Its Mythical Mooring: Reflections on Death and the Settling and Unsettling of Oregon." *Oregon Historical Quarterly* 115:3 (Fall 2014): 444–445.

Jetté, Melinda Marie, and Tim Zacharias. "The State of Oregon." In *The Uniting States: The Story of Statehood for the Fifty States*. Edited by Benjamin F. Shearer. Vol. 3. Westport, CT: Greenwood Press, 2005, 1003–1013.

Johannessen, Carl L., William A. Davenport, Artimus Millet, and Steven McWilliams. "The Vegetation of the Willamette Valley." *Annals of the Association of American Geographers* 61:2 (June 1971): 286–301.

Johansen, Dorothy O. "Introduction." In *Peter Skene Ogden's Snake Country Journal, 1826–27*. Edited by K. G. Davies and assisted by A. M. Johnson. London: Hudson's Bay Records Society, 1961.

Knuth, Priscilla. "Nativism in Oregon." *Frances Greenburg Armitage Prize Winning Essays. Reed College Bulletin* 24:2 (January 1946): 1–25.

Lang, William L. "The Chinookan Encounter with Euro-Americans in the Lower Columbia River Valley." In *Chinookan Peoples of the Lower Columbia*. Edited by Robert T. Boyd, Kenneth M. Annes, and Tony Johnson. Seattle: University of Washington Press, 250–271.

Lavender, David. "Thomas Mckay." In *The Mountain Men and the Fur Trade of the Far West*. Vol. 6. Edited by LeRoy R. Hafen. Glendale, CA: Arthur H. Clark Co., 1969, 259–277.

Lewis, David G. "Four Deaths: The Near Destruction of Western Oregon Tribes and Native Lifeways, Removal to the Reservation, and Erasure from History." *Oregon Historical Quarterly* 115:3 (Fall 2014): 414–437.

Levi, Giovanni. "On Microhistory." In *New Perspectives on Historical Writing*. Edited by Peter Burke. University Park: Pennsylvania State University Press, 1991, 93–113.

Loewenberg, Robert J. "Creating a Provisional Government in Oregon: A Revision." *Pacific Northwest Quarterly* 68:1 (January 1977): 13–24.

———. "Elijah White vs. Jason Lee: A Tale of Hard Times." *Journal of the West* 11:4 (October 1972): 636–662.

———. "New Evidence, Old Categories: Jason Lee as Zealot." *Pacific Historical Review* 47:3 (August 1978): 432–468.

———. "Saving Oregon Again: A Western Perennial?" *Oregon Historical Quarterly* 78:4 (December 1977): 332–350.

MacGregor, Alan Leander. "'Lords of the Ascendant': Mercantile Biography and Irving's *Astoria*." *Canadian Review of American Studies* 21:1 (Summer 1990): 15–30.

MacLaren, I. S. "Paul Kane and the Authorship of *A Wandering Artist*. In *From Rupert's Land to Canada*. Edited by Theodore Binnema, Gerhard J. Ens, and R. C. Macleod. Edmonton: University of Alberta Press, 2001, 225–243.

———. "Washington Irving's Problems with History and Romance in *Astoria*." *Canadian Review of American Studies* 1:1 (Summer 1990): 1–13.

Mannard, Joseph G. "Maternity . . . of the Spirit: Nuns and Domesticity in Antebellum America." In *History of Women in the United States: Historical Articles on Women's Lives and Activities*. Vol. 13: *Religion*. Edited by Nancy F. Cott. Munich: K. G. Saur, 1993, 74–92.

Marsden, Susan, and Robert Galois. "The Tsimshian, the Hudson's Bay Company, and the Geopolitics of the Northwest Coast Fur Trade, 1787–1840." *Canadian Geographer* 39:2 (Summer 1995): 169–183.

May, Jacques M. "The Ecology of Malaria." In *Studies in Disease Ecology*. Edited by Jacques M. May. New York: Hafner Publishing, 1961, 161–171.

McClintock, Thomas A. "James Saules, Peter Burnett, and the Oregon Black Exclusion Law of June 1844." *Pacific Northwest Quarterly* 86:3 (Summer 1995): 121–130.

Mckinney, F. Ann. "Kalapuyan Subsistence: Reexamining the Willamette Falls Salmon Barrier." *Northwest Anthropological Research Notes* 18:1 (Spring 1984): 23–33.

Merrill, Brent, and Yvonne Hajda. "The Confederated Tribes of the Grand Ronde Community of Oregon." In *The First Oregonians*. 2nd ed. Edited by Laura Berg. Portland: Oregon Council for the Humanities, 2007, 120–145.

Milliken, Emma. "Choosing between Corsets and Freedom: Native, Mixed-Blood, and White Wives of Laborers at Fort Nisqually, 1833–1860." *Pacific Northwest Quarterly* 96:2 (Spring 2005): 95–101.

Minthorn, Antone. "Wars, Treaties, and the Beginning of Reservation Life." In *As days go by / wiyáxayxt / wiyáa awn—Our History, Our Land, and Our People: The Cayuse, Umatilla, and Walla Walla*. Edited by Jennifer Karson. Pendleton, OR: Tamástslikt Cultural Institute, 2006, 61–92.

Minto, John. "The Number and Condition of the Native Race in Oregon When First Seen by White Men." *Oregon Historical Quarterly* 1:3 (September 1900): 296–395.

Moats, Francis I. "The Rise of Methodism in the Midwest." *Mississippi Valley Historical Review* 15:1 (June 1928): 68–88.

Morris, Ralph. "The Notion of a Great American Desert East of the Rockies." *Mississippi Valley Historical Review* 13:2 (September 1926): 190–200.

Morton, W. L. "The Significance of Site in the Settlement of the American and Canadian Wests." *Agricultural History* 25 (1951): 97–104.

Mumford, Jeremy. "Métis and the Vote in 19th-Century America." *Journal of the West* 39:3 (Summer 2000): 38–45

Munnick, Harriet. "The Earliest Three R's in Oregon, 1830–1840." *Marion County History* 5 (June 1959): 52–56.

——. "Grandma Was an Indian." *Marion County History* 7 (December 1961): 6–9.

——. "The Mission Mill at St. Paul." *Marion County History* 11 (1972–1976): 27–30.

——. "Mission Role Call." *Marion County History* 11 (1972–1976): 23–26.

——. "Oregon's First Farmer." *Marion County History* 3 (June 1957): 8–13.

——. "The Prairie That Slacum Saw." *Marion County History* 9 (1965–1968): 25–31.

——. "The Transition Decades on French Prairie, 1830–1850." *Marion County History* 4 (June 1958): 35–42.

Nelson, Herbert B. "Ruth Rover's Cup of Sorrow." *Pacific Northwest Quarterly* 50:3 (July 1959): 91–98.

Ott, Jennifer. "'Ruining' the Rivers in the Snake Country: The Hudson's Bay Company's Fur Desert Policy." *Oregon Historical Quarterly* 14:2 (Summer 2003): 166–193.

Overmeyer, Philip Henry. "Members of the First Wyeth Expedition." *Oregon Historical Quarterly* 36:1 (March 1935): 95–101.

Pannekoek, Frits. "Alexander Ross." In *Dictionnaire biographique du Canada*. Vol. 8: *1851–1860*. Edited by Francess G. Halpenny and Jean Hamelin. Toronto: University of Toronto Press, 1985, 849–852.

Pascoe, Peggy. "'A Mistake to Simmer the Question Down to Black and White': The History of Oregon's Miscegenation Law." In *Seeing Color: Indigenous Peoples and Racialized Minorities in Oregon*. Edited by Jun Xing et al. Lanham, MD: University Press of America, 2007, 27–43.

Perrine, Fred S. "Early Days on the Willamette." *Oregon Historical Quarterly* 15:4 (December 1914): 295–312.

Peterson, Jacqueline. "Sacred Encounters in the Northwest: A Persistent Dialogue." *U.S. Catholic Historian* 12 (1994): 37–48.

Peterson del Mar, David. "Intermarriage and Agency: A Chinookan Case Study." *Ethnohistory* 42:1 (Winter 1995): 1–30.

Pike, C. J. "Petitions of Oregon Settlers, 1838–1848." *Oregon Historical Quarterly* 34:3 (September 1933): 216–235.

Pipes, Nellie. "The Protestant Ladder." *Oregon Historical Quarterly* 37 (1936): 237–240.

Porter, Kenneth Wiggins. "Roll of Overland Astorians, 1809–1812." *Oregon Historical Quarterly* 43:2 (June 1933): 101–112.

Prince, Suzanne. "Marie-Louise McLoughlin." In *Dictionnaire biographique du Canada*. Vol. 7: *1836–1850*. Toronto/Quebec City: University of Toronto Press/Les Presses de l'Université Laval, 1988, 620–621.

Prucha, Francis Paul. "Two Roads to Conversion: Protestant and Catholic Missionaries in the Pacific Northwest." *Pacific Northwest Quarterly* 79:3 (October 1981): 130–137.

Raibmon, Paige. "Unmaking Native Space: A Genealogy of Indian Policy, Settler Practice, and the Microtechniques of Dispossession." In *The Power of Promises: Rethinking Indian Treaties in the Pacific Northwest*. Edited by Alexandra Harmon. Seattle: University of Washington Press, 2008, 56–85.

Ratcliff, James L. "What Happened to the Kalapuya? A Study of the Depletion of Their Economic Base." *Indian Historian* 6:3 (Summer 1973): 27–33.

Ray, Arthur J. "Diffusion of Disease in the Western Interior of Canada, 1830–1850." *Geographic Review* 66:2 (1976): 139–157.

———. "The Hudson's Bay Company and Native People." In *The Handbook of North American Indians*. Vol. 4: *History of Indian-White Relations*. Edited by Wilcomb Washburn. Washington, D.C.: Smithsonian Institution, 1988, 335–350.

Ray, Verne. "The Historical Position of the Lower Chinook in the Native Cultures of the Northwest." *Pacific Northwest Quarterly* 28 (1937): 363–372.

———. "Native Villages and Groupings of the Columbia Basin." *Pacific Northwest Quarterly* 27 (1936): 99–152.

Reid, John Phillip. "Restraints of Vengeance: Retaliation-in-Kind and the Use of Law in Old Oregon." *Oregon Historical Quarterly* 95:1 (Spring 1994): 48–92.

Reimer, Chad. "Borders of the Past: The Oregon Boundary Dispute and the Beginnings of Northwest Historiography." In *Parallel Destinies: Canadian-American Relations West of the Rockies*. Edited by John M. Findlay and Ken S. Coates. Seattle: University of Washington Press, 2002, 221–245.

Richards, Kent D. "In Search of the Pacific Northwest: The Historiography of Oregon and Washington." *Pacific Northwest Quarterly* 50:4 (November 1981): 415–444.

——. "The Methodists and the Formation of the Oregon Provisional Government." *Pacific Northwest Quarterly* 61:2 (April 1970): 87–93.

Richardson, Allan. "The Control of Productive Resources on the Northwest Coast of North America." In *Resource Managers: North American and Australian Hunter-Gatherers*. Edited by Nancy M. Williams and Eugene S. Hunn. Boulder, CO: Westview Press/American Association for the Advancement of Science, 1982, 93–112.

Robbins, William G. "The Indian Question in Western Oregon: The Making of a Colonial People." In *Experiences in a Promised Land: Essays in Pacific Northwest History*. Edited by G. Thomas Edwards and Carlos A. Schwantes. Seattle: University of Washington Press, 1986, 51–67.

——. "Willamette Eden." In *Northwest Lands, Northwest Peoples: Readings in Environmental History*. Edited by Dale D. Goble and Paul W. Hirt. Seattle: University of Washington Press, 1999, 95–110.

Robertson, James R. "The Social Evolution of Oregon." *Oregon Historical Quarterly* 3:1 (March 1902): 1–37.

Ronda, James P. "Calculating Ouragan." *Oregon Historical Quarterly* 94:3–4 (Summer-Fall 1993): 121–140.

Rushforth, Brett. "Trading Language: Chinook Jargon, Race, and Nation at Fort Vancouver, 1824–1853." In *Aboriginal Peoples and the Fur Trade: Proceedings of the Eighth Annual North American Fur Trade Conference, Akwesasne*. Edited by Louise Johnston. Cornwall, ON/Rooseveltown, NH: Akwesasne Notes, 2001, 194–199.

Rust, Richard Dilworth. "Introduction." In *Astoria*, by Washington Irving. 1976. Reprint. Lincoln: University of Nebraska Press, 1982, xxi–xxxiv.

Saler, Bethal, and Carolyn Produchny. "Glass Curtain and Storied Landscapes: The Fur Trade, National Boundaries, and Historians." In *Bridging National Borders in North America: Transnational and Comparative Histories*. Durham, NC: Duke University Press, 2010, 373–302.

Santee, J. F. "Comcomly and the Chinooks." *Oregon Historical Quarterly* 33:3 (September 1932): 271–278.

Schaeffer, Claude. "The First Jesuit Mission to the Flathead, 1840–1850: A Study in Culture Conflicts." *Pacific Northwest Quarterly* 3:3 (July 1937): 227–250.

Schroeder, John H. "Representative John Floyd, 1817–1829: Harbinger of Oregon Territory." *Oregon Historical Quarterly* 70:4 (December 1926): 333–345.

Scott, Leslie. "First Taxes in Oregon, 1844." *Oregon Historical Quarterly* 31:1 (March 1930): 1–10.

——. "Indian Diseases as Aids to Pacific Northwest Settlement." *Oregon Historical Quarterly* 29 (1928): 144–161.

———. "Oregon's Provisional Government, 1843–49." *Oregon Historical Quarterly* 30:3 (September 1939): 207–217.

Seagraves, Helen Leonard. "Oregon's 1857 Convention." *Frances Greenburg Armitage Prize Essays. Reed College Bulletin* 30: 4 (June 1952): 3–24.

Silverstein, Michael. "Chinookans of the Lower Columbia." In *Handbook of North American Indians.* Vol. 7: *Northwest Coast.* Edited by Wayne Suttles. Washington, D.C.: Smithsonian Institution, 1990, 533–546.

Sobel, Elizabeth. "An Archaeological Test of the 'Exchange Expansion Model' of Contact Era Change on the Northwest Coast." *Journal of Anthropological Archaeology* 31 (2010): 1–21.

Spencer, Omar C. "Chief Cassino." *Oregon Historical Quarterly* 34:1 (March 1933): 19–30.

Spores, Ronald. "Too Small a Place: The Removal of the Willamette Valley Indians, 1850–1856." *American Indian Quarterly* 17:2 (Spring 1993): 171–192.

Strozut, George, Jr. "Black Gold: The Story of Lake Labish." *Marion County History* 5 (June 1959): 47–49.

Swagerty, William R., and Dick A. Wilson. "Faithful Service under Different Flags: A Socioeconomic Profile of the Columbia District, Hudson's Bay Company and the Upper Missouri Outfit, American Fur Company, 1825–1835." In *The Fur Trade Revisited: Selected Papers of the Sixth North American Fur Trade Conference, Mackinac Island, Michigan, 1991.* Edited by Jennifer S. H. Brown, W. Eccles, and Donald P. Heldman. East Lansing: Michigan State University Press, 1994, 243–267.

Tanner, Elaine. "A Study of the Underlying Causes of the Depression of 1854." In *Frances Greenburg Armitage Prize Winning Essays. Reed College Bulletin* 25:3 (April 1947): 35–65.

Taylor, Herbert C., and Lester Hoaglin. "The 'Intermittent Fever' Epidemic of the 1830s on the Lower Columbia River." *Ethnohistory* 9:2 (1962): 160–178.

Taylor, Quintard. "Slaves and Free Men: Blacks in the Oregon Country, 1840–1860." *Oregon Historical Quarterly* 83:2 (Summer 1982): 153–170.

Thomas, David C. "Against the Grains: Margaret Jewett Bailey's Social and Spiritual Independence, Oregon, 1837–1854." *Methodist History* 35:1 (October 1996): 28–42.

Thomas, Russell B. "Truth and Fiction of the Champoeg Meeting." *Oregon Historical Quarterly* 30:3 (September 1929): 218–237.

Thompson, Laurence C., and M. Dale Kinkade. "Languages." In *Handbook of North American Indians.* Vol. 7: *Northwest Coast.* Edited by Wayne Suttles. Washington, D.C.: Smithsonian Institution, 1990, 30–51.

Thomson, Duane, and Marrianne Ignace. "'They Made Themselves Our Guests': Power Relationships in the Interior Plateau Region of the Cordillera Fur Trade Era." *BC Studies* 146 (Summer 2005): 3–35.

Towle, Jerry C. "Changing Geography of Willamette Valley Woodlands." *Oregon Historical Quarterly* 83:1 (Spring 1983): 66–87.

———. "Settlement and Subsistence in the Willamette Valley: Some Additional Considerations." *Northwest Anthropological Research Notes* 13:1 (Spring 1979): 12–21.

Van Kirk, Sylvia. "Tracing the Fortunes of Five Founding Families of Victoria." *BC Studies* 115/116 (Winter 1997/98): 148–179.

Vaughan, Thomas, and Martin Winch. "Joseph Gervais: A Familiar Mystery Man." *Oregon Historical Quarterly* 66:4 (December 1965): 331–362.

Vibert, Elizabeth. "Real Men Hunt Buffalo: Masculinity, Race, and Class in British Fur Traders' Narratives." *Gender and History* 8:1 (April 1996): 4–21.

Victor, Francis Fuller. "Flotsam and Jetsam of the Pacific: The *Owyhee,* the *Sultana,* and the *Mary Dacre.*" *Oregon Historical Quarterly* 2:1 (March 1901): 36–54.

Walker, James V. "Henry S. Tanner and Cartographic Expression of American Expansionism in the 1820s." *Oregon Historical Quarterly* 111:4 (Winter 2010): 416–441.

Welter, Barbara. "The Cult of True Womanhood, 1820–1860." *American Quarterly* 18:2 (Summer 1996): 151–174.

West, Elliott. "American Frontier." In *The Oxford History of the American West.* Edited by Clyde A. Milner, Carol A. O'Connor, and Martha A. Sandweiss. New York: Oxford University Press, 1994, 115–150.

West, Oswald. "Oregon's First White Settlers on French Prairie." *Oregon Historical Quarterly* 43:3 (September 1942): 198–209.

Whaley, Gray. "A Reflection on Genocide in Southwest Oregon in Honor of George Bundy Wasson, Jr." *Oregon Historical Quarterly* 115:3 (Fall 2014): 438–440.

———. "'Complete Liberty'? Gender, Sexuality, Race, and Social Change on the Lower Columbia River, 1805–1838." *Ethnohistory* 54:4 (Fall 2007): 669–695.

———. "'Trophies for God': Native Morality, Racial Ideology, and the Methodist Mission of Lower Oregon, 1834–1844." *Oregon Historical Quarterly* 107: 1 (Spring 2006): 6–35.

White, Kris A., and Janice St. Laurent. "Mysterious Journey: The Catholic Ladder of 1840." *Oregon Historical Quarterly* 97:1 (Spring 1997): 70–90.

White, Richard. "The Altered Landscape: Social Change and Land in the Pacific Northwest." In *Regionalism and the Pacific Northwest.* Edited by William G. Robbins, Robert J. Frank, and Richard E. Ross. Corvallis: Oregon State University Press, 1983, 109–128.

Williams, Glyndwr. "Peter Skene Ogden." In *Dictionnaire biographique du Canada.* Vol. 8: *1851–1860.* Edited by Francess G. Halpenny and Jean Hamelin. Toronto: University of Toronto Press, 1985, 732–736.

Wolfe, Robert J. "Alaska's Great Sickness, 1900: An Epidemic of Measles and Influenza in a Virgin Soil Population." *Proceedings of the American Philosophical Society* 126 (April 8, 1982): 92–121.

Woolworth, Stephen. "'The School is under My Direction:' The Politics of Education at Fort Vancouver, 1836–1838." *Oregon Historical Quarterly* 104:2 (Summer 2003): 228–251.

Young, Andrew W. "Donald McKenzie." In *History of Chautauqua County, New York.* 1987. Reprint. Bowie, MD: Heritage Books, 1990.

Zenk, Henry. "Kalapuyans." In *Handbook of North American Indians.* Vol. 7: *Northwest Coast.* Edited by Wayne Suttles. Washington, D.C.: Smithsonian Institution, 1990: 547–553.

———. "Notes on the Native Place-Names of the Willamette Valley Region." *Oregon Historical Quarterly* 109:1 (Spring 2008): 6–33.

———. "Tualatin Kalapuyan Villages: The Ethnographic Record." In *Contributions to the Archaeology of Oregon.* Edited by Paul W. Baxter. Portland: Association of Oregon Archeologists, 1994, 146–165.

Zenk, Henry, with Tony A. Johnson. "A Northwest Language of Contact, Diplomacy, and Identity: Chinuk Wawa/Chinook Jargon." *Oregon Historical Quarterly* 111:4 (Winter 2010): 444–461.

UNPUBLISHED SECONDARY SOURCES

Baker, Abner S. "The Oregon Pioneer Tradition in the Nineteenth Century: A Study of Recollection and Self-Definition." Ph.D. diss., University of Oregon, 1969.

Bergman, Mathias David. "Crosscultural Interactions, Interdependencies, and Insecurities in the Lower Columbia River Valley Frontier, 1810–1855." M.A. thesis, Washington State University, 2000.

Collins, Lloyd R. "The Cultural Position of the Kalapuya in the Pacific Northwest." M.A. thesis, University of Oregon, 1951.

Decker, Robert James. "Jason Lee, Missionary to Oregon: A Re-evaluation." Ph.D. diss., Indiana University, 1961.

Gandy, Shawna Lea. "Fur Trade Daughters of the Oregon Country: Students of the Sisters of the Notre Dame de Namur, 1850." M.A. thesis, Portland State University, 2004.

Hajda, Yvonne. "Mary's River Kalapuyan: A Descriptive Phonology." M.A. thesis, Portland State University, 1976.

———. "Regional Social Organization in the Greater Lower Columbia, 1792–1830." Ph.D. diss., University of Washington, 1984.

Head, Harlow Ziner. "The Oregon Donation Land Claims and Their Patterns." Ph.D. diss., University of Oregon, 1971.

Kardas, Susan. "'The People Bought This Land and the Clatsop Became Rich': A View of Nineteenth-Century Fur Trade Relations on the Lower Columbia between Chinookan Speakers, Whites, and Kanakas." Ph.D. diss., Bryn Mawr College, 1971.

Keith, H. Lloyd. "Adventure Narrative as History: Alexander Ross and *The Fur Hunters of the Far West*." Paper presented before the Pacific Northwest History Conference, April 25–26, 2004.

———. "The Historical Fictions of Ross Cox." Unpublished manuscript, November 1986.

Kinoshita, Jun R. "Little Houses on the Prairie: A Predictive Model of French-Canadian Settlement in Oregon's Willamette Valley." M.A. thesis, Oregon State University, 2004.

Martin, Douglas Dale. "Indian-White Relations on the Pacific Slope, 1850–1890." Ph.D. diss., University of Washington, 1969.

Pollard, Juliet T. "The Making of the Metis in the Pacific Northwest, Fur Trade Children: Race, Class, Gender." Ph.D. diss., University of British Columbia, 1990.

Richards, Kent David. "Growth and Development of Government in the Far West." Ph.D. diss., University of Wisconsin, 1966.

Simpson, Charles E. "The Snake Country Freemen, British Free Trappers in Idaho." M.A. thesis, University of Idaho, 1990.

Thomson, Sister Marian Josephine. "Abbé Jean-Baptiste Abraham Brouillet, First Vicar General of the Diocese of Seattle." M.A. thesis, Seattle University, 1950.

Towle, Jerry. "Woodland in the Willamette Valley: An Historical Geography." Ph.D. diss., University of Oregon, 1974.

Wright, Mary S. "The Circle Broken: Gender, Family, and Difference in the Pacific North-west, 1811–1850." Ph.D. diss., Rutgers University, 1996.

Zenk, Henry B. "Chinook Jargon and Native Cultural Persistence in the Grande Ronde Indian Community, 1856–1907." Ph.D. diss., University of Oregon, 1984.

———. "Contributions to Tualatin Ethnography: Subsistence and Ethnobiology." M.A. thesis, Portland State University, 1976.

Index

Figures are indicated by "*f*", tables by "*t*", and notes by "*n*".